Purchased by:_____

This is the first book-length treatment of the unique nature and development of Nietzsche's post-Zarathustran political philosophy. This later political philosophy is set in the context of the critique of modernity that Nietzsche advances in the years 1885–1888, in texts such as *Beyond Good and Evil, On the Genealogy of Morals, Twilight of the Idols, The Antichrist(ian), The Case of Wagner,* and *Ecce Homo.*

In this light, Nietzsche's own diagnosis of the ills of modernity is subject to the same criticism that he himself leveled against previous philosophies: that it is an involuntary symptom of the age it represents. Nietzsche is seen to be aware of his own decadence and of his complicity with the very tendencies that he dissects and deplores. By relating the political philosophy, the critique of modernity, and the theory of decadence, Daniel Conway has written a powerful book about Nietzsche's own appreciation of the limitations of both his writing style and his famous prophetic "stance."

NIETZSCHE'S DANGEROUS GAME

MODERN EUROPEAN PHILOSOPHY

This series seeks to publish a range of high-quality books on philosophers, topics, and schools of thought prominent in the Kantian and post-Kantian European tradition. The series is nonsectarian in approach and methodology and includes both introductory and more specialized treatments of these thinkers and topics. Authors are encouraged to interpret the boundaries of the modern European tradition in a broad way and to engage with it in primarily philosophical rather than historical terms.

General Editor
ROBERT B. PIPPIN, *University of Chicago*

Advisory Board
GARY GUTTING, *University of Notre Dame*
ROLF-PETER HORSTMANN, *Humboldt University, Berlin*
MARK SACKS, *University of Essex*

Some recent titles:
Frederick A. Olafson, *What is a Human Being?*
Stanley Rosen, *The Mask of Enlightenment: Nietzsche's Zarathustra*
Robert C. Scharff, *Comte After Positivism*
F. C. T. Moore, *Bergson*
Charles Larmore, *The Morals of Modernity*
Robert B. Pippin, *Idealism as Modernism*

NIETZSCHE'S DANGEROUS GAME

Philosophy in the Twilight of the Idols

DANIEL W. CONWAY

Pennsylvania State University

CAMBRIDGE
UNIVERSITY PRESS

PUBLISHED BY THE PRESS SYNDICATE OF THE UNIVERSITY OF CAMBRIDGE
The Pitt Building, Trumpington Street, Cambridge CB2 1RP, United Kingdom

CAMBRIDGE UNIVERSITY PRESS
The Edinburgh Building, Cambridge CB2 2RU, United Kingdom
40 West 20th Street, New York, NY 10011-4211, USA
10 Stamford Road, Oakleigh, Melbourne 3166, Australia

First published 1997

Printed in the United States of America

Typeset in Baskerville

Library of Congress Cataloging-in-Publication Data
Conway, Daniel W.
Nietzsche's dangerous game : philosophy in the twilight of
the idols / Daniel W. Conway.
p.   cm. – (Modern European philosophy)
Includes bibliographical references and index.
ISBN 0-521-57371-8 (hardback)
1. Nietzsche, Friedrich Wilhelm, 1844–1900 – Contributions in
political science.   I. Title.   II. Series.
JC233.N52C66   1997
193 – dc21   96-46726
                                               CIP

A catalogue record for this book is available from the British Library.

ISBN 0-521-57371-8 hardback

In Memoriam
Edward G. Ballard
my first teacher

CONTENTS

vii

ACKNOWLEDGMENTS

I wish to acknowledge my heartfelt gratitude to Robert B. Pippin, General Editor of the Modern European Philosophy series, for his unflagging support of my research. I am deeply grateful to Stephen Houlgate, Bernd Magnus, Graham Parkes, and Gary Shapiro, all of whom read earlier drafts of the manuscript and suggested important revisions. I am also greatly indebted to Brian Domino, who not only served tirelessly as my research assistant, but also directed my attention to the theory of *décadence* that emerges in Nietzsche's post-Zarathustran writings. Several other friends and colleagues have generously contributed over the years to my understanding of Nietzsche's confrontation with modernity, including Panos Alexakos, Keith Ansell Pearson, Claudia Crawford, Shannon Duval, Robert Gooding-Williams, Lawrence Hatab, Laurence Lampert, Alexander Nehamas, David Owen, Stanley Rosen, Charles Scott, John Seery, David Stern, Tracy Strong, and Michael Zimmerman. The research for this book was made possible by a grant from the Research and Graduate Study Office of the College of Liberal Arts at The Pennsylvania State University; my thanks to Dean Susan Welch and Associate Dean Raymond Lombra.

Finally, I gratefully acknowledge permission to use portions of my articles from the following publications:

"Parastrategesis, Or: Rhetoric for Decadents," *Philosophy and Rhetoric*, Vol. 27, No. 3, 1994, pp. 179–201.

"The Economy of Decadence," *The Journal of Nietzsche Studies*, Issue 9/10, 1995, pp. 77–112.

"Writing in Blood: On the Prejudices of Genealogy," *Epoché*, Vol. 3, Nos. 1–2, 1995, pp. 149–181.

"Decadence and Eternal Recurrence," *The European Legacy*, Vol. 2, No. 4, 1997.

"Standing Between Two Millennia," in *Nietzsche's Happy Returns*, ed. Duncan Large. London: Macmillan (in press).

NIETZSCHE TITLES: SOURCES AND ABBREVIATIONS

Nietzsche's Writings in German

Friedrich Nietzsche: Sämtliche Werke, Kritische Studienausgabe in 15 Bänden, ed. G. Colli and M. Montinari (Berlin: deGruyter/Deutscher Taschenbuch Verlag, 1980).
Friedrich Nietzsche: Sämtliche Briefe, Kritische Studienausgabe in 8 Bänden, ed. G. Colli and M. Montinari (Berlin: deGruyter/Deutscher Taschenbuch Verlag, 1986).

English Translations

My practice is to refer to Nietzsche's writings by citing the section (rather than the page) number of a particular book, as referenced by the following abbreviations.

Abbreviations

AC   *The Antichrist(ian)*
        [Preferred translation: Kaufmann, Walter, ed. and trans. *The Portable Nietzsche.* Viking Penguin, 1982.]
BGE   *Beyond Good and Evil*
        [Preferred translation: Kaufmann, Walter, trans. *Beyond Good and Evil.* Random House/Vintage, 1989.]
BT   *The Birth of Tragedy*

[Preferred translation: Kaufmann, Walter, trans. *The Birth of Tragedy* and *The Case of Wagner.* Random House/Vintage, 1967.]

CW   *The Case of Wagner*
[Preferred translation: Kaufmann, Walter, trans. *The Birth of Tragedy* and *The Case of Wagner.* Random House/Vintage, 1967.]

D   *Daybreak*
[Preferred translation: Hollingdale, R. J., trans., Tanner, Michael, intro. *Daybreak: Thoughts on the Prejudices of Morality.* Cambridge: Cambridge University Press, 1982.]

EH   *Ecce Homo*
[Preferred translation: Kaufmann, Walter, ed. and trans., Hollingdale, R. J., trans. *On the Genealogy of Morals* and *Ecce Homo.* Random House/Vintage, 1989.]

GM   *On the Genealogy of Morals*
[Preferred translation: Kaufmann, Walter, ed. and trans., Hollingdale, R. J., trans. *On the Genealogy of Morals* and *Ecce Homo.* Random House/Vintage, 1989.]

GS   *The Gay Science*
[Preferred translation: Kaufmann, Walter, trans. *The Gay Science: With a Prelude in Rhymes and an Appendix of Songs.* Random House/ Vintage, 1974.]

H   *Human, All-Too-Human*
[Preferred translation: Hollingdale, R. J., trans., Heller, Erich, intro. *Human, All-Too-Human: A Book for Free Spirits.* Cambridge: Cambridge University Press, 1986.]

NCW   *Nietzsche contra Wagner*
[Preferred translation: Kaufmann, Walter, ed. and trans. *The Portable Nietzsche.* Viking Penguin, 1982.]

TI   *Twilight of the Idols*
[Preferred translation: Kaufmann, Walter, ed. and trans. *The Portable Nietzsche.* Viking Penguin, 1982.]

UM   *Untimely Meditations*
[Preferred translation: Hollingdale, R. J., trans., Stern, J. P., intro. *Untimely Meditations.* Cambridge: Cambridge University Press, 1983.]

WP   *The Will to Power*
[Preferred translation: Kaufmann, Walter, ed. and trans., Hollingdale, R. J., trans. *The Will to Power.* Random House/Vintage, 1968.]

Z   *Thus Spoke Zarathustra*
[Preferred translation: Kaufmann, Walter, ed. and trans. *The Portable Nietzsche.* Viking Penguin, 1982.]

INTRODUCTION

And if a man today is praised for living "wisely" or "as a philosopher," it
hardly means more than "prudently and apart." Wisdom – seems to the
rabble a kind of escape, a means and trick for getting well out of a
dangerous game. But the genuine philosopher – as it seems to *us*, my
friends? – lives "unphilosophically" and "unwisely," above all *imprudently*,
and feels the burden and the duty of a hundred attempts [*Versuchen*] and
temptations [*Versuchungen*] of life – he risks *himself* constantly, he plays *the*
dangerous game.   (BGE 205)

This book undertakes a critical appraisal of the political philosophy that
informs the writings of Friedrich Nietzsche from the period 1885–88. The
interpretive task I have set for myself is twofold: First, I reconstruct the
revised critique of modernity that Nietzsche develops in the writings of this
period; second, I situate his post-Zarathustran political thinking within the
self-referential context of his revised critique of modernity. My specific focus
is the "symptomatological" critique of modernity that emerges in this
period, from such writings as *Beyond Good and Evil* (1886), *On the Genealogy of
Morals* (1887), *Twilight of the Idols* (1888), *The Antichrist(ian)* (1888), *The
Case of Wagner* (1888), and *Ecce Homo* (1888).

I focus on this fertile period of Nietzsche's philosophical career because
it yields the clearest formulation of his mature political thinking, as evidenced by the unprecedented self-referential turning he undertakes
therein. This turning is precipitated, I believe, by his growing awareness of
the complicity of his earlier writings – such as *The Birth of Tragedy* (1872) – in

1

the cultural malaise they presumed to treat. This period is furthermore bounded by two events of the utmost biographical importance: his belated completion of *Thus Spoke Zarathustra* in 1885 and his final departure from sanity in January of 1889.

My attention to the self-referential implications of Nietzsche's philosophy is not, in itself, novel. Friends and foes alike regularly detect a "problem" of self-reference in his critical project, noting that everything he says about his various "enemies" rebounds to discredit him as well.[1] This familiar criticism is essentially valid, inasmuch as he invariably implicates himself in his own critical tirades, but it need not prove fatal to his critique of modernity. Indeed, whereas most readers treat Nietzsche's problem of self-reference as vicious, as marking the philosophical limitations of an otherwise promising critical project, I take it as the starting point of my own investigation.

Nietzsche is the first serious critic of modernity to acknowledge his own complicity in the cultural crisis that he reveals and attempts to address. He understands not only that a philosophical confrontation with modernity must appeal to immanent standards of evaluation, but also that an immanent critique of modernity must also apply self-referentially to the critic who advances it. He has no idea, however, where his self-referential critique of modernity may lead or what conclusions it is likely to yield. Indeed, he cannot know such things, for he is in the worst possible position to evaluate objectively his own entanglements in the decadence of late modernity – hence the experimental spirit that animates his post-Zarathustran writings.

Once situated within the context of his confrontation with modernity, Nietzsche's political philosophy assumes a dramatically changed aspect. For example, this self-referential critique of modernity militates against the popular interpretation of Nietzsche as an unrepentant champion of the heroic will. While he may at one time have entrusted the redemption of modernity to a superhuman act of will, his writings from the period 1885–88 ridicule all such schemes, which invariably trade on an overestimation of the volitional resources available to agents who labor in the twilight of the idols. Modernity, he now believes, is an age beset by advanced decay, which can be neither reversed nor arrested. Any attempt to implement a political solution to the problem of modernity would only compound the decadence of modernity and possibly hasten its advance. Agents in late modernity, including Nietzsche himself, simply lack the volitional resources needed to orchestrate the redemption of the age.

My study draws its title from the passage I have summoned as the epigraph for this Introduction. Although Nietzsche says very little about these "genuine philosophers" and the "dangerous game" they play, his own post-Zarathustran confrontation with modernity provides us with an instructive example of both. To play the dangerous game is to open oneself to a degree of critical scrutiny that one cannot direct toward oneself and thereby to place oneself voluntarily in the dismembering hands of one's most ruthless critics. Nietzsche's own rendition of the dangerous game comprises those experimental rhetorical strategies that he designs in order to neutralize or compensate for the crippling effects of his own decadence.

Desperately hoping to extend his meager influence into the next millennium, he deliberately cultivates a readership that must inevitably turn against him – hence the inherent danger of his dangerous game. If his teachings are to survive the duration of modernity, safeguarded for delivery (albeit in distorted form) to the mysterious "philosophers of the future," then he must recruit wily emissaries who can negotiate the shades and shadows of the fading epoch. Although more respectful readers are both available and willing, he believes that their weakness for discipleship betrays a fatal lack of cunning and guile.

In his own case, then, the danger in question is largely attributable to his reliance on a readership he can neither trust nor control. The readers he recruits may either fail to deliver his teachings to the philosophers of the future or distort his teachings beyond recognition. Any readers who are clever enough to shelter and disseminate his untimely teachings are also sufficiently independent – we might also say traitorous – to present their own interpretations of these teachings as authoritative. Such is the danger that he must court if he is to have the influence he desires on the founding of the successor age to modernity.

Although participation in the dangerous game is voluntary, and so strategic, Nietzsche can neither foresee nor manage the consequences of his experiments. Born of excess and expenditure, the results of this dangerous game must remain largely unknown to him, but not necessarily to the readers he has trained. Having adopted an indirect route to the completion of his task, he is powerless to determine the constituency of the readership to whom he entrusts his destiny. He can only hope that he has trained his successors well and that his books contain sufficient barbs and snares to waylay unworthy readers.[2] Although he prefers to depict the dangerous game as a heroic *agon* and his own participation as an exercise of surpassing bravado, his weakness for this anachronistic romance only confirms his inability to neutralize the decadence that binds him.

Nietzsche's failure to arrive at an accurate assessment of his own decay contributes an element of danger to which he remains utterly blind, thereby compounding the native perils of his dangerous game. The "formula of decadence," he explains, is "instinctively to choose what is harmful for *oneself*" (TI 9:35). As one might expect, his own decadence manifests itself as an instinctive (and unwitting) predilection for disciples, for fawning sycophants, and for deferential flatterers. As it turns out, then, his decadence prevents him from cultivating the "perfect readers" who might deliver his teachings to the philosophers of the future. Although he wants to cultivate a heroic readership of intrepid Nietzscheans, what he needs is another matter altogether.

Indeed, despite his frequent disclaimers to the contrary, his post-Zarathustran writings evince an irrepressible anxiety of influence: He needs not only to be read, but also to be regarded, heeded, respected, revered, even idolized.[3] Vaguely aware that he is no match for the illustrious predecessors whom he arrogantly designates as his rivals, he worries to the end that he is both "too late" to salvage the remaining vital resources of modernity and "too early" to impress his stamp onto the successor epoch. Anxious that his place in history is by no means secure, he casts a reckless wager, gambling that he can somehow insulate his "children" from the decadence that besets him.

Nietzsche loses this desperate wager, but he may yet win the support of readers who are uniquely suited to the peculiar historical conditions of late modernity. Although he has failed to muster the swashbuckling warrior-genealogists to whom he hoped to entrust his teachings, he has apparently (and unwittingly) succeeded in training a revolutionary vanguard of decadent Nietzscheans, who are willing to betray even him in order to import his teachings into the next millennium. While he openly despaired of his apparent failure to found the communities of resistance that might preside over his posthumous birth as the Antichrist (EH:bge 1), his checkered reception in the twentieth century suggests that he may have been successful after all – albeit in ways unimaginable (and altogether unpalatable) to him.

Chapter 1 introduces my preferred method for reading Nietzsche against Nietzsche, such that we might extract from him the "personal confession" and "unconscious memoir" that his writings collectively essay in encrypted form. Chapters 2 and 3 attempt to reconstruct the general theory of decadence that informs his post-Zarathustran writings, focusing, respectively, on his parallel accounts of decadent souls and decadent peoples. Chapter 4 situates Nietzsche's (revised) critique of modernity within the general theory of decadence he advances, articulating his post-Zarathustran political thinking while implicating him in the moralization of decadence. Chapter 5 undertakes a critical assessment of his attempts to compensate for his besetting decadence, charting his participation (both voluntary and involuntary) in the dangerous game of parastrategesis. Chapter 6 examines his celebrated "revaluation of all values" and locates it within his complex scheme to declare war on Christian morality. Chapter 7 offers a critical appraisal of his war on Christianity, illuminating the unintended successes that may ensue from the failure of his revaluation of all values. Chapter 8 concludes the study with an evaluation of Nietzsche's cleverness, suggesting that his ingenious (albeit failed) participation in the dangerous game of para-strategesis may bespeak the inspiration of *übermenschlich* genius.

Four preliminary caveats are in order. First of all, this book ventures no sustained interpretation of Nietzsche's favorite and most influential book, *Thus Spoke Zarathustra*. While I refer to the text of *Zarathustra* throughout my study, I make no attempt to collect these various references within a fully articulated interpretive framework.[4] I have restricted my interpretive focus to the fertile period 1885–88, which follows Nietzsche's completion of *Zarathustra* in quadrapartite form. In doing so, I have attempted to take quite seriously his suggestion that his post-Zarathustran books are "fish hooks" designed to land worthy readers for *Zarathustra* – although I reject his self-serving complaint that "*there were no fish*" (EH:bge 1). In this light, it is perhaps appropriate that we investigate Nietzsche's post-Zarathustran corpus before turning to *Zarathustra* itself.

Second, I occasionally avail myself in this book of textual evidence culled from Nietzsche's letters and unpublished notes. In light of the extraordinary hardships incurred by Nietzsche in steering his books into print, I take quite seriously the decisions he made to prepare a particular text for, or withhold it from, publication. I consequently refer to the unpublished notes only in the event that such notes embellish or clarify a point independently advanced in a published book. My references to his private correspondence are similarly circumscribed. I restrict my references to those notes and letters that shed light on his own intentions and impressions in the period 1885–88.

Third, I rely throughout this study on the excellent translations of Nietzsche's writings rendered by Walter Kaufmann and R. J. Hollingdale. On those occasions when I deem necessary an alternative translation of my own design, I do so either to elicit the nuances of the passage in question or to correct for what I perceive to be an unwarranted domestication of Nietzsche's rhetorical excesses. For my translations of his private correspondence, I occasionally consult and draw from the fine translations provided by Christopher Middleton.[5]

Fourth, I have attempted throughout this study to confine my commentary on the secondary literature to the endnotes. Readers who wish not to become entangled in arcane philological and philosophical debates may safely restrict themselves to the body of the book itself.

Notes

1 Remarking on Nietzsche's attempts to orchestrate a "total revolution" in modernity, Bernard Yack concludes that "Nietzsche too must make a leap into the absurd, for the problem he seeks to resolve cannot be resolved without self-

contradiction." [*The Longing for Total Revolution* (Princeton, NJ: Princeton University Press, 1986), p. 355].

2 Jacques Derrida documents Nietzsche's reliance on such barbs and snares in *Spurs: Nietzsche's Styles*, trans. Barbara Harlow (Chicago: University of Chicago Press, 1978), especially pp. 35–45.

3 Alexander Nehamas maintains that Nietzsche wants his writing to be a part of history, that the reader's agreement or disagreement is ultimately irrelevant to Nietzsche's aim of writing himself into history [*Nietzsche: Life as Literature* (Cambrige, MA: Harvard University Press, 1985), especially chapter 7]. See also Nehamas, "Different Readings: A Reply to Magnus, Solomon and Conway," *International Studies in Philosophy*, Vol. 21, No. 2, 1989, p. 79. Nehamas thus succeeds in saving Nietzsche from the charge of "dogmatism" (a charge that Nehamas takes much more seriously than Nietzsche ever did), but only at the expense of uncomplicating the twisted motives of a remarkably complicated and decadent philosopher. As I will argue throughout this study, Nietzsche was virtually consumed by the task of cultivating a specific type of reader who might continue his life's work. He certainly wants to write himself into history, but only (or primarily) as the destroyer of Christian morality and the founder of a postmodern, tragic age.

4 Incomplete statements of my interpretation of *Zarathustra* may be found in the following essays: "Solving the Problem of Socrates: Nietzsche's *Zarathustra* as Political Irony," *Political Theory*, Vol. 16, No. 2, May 1988, pp. 257–280; "Nietzsche *contra* Nietzsche: The Deconstruction of *Zarathustra*," in *Nietzsche as Postmodernist*, ed. Clayton Koelb (Albany: State University of New York Press, 1990), pp. 91–110, 304–311; "A Moral Ideal for Everyone and No One," *International Studies in Philosophy*, Vol. 22, No. 2, 1990, pp. 17–30. For a superbly philological interpretation of *Thus Spoke Zarathustra*, see Laurence Lampert, *Nietzsche's Teaching* (New Haven, CT: Yale University Press, 1986).

5 *Selected Letters of Friedrich Nietzsche*, trans. and ed. Christopher Middleton (Chicago: University of Chicago Press, 1969).

READING THE SIGNS OF THE TIMES:
NIETZSCHE CONTRA NIETZSCHE

I am, in questions of *décadence,* the highest authority on earth.
        Letter to Malwida von Meysenbug on 18 October 1888.[1]

Thus scribbled Nietzsche in the twilight of his sanity, just months before his storied collapse in Turin. Lest we dismiss this extraordinary claim as an epistolary exaggeration (designed, perhaps, as a private bit of braggadocio between close friends), let us take note of the following passage, which was written at approximately the same time as the letter just cited. Intending to demonstrate publicly the extent of his formidable "authority," Nietzsche rhetorically asks, "Need I say after all this that in questions of *décadence* I am *experienced?*" (EH:wise 1).

Although Nietzsche had thoroughly researched the problem of decadence, his "authority" was not merely academic in nature. Nor was his "experience" in "questions of *décadence*" culled exclusively from the pseudo-scientific literature that proliferated in Europe and Great Britain in the 1880s. The problem of decadence was not only the intellectual fiefdom he had recently staked out for himself, but his "physiological" destiny as well. Nietzsche, it seems, knew whereof he spoke: "I am, no less than Wagner, a child of this time; that is, a *décadent.* But I comprehended this, I resisted it. The philosopher in me resisted" (CW P). His decadence is sufficiently pronounced, he announces in his autobiography, that he is "already dead as [his] father, while as [his] mother [he] is still living and becoming old" (EH:wise 1).

In itself, Nietzsche's decadence should come as no surprise either to his faithful readers or to students of *fin de siècle* European culture. Indeed, the writings from all periods of his career are rife with signs of creeping degeneration: periodic lapses into romanticism and resentment; delusions of grandeur; irrational appeals to race and power; wholesale denunciations of modernity; sociopathic idealizations of solitude, nomadism, and autarky; adolescent fantasies of virile leaders and chivalrous warriors; beatific visions of the gods, heroes, and monsters whose advent he prophesies; an unquenchable thirst for revenge and redemption; an anachronistic reverence for "noble" ideals; and so on.

In fact, we need not take Nietzsche's word for the malady that besets him, for a great deal of independent – if not altogether reliable – evidence of his decay is readily available. His decadence was independently "diagnosed" at least as early as 1892, in Max Nordau's shrill (but influential) study *Entartung*. In a typical passage from his discussion of "Ego-Mania," Nordau writes:

> From the first to the last page of Nietzsche's writings the careful reader seems to hear a madman, with flashing eyes, wild gestures, and foaming mouth, spouting forth deafening bombast; and through it all, now breaking out into frenzied laughter, now sputtering expressions of filthy abuse and invective, now skipping about in a giddily agile dance, and now bursting upon the auditors with threatening mien and clenched fists.[2]

Closer to home, though no less disturbing, are the observations of those who knew Nietzsche best. Allusions to some form of degeneration or decline are found in virtually all accounts of his life, from the diagnosis filed by Dr. Wille in Basel ("mental degeneration")[3] to the retrospective anecdotes recorded by friends, relatives, correspondents, and colleagues.[4] His decadence was so widely acknowledged, in fact, that Elisabeth Förster-Nietzsche was remarkably successful in her shameless endeavors to promote a cult following for the tragically stricken idiot savant who had once been her brother.

Although virtually unanimous in their pronouncement of Nietzsche's decadence, his contemporaries were largely ignorant of his own uncanny anticipation of this diagnosis. As we have seen, he occasionally pronounces himself decadent in his correspondence from 1888, but only selectively and almost exclusively to women. He briefly bears witness to his decadence in *The Case of Wagner,* which was published by Naumann in September 1888, but *Ecce Homo,* which he penned as a pre-emptive strike against critics like Nordau, did not appear in print until 1908. The complexities introduced by a *self-referential* theory of decadence were consequently lost on his contemporary readers and critics, many of whom presented their "original" diagnoses as the final word on the strange case of Herr Nietzsche. Thus began a lively tradition of interpretation, born of ignorance and secondhand testimony that endures to this day, as expert observers solemnly file diagnoses of Nietzsche that he himself has already advanced.

The candor of his pronouncement of his own decay is especially remarkable in light of the central role that the diagnosis of decadence plays in his revised critique of modernity. While charges of decadence flew rather freely in the closing decades of the nineteenth century,[5] Nietzsche took quite seriously the notion that physiological degeneration could be detected and measured not only in individuals, but in epochs and peoples as a whole. He consequently revamped the critical apparatus of his entire philosophy, installing as its centerpiece his own theory of decadence.

In his post-Zarathustran writings, he thus contends that the accomplishments in which modernity takes its greatest pride, the spread of democratic reforms and the ascension of liberal ideals, are in fact symptoms of the decay of political institutions and of European culture in general. The primary targets of his post-Zarathustran critique of modernity – democracy, liberalism, Christianity, Enlightenment, Wagnerian opera, German *Bildung* – all stand in a state of irrecuperable crisis. Modernity, he now proclaims, is an age beset by advanced decadence, which political countermeasures are powerless to reverse. *Late* modernity, the anemic epoch in which he labors, is destined to enact the grisly death throes of the age as a whole. Modernity shares this epigonic destiny, we now learn, with its greatest critic.

Nietzsche's pronouncement of his own decay thus attests publicly to a decisive turning in the development of his critical philosophy. This turning was precipitated by his growing awareness of and attention to the self-referential implications of his original critique of modernity, which he developed in such early works as *The Birth of Tragedy* (1872). In his 1886 "Attempt at a Self-Criticism," for example, he ruthlessly exposes the complicity of *The Birth of Tragedy* in the romantic pessimism it ostensibly sought to dispel. In a passage that Wilamowitz-Möllendorff might have envied for its biting sarcasm, Nietzsche asks himself:

> But, my dear sir, what in the world is romantic if *your* book is not? Can deep hatred against "the Now," against "reality" and "modern ideas" be pushed further than you pushed it in your artists' metaphysics? believing sooner in the Nothing, sooner in the devil than in "the Now?" . . . Is your pessimists' book not itself a piece of anti-Hellenism and romanticism? (BT P7)

As this passage confirms, Nietzsche now realizes that his desire to orchestrate a rebirth of tragic culture actually manifests the cultural crisis he had (fatuously) presumed to address. The guiding conviction that modernity stands in need of redemption, that its goals and accomplishments fall short of some shadowy trans-historical standard of cultural "health," is itself symptomatic of the facile moralizing that he now associates with decadence.[6]

Although Nietzsche publicly announces his self-referential turning in 1886, in the retrospective prefaces that he appends to his pre-Zarathustran books,[7] this turning actually commenced a year or so earlier. Having gained some salutary critical distance from his beloved *Zarathustra,* he resolved late in 1884 to add a fourth, self-parodic installment to his masterpiece, which he had proclaimed "complete" in tripartite form only one year earlier. The period 1885–88 thus falls in the shadow of the failure of the tripartite *Zarathustra* and of Nietzsche's recognition of this failure. Indeed, his decision to pen a fourth installment to *Zarathustra* was prompted in part by his realization that the failure of the tripartite *Zarathustra,* like the book itself, is strongly and inadvertently autobiographical.[8] To investigate this unintended autobiography is the guiding aim not only of his post-Zarathustran writings, but of my study as well.

The trajectory of Nietzsche's post-Zarathustran thought thus describes a turning inward as he attempts to situate himself within the ongoing crisis of modernity. Abandoning the pose of the detached physician of culture and along with it the pretense of a transcendent, ahistorical standpoint, he now immerses himself in the decadence of his age. Emboldened rather than humbled by the forfeiture of his "objectivity," he now attempts to turn his decadence to the advantage of his (revised) critical project. He consequently advances in his post-Zarathustran writings an immanent critique of modernity, which culminates in his pronouncement of his own decay. This pronouncement in turn announces the completion of his period of "convalescence": He is now sufficiently healthy that he can resist – though not throw off – the decadence that besets him (EH:clever 9). This resistance to decadence comprises the entirety of his post-Zarathustran political engagement with modernity.

Nietzsche's turning inward thus furnishes the justification for our renewed attention to the political philosophy that emerges from his post-Zarathustran writings. Prior to this turning, he had shared Zarathustra's distaste for personal political involvement, preferring the comfortable detachment of the diagnostician to the frenzied engagement of the legislator. He more readily fancied himself a tactician and planner, an *éminence grise* perhaps, but never more than a prelude to the mysterious lawgivers who will someday right the listing bark of humanity. While his post-Zarathustran writings continue to emphasize the preparatory contributions of his work, they also evince his desire to preside over the timely demise of modernity and to legislate favorable conditions for the founding of the successor epoch. In *The Antichrist(ian)* he boldly declares war on Christianity, and he promises in his correspondence from late 1888 and early 1889 to assassinate the religious and secular leaders of Europe.

While it may be tempting to attribute this unprecedented flurry of legislative activity to incipient madness,[9] his newly awakened political consciousness actually constitutes a logical extension of his inward turning. His philosophy becomes overtly and directly political, that is, only when he resolves to read himself into his own critique of modernity. It is precisely *his* complicated role in the decadence of his age that has heretofore eluded his confrontation with modernity. He is not only the faithful chronicler of his disintegrating epoch, but its representative exemplar as well. In order to take the full measure of modernity and thus bring to completion his (revised) project of critique, he must either take the measure of his own soul or prepare others to do so for him. Toward this end, his writings from 1888 comprise two noteworthy gestures of self-disclosure, both of which expose the extent of his own complicity in the crisis of modernity: (1) his pronouncement of his own decadence; and (2) his *volte-face* advocacy of truth. These two gestures govern the turning described in his post-Zarathustran writings, and they anchor the critical confrontation that he arranges between his readers and himself.

What are we to make of Nietzsche's attempt to derive an immanent critique of modernity from his personal experience of decadence? On the one hand, this curious gambit may enable him to avoid some of the nagging epistemic problems that arise when self-styled physicians of culture exempt themselves and their critical standpoints from the general theories they advance. Hegel, it is often said, cannot account to finite spirits for his uncanny familiarity with the crepuscular peregrinations of the owl of Minerva. Marx, some critics insist, cannot defend the validity of his deduction of the laws of history within the terms of the theory of history he advances. Freud, critics often observe, cannot reconcile his later forays into philosophical anthropology (including his timely "discovery" of Thanatos) with the basic principles of psychoanalysis. Heidegger is similarly chastised for failing to justify the preternatural confidence with which he inventories the erratic "gifts" of Being. And Wittgenstein's gnomic allusions to a rank ordering of disparate "forms of life" are often said to founder on the shoals of solipsism.[10]

No such *aporia* vitiates Nietzsche's revised critique of modernity, which actually manifests the decadence it purports to document. His pronouncement of his own decay effectively tables the difficult methodological questions that plague most critics of culture. Having forfeited his claim to a foundational critical standpoint, Nietzsche is "free" to pursue a genuinely immanent critique of modernity independent of the metaphysical contrivances in which diagnosticians of culture customarily traffic. He consequently eschews the false optimism and hollow boosterism of the Enlightenment, offering instead a cold, pragmatic account of an age sputtering inexorably toward exhaustion. Deviating from the established practice of predecessor physicians of culture, he refuses to prescribe redemptive measures for modernity; he undertakes instead to steer his dying epoch toward a timely and fitting repose. In the twilight of the idols, philosophy has once again become a preparation for death.

On the other hand, it is not the usual practice of aspiring critics of

culture to undermine the philosophical standpoints from which their respective diagnoses arise. Even those philosophers who expressly promote
some version of historicism are usually careful to arrange for themselves a
generous, ahistorical loophole. Yet Nietzsche commands no external perspective on modernity as a whole, and he admittedly attains his immanent
critical standpoint only by immersing himself in the constitutive decadence
of the age. He may avoid the epistemic *aporia* that haunts rival critics of
modernity, but only because he courts an equally unappealing paradox of
self-reference. Why should anyone take seriously the diagnoses advanced by
a self-avowed decadent?[11] Zarathustra's pointed riposte – "Physician, heal
thyself!" – thus rebounds to mock Nietzsche's decision to resume his critique of modernity. Indeed, if he truly shares in the besetting sickness of his
age, then should he not surrender himself to the political quarantine that
he prescribes for all other pathogenic agents?

To those who wish to discredit Nietzsche's grim appraisal of modernity,
he certainly supplies sufficient reason. These are, after all, the idle speculations of a decadent philosopher, and they may be justifiably dimissed as
pathological expressions of his decay.[12] Critics who pledge allegiance to the
project of Enlightenment, to liberal ideals and democratic reforms, or to
the continued progress and greater glory of humankind may confidently
reject his critique of modernity as a decadence-induced delusion.[13] To be
sure, he appeals to a fairly elaborate theory of decadence, into which he
invests a wealth of original insights into philosophy, psychology, anthropology, and history. Yet he can offer no further justification for this theory,
which originates in a critical perspective that is itself tinctured with decay.[14]

To those in whom this critique strikes a resonant chord, Nietzsche lends
an articulate voice, but nothing more. For such readers, his critique of
modernity stands (or falls) strictly on its own merits as a map of the existential landscape of late modernity. The promise of his critique cannot be
determined in advance from a consideration of his epistemic framework
and critical method, both of which betray the deformative influence of his
own decadence. Moreover, since we have never before witnessed the death
of an epoch from the inside, we have no empirical means of confirming or
disputing the jeremiad he so forcefully advances. Those who endorse his
critique of modernity must consequently make it their own, concocting
additional theoretical support if possible and compensating for his decadent influence in any event.

In light of Nietzsche's apparent stumble into the snare of self-reference,
we might at this juncture dismiss his post-Zarathustran critique of modernity.[15] We are perfectly justified on epistemic grounds in doing so, for he has
told us that in themselves all such theories are mere "stupidities" (TI 2:2).
Following his interpretive lead, we might confidently reduce his post-
Zarathustran critique of modernity to a cluster of telltale symptoms that

collectively signify the (relative) health of his underlying physiological condition. We might furthermore cite his own, acerbic exposé of philosophy
itself: "Gradually it has become clear to me what every great philosophy so
far has been: namely, the personal confession of its author and a kind of
involuntary and unconscious memoir" (BGE 6).

Nietzsche's qualifying modifier – "so far" – is indeed beguiling, but we
have no good reason to exempt him from his general account of philosophers. In fact, if he is right about the unconscious motives of philosophers,
then we should fully expect him to issue himself some such self-exculpatory
caveat. On his own symptomatological terms, then, his critique of modernity may tell us a great deal about the state of his diseased soul but virtually
nothing about his age as a whole. His "unconscious memoir," though potentially titillating, will simply confirm his public admission of his own decadence. What more do we need to know?

One might think that Nietzsche's pronouncement of his own decadence
would simplify the task of assessing his confrontation with modernity. But in
fact the reverse may be true. For some readers, at least, his self-referential
disclosure only complicates the task of interpretation, for it introduces into
his writings a doubled texture.[16] The post-Zarathustran Nietzsche now
speaks from both sides of his mouth: as an "objective" chronicler of decadence, to be sure, but also as a paradigmatic decadent in his own right. In
order to assess the merit of his confrontation with modernity, we must
consequently attempt to separate, if possible, his general theory of decadence from the autobiographical corroboration he unwittingly provides of
it. This complex task requires, in turn, that we read Nietzsche (the theorist
of decadence) against Nietzsche (the exemplar of decadence).

My goal here is to orchestrate a peritropaic confrontation with Nietzsche
that is consistent both with his own revised critical project and with his
larger political aims (which are often obscured by the perturbations introduced by his periodic afflictions with decadence). The untraditional aims of
this peritropaic confrontation in turn call for a traditional interpretive approach. I am concerned to reconstruct and establish what Nietzsche actually
said in his post-Zarathustran writings, as opposed to what he might (or
should) have said in light of his various insights and experiments. I consequently strive to "do" very little with (or to) Nietzsche, intending instead to
document and assess what he "does" on his own. Before putting Nietzsche
"to work," that is, I am concerned to identify the forms of work to which he is
uniquely suited.

My specific strategy for reading Nietzsche against Nietzsche is to reconstruct his general theory of decadence and subsequently to deploy this
theory to determine the limitations of his own self-understanding. The self-
referential application of this general theory of decadence thus furnishes us
with a Nietzschean lens through which we may view him more accurately

(and more "objectively") than he can view himself. A strategic appropriation of this lens should in turn enable us to detect those symptoms of his own decay that he either neglects or misinterprets.

In order for this peritropaic strategy to commence, however, we must rehabilitate or at least bypass the vicious circle on which it trades. Nietzsche's general theory of decadence cannot be used to investigate the condition of his soul if in fact the construction of this theory rests primarily (if not exclusively) on a generalization from the particular facts of his own decadence. Conversely, his symptoms of decay cannot be summoned to corroborate the general theory if in fact the diagnosis of his decadence is derived exclusively from the general theory iself. In order to tame this circle, it would seem that we require an independent confirmation of either the general theory itself or Nietzsche's personal case history.

Lacking the empirical evidence needed to advance an independent confirmation either of Nietzsche's decadence or of his general theory of decadence, I have adopted instead a parametric method in which the truth (or fact) of his own decay is arbitrarily fixed as a constant. This parametric method is appropriate to my investigation because I am ultimately concerned to establish neither the truth of Nietzsche's theory of decadence nor the accuracy of his own self-diagnosis. I am concerned instead to elicit his involuntary exemplification of the age he represents, and to this end the parametric method is apposite.

When fixed as a parameter, Nietzsche's decay corroborates his general theory of decadence, which can then be used, with a greater degree of confidence, to determine the extent of his complicity in the alleged sickness of his age. His general theory of decadence thus provides us with a more "objective" account of his condition, which serves to counterbalance his own, self-serving accounts of his struggle with decadence. The truth of this general theory of decadence, as of the critique of modernity it underwrites, is therefore irrelevant to the peritropaic confrontation I wish to orchestrate. Indeed, the enduring value of Nietzsche's confrontation with modernity is strictly heuristic, residing not in its accuracy or truth, but in its capacity to disclose and decipher the "unconscious memoir" that his post-Zarathustran writings essay in encrypted form. The parametric method I have adopted for this study is thus designed to illuminate the unintended by-products of Nietzsche's failed, quixotic attempt to take the measure of modernity.

Most important, this parametric method allows us to chart the advance and manifestations of Nietzsche's own decadence, in accordance with the general theory he articulates in his post-Zarathustran writings. He consistently defines *decadence* as a degenerative physiological condition, which characteristically manifests itself as: a growing disparity between the cognitive and volitional resources at one's disposal; a yawning chasm that divorces intention from accomplishment; the widening gulf that separates what one wants from what one needs; and, most succinctly, an irreversible weakness of will. Armed with this definition, we may situate our own symptomatological reading of Nietzsche in the context of the general theory he advances.[17]

For example, we may confidently identify and expose his various schemes to exempt himself from his general theory of decadence. Much to the surprise and disappointment of his faithful readers, Nietzsche regularly violates his own best insights, shamelesssly appealing to privileges and pre-rogatives that he has expressly disallowed to others.[18] According to the terms of his own general theory, however, precisely this sort of recidivism is to be expected of any decadent. Beset by a crippling *akrasia,* he involuntarily lapses into the very metaphysical prejudices that he has so artfully debunked. By reading Nietzsche against Nietzsche in this way, we are able to assay carefully his critique of modernity while acknowledging nonetheless that it issues forth from a decadent philosopher. He has warned us that all great sages are teachers of decline (TI 2:1), and we may turn this warning to our own advantage if we properly situate him within the context of his own diagnosis.

This peritropaic strategy thus takes seriously Nietzsche's general critique of modernity, while interpreting his account of his own decadence – its virulence, periodicity, symptoms, and consequences – as itself a symptom of decay. This problem of self-reference is illuminated by Nietzsche's preferred image of himself as a physician of culture. Whereas his accounts of the effects of decadence on others invariably cite a systemic failure of diagnostic faculties, his reckoning of the disruptions induced by his own decadence presents no challenge to his own diagnostic authority. Rival physicians of culture are cashiered by the onset of decadence, but Nietzsche himself heroically exploits his decadence to expand and sharpen his diagnostic skills (EH:wise 1). He only exacerbates the reader's interpretive dilemma by then proposing the penchant for self-misdiagnosis as a prime symptom of decadence.

When Nietzsche speaks of decadence in general or in others, I take him to be more or less credible – although, as we have seen, nothing much rests on the ultimate truth of his diagnoses. When he expounds upon his own decadence, however, he is an unreliable, "interested" witness, as his general theory would suggest of any decadent. His pronouncement of his own deca-dence may strike some readers as disarming, insofar as he appears to in-clude himself within the terms of his own critique, but he is in fact not free to assess accurately the condition of his own soul. Indeed, this is a freedom that no decadent enjoys; a definitive self-knowledge is apparently available only to those who have no need of it. Nietzsche clearly knows that he is decadent (though the source of his knowledge may be suspect), but this is all he knows about his condition. Although his interpretations of his illness are invariably mistaken and self-serving, he has already identified this particular brand of misdiagnosis as a typical sign of advanced decay. In fact, he regularly identifies the involuntary recourse to "bad philology" as a prime symptom of decadence in others.

The trajectory of Nietzsche's post-Zarathustran turning thus describes neither a graceful arc nor a golden circle, but a jagged inward spiral, which winds ever tighter as it penetrates the layers of unconscious prejudice that texture his thought. This spiral is set in motion by Nietzsche, by virtue of his pronouncement of his own decadence. But only his readers can continue the violent, invasive progress of this inward spiral by forcibly laying bare the internal folds in the economy of his soul and thought. Stolidly disregarding the various exemptions and privileges he creatively claims for himself, his readers can deploy his own critical analyses to reveal the dual role that he plays in his diagnosis of modernity: He is subject and object, physician and patient, analyst and analysand.

Nietzsche's acknowledged situation within the cultural malaise he presumes to treat thus accounts for both the novelty and the insight of his confrontation with modernity. It is not simply that his post-Zarathustran writings allow the reader to refract his critical strategies back upon themselves, as champions of deconstruction have long insisted. No author can effectively legislate against this sort of violence and appropriation, and Nietzsche certainly realized as much (EH:destiny 1). The imperative to press his critique of modernity to its logical, self-referential conclusion actually issues from Nietzsche himself, as an integral, strategic component of his revised political project. He not only enables his readers to detect and to thwart his involuntary schemes to exempt himself from his confrontation with modernity, but also trains them in the symptomatological method of criticism he practices. He thus furnishes the psychological insights, rhetorical strategies, and historical case studies needed to subject him to the diagnostic categories of his own critique. Within the context of his revised critical project, his pronouncement of his own decadence thus functions as a gesture of provocation, as an invitation to read Nietzsche against Nietzsche. Unlike other critics of modernity, he actually dares his readers to extract from him his "personal confession" and "unconscious memoir."

This invitation to read Nietzsche into his own critique of modernity serves to mitigate and perhaps to recuperate the paradox of self-reference in which he has ensnared himself. That he has strategically courted this paradox, thereby providing his readers with a novel point of entry into his thought, may be sufficiently provocative to discourage us, if only temporarily, from dismissing his critique of modernity on the epistemic grounds outlined earlier. In that event, his strategic gesture of provocation would serve as the rhetorical pivot he needs in order to divert his readers' attention from what he says to what he does, from his conscious "sayings" to his unintended "showings."[19] By publicly pronouncing his own decadence, he effectively reveals to his readers (but not to himself) a previously unexplored dimension of his philosophy in which he unwittingly enacts the tensions and contradictions of the age he represents.

Reading Nietzsche against Nietzsche in this way thus illuminates the *performative* dimension of his philosophy, in which he involuntarily divulges his personal confession and unconscious memoir. These unwitting performances bathe him in a decidedly unflattering (i.e., all-too-human) light: He is exposed as bourgeios, romantic, resentful, self-deceived, petty, meek, confused, lonely, naive, childish – as anything but the self-styled prophet of extremity who bullies his readers and bellows into the night. At these points of limitation, he involuntarily signifies the contradictions of his age, enacting an embodied critique of modernity that his readers might juxtapose with the discursive critique he deliberately advances. When forcibly subsumed under his own diagnostic categories, he literally becomes a sign of his times, onto whom modernity has inscribed its distinctive, indelible scrawl. Taking seriously his pronouncement of his own decay consequently enables us to continue his self-referential turning, allowing us to reduce him, as he reduced all others, to a constellation of telling symptoms.

Thus, we gain a preliminary glimpse of the fruits to be reaped from the peritropaic strategy I have outlined. Nietzsche's post-Zarathustran writings actually essay two critical appraisals of modernity: a *discursive* critique of modernity, in which he diagnoses widespread decay and prescribes a timely death for his age, and a *performative* critique of modernity, in which he involuntarily embodies the signature tensions of the age as a whole. This latter critique, I contend, is more promising and valuable, at least on Nietzschean grounds, but it is also unwitting and unintentional. It can be approached only indirectly, through a symptomatological interpretation of the former critique.

The enduring value of Nietzsche's discursive critique thus lies not in the diagnoses it directly advances of modernity, the truth of which must remain unknown to us, but in the encrypted diagnosis that it indirectly advances of its unsuspecting author. Indeed, the only way to gain access to Nietzsche's embodied critique of modernity is to interpret his discursive critique as symptomatic of the underlying condition of his soul. For just such an operation of symptomatological reduction, however, he has provided us with ample precedents and a surprisingly complete translational matrix.

Nietzsche may fail in his avowed intention to take the discursive measure of his age, but he unwittingly succeeds in embodying the fragmentary ethos of modernity. Although unaware of the uses to which they will be put, he provides the tools and insights that his readers need in order to derive an unintended success from his inevitable failures. His more promising critique of modernity is etched not on the pages of his post-Zarathustran writings, but on the swollen, scarred surface of his tormented soul, as enacted in the contradictions and prejudices that define (and limit) him as a thinker. His failure to divine the logos of his age actually contributes to our greater appreciation of the governing pathos of modernity. From his philosophical successes and failures, that is, we may acquire an enhanced sense of what it is like to be ineluctably modern.

As a sign of his troubled times, Nietzsche may actually contribute, as he hoped, to the founding of the successor epoch to modernity – albeit in ways unimaginable to him. For example, his own unique enactment of Christian morality may be sufficient to convince the philosophers of the future to proscribe the practices of Christian morality and to disenfranchise the priestly class. In that event, he would be "born posthumously" as the Antichrist, as the destroyer of Christian morality – but not for the reasons he anticipates. Indeed, only as the apotheosis of Christian morality, rather than as its "other," will he influence the founding of the postmodern, tragic age:

> I should actually risk an order of rank among philosophers depending on the rank of their laughter – all the way up to those capable of *golden* laughter. And supposing that gods, too, philosophize, which has been suggested to me by many an inference – I should not doubt that they also know how to laugh the while in a superhuman [*übermenschliche*] and new way – and at the expense of all serious things. Gods enjoy mockery: it seems they cannot suppress laughter even during holy rites. (BGE 294)

Notes

1 *Friedrich Nietzsche: Sämtliche Briefe, Kritische Studienausgabe in 8 Bänden*, ed. G. Colli and M. Montinari (Berlin: deGruyter/Deutscher Taschenbuch Verlag, 1986), Vol. 8, No. 1131, p. 452.

2 Max Nordau, *Degeneration* (Lincoln: University of Nebraska Press, 1993), p. 416.

3 Cited in Ronald Hayman, *Nietzsche: A Critical Life* (New York: Oxford University Press, 1980), p. 337.

4 Lou Salomé interprets Nietzsche's decadence in the heroic, spiritual terms he favored, but she nevertheless cleaves to the standard account of his decline: "Already here, we can recognize clearly its spiritual origin: it is a secret anguish that prompts his passionate spirit to endure the constant crush of knowledge and stream of ideas. . . . What he found to be taking place within himself signaled a generalized danger that threatened his own time; and this escalated itself later into a deadly threat posed against all of mankind, a notion that called upon him to become mankind's redeemer and savior" [*Nietzsche*, ed. and trans. Siegfried Mandel (Redding Ridge, CT: Black Swan Books, 1988), pp. 42–43].

5 For a thorough study of the emergence and development of the concept of decadence in the philosophical and scientific literature of late-nineteenth-century Europe, see Daniel Pick, *Faces of Degeneration: A European Disorder c. 1848–1918* (Cambridge: Cambridge University Press, 1989).

6 John Sallis advances an ambitious double reading of *The Birth of Tragedy* in *Crossings: Nietzsche and the Space of Tragedy* (Chicago: University of Chicago Press,

1991). In articulating a highly original interpretation of the "crossings" enacted in *The Birth of Tragedy*, however, Sallis makes very little use of the double-crossings Nietzsche inscribes into his "Attempt at a Self-Critique," instead "deferring consideration of the way in which [it] inscribe[s], retrospectively, the space of reading and writing *The Birth of Tragedy*" (pp. 10–11).

7   In his commentary on the prefaces of 1886, Claus-Artur Scheier persuasively argues that the prefaces collectively constitute an event of self-presentation and self-annunciation on Nietzsche's part [*Friedrich Nietzsche. Ecce Auctor: Die Vorreden von 1886*, collected and introduced by Claus-Artur Scheier (Hamburg: Felix Meiner Verlag, 1990), pp. vii–xxxii]. On the pivotal importance of Nietzsche's retrospective prefaces, see Keith Ansell-Pearson, "Toward the *Übermensch*: Reflections on the Year of Nietzsche's Daybreak," *Nietzsche-Studien*, Vol. 23, pp. 124–145; and my own essay, "Nietzsche's Art of This-Worldly Comfort: Self-Reference and Strategic Self-Parody," *History of Philosophy Quarterly*, Vol. 9, No. 3, July 1992, pp. 343–357.

8   Several commentators have speculated that Nietzsche limited the publication and distribution of Part IV of his *Zarathustra* in order to avoid offending those friends and acquaintances who are lampooned in his sketches of the buffoonish "higher men." In light of the strongly autobiographical character of Part IV, however, he may have been more concerned to avoid embarrassing himself. As he explains to Franz Overbeck in a letter of 31 March 1885, Part IV of *Zarathustra* comprises his attempt to "reckon the sum of a deep and hidden life" (*Sämtliche Briefe*, Vol. 7, No. 589, p. 34).

9   See, e.g., Tracy Strong's excellent essay "Nietzsche's Political Aesthetics," collected in *Nietzsche's New Seas: Explorations in Philosophy, Aesthetics and Politics*, ed. Michael Allen Gillespie and Tracy B. Strong (Chicago: University of Chicago Press, 1988), pp. 153–174.

10 For an insightful survey of the methodological problems facing self-appointed physicians of culture, especially with respect to Nietzsche and Marx, see Nancy S. Love, *Marx, Nietzsche, and Modernity* (New York: Columbia University Press, 1986), especially chapters 1 and 7.

11 Jürgen Habermas, who is perhaps the most impassioned critic of Nietzsche's political project, thus argues that "Nietzsche enthrones taste . . . as the organ of a knowledge beyond true and false, beyond good and evil. But he cannot legitimate the criteria of aesthetic judgment that he holds on to because he transposes aesthetic experience into the archaic, because he does not recognize as a moment of reason the critical capacity for assessing value that was sharpened through dealing with modern art – a moment that is still at least procedurally connected with objectifying knowledge and moral insight in the processes of providing argumentative grounds" [*The Philosophical Discourse of Modernity: Twelve Lectures*, trans. Frederick G. Lawrence (Cambridge, MA: MIT Press, 1987), p. 96].

12 Nietzsche's original title for *Twilight of the Idols* was perhaps more accurately descriptive of his post-Zarathustran enterprise: *The Idleness of a Psychologist*.

13 Martha C. Nussbaum maintains, for example, that Nietzsche "does not see what socialism is trying to do" because he "does not get the basic idea [of socialism]" ["Pity and Mercy: Nietzsche's Stoicism," collected in *Nietzsche, Genealogy, Moral-*

ity: Essays on Nietzsche's "On the Genealogy of Morals," ed. Richard Schacht (Berkeley: University of California Press, 1994), p. 159]. While Nussbaum may ultimately be right about Nietzsche's failure to appreciate the inherent wisdom and justice of socialism, her conjecture that "he probably never saw or knew an acutely hungry person, or a person performing hard physical labor" (p. 159) is exceedingly difficult to square with the fact, for example, of his voluntary service as a medical orderly in the Franco-Prussian War. For Nietzsche's impressions of war and military service, see his correspondence from August–September 1870 in *Sämtliche Briefe*, Vol. 3, No. 89–101, pp. 133–145.

14   See, e.g., Habermas, *The Philosophical Discourse of Modernity*, pp. 92–97. On the other hand, Richard Rorty has recently urged philosophers and political theorists to abandon their quest for justification at the metanarrative level. A historicist influenced by Nietzsche, Rorty believes that the search for a trans-historical justification of liberalism causes more harm than the allegedly oppressive practices of liberal democracies [*Contingency, Irony and Solidarity* (Cambridge: Cambridge University Press, 1989), especially chapters 3 and 4].

15   This is the interpretive tack taken, for example, by Habermas, who insists that in Nietzsche's critique of modernity, "The aesthetic domain, as the gateway to the Dionysian, is hypostatized instead into the other of reason. The disclosures of power theory get caught up in the dilemma of a self-enclosed critique of reason that has become total . . . [Nietzsche] could muster no clarity about what it means to pursue a critique of ideology that attacks its own foundations" (*The Philosophical Discourse of Modernity*, p. 96). Although Habermas is perfectly justified in dismissing Nietzsche's post-Zarathustran critical project, I hope to show in this study that he is mistaken to conclude both that Nietzsche fetishizes the "other" of reason and that a self-referential critique of modernity can yield no insights into the governing ethos of the age.

16   For a thorough treatment of the self-referential scope of Nietzsche's irony, see Ernst Behler, *Irony and the Discourse of Modernity* (Seattle: University of Washington Press, 1990). Behler characterizes Nietzsche's irony as "a self-critical awareness of our linguistic embeddedness," which anticipates Derridean deconstruction (p. 112).

17   My peritropaic strategy is indebted to Henry Staten's "psychodialectical" reading of the complex libidinal economy of Nietzsche's texts, in *Nietzsche's Voice* (Ithaca, NY: Cornell University Press, 1990), especially chapter 1.

18   Tracy Strong maintains that Nietzsche's self-referential insights signal the end of his career as a physician of culture. Applauding Nietzsche's "perspectivism," Strong contends that "the perspectival understanding of the world . . . makes it impossible for the writer to pretend to be the physician of culture – all that one says must also be said about oneself" ("Text and Pretexts: Reflections on Perspectivism in Nietzsche," *Political Theory*, Vol. 13, No. 2, May 1985, p. 178). While Strong helpfully illuminates some important philosophical advantages of the position known as "perspectivism," he neglects to note that Nietzsche does continue "to pretend to be the physician of culture." In fact, Nietzsche points to his own experience with decadence as providing him with sufficient justification for his diagnostic enterprise (EH:wise 2). The self-referential insight that his diagnoses must also apply to him certainly alters the orientation of his

critical enterprise, but it in no way leads him (as Strong suggests it must) to abandon the project of articulating a definitive critique of modernity.

19   I am indebted here to Charles E. Scott's lucid explanation of the complex operation of "recoil" in Nietzsche's thought, in *The Question of Ethics: Nietzsche, Foucault, Heidegger* (Bloomington: Indiana University Press, 1991), especially pp. 13–19.

2

THE ECONOMY OF DECADENCE

All great problems demand *great love,* and of that only strong, round, secure spirits who have a firm grip on themselves are capable. It makes the most telling difference whether a thinker has a personal relationship to his problems and finds in them his destiny, his distress, and his greatest happiness, or an "impersonal" one, meaning that he can do no better than to touch them and grasp them with the antennae of cold, curious thought.   (GS 345)

Nothing has preoccupied me more profoundly than the problem of *décadence* – I had reasons.   (CW P)

The profundity that Nietzsche attaches to his preoccupation with "the problem of *décadence*" may strike even his most loyal readers as exaggerated. Not until 1888 does he import the French term *décadence* into his philosophical vocabulary, and only in the flickering twilight of his sanity, in such testimonial books as *Ecce Homo* and *The Case of Wagner,* does he explicitly pronounce his own decay.[1]

Nietzsche's pronouncement of his own decadence is, moreover, as obscure as it is candid. Like most of the themes and topics that dominate his later writings, "decadence" receives neither a formal introduction nor a sustained analysis. He apparently believes that decadence afflicts ages, epochs, peoples, and individuals, but he nowhere ventures a detailed account of the phenomenon of decay. In light of the currency of theories of decadence in the 1880s, he may have supposed his readers to be thoroughly familiar with his use of the term. Or, less charitably, he may have hoped to distract his readers from his failure to develop an adequately articulated account of decadence. Indeed, he occasionally employs the term so loosely as to convey nothing more than his general sense of disgust and disapprobation. In any event, it comes as no surprise that Nietzsche's theory of decadence and, a fortiori, its self-referential application have received very little attention from scholars.[2]

Nietzsche's reckoning of his preoccupation may nevertheless be both accurate and illuminating. Although the term *décadence* appears in his published writings only in 1888, the synonymous term *Entartung* (degeneration) appears as early as 1883, in Zarathustra's speech on "The Gift-giving Virtue," where degeneration is deemed "bad and worst of all," that which "we always infer where the gift-giving soul is lacking" (Z I:22).[3] Nietzsche furthermore employs the related terms *Niedergang* and *Verfall* at least as early as 1886, in the retrospective prefaces that he appends to his pre-Zarathustran books. He thus appeals to some concept of decadence, if not to the term itself, throughout the entire post-Zarathustran period of his career.[4] The belated emergence of an incomplete theory of decadence furthermore serves to unify the otherwise fragmented critical dimension of his post-Zarathustran thought, such that he might finally articulate the critique of modernity toward which he has gestured darkly throughout his career. Only upon acknowledging his own decadence, his own complicity in the cultural crisis he has presumed to treat, does Nietzsche glimpse his problem, his destiny, in its entirety. Although the problem of *décadence* has burdened him throughout his philosophical career – indeed, throughout his entire life – only in 1888 can he finally lend voice to the nature and profundity of this preoccupation. Racing feverishly against a fate he vaguely anticipated, he produced five books in the final year of his sanity, all of which contribute to the articulation of an inchoate theory of decadence.

Despite this late burst of creative productivity, however, Nietzsche's theory of decadence remains both largely implicit and incomplete. In order to evaluate his diagnosis of modernity, as well as its self-referential application, we must first reconstruct and render explicit the account of decadence that informs his post-Zarathustran writings.

The Physiology of Decadence: Mapping The "Invisible" Body

In his writings from the year 1888, especially *Twilight of the Idols*, Nietzsche consistently defines decadence as an organic disorder that involves, in alternate expressions, "the degeneration of the instincts" (TI 9:41) or "the disgregation of the instincts" (TI 9:35). He also offers the following two "formulae of decadence," both of which treat decadence as an instinctive, involuntary enactment of self-dissolution: "Instinctively to choose what is harmful for *oneself*" (TI 9:35; cf. TI 9:39, AC 6); and the *need* to "fight the instincts" (TI 2:11). Continuing this theme of ineluctable self-destruction, he goes so far as to claim that "every mistake in every sense is the effect of the degeneration of instinct [*Instinkt-Entartung*], of the disgregation of the will: one could almost define all that is *bad* in this way" (TI 6:2).

In all of these passages, Nietzsche characterizes decadence as a corruption or clash of the instincts, on which individuals and peoples customarily (and unreflectively) rely to guide their everyday behavior. His emerging theory of decadence thus reflects the burgeoning influence of his pioneering investigations into depth psychology. Throughout his post-Zarathustran writings, he consistently treats conscious intentions, volitions, and actions as derivative manifestations of a more basic, vital core of animal agency:

> Man, like every living being, thinks continually without knowing it; the thinking that rises to *consciousness* is only the smallest part of all this – the most superficial and worst part – for only this conscious thinking *takes the form of words, which is to say signs of communication,* and this fact uncovers the origin of consciousness. (GS 354)

Thus interpreted, the "surface- and sign-world" of consciousness not only yields its privileged, regal position within the realm of human activity, but also bespeaks the depth – hitherto unacknowledged and unexplored – of the human psyche. Having reduced consciousness to a surface expression of an underlying deep structure, Nietzsche consequently locates the genuine source of "thinking" and of all human endeavors in the invisible, unconscious drives and impulses that animate all of animal activity. From (at least) 1885 onward, in fact, he unwaveringly cleaves to a drive- and impulse-based model of human agency.[5] As we shall soon see, this depth-psychological model of human agency serves as the basis and foundation for his account of decadence as an internecine clash of instincts.

Although Nietzsche tends to describe decadence as an organic, physiological disorder, he also understands human physiology to be continuous with, if not finally indistinguishable from, human psychology. "All psychology so far," he insists, "has got stuck in moral prejudices and fears; it has not dared to descend into the depths" (BGE 23). In order to precipitate this daring descent, he attempts to account for the whole of human interiority as a development and ramification of the basic organic principles of "animal psychology." His unprecedented turn inward, whereby he cruelly probes his own lacerated psyche, reveals to him that animal activity, of which human activity is merely a complicated instance, is always the encrypted surface expression of the operation of primal drives and impulses:

> Every animal . . . instinctively strives for an optimum of favorable conditions under which it can expend all its strength [*Kraft*] and achieve its maximal feeling of power [*Machtgefühl*]; every animal abhors, just as instinctively and with a subtlety of discernment that is "higher than all reason," every kind of

intrusion or hindrance that obstructs or could obstruct this path to the optimum. (GM III:7)

This postulate of a primal, instinctual life activity common to all animal species thus anchors Nietzsche's depth psychology in the naturalism that ostensibly frames his post-Zarathustran critical project.[6] Rehabilitating his useless training in classical philology, he now characterizes the psychologist as "a reader of signs" (H I P8).[7]

Promising to inaugurate a "proper psycho-physiology" (BGE 23), Nietzsche undertakes a pathology of the human animal organism, whereby he records and interprets the signs of its underlying deep structure. A conventional pathological investigation, however, is inadequate to Nietzsche's purposes, for the human body as understood and treated by orthodox physiologists is an unreliable indicator of its enabling vitality. Decadence is predicated not of the visible, corporeal body, but of the "invisible," instinctual body, the subsystem of drives and impulses that propagates the native vitality of the animal organism. Whereas the visible body invariably (if erratically) manifests the prevailing condition of its governing system of instinctual regulation, only the invisible body directly bears the affliction of decadence. In order to render a diagnosis that is both empirically verifiable and faithful to his naturalism, Nietzsche must approach the invisible body indirectly, through his interpretation of the symptoms involuntarily manifested by the visible body.

Nietzsche derives indirect support for this evolving depth-psychological model of agency (and so for his emerging theory of decadence) from his speculative forays into philosophical anthropology. Intending to deliver a strictly naturalistic account of the origin of consciousness, he directs our attention to "the most fundamental change [man] ever experienced – that change which occurred when he found himself finally enclosed within the walls of security and of peace" (GM II:16). Describing the response of human animals to the (repressive) demands of civil society, he explains that

> in this new world they no longer possessed their former guides, their regulating, unconscious and infallible drives: they were reduced to thinking, inferring, reckoning, co-ordinating cause and effect, these unfortunate creatures; they were reduced to their "consciousness," their weakest and most fallible organ! (GM II:16)

Nietzsche thus locates the ultimate source and necessity of decadence in the illness of the "bad conscience" (GM II:16), which obliges individual human beings to exhaust their native vitality in the struggle to refuse the incessant demands of their natural, instinctual heritage. In exchange for the peace and security promised by civil society, that is, human animals must forfeit the natural state of well-being (and internal regulation) associated with the instantaneous discharge of their primal drives and impulses. In order to honor the founding taboos of civil society, they now must rely primarily on consciousness, a feeble organ of relatively recent emergence, to regulate their animal vitality. In an effort to simulate natural principles of regulation within the walls of civil society, human beings preside over the implementation of instinct systems, which impose an artificial order upon the amoral drives and impulses.

As one might expect from Nietzsche's account, consciousness has proven to be an extremely inefficient organ of internal regulation. Consciousness "is in the main *superfluous*" (GS 354), involving "an exertion which uses up an unnecessary amount of nervous energy" (AC 14). Indeed, human animals must pay dearly to afford, even temporarily, the extravagant luxury of renouncing the unconscious regulation furnished them by Nature:

> All instincts that do not discharge themselves outwardly *turn inward* – this is what I call the *internalization* of man. Thus it was that man first developed what was later called his "soul." The entire inner world, originally as thin as if it were stretched between two membranes, expanded and extended itself, acquired depth, breadth and height, in the same measure as outward discharge was *inhibited*. (GM II:16)

In order to enjoy the fruits of civil society, the human animal must expend a great deal of its native vitality simply to sustain the artificial introjection of its natural instincts, which in turn exerts an inordinate strain on the newborn soul. Compensating on the one hand for the deficiencies of consciousness as a regulative organ, while enduring on the other hand the inwardly directed discharge of its ever-active drives and impulses, human animals prematurely exhaust their store of native vitality in an attempt to regulate the overtaxed economy of their natural organisms.

The clash of instincts that Nietzsche associates with decadence is therefore the inevitable result of the artificial mode of internal regulation required by civilization and imposed by consciousness. Healthy peoples and individuals can temporarily enforce this artificial mode of regulation, but the eventual cost to them and their successors is enormous. Indeed, decadent peoples and individuals must bear the expense of the squandered vitality of their predecessors in the form of an instinctual discord they cannot afford to quell: "Such human beings of late cultures and refracted lights will on the average be weaker human beings: their most profound desire is that the war they *are* should come to an end" (BGE 200).

Throughout his post-Zarathustran writings, Nietzsche consistently refers to the invisible body as the "soul." Although his terminological preference is both anachronistic and potentially misleading, his attention to the soul is perfectly consistent with the naturalistic orientation of his post-Zarathustran philosophy. He explains, for example, that his prepotent critique of subjectivity banishes only the "soul atomism" that has stalled the progress of psychological investigation hitherto and not the "soul-hypothesis" itself (BGE 12). He consequently proposes as alternative formulations of this hypothesis the "mortal soul," the "soul as subjective multiplicity," and the soul "as social structure of the drives and affects" (BGE 12).

As these alternative versions of the soul-hypothesis collectively suggest, Nietzsche's account of the invisible body is far closer to a kind of functionalism than to any of the reductionist versions of materialism that were current in the latter half of the nineteenth century.[8] In keeping with his self-imposed ban on supernatural principles of explanation, he understands the soul strictly in terms of the complex of functions attributable to it through empirical observation. He consequently attempts to offer an account not of the content or material of the soul, but of its form and function; he articulates a model not of what the soul is, but of what it does.[9] He thus portrays the soul as a "social structure of the drives and affects," but not because he has direct, empirical proof of these drives and affects in operation; they remain, by definition, invisible to us. He posits the existence of the unconscious drives and affects in order to model, and so to account for, the activity and functions that he attributes to the soul.

In deriving a strictly functionalist account of the soul, Nietzsche is furthermore determined to avoid the soul–body dualisms that have thwarted the progress of all philosophy and psychology hitherto. The soul is not a metaphysical entity or substance distinct from the body, but an instinctual, substructural modality of the body. The invisible body, or soul, is the visible body in excess of itself. It is always the case, then, that his references to particular states of the soul can be translated into accounts of specific modalities of embodiment. Following Zarathustra, in fact, we might say that the soul is the body (Z I:4), provided that we continue to regard both body and soul from the "scientific," symptomatological perspective that Nietzsche claims to command in his post-Zarathustran writings. Indeed, Nietzsche's attempt to map the functional topography of the soul should be understood within a larger, more ambitious campaign to rethink the human animal organism as a dynamic, instinct-regulated machine or engine.[10] As we shall see later in more detail, neither the visible body nor the soul possesses the originary causal efficacy that is commonly associated with human agency. The visible body is in large part an involuntary coded expression of the soul, whereas the soul is a (largely) passive conduit of the undifferentiated vital forces that flow through it.[11]

In order to convey his functionalist account of the invisible body, Nietzsche regularly figures the soul as a vessel or receptacle that contains and reserves the vital forces propagated by its constituent drives and impulses. In the interest of psychic "hygiene," he thus reminds us that "the filth of the soul also requires sewers with pure and purifying waters in them, it requires rapid streams of love and strong, humble, pure hearts who are willing to perform such a service of non-public hygiene" (GS 351). In his writings from the period 1885–88, he also introduces an electrostatic model of selfhood and agency, which he deploys alongside the more familiar hydrological model he has employed since his youth. In both cases he presents the soul as a receptacle that channels and discharges a reservoir of vitality, which in turn is fed by streams (of water or energy) that originate beyond its periphery.[12] Zarathustra confidently invokes this sumptuary image of the soul in his salutation to the sun: "Bless the cup that wants to overflow, that the water may flow from it golden and carry everywhere the reflection of your delight. Behold, this cup wants to become empty again, and Zarathustra wants to become man again" (Z P1).

In figuring the soul as a receptacle, Nietzsche both adopts and adapts the Platonic model of the soul as an *oikos*, or household. He thus conceives of the soul, again in strictly functionalist terms, as the home of the primal drives and impulses.[13] For Nietzsche as for Plato, the primary attraction of the figure of the *oikos* is its immediate suggestion of the need for a regimen of internal regulation. A strong, vital household must be constantly guarded and fortified, its perimeter clearly defined and tenaciously secured, in order that it might both preserve and expand its precious holdings.[14] Nietzsche consequently introduces himself and his kindred "men of knowledge" by attesting to the primacy they assign to good housekeeping: "There is one thing alone we really care about from the heart – 'bringing something home.' Whatever else there is in life, so-called 'experiences' – which of us has sufficient earnestness for them? Or sufficient time?" (GM P1).

The figure of the *oikos* also serves to fortify Nietzsche's postulated analogy between souls and peoples, for it effectively inscribes the conceptual space that falls midway between microcosm and macrocosm. If the soul is an *oikos* writ small and if a people or epoch is an *oikos* writ large, then Nietzsche, like Plato before him, can transit effortlessly between the two poles of his political philosophy. As we shall see in the next chapter, his reliance on the Platonic model of the *oikos* thus enables the political extension of his account of decadent souls to encompass decadent peoples and ages as well. Following Plato's lead in the *Republic*, he treats peoples and ages as mortal souls writ large.

Nietzsche deploys the figure of the *oikos* in order to convey the importance of the regulatory role played by the instincts in the maintenance of the soul. Indeed, any regnant system of instincts constitutes a literal *economy* within the soul, both legislating and enforcing the governing law of the household.[15] Since a regular pattern of expenditure is the most reliable sign of a dominant instinctual system at work, the healthy soul is in fact a sumptuary, incontinent vessel – not unrelated to the leaky containers Socrates associates with intemperance in the *Gorgias*.[16] Siding with Callicles, Nietzsche thus announces that "the price of fruitfulness is to be rich in internal opposition; one remains young only as long as the soul does not stretch itself and desire peace" (AC 3).

Decadent souls, which lack the structural organization and integrity provided by a single, dominant instinctual system, are therefore failed households. They cannot distinguish friend from foe, kin from stranger, virtue from vice, treasures from trash, or triumph from collapse. Hence, Nietzsche's account of decadence as an inexorable march toward dissolution: "*Instinctively* they prefer what disintegrates, what hastens the end" (TI 9:39). Whereas healthy souls are instinctually fortified to maintain strict control over their patterns of influx and expenditure, jealously guarding their native holdings while also scheming to increase them, decadent souls instinctively throw open their gates and portals, giving away what is truly precious and standing guard only over barren larders. Decadent souls may not suffer from the incontinence that characterizes healthy souls – priestly legerdemain transforms this lack into their signal virtue – but only because they can barely muster the requisite vitality to operate as viable households.

The health and well-being of the soul, as of any household, are therefore dependent upon the regimen of internal regulation that determines the magnitude and frequency of all intake, reflux, and expenditure: "To sense that what is harmful is harmful, to be *able* to forbid oneself something harmful, is a sign of youth and vitality" (CW 5). The imposition onto the drives and impulses of a principle of organization actually serves to strengthen the soul, enabling it to propagate a greater volume and more variant flow of vital forces. Just as a wealthy household naturally excretes its lesser holdings in order to accommodate the richer treasures it covets and acquires, so a healthy soul regularly squanders its native resources in order to secure an even greater capacity for the propagation and discharge of vital forces. The failure or decay of any such principle of organization not only renders inefficient the soul's regulation of propagation and discharge, but also compromises the structural integrity of the soul itself. On Nietzsche's adaptation of the model of the *oikos*, this regimen of internal regulation is supplied by the instincts, which regulate the flow of vital forces through the soul itself.

Nietzsche ultimately prefers a starkly naturalistic account of the *oikos*, as a transient, self-regulating subsystem sheltered within the undifferentiated plenum of will to power. Hoping to purge his philosophy of its residual anthropocentrisms, he occasionally presents the soul as an embodied energy circuit through which undifferentiated forces circulate and flow in accordance with amoral principles of internal self-regulation. For Nietzsche, the soul is no inert container, but a surging, pulsating capacitor, which continuously propagates and discharges its native holdings of forces.

As the figure of the capacitor suggests, the natural activity of the soul extends no further than the unconscious expenditure of native forces in spontaneous bursts of creative self-expression. This is its sole function, which it involuntarily performs in utter indifference to external obstacles and internal constraints. Even the self-preservation of the organism is subordinated to the maintenance of the soul's natural, unconscious rhythm of propagation and discharge:

> The really fundamental instinct of Life . . . aims at *the expansion of power* and, wishing for that, frequently risks and even sacrifices self-preservation. . . . The struggle for existence is only an *exception*, a temporary restriction of the will to Life. The great and small struggle always revolves around superiority, around growth and expansion, around power – in accordance with the will to power which is the will to Life. (GS 349)

Nietzsche thus conceives of the soul as the human animal organism functioning in its most primal, uncomplicated, and rudimentary form, as a pure, amoral engine of will to power (BGE 13). Hewing strictly to the stringent naturalism of his post-Zarathustran philosophy, he accords the soul no justificatory *telos* or metaphysical birthright, vowing instead to scour the "eternal basic text of *homo natura*" of its supernatural accretions (BGE 230).

Trieb and Instinkt

The emergence of Nietzsche's theory of decadence coincides with an important refinement of his evolving depth-psychological model of the soul: his distinction between drive or impulse (*Trieb*) and instinct (*Instinkt*). The implementation of this distinction enables him to claim indirect empirical access to the "social structure" of the drives and impulses housed within the soul through his observation of discernible patterns of instinctual behavior.

Up until 1888, Nietzsche treats the terms *Trieb* and *Instinkt* as roughly synonymous, and faithful Anglophone translators have honored this practice. He employs both terms in contradistinction to the faculties and operations traditionally associated with human consciousness, for he intends both terms to refer in general to the primal, unconscious vitality that human beings share (and discharge) in common with all other members of the animal kingdom. In his account of the "origin of the bad conscience," for example, he employs the two terms interchangeably to refer to the unconscious animal activity that is forced inward at the onset of civilization (GM II:16).[17] He consistently maintains this use of *Trieb* throughout his career, but his writings from the year 1888 suggest the development of a subtle distinction between *Instinkt* and *Trieb*. While the two terms remain extensionally equivalent in the writings of 1888, denoting the unconscious drives that discharge themselves in the natural propagation of animal vitality, they are no longer intensionally equivalent. In *Twilight*, Nietzsche consistently reserves the term *Instinkt* to refer to any specific organization of the drives and impulses, as determined by the dominant mores of the particular people or epoch in question. It is precisely this task of cultivating instincts, of ruthlessly imposing order and rule onto the natural, spontaneous discharge of the drives and impulses, of creating a "morality of mores," that occupied the entire prehistory of the human animal (GM II:2).

Nietzsche's precise use of the term *Instinkt* in 1888 thus designates any specific set of conditions, imposed by and inculcated through civilization, under which the drives and impulses are trained to discharge themselves. The aim of this process of acculturation is to provide individual souls with the cultural (i.e., artificial) equivalent of those natural instincts that the human animal has forsaken in exchange for the peace and security of civil society. Disciplined to enact a trusty set of pre-reflective patterns of response to foreseeable exigencies, individuals might minimize their vexed reliance on a conscious regulation of their animal organisms. Nietzsche consequently applauds Manu's attempt

> step by step to push consciousness back from what had been recognized as the right life (that is, *proved* right by a tremendous and rigorously filtered experience), so as to attain the perfect automatism of instinct – that presupposition of all mastery, of every kind of perfection in the art of life. (AC 57)

What philosophers have traditionally called "morality" largely amounts to a confused (and cowardly) attempt to impose instinctual order onto the chaotic drives and impulses of the soul. While philosophers and moralists hitherto have been satisfied simply to cultivate any kind of instinctual organization of the soul, usually settling for some imperious form or another of castratism, Nietzsche undertakes an evaluation and rank ordering of the various systems of instinctual order that have prevailed in the course of human history. This distinction between *Trieb* and *Instinkt* thus enables him to incorporate into his evolving model of the soul an additional dimension of complexity. The unconscious drives and impulses compose the circulatory network of the soul, while the instincts constitute the patterns of regulation that govern the internal operations of this network. On this amended model of the soul, the drives and impulses themselves remain "invisible," but the instincts admit of indirect empirical observation by virtue of the traces they manifest in detectable, public patterns of behavior.

This distinction between *Trieb* and *Instinkt* also enables Nietzsche to specify the precise locus of decay within the invisible body. When he describes decadence as the loss or disintegration of the instincts, he does not mean that the underlying drives have somehow decomposed, but that their previous configuration has been compromised. Decadence thus pertains not to the drives and impulses per se, but to the instincts, to the systems of internal organization that regulate the discharge of the drives and impulses: "I call an animal, a species, or an individual corrupt [*verdorben*] when it loses its instincts, when it chooses, when it prefers, what is disadvantageous for it" (AC 6).[18] Only the instincts undergo decay and become "reactive," which means that the drives and impulses no longer work harmoniously toward a collectively desirable end. As an instinctual system decays, its constituent drives and impulses fall – amorally and indifferently – under a successor principle of organization, continuing all the while their natural activity of propagating and discharging the native vitality of the organism. For this reason, Nietzsche occasionally equates the decay of a system of instincts with the *disgregation* (rather than the deterioration) of its constituent drives and affects.

Instinctual decay involves either the reconfiguration of the drives and impulses under a novel, unhealthy principle of organization or the "anarchy" that ensues when no single system of instincts emerges as dominant. Nietzsche more regularly associates the decadence of modernity with this latter model, pointing to the internecine clash between fragmentary instinctual systems, but both alternatives are equally unappealing. In either event, the soul is guided by a principle of organization that properly belongs to another time or place, perhaps to another people or race altogether. The ensuing clash of atavistic instinctual systems riddles the soul with open sumps and circuits, which introduce an element of endogenous wastage into the already-strained economy of the soul. Rather than discharge its vitality in outward creative expressions, the discordant soul largely exhausts itself in an internal conflict between competing instinctual systems.

Nietzsche does not mean to imply, however, that it is somehow possible to restore the drives and impulses to their "original" or "raw" form, independent of all acquired patterns of organization. As a creature uniquely reliant for survival upon its nascent interiority, the human animal is defined by the mediated, principled expression of its native vitality. Although Nietzsche occasionally employs "instinct" as a term of valorization to designate those rare, "aristocratic" principles of organization that merit his approval, the absence of instinctual organization is in fact unintelligible to him. As an afterbirth of civilization itself, the human soul exists only as the product of training and cultivation, in accordance with the demands of civilization. Nietzsche roundly (and unfairly) ridicules Rousseau for believing that some untamed "noble savage" lurks within the human breast, hungrily awaiting its release from the chains of culture and convention.[19] The decay of a regnant system of instincts does not unleash our primal animal nature in its pure, unbridled fury, but simply enables the regency of another system (or of a *bricolage* of system fragments), *ad infinitum*.

Indeed, the goal of Nietzsche's politics is not to strip away the layers of instinct that stifle the spontaneous expression of our primal drives and impulses, but to perfect the process of acculturation whereby the drives and impulses become fully civilized. Since the drives and impulses invariably fall under some principle of organization or another, he wonders, why consign to chance what has been and can again be amenable to human design? He hopefully anticipates the completion of our transition from natural animal to human animal, at which time some exemplary individuals might enjoy the luxury of "returning to nature," of yielding altogether to their (fully civilized) drives and impulses (TI 9:48).[20] In this respect, Goethe affords us a glimpse of the promise the future holds, for "he disciplined himself to wholeness, he *created* himself. . . . Goethe conceived a human being who . . . might dare to afford the whole range and wealth of being natural, being strong enough for such freedom" (TI 9:49).

Nor does Nietzsche mean to imply that the decay or imposition of any single instinctual system is particularly disastrous or beneficial for its constituent drives and impulses. The invisible body is an irresistably active engine of propagation and discharge, and it continues its animal activity in utter indifference to the instinctual systems imposed upon it. The overworked distinction between "active" and "reactive" forces thus pertains not to the drives and impulses themselves, but to the instinctual systems under which they are organized.[21] Indeed, the drives and impulses do not distinguish, as Nietzsche does, between "healthy" and "decadent" configurations of their enabling networks, or between active and reactive systems of instinctual organization. Despite his occasional wishes to the contrary, the human soul displays neither a natural affinity for healthy instincts nor a natural aversion to decadent instincts. Whereas an instinctual system is a human artifice, perfected and imposed by human beings in an attempt to orchestrate a temporary convergence between *nomos* and *physis,* the unconscious drives and impulses belong solely to Nature, from which they inherit their implacable indifference to human design.

Nietzsche's late distinction between *Trieb* and *Instinkt* serves the further purpose of supplying his critical philosophy with a more solid, empirical foundation. While he claims no direct access to the basic network of unconscious drives and impulses, he believes that an indirect access to them is available through a "scientific" interpretation of the observable patterns of behavior through which the instincts invariably express themselves. His writings from the year 1888 consistently treat the instincts as manifesting themselves in acculturated, habitual, pre-reflective patterns of behavior. He consequently applauds the findings of Zopyrus, the itinerant physiognomist who (correctly) diagnosed the ugly Socrates as a "cave of bad appetites" (TI 2:9).

By carefully observing an individual's outward, instinctual behavior, Nietzsche can similarly deduce the principle of organization (or lack thereof) that governs the individual's underlying substructure of drives and impulses. Instincts do not admit of direct observation, but their surface traces function as signs of the "social structure" that prevails within the invisible body. He thus insists that "the values of a human being betray something of the *structure* of his soul" (BGE 268). As Freud would similarly conclude several years later, a "scientific" defense of depth psychology must establish an empirical link between the invisible activity of the unconscious drives and an established database of observable phenomena. Just as Nietzsche points to "instinctive" patterns of behavior as reliable signs of the principle of organization that governs underlying drives and impulses, so Freud tirelessly documents the empirical data furnished by dreams, mischievements, parapraxes, and the like.

For all of Nietzsche's confidence in pronouncing the decadence of various peoples and ages, however, his forays into depth psychology stray dangerously far from the naturalism that supposedly anchors his post-Zarathustran critical philosophy. While he consistently couches his symptomatology in empirical, naturalistic terms, his constant appeal to the unconscious drives and regulatory instincts remains to some extent speculative. Because the invisible body, by definition, defies direct empirical observation, the very existence of the unconscious drives and impulses remains to some extent hypothetical. The only observable traces of physiological decay lie in those mysterious encrypted symptoms that Nietzsche alone can interpret.

He insists that the native vitality of the invisible body can be measured with a "dynamometer" (TI 9:20), implying that such measurements would help to secure the tenuous empirical grounding of his critical philosophy. The precise calibration he has in mind for this wondrous instrument, however, such that it might accurately detect instinctual disarray, remains a secret to all but him.[22] In any event, he advances no reproducible method or system whereby others might scientifically confirm or dispute the findings on which he bases his diagnoses. That the human body is amenable to the semiotic strategies he introduces follows only from his postulate – untested and unproved – that human beings rely indirectly on the drives and impulses characteristic of all animal life. If we were to reject this postulate or even suspend it in skeptical abeyance, then Nietzsche's appeal to the invisible body, as well as the symptomatological turn it enables, would probably hold little scientific credence.[23]

In Vita Veritas

In order to continue our reconstruction of Nietzsche's theory of decadence, we must now investigate the *vitalism* that it presupposes and conveys. If all animal activity is a ramification, as he postulates, of the unconscious propagation of vital forces, then all value judgments are ultimately reducible to a measure of the native vitality involuntarily expressed by the soul or souls in question. Nietzsche's vitalism thus emerges in his post-Zarathustran writings as the ground, or source, of the various normative judgments he advances. Throughout his writings from the period 1885–88 and especially in the books written in his final year of sanity, Nietzsche evinces his ever-strengthening commitment to a form of vitalism. He regularly insists that one's prospects for flourishing, for attaining nobility and greatness, depend in complicated ways on the quantity and quality of the native vitality that one's soul reserves and expends. In fact, this experiment with vitalism stands as the central, unifying theme of his post-Zarathustran writings: All of his critical evaluations, pro and contra, ultimately rest on his appeal to the store of vital "stuff" that the souls in question propagate and discharge. His vitalism also links the critical project of his post-Zarathustran period with the hylozoism of his youth, thereby announcing the homecoming of his own soul.[24] As he says of all philosophers:

> Their thinking, is, in fact, far less a discovery than a recognition, a remembering, a return and a homecoming to a remote, primordial, and inclusive household of the soul, out of which these concepts grew originally: philosophizing is to this extent a kind of atavism of the highest order. (BGE 20)

The critical dimension of Nietzsche's post-Zarathustran writings trades on a simple, dichotomous typology. When evaluating art, philosophy, law, ethics, politics, and all other creative human endeavors, he characteristically inquires: Does the activity in question signify a *deficiency* or an *excess*, a *lack* or a *surfeit*, *depletion* or *nimiety*, *sacrifice* or *squandering*? Of the value judgments pertaining to good and evil, for example, he thus inquires:

> Have they hitherto hindered or furthered human prosperity? Are they a sign of distress, of impoverishment, of the degeneration of Life? Or is there revealed in them, on the contrary, the plenitude, force, and will of Life, its courage, certainty, future? (GM P3)

He similarly insists that a work of art is produced either from overfullness or from privation, and as such is symptomatic of the relative "health" of the artist in question (BT P1, GS P2). Bearing witness to the centrality of his vitalism, he thus explains that "regarding all aesthetic values I now avail myself of this main distinction: I ask in every instance, 'is it hunger or superabundance that has here become creative?'" (GS 370).[25] He pursues a similar distinction between two basic types of philosophers: "In some it is their deprivations that philosophize; in others, their riches and strengths. The former *need* their philosophy. . . . For the latter it is merely a beautiful luxury" (GS P2).[26] Indeed, his vaunted critique of metaphysics ultimately turns on his interpretation of metaphysical judgments as symptoms of an underlying condition that bespeaks either a superfluity or deficiency of vital resources:

> All those bold insanities of metaphysics, especially answers to the question about the *value* of existence, may always be considered first of all as the symptoms of certain bodies. And if such world affirmations or world negations *tout court* lack any grain of significance when measured scientifically, they are the more valuable for the historian and psychologist as hints or symptoms of the body, of its success or failure, its plenitude, power, and autocracy in history, or of its frustrations, weariness, impoverishment, its premonitions of the end, its will to the end. (GS P2)

In all such examples of his critical philosophy at work, Nietzsche bases his distinctions and subsequent evaluations on an appeal to the native vitality of the individual or artifact in question. Throughout the post-Zarathustran period of his career, he employs various designations for the basic, constitutive "stuff" of human agency, including *affect, energy, force, health, life, power, strength, vitality,* and *will*. All of these terms carry a strongly positive connotation for him, and he invariably prefers those activities, individuals, organizations, and institutions that manifest an excess – either quantitative or qualitative – of the stuff in question. His failure (or refusal) to arrive at a satisfactory technical term for this basic vital stuff contributes to the vagueness and generality of his post-Zarathustran political thinking, for he tends to employ these terms interchangeably in his various diagnoses of health and decay.

The numbingly simple dichotomies for which Nietzsche is often lampooned – healthy versus decadent, strong versus weak, active versus reactive, and so on – are all products of the vitalism that informs his post-Zarathustran critical philosophy. Interpreting the decadence of modernity within the framework of this vitalism, he explains that "the decrease in instincts which are hostile and arouse mistrust . . . represents but one of the consequences attending the general decrease in *vitality* [*Vitalität*]" (TI 9:37). Passages such as this presuppose (and reflect) Nietzsche's turn to symptomatology, which he deploys in his post-Zarathustran writings as his favored method of critical inquiry. Through symptomatology, he claims to gain indirect access to the structure of the invisible bodies he investigates. Yet the turn to symptomatology and the blunt dichotomies that follow this turn would be unintelligible outside the framework of his vitalism. Explicitly linking his symptomatology with his vitalism, he maintains that "every individual may be scrutinized to see whether he represents the ascending or the descending line of Life" (TI 9:33). Indeed, his vitalism serves as the fixed background of his post-Zarathustran thought, against which we might chart the various developments in his revised critical method.

While Nietzsche's philosophical experiment with vitalism is unique to his post-Zarathustran writings, his personal commitment to vitalism is not.[27] Influenced both by Emerson and the Romantic poets, his earliest notes and essays convey a pantheistic reverence for the transcendent force or deity that infuses individuals with the vitality they derivatively express.[28] His promising career as a philologist was ruined, in part, by his insistent association of Dionysus with the trans-individual agency – or *Ur-eine* – that breathed an intoxicating vitality into the otherwise lifeless Apolline forms of Greek tragedy. The books of his middle period depart from the implicit vitalism of his early period, but they are also symptomatic, or so he claims, of a nearly fatal bout with romantic pessimism (H II P7). His "positivistic" campaign to purge his philosophy of its vitalism thus reflects the waning vitality of his own life. As he begins to "convalesce" (GS P1), his commitment to vitalism resumes a prominent and central place within the economy of his thought.

Nietzsche's vitalism re-enters his philosophy unannounced, smuggled in by way of his turn to symptomatology in 1885.[29] His vitalism quickly takes root, gradually transforming the basic orientation of his entire philosophical project. The signature teachings of his post-Zarathustran period – historicism, perspectivism, nihilism, will to power, symptomatology, fatalism – all arise and take shape within the context of his experiment with vitalism.[30] The categories and vocabulary of vitalism dominate Parts I and II of *Beyond Good and Evil*, even to the point of distraction. At all decisive junctures Nietzsche appeals, usually without elaboration or clarification, to the substructure of drives and impulses that all other philosophers, psychologists, and physiologists have failed to capture in their "prejudiced" accounts of human agency. Parts I and II of *Beyond Good and Evil* furthermore link his experiment with vitalism to his "hypothesis" of the will to power; he intends the latter to serve the former, and he continues his experiment with vitalism even after the novelty of the will to power begins to fade. In fact, his notorious attempt in *Beyond Good and Evil* to account for the entirety of human activity in terms of the desire for enhanced power is replaced by, or subsumed under, his later attempt to account for the entirety of Life in terms of the natural, amoral discharge of vital forces.

His symptomatology receives its first sustained test in the *Genealogy*, whose occasional lapses are perhaps attributable to the novelty of the vitalism at work therein. His avowed goal in Essay I of the *Genealogy*, for example, is not to advance a normative evaluation of "slave morality," but to interpret the contemporary predominance of slave morality as a sign of the underlying condition (and development) of the human soul. He of course fails to observe the line he draws between description and prescription, relying on his rhetoric to convey his own pre-philosophical, "unscientific" prejudices against slave morality. His "genealogy of morals" thus represents a first, largely unsuccessful attempt to deploy the "objective" critical method that would soon evolve into symptomatology.

The critical apparatus of vitalism-cum-symptomatology is firmly in place by the time he writes *Twilight of the Idols*, a book in which he extends his symptomatology to encompass entire peoples and ages; here the diagnosis of modernity as a *decadent* age receives its first full formulation. In all of the writings from 1888, his growing reliance on the concept of Life attests to the ascendency of his vitalism. Finally, in *Ecce Homo* and *The Case of Wagner*, he applies to himself the vitalistic categories that now dominate his thought, describing the descensional and ascensional trajectories of his own life, respectively, as decreases and increases in vitality (*Vitalität*) (EH:wise 1). Generalizing this insight in *The Case of Wagner*, he remarks that "every age" either "has the virtues of *ascending* life" or it "represents declining life" (CW E).

Nietzsche's experiment with vitalism thus furnishes the context for his anachronistic attempt to defend an order of rank among human types. In his post-Zarathustran writings, he measures human flourishing strictly in terms of the depth and plasticity of the soul, as evidenced by its capacity to propagate and discharge its native vitality. Indeed, the virtues and good works that figure so prominently in voluntaristic accounts of "moral worth" are conspicuously absent from his vitalistic account of human flourishing. Speaking on behalf of an anonymous "philosopher," he thus proposes a strictly formal, extra-moral ideal of human flourishing:

> He shall be greatest who can be loneliest, the most concealed, the most deviant, the human being beyond good and evil, the master of his virtues, he that is overrich in will. Precisely this shall be called *greatness:* being capable of being as manifold as whole, as ample as full. (BGE 212)

As several commentators have observed, Nietzsche offers no reliable table of virtues, no surefire recipe for *Übermenschlichkeit*.[31] His "manifold-ample" measure of greatness is deliberately devoid of particular content and pre-scription, for it reflects the amoral vitalism on which it trades.[32]

As this account of greatness indicates, the key to human flourishing thus lies exclusively in one's sumptuary capacity to afford the involuntary expen-ditures required for "superhuman" self-expression:

> The genius, in work and deed, is necessarily a squanderer: that he squanders himself, that is his greatness. The instinct of self-preservation is suspended, as it were; the overpowering pressure of outflowing forces forbids him any such care and caution. . . . He flows out, he overflows, he uses himself up, he does not spare himself – and this is a calamitous, involuntary fatality, no less than a river's flooding the land. (TI 9:44)

The exemplary human beings whom he praises thus share a common phys-iological destiny: They involuntarily squander themselves, thereby unleashing a potentially mortal expenditure of "outflowing forces." At the pinnacle of this vitalistic order of rank, Nietzsche installs the enigmatic *Übermensch.*

His fertile image of the genius as a natural disaster, as a swollen river that spontaneously floods the surrounding countryside, is designed to convey the amoral account of genius that his vitalism suggests. Exemplary human beings are to be admired and cherished for their profligacy, but they are neither to be congratulated nor to be chastised for their involuntary expenditures of vitality. Exotic specimens of overflowing health are no more responsible for their "physiological" destiny than the cripples and fragments who induce in Zarathustra a contempt for humankind as a whole (Z II:20). Here we see that Nietzsche's experiment with vitalism also serves his campaign to emigrate "beyond good and evil," whereby he might "leave the illusion of moral judgments *beneath* himself" (TI 7:1).

This amoral model of human flourishing is also helpful in situating the *noble* soul within the typology of vitalism. Indeed, Nietzsche's famous distinction between *noble* and *base* is eventually replaced by, or subsumed under, the later, more "objective" distinction between *healthy* and *decadent.* In his post-Zarathustran writings, both distinctions are supposed to comprise purely formal (and morally neutral) concepts of designation, independent of the specific content or manifestation of the activities involved; for this reason, he often attributes the same actions and traits to noble and base souls alike. Noble souls are distinguished simply by their enhanced, natural capacity to express themselves through an involuntary expenditure of their native vitality:

> Whoever has a soul that craves to have experienced the whole range of values and desiderata to date . . . needs one thing above everything else: the *great health* – that one does not merely have but also acquires continually, and must acquire because one gives it up again and again, and must give it up. (GS 382)

Owing to the "*great health*" that enables its Faustian quest to experience "the whole range of values and desiderata to date," the noble soul comes to resemble Nature itself, which Nietzsche describes as "wasteful beyond measure, indifferent beyond measure" (BGE 9). Because of its capacity for squandering its excess energies and resources, the noble soul thus represents both a "return to Nature" and an "ascent" to Nature (TI 9:48). Invoking this prodigal image of Nature, Nietzsche thus alludes to the strictly "naturalistic" ideal he foresees for the post-nihilistic age to come: "Another ideal runs ahead of us, . . . the ideal of a spirit who plays naively – that is, not deliberately but from overflowing power and abundance – with all that was hitherto called holy, good, untouchable, divine" (GS 382). As we have seen, however, any "return to Nature" on the part of mortal souls is only temporary, only illusory. Even the greatest human exemplars must eventually resume their appointed places within the restricted economy of Life.

Because Nietzsche's experiment with vitalism contradicts some of his most influential anti-metaphysical insights, many scholars are reluctant to acknowledge its presence in, much less its centrality to, his post-Zarathustran thinking.[33] In light of his penetrating critique of metaphysics and his ridicule of the Kantian *Ding an sich*, one might conclude that he should know better than to experiment with a metaphysically freighted vitalism. Part of the problem here lies, however, in the anachronistic insistence that he lie in a Procrustean bed of "postmodern" design, that he anticipate and thereby legitimate the philosophical anxieties of his twentieth-century scions.[34] Nietzsche may have raised some of the guiding questions of postmodern philosophy, but his own unique attempts to answer these questions – witness, for example, his experiment with vitalism – are often exceedingly difficult to reconcile with the avowed aims of his postmodern heirs.

Nietzsche's Critique of Agency

Nietzsche's experiment with vitalism dramatically expands the scope of his critique of subjectivity. He not only exposes the ego and the will as metaphysical fictions, but also challenges the very notion of individual agency. Far from the champion par excellence of the heroic will, as he is so commonly portrayed, Nietzsche stands as the most radical critic of voluntarism itself. Indeed, if we accept his full critique of subjectivity, then we must be prepared to view individual "subjects" not as causal agents, but as passive conduits of the will to power.

In an oft-cited passage from the *Genealogy*, Nietzsche avers that the metaphysical subject, understood here as an identity-preserving substratum in which accidental properties alternately inhere, is nothing more than a "fiction" endemic to folk psychology:

> But there is no such substratum; there is no "being" behind doing, effecting, becoming; "the doer" is merely a fiction added to the deed – the deed is everything. The people [*Volk*] in fact double the deed; when they see the lightning flash, it is the deed of a deed: they posit the same event first as cause and then a second time as its effect. (GM I:13)

Despite the widespread enthusiasm for this critique of subjectivity, its full implications are not generally acknowledged. For if the metaphysical subject is a fiction of folk psychology, then surely its constituent agencies – such as the will – are fictions as well.

Nietzsche makes precisely this point in his textbook debunking of "The Four Great Errors" in *Twilight of the Idols*. He begins by exposing the alleged causality of the will as an external projection of an "inward fact" – namely, the experience of oneself as a causally efficient agent in the world. The progress of psychology, however, modest as it is, reveals that the metaphysical will, a spectral agency allegedly responsible for translating beliefs into deeds, is nothing more than a "phantom," a "will-o'-the-wisp" (TI 6:3) that was "invented essentially for the purpose of punishment, that is, because one wanted to impute guilt" (TI 6:7). In a parlance reminiscent of his critique of subjectivity in the *Genealogy*, he exposes the metaphysical will as a hoary fiction of folk psychology:

> The most ancient and enduring psychology was at work here and did not do anything else: all that happened was considered a doing, all doing the effect of a will. . . . A doer (a "subject") was slipped under all that happened. It was out of himself that man projected his three "inner facts" – that in which he believed most firmly: the will, the spirit, the ego. (TI 6:3)

He consequently ridicules those "philosophers [who] are accustomed to speak of the will as if it were the best-known thing in the world" (BGE 19). He singles out his *Erzieher*, Schopenhauer, who "has given us to understand that the will alone is really known to us, absolutely and completely known, without subtraction or addition" (BGE 19).

Although the metaphysical will is nothing more than a fiction of folk psychology, its currency is attributable to the attempt to account for a phenomenon that Nietzsche takes quite seriously: the experience of oneself as a causally efficient agent. He consequently undertakes to explain the provenance of this experience, but without recourse to the metaphysical contrivances of folk psychology: "The old word 'will' now serves only to denote a resultant, a kind of individual reaction, which follows necessarily upon a number of partly contradictory, partly harmonious stimuli: the will no longer 'acts' or 'moves'" (AC 14). He thus advances a strictly phenomenalistic account of the experience associated with "willing," of which the metaphysical will represents a clumsy hypostatization.[35]

Vowing to scour the phenomenal experience of willing of its noxious metaphysical accretions, he offers these observations: (1) "In all willing there is, first, a plurality of sensations [*Gefühlen*]"; (2) "just as sensations [*Fühlen*] (and indeed many kinds of sensations) are to be recognized as ingredients of the will, so, secondly, should thinking also: in every act of will [*Willensucht*] is a commanding thought"; (3) "the will is not only a complex of sensation and thinking [*Fühlen und Denken*], but also an *affect,* and specifically the affect of the command" (BGE 19).[36]

The intimate relationship between will and affect is central to Nietzsche's phenomenalism, for it provides a point of contact between the invisible body and the world.[37] The complex phenomenal state associated with willing is achieved only when one attains a threshold level of affective engagement with the world.[38] This requires, in turn, that one identify a goal upon which the will might blindly fasten itself, in the pursuit of which one might invest one's ownmost affective energies. In order to sustain a vital level of affectivity in the absence of the unreflective direction provided by Nature, one needs a goal to focus, channel, and enhance one's affective engagement with the world. According to Nietzsche, "The basic fact [*die Grundthatsache*] of the human will [is] its *horror vacui: it needs a goal* [*Ziel*] – and it would rather will nothingness than not will [*das Nichts wollen, als nicht wollen*]" (GM III:1).

A goal is needed, he explains, to justify the suffering endemic to life and to silence the Silenian refrain – "In vain! [*Umsonst!*]" – that echoes throughout an otherwise meaningless existence (GM III:28). Because the will has no natural object, it attaches itself promiscuously to any goal whose pursuit promises to ensure a threshold level of affective engagement. Indeed, the "last will of man" is achieved when the sole remaining goal capable of exciting a vital level of affective investment is that of self-annihilation: the will never to will again (GM III:1). Nietzsche thus employs the term *goal* in a strictly functional sense to refer to any end whose pursuit can be "justified" in an interpretive context that excites a vital level of affective investment and thus engages the will.

Strictly speaking, then, there is no will, but only willing, which Nietzsche describes as "something *complicated,* something that is a unit only as a word" (BGE 19). What metaphysicians characteristically hypostatize as the "will" is simply the enhanced feeling of power (*Machtgefühl*) that gives rise to an experience of causal efficacy.[39] This enhanced feeling of power, in turn, is an epiphenomenal result of the configuration of the soul under a specific principle of organization, or set of instincts: "In this way the person exercising volition adds the feelings of delight of his successful executive instruments, the useful 'underwills' or undersouls – indeed, our body is but a social structure composed of many souls – to his feelings of delight as commander" (BGE 19). It is this enhanced feeling of power that alone assures the human animal that its threshold level of vitality has been attained; it thus functions to alert the human animal that it currently operates under a viable principle of internal regulation. Nietzsche's appeal to this feeling of power as a standard of relative health (or decay) thus reflects, or so he believes, the naturalism that guides his symptomatological investigations.

While the *experience* of willing is both simple and unitary – hence the confusion shared by orthodox metaphysicians and folk psychologists alike – this experience belies the complexity of its underlying configuration of drives and affects. Indeed, the soul experiences itself as a unified, efficient force only when its constituent drives and affects work together to ensure an unimpeded propagation of agency: "*L'effet c'est moi:* what happens here is what happens in every well-constructed and happy commonwealth; namely, the governing class identifies itself with the successes of the commonwealth"

(BGE 19). *Willing* thus refers not to the handiwork of a spectral agency, but to the complex phenomenal state that attends the organization of the drives and affects into a "happy commonwealth." Because the invisible body is a "social structure composed of many souls" (BGE 19), the appropriate "political" organization of these souls (or undersouls) will enable the enhanced feeling of power that accompanies a robust propagation of agency. He consequently insists that "the 'unfree' will is mythology; in real life it is only a matter of *strong* and *weak* wills" (BGE 21).

Hence the importance for Nietzsche of cultivating strong, monopolistic instincts: Only when properly organized and configured do the unconscious drives and impulses attain a propagation of vitality that is commensurate with the feeling of power that he associates with willing. The decay of instinct thus results in a "weakness of the will," which he defines as "the inability *not* to respond [impulsively] to a stimulus" (TI 5:2). A capacitor is damaged not by a quantitative shortage of vital resources, but by a structural incapacity to channel its resources effectively and efficiently. He consequently defines *decadence* in terms of the "disgregation of the will" (TI 6:2), a process whereby the drives and affects become (dis)organized in such a way that their subsequent "aggregation" can no longer produce a feeling of power.[40] The disgregation of the will instead produces a "feeling of physiological inhibition," which Nietzsche associates with "deep depression, leaden exhaustion, and black melancholy" (GM III:17).

Nietzsche occasionally attempts an even more fundamental analysis of decadence, explaining the disgregation of the will in terms of an entropic deformation in the circulatory system of the soul. Although he conceives of the "world" of will to power as a boundless, undifferentiated plenum, he also believes that this "powerful unity . . . undergoes ramifications and developments in the organic process" (BGE 36). The entirety and complexity of human psychology, he consequently insists, can be understood in terms of the organic differentiation and diversification of the will to power (BGE 23). Toward this end, he outlines a three-stage "morphology" of the uniquely human manifestations of will to power: (1) The most basic manifestation of agency is that of the undifferentiated, anorganic will to power, which, in the process of suffusing capacitors with vitality, (2) propagates itself through an invisible, ramifying network of drives and impulses, (3) which in turn manifests itself, by virtue of the affective engagement it enables, as observable (albeit encrypted) patterns of "instinctual" behavior. He consequently refers to the will to power as a "*pre-form* [*Vorform*] of Life" and to the "life of the drives [*Triebleben*]" as a "ramification" of the will to power (BGE 36).

This three-stage morphology of the will to power thus furnishes the context for his account of the disgregation of the will. Influenced by the anti-materialist atomisms promulgated by Boscovich, Lange, and others, he presents the "world" of will to power as a dynamic whirl of quanta (or "centers") of force.[41] Each quantum of force is defined not in terms of a material essence or substratum, but only in terms of its differential "effects" on other quanta of force within the plenum. He thus proposes, in a famous notebook entry, that "a 'thing' is the sum of its effects, synthetically united by a concept, an image" (WP 551). His hypothesis of will to power thus suggests an account of the world as an immeasurably dense, undifferentiated whole, which is not the sum of the constituent "parts" inhabited (and hubristically "explained") by human beings.[42] If quanta of force are isolated and defined only in terms of their differential relations to other quanta of force, then any attempt to measure the world itself, through an aggregation of all known quanta of force, is doomed to failure and folly.[43]

At the organic level of ramification and differentiation of will to power, the invisible body propagates quanta of force through its circulatory network of drives and impulses.[44] The internal flow of these quanta of force, which is determined in volume and regularity by the regnant configuration of the instincts, thus accounts for the vitality embodied by "individual" human beings. By means of an efficient propagation of quanta of force, a system of instincts thus enables the phenomenal sensations of empowerment and efficacy.[45] Nietzsche consequently explains that "a quantum of force [*Kraft*] is equivalent to a quantum of drive, will, effect – more, it is nothing other than precisely this very driving, willing, effecting" (GM I:13).[46] The enhanced feeling of power associated with willing thus signifies (to the symptomatologist) an unimpeded flow of these quanta of force through the circulatory system of the healthy capacitor. *Willing* thus refers to a specific disposition – both quantitative and qualitative – of the quanta of force propagated and discharged by the capacitor.

Embracing Lange's principles of the "conservation of energy" and the "indestructability of matter," Nietzsche insists that these basic quanta of force cannot be destroyed.[47] They can, however, fall under anarchic or ochlocratic principles of aggregation in the "social structure of the drives and affects," which invariably effect a vital entropy. The quantity of vital forces within the soul remains constant, but in the event of a clash of competing instinct systems, these quanta of force become (dis)aggregated in configurations that are qualitatively incapable of sustaining a feeling of power. He consequently equates decadence with "the anarchy of atoms" (CW 7), which in turn occasions the experience of weakness of the will.[48]

The advance of decadence thus cripples the soul as an efficient capacitor. Bereft of the instinctual reinforcement that hitherto ensured its structural integrity, the soul devolves into a distended, flaccid casing for the vital forces that now course aimlessly throught it: "Everywhere paralysis, arduousness, torpidity or hostility and chaos: both more and more obvious the higher one ascends in forms of organization. The whole no longer lives at all: it is

composite, calculated, artificial, and artifact" (CW 7). While the disgregation of the will signals a crisis in the invisible body, a vigilant symptomatologist can indirectly detect this crisis by charting its symptoms in the "visible"
body. As "the typical signs" of decay, Nietzsche lists selflessness, depersonal-
ization, the loss of a center of gravity, and neighbor love (EH:destiny 7).

He consequently understands "health" in terms of an integration of the
will and "decadence" in terms of a disgregation of the will. Indeed, he often
characterizes decadence as a *weakness of the will,* by which he means any
failure of the instincts to maintain the specific organization of drives and
impulses needed to sustain a threshold level of affective engagement, which
occasions, in turn, the enhanced feeling of power associated with willing.
Weakness of the will thus designates the failure or corruption of any regnant
system of instincts.

The disgregation of the will leaves the soul a sclerotic capacitor, which
becomes increasingly unable to propagate and discharge its native vitality.
Decadence consequently manifests itself as a volitional crisis, or *akrasia,*
which prevents individuals from acting in their own best interests.[49] The
decadent soul must therefore accommodate within its collapsing economy
an ever-widening gulf between the cognitive and volitional resources at its
disposal, and it must compensate for the relative deficiency of will that
ensues. Indeed, decadent individuals are not typically unaware of their
condition or of the mistakes they involuntarily commit; they simply lack the
volitional resources needed to implement their cognitive insights. They
often know their destiny, but they are powerless to alter it.

This detour through Nietzsche's phenomenalism delivers us to the arch-
principle of his vitalism: *Willing* is the key to human flourishing. The
capacity for willing, for the reserve and discharge of one's native vitality,
alone determines the richness (or poverty) of one's experiences. Nobility,
happiness, greatness, power, strength – all are functions of willing, which is
itself the phenomenal state that accompanies the attainment of a threshold
level of affective engagement. In a passage that is rarely taken seriously, but
which fits neatly within the context of his vitalism, Nietzsche explicitly
defines *happiness* as "the feeling that power is growing, that resistance is
overcome," and he identifies as *good* "everything that heightens the feeling
of power in man" (AC 2). In a similar vein, he suggests that "one could
almost define all that is bad" in terms of the "disgregation of the will" (TI
6:2). We find ugliness abhorrent, he explains, simply because it stands as a
sign or reminder to us of decay (TI 9:20).

As Nietzsche sees it, "will" has always referred to the complex configuration of affective engagement that issues in an enhanced feeling of power.
Owing to the "crude fetishism" served by "the basic presuppositions of the
metaphysics of language" (TI 3:5), however, human beings eventually fall
captive to the supernatural principles they fashion for themselves. Only

under the metaphysical aegis of folk psychology, that is, did *will* acquire a castrative connotation, as it became identified with the successful suppression of particular affects. Nietzsche stubbornly continues to employ the term *will*, but only within the context of his phenomenalism, wherein it refers not to some spectral regent presiding over the body, but to the specific experience that attends the attainment of a threshold level of affective engagement.

Nietzsche thus accounts for willing in strictly phenomenalistic terms, as the experience of oneself as a causally efficient agent in the world. (As the example of slave morality indicates, of course, this enhanced feeling of power need bear no objective correlation to any state of affairs in the real world.) He consequently characterizes "the feeling of life in general" in terms of "will and desire" and "all that produces affect" (GM III:13). He furthermore associates this experience of causal efficacy with its attendant feeling of freedom: "His animal *vigor* has . . . become great enough for him to attain that freedom which overflows into the most spiritual regions and allows one to recognize: *this* only I can do" (EH:clever 2). In a related passage, he identifies *will to power* as his preferred term for "the *instinct for freedom*" (GM II:18). Although Nietzsche's account of the quasi-mythic "nobles" suggests that this instinct for freedom may at one time have been linked to the actuality of freedom, his phenomenalistic account of willing brackets all such questions of objective correlation, restricting itself exclusively to the *experience* of freedom.

"Life Itself Is Will to Power"

The centrality and importance of Nietzsche's vitalism is confirmed in his post-Zarathustran writings by his appeal to Life as the basic organic differentiation of the will to power. Although human "agents" constitute moments within the plenum of will to power, their only access (cognitive or volitional) to will to power is indirect, through their immersion in Life itself. Perhaps because nothing substantive can be predicated of that which constitutes the whole, Nietzsche's post-Zarathustran writings announce an important shift in focus: from the boundless economy of will to power to the restricted, organocentric economy of Life.

In an irony that is easily misplaced, Nietzsche's full critique of the metaphysical will emerges as the product of his attempt to take seriously the notion that the will is the sole efficient cause of human agency. While introducing his hypothesis of the will to power, he claims:

> The question is in the end whether we really recognize the will as *efficient*, whether we believe in the causality of the will: if we do . . . then we have to experiment with the hypothesis *that the will alone is causal.* "Will," of course, can

affect only "will" – and not "matter" (not "nerves," for example). (BGE 36, emphasis added)

This experiment might seem to confirm the popular interpretation of Nietzsche as a champion of the metaphysical will, for he attempts here to defend his belief in "the causality of the will." If "the will alone is causal," however, then the "efficient" will in question can no longer be identified with that puny homunculus whose sole power lies in transforming natural impulses into sins. In order to accommodate the hypothesis that the will alone is causal, Nietzsche must supplant that alleged mover of matter, the metaphysical will, with a more powerful and pervasive agency, which he calls "will to power."

He famously wonders whether "all mechanical occurrences are not . . . effects of will" (BGE 36), which leads him to the more radical hypothesis that "our entire instinctual life [is] the development and ramification of *one* basic form of the will – namely, of the will to power" (BGE 36). His signal contribution to psychology, he explains, is "to understand it as morphology and *the doctrine of the development of the will to power*" (BGE 23). He thus proposes that "all efficient force" is, in its most basic form, "will to power" (BGE 36).[50] In order to take seriously the causality of the will, now understood in terms of the undifferentiated, hylozoic will to power, he reverses the traditional relation of cause and effect. He traces the "Four Great Errors" of philosophical explanation to a common, uncritical faith in the individual subject as the causally efficient originator of action (TI 6). This account is conducive to error because it confuses the effect or expression of agency – namely, the will – with its cause: "The will no longer moves anything, hence does not explain anything either – it merely accompanies events; it can also be absent" (TI 6:3).

But if the will does not cause action, then the source of the agency attributed to individual "subjects" must lie elsewhere. Having "reduced" the individual soul to an amoral capacitor of vital forces, Nietzsche locates the source of the agency popularly ascribed to individuals outside (and logically prior to) the capacitor itself. The individual human being is not the origin or cause of agency, but its expression or effect: "When we speak of values, we speak with the inspiration, with the way of looking at things, which is part of Life: Life itself forces [*zwingt*] us to posit values; Life itself values through us when we posit values" (TI 5:5). Within the context of Nietzsche's vitalism, then, individuals are not so much agents as patients through whom Life irrepressibly expresses itself in the positing of values.

This important passage not only militates against the robust voluntarism that is popularly attributed to Nietzsche, but also suggests a further identification of the primordial agency that "values through us." This cryptic allusion to Life calls to mind his famous proclamation that "A living thing seeks above all to *discharge* its strength – Life itself is *will to power*" (BGE 13). Further embellishing this identification of Life with will to power, he notoriously maintains that

> Life itself is *essentially* appropriation, injury, overpowering of what is alien and weaker. . . . "Exploitation" does not belong to a corrupt or imperfect and primitive society: it belongs to the *essence* of what lives, as a basic organic function; it is a consequence of the will to power, which is after all the will of Life. (BGE 259)

Taken together, these passages situate the elusive teaching of will to power squarely within the context of Nietzsche's vitalism. *Life* is simply his preferred designation for the will to power at its most basic, undifferentiated level of *organic* ramification, that which all animate beings, independent of the complexity of their respective morphologies, share as a common link and provenance.[51] At the uniquely human level of organic differentiation and complexity, Life thus functions as the primordial, trans-individual agency that endows individual souls with the vital forces they propagate and expend. He thus figures Life as a trans-personal force that spontaneously overflows itself in a sumptuary expression of its unquenchable vitality.

Nietzsche consequently locates decadence in the natural, inevitable failure of the invisible body to sustain an efficient propagation through itself of the will to power. He refers to Life as the "foundation [*Grundbau*] of the affects" (BGE 258), and he subsequently equates "the decline of Life" with "the decrease in the power to organize" (TI 9:37). A tremendous (and eventually mortal) collision transpires at the interface of will to power, or Life, and its transient human capacitors. Like a raging torrent that is temporarily channeled and tamed, the will to power gradually wears down its capacitors with a relentless surge of vitality, eventually obliterating the locks and dams that were engineered to harness its boundless power. Bereft of the structure and organization supplied hitherto by an effective system of internal regulation, the invisible body continues to channel and discharge quanta of will to power, but now at the expense of its own structural integrity and "health." The disgregated drives and impulses of a decadent soul are (dis)organized in such a way that any further propagation of quanta of force threatens to cripple the soul as a capacitor. Of course, the will to power itself is oblivious to all such qualitative "limitations" of its natural sumptuary expression. Unlike Nietzsche, the amoral will to power does not distinguish between healthy and decadent bodies; it expresses itself indiscriminately through either type of engine and eventually exhausts both.

Although constitutive of human agency and creativity, the will to power exhibits no discernible attunement either to the fate of humankind in general or to the concerns of particular human beings. In fact, the will to power is utterly indifferent to its destructive effects on the capacitors and conduits through which it propagates itself. While the will to power cannot be tamed by human legislation, it can be harnessed and directed to the temporary service of human ends. A successful cultivation of the will to power requires, however, a capacitor fortified and trained to withstand the constant impact of the boundless agency that courses through it. To produce such capacitors, to enforce instinctual regulation as a matter of design, is the overarching goal of Nietzsche's politics.

Nietzsche's identification of Life with will to power thus facilitates the continued development of his experiment with vitalism.[52] Reconciled, perhaps, to the futility (and residual anthropocentrism) of ascribing positive attributes to an undifferentiated Whole, he concerns himself in his post-Zarathustran writings with an exploration of the will to power in its differentiated ramifications. While his repeated identification of Life with will to power might suggest that he treats the two terms as equivalent or perhaps as synonymous, the morphological inflection of his investigation suggests otherwise. Rather than abandon his "hypothesis" that the world in its most basic, undifferentiated incarnation is will to power, he instead shifts his interpretive focus to the uniquely organic ramification of will to power, which he calls Life.[53]

Whereas the will to power in its most primordial state is boundless, hylozoic, indifferent, and amoral, Life remains bounded by a horizon of anthropocentric preferences and values. To live, according to Nietzsche, is to legislate a hierarchy of values with the human at its center: "Living – is that not precisely wanting to be other than this Nature? Is not living – estimating, preferring, being unjust, being limited, wanting to be different?" (BGE 9).[54] Life itself requires us to legislate, to design, to register preferences – in short, to "deviate" from Nature and regulate the economy of Life. The internal regulation of the economy of Life is thus restricted by the non-negotiable human need for nomothesis.

Nietzsche's vitalism has occasioned a great deal of confusion, for he often appeals to Life as a standard, or principle of selection, whereby he justifies his dubious rank orderings of various manifestations of the will to power. For example, he reserves his greatest enmity for those opponents whom he deems "inimical to Life," and he apparently expects his readers to appreciate (if not share) his enmity. He also indulges himself a similar equivocation on the term *will to power.* On the one hand, he employs the term literally to designate the boundless, amoral agency that propagates itself through human capacitors. On the other hand, he employs the term synechdochically to designate the system of instincts that best provides for the unimpeded propagation of vitality.

This latter, synechdochical sense of *will to power* often conveys an (illicit) evaluative connotation, as Nietzsche attempts to distinguish between instinctual systems that enable greater and lesser expressions of vitality. He often traffics in synechdoche, for example, when referring to the loss or disintegration of specific instinctual systems:

> Liberal institutions cease to be liberal as soon as they are attained: later on there are no worse and no more thorough injurers of freedom than liberal institutions. Their effects are known well enough: they undermine the will to power; they level mountain and valley, and call that morality. (TI 9:38)[55]

Or more succinctly: "Where the will to power is lacking there is decline" (AC 6).

It is this weakness for equivocation that leads Nietzsche to derive (dubious) qualitative judgments from his reckoning of the purely quantitative dispositions of the will to power.[56] The will to power per se is never lacking or deficient in any respect. All perceived limitations and their moral residues are predicated only of specific human ramifications of will to power and thus only of the human capacitors that serve as its conduits. Of course, the perceived limitations of these capacitors, which are also configurations of will to power, are only illusory, evincing nothing more than the all-too-human wish that the will to power exhibit some measure of moral attunement to the anxieties of its transient human subsystems.

A similar equivocation on the term *Life* accounts for his occasional and equally unwarranted claims that Life favors those instinctual systems that accommodate excessive expressions of will to power. When at his best, he realizes that Life itself is utterly indifferent to the quantity and quality of forms that unfold within its omniplex plenitude. Although Life comprises a subsystem of Nature, a naturalistic account of Life commands no epistemic advantage over an antinatural or supernatural account of Life. In fact, Life itself is ultimately indifferent even to Nietzsche's own vitalism, for Life requires simply that human beings posit values; it registers no documented preference for the particular pro-Life values that Nietzsche prefers. Even the ascetic ideal, which apparently sponsors an assault on Life itself, functions to preserve certain forms of (degenerating) Life (GM III:13). When lawgivers and philosophers intervene to nurture particular forms of Life, they act solely on their own authority, in accordance only with their own legislative preferences.

The "doctrine" of the will to power was never so dear to Nietzsche as it is to his twentieth-century readers. Despite the weight assigned this "teaching" by his self-appointed executors and by Heidegger, the will to power hardly qualifies as the centerpiece of his post-Zarathustran writings. After being introduced (and subsequently neglected) by Zarathustra (Z II:12),[57] the teaching of will to power figures prominently for Nietzsche only in his initial post-Zarathustran book, *Beyond Good and Evil*, where it is identified as both a "hypothesis" and a "supposition." Following this initial experiment in *Beyond Good and Evil*, his enthusiasm for the hypothesis of the will to power noticeably declines (at least in his published writings).[58]

His subsequent books employ the term only infrequently, referring more regularly either to Life or to Nature as the primordial agency that suffuses capacitors with the vital forces they propagate. While he continues to experiment in his notebooks with the will to power as an anti-metaphysical principle of identity-in-difference, as a fluid network of orphaned texts and floating signifiers,[59] he only rarely incorporates such musings into his published writings – despite numerous opportunities to do so.[60] The enormous attention paid by scholars to the "doctrine" of the will to power, especially as the key to Nietzsche's mature philosophy, is therefore somewhat misplaced, insofar as he employed this doctrine primarily as a vehicle for the conveyance of his more basic and enduring experiment with vitalism. Indeed, whereas the novelty of the will to power quickly fades, he retains to the end the vitalism that this doctrine was introduced to serve.[61]

Nietzsche gamely endeavors to view the world "from inside," as "will to power and nothing else" (BGE 36), but the enormity of his task, he realizes, virtually eclipses his own modest philosophical achievements. Supernatural vestiges of the world viewed "from outside" continue to haunt his experiments with vitalism and will to power, causing him to relapse recidivistically into the metaphysical prejudices he has so expertly debunked. The world viewed from inside thus remains a project rather than an accomplishment.[62] Indeed, the genius of Nietzsche's hypothesis of will to power lies not in its success in securing for us a glimpse of the world viewed from inside, but in its suggestion that the failure to do so need not constitute a dead end. He thus invites his readers to collaborate on an experiment that he knows may take centuries, even millennia, to complete. The Platonic sun may be a cold, dead star, but its light will continue to reach – and blind – our eyes for some time to come.

The Full Critique of Voluntarism

In eschewing the metaphysical fictions of folk psychology, Nietzsche advances a radical critique of human agency that divests individual "agents" of the causal efficacy they hold so dear. The relevant compass of human volition extends only to the "directing force" of agency, whereby "individuals" determine the specific expression of the vitality they involuntarily reserve and discharge. When placed within the context of his vitalism, which severely limits the ambit of human volition, Nietzsche's theory of decadence per se is not as deflationary as it might at first appear. While the "driving force" of agency is rendered entropic by the onset of decadence, some decadents nevertheless retain their command over the directing force of agency.

Nietzsche's full critique of subjectivity thus calls into question the very notion of individual agency. The human soul, indirectly known through its observable patterns of "instinctual" behavior as an invisible network of drives and impulses, is a capacitor that amorally discharges its native endowment of vitality, which Nietzsche calls "will." The pervasive, trans-personal agency that enables animate entities as capacitors, suffusing them with vitality, is Life, which itself comprises all organic differentiations of the primordial will to power. The individual is therefore nothing more than an artificially designated – albeit functional – configuration of will to power:

> The single one, the "individual," as hitherto understood by the people and the philosophers alike, is an error after all: he is nothing by himself, no atom, no "link in the chain," nothing merely inherited from former times; he is the whole single line of humanity up to himself. (TI 9:33)

This deflationary account of the individual, he furthermore insists, constitutes the logical conclusion of his "hypothesis" that the will alone is causal.

As this passage suggests, Nietzsche ascribes originary agency only to Life, or will to power. He attributes only a derivative agency to that which philosophers call the "individual subject," which he sees as nothing more than a transient reflux vortex within the unquenchable plenum of Life. The accidental occasion of these vortices within the economy of Life invests individuals with the residual agency they involuntarily propagate.[63] His full critique of agency thus exposes the uniquely modernist preoccupation with the individual, as a (potentially) autonomous, self-regulating subject, as a fatuous piece of voluntaristic *niaiserie*. The Enlightenment project has not so much failed (as Nietzsche's readers often report him to claim), as it has never actually been in a position to commence:[64] "Today the individual still has to be made possible by being pruned: possible here means *whole*" (TI 9:41).

Nietzsche's displacement of individual agency into the "whole single line of humanity itself" indicates that his critique of subjectivity also comprises a critique of human agency, for the integrity of the individual is traditionally linked to the causal efficacy of the will.[65] Individual human "agents" are simply the embodied media through which the will to power amorally propagates itself:

> Is the "goal," the "purpose," not often enough a beautifying pretext, a self-deception of vanity after the event that does not want to acknowledge that the ship is *following* the current into which it has entered accidentally? That it "wills" to go that way *because it – must?* that is has a direction, to be sure, but – no helmsman at all? (GS 360)

Nietzsche thus limits his critique of agency to a debunking of the metaphysical fictions enshrined by folk psychology. Stopping far short of the anti-metaphysical anti-position favored by his postmodern interpreters, he displaces (rather than banishes) the agency popularly attributed to individual human beings.[66] He apparently conceives of Life (or will to power) as the ontological condition, ground, or event of the possibility of all manifestations of individual agency.[67] In the vitalistic writings of his post-Zarathustran period, that is, Life (or will to power) stands as the grand, trans-personal "doer" behind all "deeds." Although Nietzsche is accurately described as the "philosopher of power," he is dangerously misappropriated as a champion of individual agency, for the power he discloses is neither native to nor commanded by individual subjects. If anything, his philosophy of power summarily reduces all individual agents to conduits of the amoral, trans-individual will to power.

The enhanced feeling of power that Nietzsche associates with virtuosity and nobility of soul is not the product of "good works" legislated by the metaphysical will, but an epiphenomenon of the propagation of vital forces through the mortal soul. Reversing a hoary Socratic dictum, he consequently insists:

> A well-turned-out human being, a "happy one," *must* perform certain actions and shrinks instinctively from other actions; he carries the order, which he represents physiologically, into his relations with other human beings and things. In a formula, his virtue is the *effect* of his happiness. (TI 6:2)

Preferring the teachings of Buddhism to those of Christianity, he consequently applauds the Buddha for conforming his morality to the "hygienic" demands of Nature: "It is *not* morality that speaks thus; thus speaks physiology" (EH:wise 6).

Human flourishing is therefore a remote and attenuated expression of one's physiological destiny. While individuals enjoy limited control over the precise expression of their native vitality, they can neither alter nor augment the vital resources at their disposal. Decadent individuals, for example, cannot help but enact their constitutive contradictions: "Instinctively to choose what is harmful for *oneself,* to feel attracted by 'disinterested' motives, that is virtually the formula of decadence" (TI 9:35).

Nietzsche's celebrated emigration "beyond good and evil" thus involves his attempt to distance himself from the "ancient and enduring psychology" (TI 6:3) that he associates with "the metaphysics of the hangman" (TI 6:7). In order to avoid the confusion of cause and effect that has plagued all philosophers hitherto, he "demands" that the philosopher "take his stand *beyond* good and evil and leave the illusion of moral judgments *beneath* himself. . . . Morality is mere sign language, mere symptomatology: one must know what it is all about to be able to profit from it" (TI 7:1). A moral judgment is illusory insofar as it erroneously identifies individual "subjects" as the source or cause of the agency they involuntarily propagate. If individuals are merely capacitors of vital forces, then they can be held responsible neither for their respective endowments of vital forces nor for the economic laws that they invariably obey. If the origin of "human" agency resides beyond the derivative volition of individual human beings, then it makes no sense to blame (much less punish) individuals for the agency they involuntarily enact. As he observes with respect to the "lambs" and the "birds of prey," "To demand of strength that it should *not* express itself as strength . . . is just as absurd as to demand of weakness that it should express itself as strength" (GM I:13).

Nietzsche resolves to stand beyond good and evil not simply because he opposes the particular ascetic disciplines employed by Christian morality, but also because the model of agency they presuppose is incompatible with the vitalism he now endorses:

> One is in a state of hope *because* the basic physiological feeling is once again strong and rich; one trusts in God *because* the feeling of fullness and strength gives a sense of rest. Morality and religion belong altogether to the *psychology of error:* in every single case, cause and effect are confused; or truth is confused with the effects of *believing* something to be true; or a state of consciousness is confused with its causes. (TI 6:6)

He consequently rejects all moralities that trade on the metaphysical apparatus of will, responsibility, blame, and guilt.

In order to correct for the confusion of cause and effect that gives rise to the metaphysics of morals, Nietzsche exposes moral evaluation as a wayward species of aesthetic evaluation. Exemplary human beings are to be admired for their expressions of vitality – as one might admire any piece of Nature that has turned out well – but they do not deserve our moral approbation. Cesare Borgia is no more responsible for the exotic, overflowing health he embodies than is Wagner for the decadent romanticism of his late operas. Nietzsche openly celebrates titanic explosions of vitality and will, but he neither recommends nor prescribes them to his late modern readers.[68] While this refusal on his part is often interpreted as a Zarathustran gesture of paternalism, designed to promote the autonomy of his sluggish readers, nothing could be further from the truth. He eschews normative exhortations because they trade on the confusion of cause and effect that he has exposed lying at the heart of the metaphysics of morals. Indeed, the "ought" gradually disappears from his post-Zarathustran philosophy as he realizes that individuals cannot help but express the native vitality with which they are endowed. To urge his readers to enact a vitality they do not possess, as Zarathustra comically implores his *allzumenschlich* auditors, would be to reproduce the signature error of all priests and moralists.[69]

The prescriptive dimension of Nietzsche's post-Zarathustran thought consequently extends only to the specific expression of the vitality that individuals involuntarily propagate. Directing our attention to "one of [his] most essential steps and advances," he rehearses the following distinction between "two kinds of causes that are often confounded":

> I have learned to distinguish the cause of acting from the cause of acting in a particular way, in a particular direction, with a particular goal. The first type of cause is a quantum of dammed-up energy that is waiting to be used up somehow, for something, while the second kind is, compared to this energy, something quite insignificant, for the most part a little accident in accordance with which this quantum "discharges" itself in one particular way – a match versus a ton of powder. (GS 360)

Only this second kind of cause falls within the legitimate compass of human volition. While certain individuals enjoy some influence over the specific expression of their native vitality, the condition of their souls, as well as the capacity of expendable resources at their disposal, are largely a matter of their unalterable destiny.

Lest we dismiss this account of volition as simply too impoverished, Nietzsche cautions us to beware of popular prejudice:

> People are accustomed to consider the goal (purposes, vocations, etc.) as the *driving force*, in keeping with a very ancient error; but it is merely the *directing force* – one has mistaken the helmsman for the steam. And not even always the helmsman, the directing force. (GS 360)

Taken together, these two passages demonstrate that he likens the directing force of agency to a match, and the driving force to a ton of gunpowder. While the directing force of agency is, relative to the driving force, quantitatively insignificant, it is potentially momentous in the qualitative terms that human beings alone find interesting. The humble helmsman cannot possibly generate sufficient energy to propel the vessel he steers, but he can nevertheless influence the ship's initial course and ultimate destination.

Individuals are not responsible for the quanta of force they involuntarily propagate, but they can under certain conditions determine the qualitative disposition of these quanta. Although restricted to a command of the directing force of the agency they involuntarily enact, certain human beings enjoy sufficient volitional latitude to determine the expression of their native vitality. We must be careful, moreover, not to overestimate even this limited sphere of volition, for in many cases the directing force exerted by the helmsman may itself belong to the figments of folk psychology.

Nietzsche's imagery of the match and the gunpowder thus suggests that a strategic disposition of one's residual vitality can ignite an explosion of dammed-up forces. The amoral will to power may be utterly indifferent to its specific modes of expression, but human beings can occasionally exploit this indifference to serve their own ephemeral ends. As we shall see more clearly in the next chapter, Nietzsche presents himself as the match that will set off the explosion that brings modernity itself to a timely close.

As the greatest critic of the tranformative power of the will, Nietzsche is egregiously miscast as a (failed) radical voluntarist. In fact, when placed within the context of his vitalism, his full critique of agency militates against the standard interpretation of him as the champion par excellence of the heroic will. To the healthy, prescriptions of health are superfluous, whereas to the sick they are cruel. Contrary to popular prejudice, he offers no plan for restoring decadent souls to a more robust standard of vitality. He is interested neither in prescribing a recuperative system of instincts nor in rallying the anemic and infirm to unlikely feats of heroism and nobility. Decadent souls can do nothing but enact their constitutive chaos, expressing themselves creatively in their own self-destruction.

To the decadent souls whom he diagnoses, Nietzsche offers no cures, no therapies, and no hopes for a regimen of self-constitution that might make them whole. In a notebook entry, he ridicules the idea that we might combat decay simply by easing the experience of discomfort that attends it: "The supposed remedies of degeneration are also mere palliatives against some of its effects: the 'cured' are merely one type of the degenerates" (WP 42). Socrates' ugly face betrays not only an ugly character, but also the fatality of an ugly character. So for modern decadents as well: Cosmetic surgery can salvage a misshapen face, but not a broken soul. Decadent individuals can hope at best to rechristen their constitutive ugliness as an alternative form of beauty; in order to receive this dubious service, they must consult their local philosophers and priests.

Decadence must run its inexorable course, gradually exhausting those protective instincts that might otherwise have resisted its advance (EH:wise 6). Any recuperative scheme that claims otherwise is guilty of confusing the effects (or signs) of decay for its cause:

> This young man turns pale early and wilts; his friends say: that is due to this or that disease. I say: that he became diseased, that he did not resist the disease, was already the effect of an impoverished life or hereditary exhaustion. (TI 6:2)

Like all decadents, this young man must enact the mortal drama scripted for him: "One anti-natural step virtually compels the second" (EH:h 3). It matters not that he acknowledges his role, discerning perhaps the familiar trajectory of the advancing plot, for his crippled will can muster no effective protest. Nor can he rely on his instincts to guide him to a healthier form of life, for it is precisely the failure of his instincts to collaborate harmoniously that has sealed his demise. In Nietzsche's post-Zarathustran writings, in fact, "physiology" becomes destiny.

Notes

1 Nietzsche apparently borrows the term *décadence* from Paul Bourget, whose *Essais de psychologie contemporaine* (Volume I) appeared in 1883. Nietzsche was especially influenced by a section of Bourget's sketch of Baudelaire, entitled *Théorie de la décadence* (pp. 19–26), which he subsequently endorses and expands upon (EH:clever 5). Nietzsche names Bourget as one among a number of "inquisitive and yet at the same time . . . delicate psychologists . . . in contemporary Paris" (EH:clever 3). He also refers approvingly to Bourget in letters to Resa von Schirnhofer on 11 March 1885 and in June 1885 [*Friedrich Nietzsche: Sämtliche Briefe, Kritische Studienausgabe in 8 Bänden*, ed. G. Colli and M. Montinari (Berlin: deGruyter/Deutscher Taschenbuch Verlag, 1986), Vol. 7, No. 578, p. 18; No. 607, p. 59]. For a summary account of the extent of Bourget's influence on Nietzsche, see Walter Kaufmann, *Nietzsche: Philosopher, Psychologist, Antichrist*, 4th Edition (Princeton, NJ: Princeton University Press, 1974), p. 73.

2 Notable exceptions to this rule include Daniel Ahern, *Nietzsche as Cultural Physician* (University Park: Pennsylvania State University Press, 1995), especially chapters 1–2; Brian G. Domino, "Nietzsche's Republicanism," Doctoral Thesis, Pennsylvania State University, 1993; and Henning Ottman, *Philosophie und Politik bei Nietzsche* (Berlin: deGruyter, 1987), especially Part C, Section IV.

3 For a thorough account of Nietzsche's reliance on the imagery and vocabulary of *décadence*, see Brian Domino, "Nietzsche's Republicanism," pp. 133–144.

4 In his 1886 preface to *The Birth of Tragedy*, for example, he associates "decline, decay, [and] degeneration" with "weary and weak instincts" (BT P1).

5 On the development of Nietzsche's reliance on a drive-based model of agency, see the excellent study by Graham Parkes, *Composing the Soul* (Chicago: University of Chicago Press, 1994), especially chapters 7–8.

6 For a succinct and sympathetic account of the naturalism that informs Nietzsche's critical philosophy, see Richard Schacht, "Nietzsche's *Gay Science*, or, How to Naturalize Cheerfully," collected in *Reading Nietzsche*, ed. Robert C. Solomon and Kathleen M. Higgins (New York: Oxford University Press, 1988), pp. 68–86.

7 On Nietzsche's ingenious transformation of philology from the science of interpreting "dead" texts into the science of interpreting "live" bodies, see Eric Blondel, *Nietzsche: The Body and Culture: Philosophy as a Philological Genealogy*, trans. Seán Hand (Stanford, CA: Stanford University Press, 1991), chapter 8.

8 On Nietzsche's fascination with and knowledge of anti-materialist revisions of atomism, see George J. Stack's seminal study *Nietzsche and Lange* (Berlin: deGruyter, 1983), pp. 224–236.

9 For Nietzsche's attempt to explain what the soul is *like* (rather than what it *is*), see Parkes, *Composing the Soul*, pp. 7–8, 171–173.

10 My attention to the trans-human dimensions of Nietzsche's philosophy is indebted to Gilles Deleuze, "Nomad Thought," trans. David B. Allison, collected

in *The New Nietzsche: Contemporary Styles of Interpretation,* ed. David B. Allison (New York: Delta Books, 1977), pp. 142–149.

11　Perhaps no scholar has contributed more to our understanding of Nietzsche's proto-phenomenology of the body than Blondel, in *Nietzsche,* especially chapters 2 and 9. According to Blondel, Nietzsche approaches the body through metaphor, because metaphor allows him to speak *within* metaphysics and yet speak *about* that which metaphysics excludes (and tortures): the body. Nietzsche's "double discourse" subverts itself, to be sure, but only in this way can he avoid a metaphysical hypostatization of the body, which "shows" itself through the collision and reflux of the metaphors Nietzsche fashions (p. 28).

12　On the development of Nietzsche's hydrological model of the soul, see Parkes, *Composing the Soul,* pp. 143–155.

13　My discussion of the soul as a figural household is indebted to Parkes, ibid., pp. 43–44.

14　I explore Nietzsche's use and abuse of the *oikos* as an image of the soul in my *Nietzsche and the Political* (London: Routledge, 1997), pp. 58–60.

15　My attention to the libidinal economy of Nietzsche's writings is indebted to Henry Staten's provocative study *Nietzsche's Voice* (Ithaca, NY: Cornell University Press, 1990). Nietzsche's theory of decadence provides a promising organic basis, I believe, for the complex internal drama that Staten captures under the term "psychodialectic" (p. 31). Nietzsche's attention to the economy of the soul thus furnishes an independent, extra-textual model for the textual economies that Staten wishes to chart.

16　*Gorgias* 493–494. In response to Socrates' stated preference for temperate, self-controlled souls, Callicles retorts, "The pleasure depends on the superabundance of the influx" [*The Dialogues of Plato,* Volume 1, trans. Benjamin Jowett (New York: Random House, 1937), pp. 553–554].

17　In the context of the Darwinesque analogy that he proposes to explain the origin of the bad conscience, he describes the loss on the part of the first land animals of "their former guides, their regulating, unconscious and infallible drives [*Triebe*]" in apposition to the disvaluation and suspension of their "instincts [*Instinkte*]" (GM II:16).

18　Although Nietzsche does not use the term *decadence* in this passage, his definition here of *corruption* is virtually the same as his definition of *decadence* at TI 9:35 and 9:39.

19　Nietzsche's geuinue debts to Rousseau are judiciously reckoned by Keith Ansell-Pearson in *Nietzsche contra Rousseau* (Cambridge: Cambridge University Press, 1991).

20　For a compelling account of the psychological conditions under which the (self-)creative individual might "return to Nature," see Parkes, *Composing the Soul,* pp. 363–371. Parkes persuasively suggests that if one assiduously disciplines one's multiple drives and impulses, then eventually "control can be relaxed, one can dare to be natural, and the multiplicity will spontaneously order itself" (p. 377).

21　The currency of this distinction is most directly attributable not to Nietzsche himself, but to Gilles Deleuze, *Nietzsche and Philosophy,* trans. Hugh Tomlinson (New York: Columbia University Press, 1983), especially chapter 2. Deleuze proposes this distinction as the guiding typology of Nietzsche's thought, and he often employs it in synonymy to Nietzsche's own distinction between "health" and "decadence."

22 Nietzsche insists that "one can measure the effect of the ugly with a dynamometer. . . . The ugly is understood as a sign and symptom of degeneration: whatever reminds us in the least of the degeneration causes in us the judgment of 'ugly'" (TI 9:20). In his notes, he similarly maintains that "the muscular strength of a girl increases as soon as a man comes into her vicinity; there are instruments to measure this" (WP 807) [*Friedrich Nietzsche: Sämtliche Werke, Kritische Studienausgabe in 15 Bänden*, ed. G. Colli and M. Montinari (Berlin: deGruyter/Deutscher Taschenbuch Verlag, 1980), Vol. 13, 17[5], pp. 526–527].

23 As a solitary pioneer in the field of depth psychology, Nietzsche was bound to derive dubious and flawed theories from his own evolving models of explanation. A more polished, and in many respects more persuasive, attempt to deduce the state of the soul from a symptomatological interpretation of observable behavior is found in Allan Bloom, *The Closing of the American Mind* (New York: Simon and Schuster, 1987). While "blaming" Nietzsche for the value-relativism that has corrupted higher education in the United States, Bloom perfects Nietzsche's symptomatological method of criticism in his appraisal of the condition of the souls of contemporary college students.

24 On the hylozoic musings of the young Nietzsche, see Parkes, *Composing the Soul*, pp. 35–42.

25 In a related claim, Nietzsche decrees that "aesthetics is tied indissolubly to these biological presuppositions [namely, of declining or ascending life, respectively]: there is an aesthetics of *decadence,* and there is a *classical* aesthetics" (CW E).

26 This preface, along with Book 5 and the appendix of "Songs," did not appear in the original 1882 edition of *The Gay Science*. They were added to the original text for the new edition in 1887, and they properly belong in a grouping with the other post-Zarathustran writings.

27 Blondel displaces Nietzsche's vitalism by relegating it to the realm of metaphor (*Nietzsche,* pp. 201–238). According to Blondel, Nietzsche's recourse to the metaphor of vitalism enables him simultaneously to discuss the body and to cancel the metaphysical implications of this discussion. The problem with Blondel's interpretation is that "extra-metaphorical" concerns motivate Nietzsche's recourse to metaphor. He takes quite seriously and literally the conclusions he derives from his vitalistic model of human agency. Unless Blondel is willing also to relegate all of philosophy and politics to the realm of metaphor, his strategy for containing Nietzsche's vitalism must fail.

28 Parkes's *Composing the Soul* essays a lapidary biography of the young Nietzsche. I am especially indebted to his discussion of the influences on Nietzsche of Goethe, Byron, Hölderlin, and Emerson (pp. 23–48). See also Ronald Hayman, *Nietzsche: A Critical Life* (New York: Oxford University Press, 1980), pp. 40–49; Frederick Love, *Young Nietzsche and the Wagnerian Experience* (Chapel Hill: University of North Carolina Press, 1963), pp. 4–18; and Carl Pletsch, *Young Nietzsche: Becoming a Genius* (New York: Macmillan/Free Press, 1991), pp. 51–62.

29 This turning begins, I believe, with Nietzsche's decision to add a fourth, self-parodic part to *Zarathustra*. The works that immediately followed – *Beyond Good and Evil* and the retrospective prefaces – all implement a symptomatological method of inquiry that is largely missing from the pre-Zarathustran writings.

;0 The attempt to excise all vestiges of metaphysics, including vitalism, from Nietzsche's post-Zarathustran writings may yield a Nietzsche who is consistent with his alleged post-metaphysical insights, but it also succeeds in eviscerating these problematic books. One such attempt is made by Richard Rorty, in *Contingency, Irony, Solidarity* (Cambridge: Cambridge University Press, 1989), especially chapters 2 and 5. I address the violence involved in Rorty's interpretive strategy in "Disembodied Perspectives: Nietzsche contra Rorty," *Nietzsche-Studien*, Vol. 21, 1992, pp. 281–289.

31 This claim is found in Alexander Nehamas, *Nietzsche: Life as Literature* (Cambridge, MA: Harvard University Press, 1985), chapter 7. Rather than bemoan Nietzsche's failure to articulate a positive moral position, Nehamas applauds him for his perspectivalist restraint. According to Nehamas, Nietzsche's "failure" here is both deliberate and benevolent, for he wants to avoid at all costs dogmatically influencing his readers. In the end, Nietzsche is able to observe the moral strictures of his perspectivism and convey his ideal through the (nondogmatic) self-exemplification achieved in *Ecce Homo*. As Robert Ackermann points out, however, Nehamas's interpretation is influenced by his selectively Apollinian reading of Nietzsche's project: "The most worrisome aspect here for Nehamas is that a personal style might prove to be integrated but morally repulsive. If this problem could be solved, *Übermenschen* could meet like Rotarians, each with a colorful and unmistakable personality, ready to engage in a provocative Monday luncheon conversation" ["Current American Thought on Nietzsche," in *Nietzsche Heute: Die Rezeption seines Werkes nach 1968*, ed. Sigrid Bauschinger, Susan L. Cocalis, and Sara Lennox (Bern: A. Francke Verlag, 1988), p. 134].

32 As Ackermann notes, "There cannot be a specific code for *Übermenschen* . . . because the *Übermensch*, poised and sensitive at the cutting edge of Dionysian flux, cannot anticipate what will be demanded by Dionysus from one moment to the next. Moral codes which involve maximizing fixed values over time are simply not useful in this situation" (*Nietzsche Heute*, p. 135).

33 A notable exception here is Lester H. Hunt, who offers a sympathetic reading and defense of Nietzsche's vitalism in *Nietzsche and the Origin of Virtue* (New York: Routledge, 1991), pp. 111–130.

34 Representative of a self-described "postmodern" approach to Nietzsche is Mark Warren's *Nietzsche and Political Thought* (Cambridge, MA: MIT Press, 1988). According to Warren, "The innovative aspects of [Nietzsche's] philosophy find little expression in his overt politics. What he does, unsuccessfully, is combine a postmodern philosophy with a premodern politics" (p. 209). Warren goes so far as to claim that "in spite of the contributions of Nietzsche as a philosopher to contemporary political thought, he lacks a politics adequate to his philosophy. It follows that Nietzsche as a political philosopher must be rejected, leaving the politics of his philosophy still to be determined" (p. 210). While Warren offers various accounts of the "inadequacy" of Nietzsche's politics, he seems most

uncomfortable with Nietzsche's apparent contention that "exploitation, domination, struggle, mastery over others, and hierarchy" are endemic to political life per se (pp. 207–248). Rather than refute or discredit (much less explore) this contention, Warren announces that it "violates the intellectual integrity of [Nietzsche's] philosophical project" (p. 208).

35 I am indebted here to Warren's excellent reconstruction of Nietzsche's "phenomenology of agency," in ibid., pp. 126–130. I believe that Warren may mean "phenomenalism" rather than "phenomenology."

36 In one of his few published references to the position known as "perspectivism [*Perspektivismus*]," Nietzsche explicitly associates this position with phenomenalism (*Phänomenalismus*) (GS 354).

37 For a thoughtful treatment of Nietzsche's phenomenalism within the context of his understanding of science, see Babette Babich, *Nietzsche's Philosophy of Science: Reflecting Science on the Ground of Art for Life* (Albany: State University of New York Press, 1994), pp. 109–119. In order to accommodate the link that Nietzsche preserves between his phenomenalism and a world for which science cannot exhaustively account, Babich proposes to situate his phenomenalism within his "hyperrealism," by which she means to refer to "the world in its ambiguity and constant flux as chaos" (p. 109).

38 In a note from 1887, Nietzsche lists the following among his "fundamental innovations": "In place of 'epistemology,' a perspectival theory of affects (to which belongs a hierarchy of the affects; the affects transfigured; their superior order, their 'spirituality'" (WP 462). For an investigation of Nietzsche's "perspectival theory of affects," see Martin Heidegger, *Nietzsche, Volume 3: The Will to Power as Knowledge and as Metaphysics*, ed. David Farrell Krell, trans. Joan Stambaugh, David Farrell Krell, and Frank A. Capuzzi (San Francisco: HarperCollins, 1991).

39 While outlining "a psychology of the artist," for example, Nietzsche maintains that "what is essential in [the frenzy of an overcharged and swollen will] is the feeling of increased strength and fullness" (TI 9:8).

40 For a provocative investigation into the potentially affirmative consequences of decadence, especially for the possible reconfiguration of individual agency, see Werner Hamacher, "'Disgregation des Willens': Nietzsche über Individuum und Individualität," *Nietzsche-Studien*, Vol. 15, 1986, pp. 306–336.

41 For a promising reconstruction of Nietzsche's hypothesis of will to power, see Richard Schacht, *Nietzsche* (London: Routledge, 1983), pp. 216–224. Schacht's reliance on the unpublished notebooks tends to obscure the corrective modifications of the "hypothesis" of will to power that Nietzsche himself incorporates into his published writings.

42 On the "hyperrealism" conveyed by Nietzsche's account of the world as will to power, see the stimulating discussion by Babich, in *Nietzsche's Philosophy of Science*, pp. 109–119.

43 In a famous (but apparently discarded) notebook entry, Nietzsche proposes that the world in its entirety is simply an undifferentiated plenum of will to power: "And do you know what 'the world' is to me? Shall I show it to you in my mirror? This world is a monster of energy, without beginning, without end; a firm, iron magnitude of force that does not grow bigger or smaller, that does

not expend itself but only transforms itself; as a whole, of an unalterable size, a household without expenses or losses, but likewise without increase or income . . . *This world is the will to power – and nothing besides!* And you yourselves are also this will to power – and nothing besides!" (WP 1067).

44 In his letter to Köselitz on 20 March 1882, Nietzsche credits Boscovich with replacing matter with force (*Kraft*) as the central focus of physics and cosmology (*Sämtliche Briefe*, Vol. 6, No. 213, pp. 183–184). For a definitive reckoning of Nietzsche's debts to Boscovich and Lange, see Stack, *Nietzsche and Lange*, especially chapter 9.

45 In a notebook entry from 1887, Nietzsche thus scribbles: "What determines rank, sets off rank, is only quanta of power, and nothing else" (WP 855). In the following year he adds, "What determines your rank is the quantum of power you are: the rest is cowardice" (WP 858).

46 In a notebook entry from 1888, Nietzsche thus insists that "if we eliminate these additions, no things remain but only dynamic quanta, in a relation of tension to all other dynamic quanta: their essence lies in their relation to all other quanta, in their 'effect' upon the same" (WP 635).

47 See Stack, *Nietzsche and Lange*, pp. 35–36.

48 For a detailed study of Nietzsche's various experiments with atomism, see James Porter, "Nietzsche's Atoms," in *Nietzsche und die antike Philosophie*, ed. Daniel W. Conway and Rudolf Rehn (Trier: Wissenschaftlicher Verlag, 1992), pp. 47–90.

49 Warren has persuasively demonstrated the centrality of a "crisis of human agency" to Nietzsche's understanding of modernity (*Nietzsche and Political Thought*, chapters 1–2). Rather than view this "crisis" in terms of the "natural," descensional trajectory of modernity, however, Warren attributes the crisis to the onset of *nihilism,* a term that refers, he believes to *"situations in which an individual's material and interpretive practices fail to provide grounds for a reflexive interpretation of agency"* (p. 17). While this definition of *nihilism* bears a family resemblance to Nietzsche's concept of decadence, Warren's various accounts of the "causes" of nihilism (e.g., pp. 18–19) suggest a significant departure from Nietzsche's own symptomatological method. In fact, Warren's understanding of nihilism as a species of alienation would seem to betray the confusion of cause and effect that Nietzsche is keen to debunk.

50 According to Maudemarie Clark, Nietzsche's argument in BGE 36 "depend[s] on the causality of the will, something he nowhere accepts" [*Nietzsche on Truth and Philosophy* (Cambridge: Cambridge University Press, 1990), p. 217]. Clark thus maintains not only that "Nietzsche gives us very strong reason to deny that he accepts the argument of BG 36," but also that his exercise in self-subversion is "quite deliberate" (p. 218). This exciting appeal to Nietzsche's esotericism, however, not only is abrupt – Clark offers no sustained account of the rhetorical strategies involved or the ends to which they are deployed – but also works equally well *against* the anti-metaphysical interpretation of the will to power that she favors. Clark assures us that "Nietzsche is challenging us to look for an explanation" of will to power (p. 218), but she never returns to discuss the important moral claims her assurance presupposes. That Clark herself (or anyone else) feels challenged by Nietzsche's rhetorical indirections is one thing; that Nietzsche himself is intentionally responsible for issuing this challenge is

another thing altogether. Finally, Clark fails to demonstrate that Nietzsche's "experiment" in BGE 36 is incompatible with his critique of the causality of the will (p. 217). The former "supposes" that will can affect only will, whereas the latter ridicules the notion that will can affect matter. While Nietzsche may ultimately reject the "will – will" mode of causality that he proposes in BGE 36, as Clark plausibly insists (p. 217), he need (and should) not appeal to his critique of the "will – matter" mode of causality in order to do so.

51 On the relationship of Life to will to power, see Karl Jaspers, *Nietzsche: An Introduction to the Understanding of His Philosophical Activity*, trans. Charles F. Wallraff and Frederick J. Schmitz (South Bend, IN: Regnery/Gateway, 1965), pp. 293–302.

52 Were Clark to acknowledge Nietzsche's identification of Life with will to power, her anti-metaphysical interpretation of the will to power would become even more difficult to defend, if only because she would be obliged to account for several metaphysically freighted passages from *Twilight of the Idols*. Clark claims to extract from Nietzsche "what amounts to an admission that life itself is not will to power" (*Nietzsche on Truth and Philosophy*, p. 225), but this "admission" largely depends for its purchase on her questionable equation of *Macht-Wille* (BGE 44) with *Wille zur Macht* (p. 225). In any event, Clark fails to explain why – save for her own hermeneutic presuppositions – we should lend more credence to this cryptic admission than to Nietzsche's vitalism or to his explicit claims that "life *is* will power."

53 In a parallel development, his post-Zarathustran writings identify Nature as an even more basic morphological differentiation of the will to power, one that comprises the whole of Life within its boundless economy. Although less fully developed than his discussions of Life, his occasional appeals to Nature represent his most ambitious (and successful) attempts to rid his philosophy of its anthropocentric prejudices. As described by Nietzsche in his post-Zarathustran writings, Nature is unbounded, independent of and indifferent to the peculiar needs and demands of Life. Nature admits of no other, whether hospitable or hostile to Life, that imposes conditions upon the internal regulation of its economy. To those philologically inept "physicists" who claim to deduce democratic principles from the canon of natural law, he rejoins, "Somebody might come along who, with opposite intentions and modes of interpretation, could read out of the same 'Nature,' and with regard to the same phenomena, rather the tyrannically inconsiderate and relentless enforcement of claims of power" (BGE 22). For a sustained discussion of the distinction between Life and Nature, see my essay "Returning to Nature: Nietzsche's *Götterdämmerung*," in *Nietzsche: A Critical Reader*, ed. Peter Sedgwick (London: Blackwell, 1995).

54 Nietzsche's ridicule of the Stoics militates against any transcendence of the restricted economy of Life. Death alone links human beings to a general economy – namely, that of Nature, in which expenditure transpires unrestricted by conditions of exchange. Within the restricted economy of Life, all expenditure is channeled through the ascetic ideal, which ultimately governs (and restricts) the economies of all human organisms.

55 In those passages where Nietzsche describes the will to power as "lacking" or "declining," he invariably locates the perceived lack or deficiency in the human

capacitor and its expression of the will to power. He thus observes, for example, that "wherever the will to power declines in any form, there is invariably also a physiological retrogression, decadence" (AC 17).

56 Stanley Rosen locates in Nietzsche's unwarranted celebrations and condemnations the final unfolding of the logic of the modern scientific Enlightenment: "The search for truth leads directly to nihilism and the death of the spirit . . . theology, metaphysics and ontology are all utter nonsense" [*The Ancients and the Moderns: Rethinking Modernity* (New Haven, CT: Yale University Press, 1989), pp. 198–199].

57 Although Zarathustra first mentions the will to power at Z I:15, he does not attempt an explanation of this difficult concept until Z II:12. On Nietzsche's "discovery" of the will to power, see Kaufmann, *Nietzsche*, pp. 198–207.

58 Nietzsche's famous and oft-cited proclamation that "*this world is the will to power – and nothing besides!*" appears in a notebook entry from 1885, at which time he was assembling the materials for *Beyond Good and Evil*, the only published work in which the will to power figures prominently; resonances of this entry are to be found, for example, in BGE 36. In those notebook entries from 1887–88 that similarly treat the immanence of the world, the thesis of will to power is conspicuously deemphasized. By 1888 he has also changed the title of his proposed *Hauptwerk* from *The Will to Power* to *The Revaluation of All Values*.

59 A compelling reconstruction and defense of Nietzsche's unpublished theory of will to power is advanced by Ruediger Hermann Grimm, in *Nietzsche's Theory of Knowledge* (Berlin: deGruyter, 1977), especially chapter 1. See also Nehamas, *Nietzsche*, chapter 3.

60 Bernd Magnus persuasively emphasizes the finality with which Nietzsche abandoned his plans for *The Will to Power,* most recently in *Nietzsche's Case: Philosophy as/and Literature* (with Stanley Stewart and Jean-Pierre Mileur) (New York: Routledge, 1993), pp. 37–46.

61 Even if we accept Clark's astute contention that the "cosmological" doctrine of will to power is inconsistent with Nietzsche's critique of metaphysics (*Nietzsche on Truth and Philosophy*, p. 213), the question of his ownmost metaphysical prejudices remains open. He may "know better" than to traffic in a priori metaphysical speculations, as Clark persuasively demonstrates, but this knowledge alone need (and does) not prevent him from doing so. His theory of will to power, or the vitalism it serves, may not be philosophically consistent with (some of) his other insights, but this inconsistency is itself perfectly consistent with his general account of the activity of philosophizing. Clark's preference for a strictly consistent, Apollinian Nietzsche is certainly understandable, but is it warranted on Nietzschean grounds? Would this Nietzsche not stand suspiciously immune to the criticisms that Nietzsche levels against all philosophers?

62 Nietzsche's failure to gain access to the world viewed "from inside" would appear to confirm Heidegger's famous critique: "This makes clear in what respect the modern metaphysics of subjectness is consummated in Nietzsche's doctrine of will to power as the 'essence' of everything real" ["The Word of Nietzsche: God is Dead," *The Question Concerning Technology and Other Essays*, trans. and ed. William Lovitt (New York: Harper & Row, 1977), p. 83]. Al-

though Nietzsche failed to extricate himself from what Heidegger calls "metaphysics," it is not at all clear that he consistently intended to overcome or overturn the entire metaphysical tradition; nor is it clear what such a project could have meant to him, especially in the post-Zarathustran period of his career. Indeed, his pronouncement of his own decadence calls into question the precise nature of the "failure" Heidegger attributes to him. On the question of Nietzsche's vexed relationship to metaphysics, see Wolfgang Müller-Lauter, "Nietzsche's Teaching of Will to Power," trans. Drew E. Griffin, *Journal of Nietzsche Studies*, No. 4–5, Autumn 1992–Spring 1993, pp. 37–101.

63 It is perhaps noteworthy that, despite this conclusion, he generally eschews the language and vocabulary of machine systems, which his hypothesis would appear to endorse. He continues to speak of subjects in traditional moral and metaphysical terms as (failed) agents. Although philosophically poised, that is, to explore more thoroughly the anti- and trans-subjective projects taken up, for example, by Deleuze and Guattari in *Anti-Oedipus*, he evidently elected not to do so. As his account of decadence perhaps suggests, all such projects remain philosophically underdeveloped, for he lacks the categories and vocabularies he would need in order to express a truly trans-subjective account of agency. In an apparent concession to his limitations as a philosopher, he continues to use the terms and categories whose inadequacy he has already exposed, thereby restricting his critique of agency to an immanent assault.

64 For an influential account of Nietzsche as a (self-implicating) critic of the Enlightenment, see Alasdair MacIntyre, *After Virtue* (Notre Dame, IN: Notre Dame University Press, 1984), chapter 9.

65 For a positive interpretation of Nietzsche's critique of individual agency, see Hamacher's treatment of "the *Überleben* of Life," in "Disgregation des Willens," pp. 316–323.

66 Warren applauds Nietzsche's "postmodern" campaign to rethink agency in non-metaphysical terms, but Nietzsche's critique of agency is in fact far more radical than the critique Warren imputes to him. According to Warren, Nietzsche's genius lies in "his removal of the categories of agent-unity that lie behind the ideals of Westen culture . . . out of the realm of the metaphysically given (where they serve as assumptions divorced from practices) and into the realm of human morals or goals (where they can be conceived as projects)" (*Nietzsche and Political Thought*, p. 157). Agency is not something immediately granted by virtue of one's metaphysical birthright, but something one achieves, in concrete historical contexts of practices and values. Warren consequently emphasizes the influence of any particular historical epoch in determining the range of powers available to subjects, but he retains the model of the individual subject as the causally efficient originator of (historically defined) agency. He is not opposed, it turns out, to conceptions of agency rooted in individual subjectivity, but only to those conceptions of agency that cast the conditions of subjectivity in "metaphysical" stone (p. 189). Although he recommends Nietzsche's "post-modern philosophy of power" because it supposedly opens up a "broad range of political possibilities" (p. 246), in fact, Nietzsche's vitalism not only displaces the agency of all "subjects," but also disempowers all residents of a decadent epoch. The "postmodern" insights that Warren finds attractive in

Nietzsche's philosophy are in fact more restrictive of individual agency than the retrograde political commitments for which Warren chastises Nietzsche.

67   Nietzsche perhaps confirms this interpretation in a cryptic notebook entry from 1888: "The will to power not a being, not a becoming, but a *pathos* – the most elemental fact from which a becoming and effecting first emerge" (WP 636). Several commentators, including Tracy Strong, in *Friedrich Nietzsche and the Politics of Transfiguration* (Berkeley: University of California Press, 1975), pp. 232–234, and Warren, *Nietzsche and Political Thought*, pp. 130–138, have based anti-metaphysical interpretations of the will to power on this notion of pathos, but Nietzsche's idea here remains sufficiently obscure to justify his decision not to include it in any of his published writings.

68   Müller-Lauter suggests that a moral "proclamation" issues forth from Nietzsche's teaching of will to power, once this teaching is considered in its inescapable "circularity": "His philosophy of the will to power cannot have a merely contemplative character. It itself is the expression of willing-power. . . . But the basic change is still to come. It is not only valid to reflect on its necessity; it must be summoned. Nietzsche becomes the *proclaimer* out of his understanding of the real as the will to power" ("Nietzsche's Teaching of Will to Power," pp. 78–79). The proclamation Müller-Lauter has in mind is not directed necessarily to Nietzsche's contemporaries or, for that matter, to any specific audience, but simply to those who can afford to see themselves as will to power. Were Müller-Lauter to emphasize the conditions of the reception of this proclamation, rather than Nietzsche's "moral" role in issuing it, the disappearance of the "ought" from Nietzsche's philosophy would perhaps be more evident.

69   In a note from 1888, which echoes several others from that year, he writes, "Basic insight regarding the nature of decadence: *its supposed causes are its consequences*" (WP 41; cf. WP 42–45).

3

PEOPLES AND AGES: THE MORTAL SOUL
WRIT LARGE

The whole of the West no longer possesses the instincts out of which institutions grow, out of which a *future* grows: perhaps nothing antagonizes its "modern spirit" so much. One lives for the day, one lives very fast, one lives very irresponsibly: precisely this is called "freedom." That which makes an institution an institution is despised, hated, repudiated: one fears the danger of a new slavery the moment the word "authority" is even spoken out loud. This is how far decadence has advanced in the value-instincts of our politicians, of our political parties: *instinctively* they prefer what disintegrates, what hastens the end.   (TI 9:39)

Introduction

Nietzsche's experiment with vitalism precipitates his post-Zarathustran rejection of voluntarism. The general condition of an age or a people determines what human "agents" can and cannot do. As involuntary expressiosns of a particular age or people, individual agents have no choice but to reflect and reproduce the (relative) vitality of the age or people for which they stand. Representatives of a decadent age or people cannot help but express its constitutive decadence; the inauguration of a healthy epoch lies beyond the volitional resources at their disposal.

In his writings from the period 1885–88, Nietzsche consistently treats individual human beings as the embodied media through which an age or people expresses its native vitality. As involuntary "symptoms" of the peoples and ages they represent, individuals cannot be abstracted unintelligibly from the historical context that defines their agency and vitality. In one of

67

the more controversial elements of his mature political philosophy, he thus treats peoples and ages as organic forms in their own right, whose documented rise and fall follow a natural cycle of growth and decay. In order to account, in turn, for the vitality and health of entire peoples and ages, he consequently expands his functionalist model of the soul. He conceives of peoples and ages as souls writ large, and this postulated analogy dominates his post-Zarathustran political thinking.[1]

The political extension of Nietzsche's organic model of the soul thus enables him to present himself as a qualified diagnostician of entire peoples and ages – despite his scorn for the pretensions of all predecessor physicians of culture. Just as he can discern and interpret telltale symptoms in individual bodies, so can he diagnose sick and healthy peoples and ages. He consequently imports the diagnostic categories of his symptomatology into political philosophy, similarly describing peoples and ages as either "strong" or "weak," "healthy" or "decadent," "overfull" or "exhausted." Like the invisible bodies on which Nietzsche models them, peoples and ages naturally propagate the forces that circulate and flow through them, discharging their native vitality in spontaneous expenditures of creative self-expression. Each people or age is similarly endowed with a will, from which arise its signature institutions, which in turn play a regulative structural role analogous to that of the instincts within the economy of the soul (TI 9:39).

Like the individual souls on which they are modeled, ages and peoples thus function as capacitors, which amorally propagate and discharge the vital forces they hold in reserve. Indeed, Nietzsche apparently conceives of peoples and ages as *macro*-capacitors, of which their constituent souls, or *micro*-capacitors, are reproductions in miniature. Extending his figure of the soul as a vessel or receptacle of vital forces, he explains that "great men, like great ages, are explosives [*Explosiv-Stoffe*] in which a monstrous force [*Kraft*] is stored up" (TI 9:44). Based on this postulated analogy between micro- and macro-structures, he undertakes to extend his symptomatology to interpret the condition of entire peoples and ages. As organic forms in their own right, macro-capacitors too are susceptible to systemic afflictions of decadence – hence his famous diagnosis of modernity as an age beset by irreversible decay.

It is not simply the case, however, that micro- and macro-capacitors bear a functional resemblance to one another. Nietzsche views individual souls as emanations or reflections of their respective people or age, from which they "inherit" their ineluctable vitality and destiny. As he explains in an early essay, the ambit of human agency is always constrained by our "chains" to the past:

> Since we are the outcome of earlier generations, we are also the outcome of their aberrations, passions and errors, and indeed of their crimes; it is not

possible wholly to free oneself from this chain. If we condemn these aberrations and regard ourselves as free of them, this does not alter the fact that we originate in them. (UM II:3)

Refining this point later in his career, he grimly cinches the chains of history, reducing the individual to an unalterable moment within a grand fatality:

> But even when the moralist addresses himself only to the single human being and says to him, "You ought to be such and such!" he does not cease to make himself ridiculous. The individual human being is a piece of *fatum* from the front and from the rear, one law more, one necessity more for all that is yet to come and to be. To say to him, "Change yourself!" is to demand that everything be changed, even retroactively. (TI 5:6)

Although peoples and ages too fall indiscriminately within the plenum of this unalterable fatality, Nietzsche nevertheless assigns a certain priority to macro-capacitors. Just as the sun determines the periodicity and luminescence of moonlight, or as a mountain spring determines the volume and flow of the streams that descend from it, so the vitality of the macro-capacitor determines the health of its corporate micro-capacitors. The vitality of the macro-capacitor is ultimately determined by Life itself.

Nietzsche locates the source of the homology between micro- and macro-structures in the instinctual systems that organize and regulate the invisible bodies of individual human beings. The instincts operate as regulatory systems at the level of the micro-capacitors, but they are created and maintained (or not) at the level of the macro-capacitor. The regnant instincts of any people or age are cultivated and reinforced in individual souls by the signature institutions of the people or age in question. These institutions include not only the visible forms of political organization familiar to modernity, but also the pre-political customs, habits, folkways, and mores that silently infuse a people or age with its unique vitality and character. This interface between institutions and instincts not only links the political macrosphere with the political microsphere, but also serves as the basis of Nietzsche's postulated analogy between souls and peoples. As we shall see, he supports his diagnosis of modernity by exposing the senescence of our guiding institutions.

This linkage between microsphere and macrosphere is already implicit in the political metaphor Nietzsche employs to recommend his depth-psychological model of the soul. Echoing Plato's duplex account of justice in the *Republic*, he prescribes an alignment or symmetry between the prevailing macro-capacitor and its micro-constituents: "*L'effet c'est moi:* what happens here is what happens in every well-constructed and happy commonwealth; namely, the governing class identifies itself with the successes of the commonwealth" (BGE 19). In order to foster the health and vitality of each constituent soul, a people must legislate and secure the conditions of a "well-constructed and happy commonwealth." With respect to macro- and micro-capacitors alike, that is, *nomos* must gently shape *physis* into forms that are hospitable to human design.

The primary formative role of any people or age is to oversee the husbandry of the soul. By means of a constellation of sustaining institutions, the people or age fashions individual souls into fortified capacitors, thereby investing human agents with the capacity for an ever-greater expenditure of vitality. *This* is the task of culture whereby individuals receive the education and cultivation needed to flourish within the vital boundaries established by the prevailing macro-capacitor. In a well-constructed and happy commonwealth, the instincts that preside over the internal regulation of micro-capacitors will consequently reflect and reproduce the principles of organization established in the cognizant institutions of the macro-capacitor.

Extending his borrowed figure of the *oikos* into the political macrosphere, Nietzsche conceives of ages and peoples as grand households, each of which determines for its corporate souls the arch-principles of effective householding. While the economy of the micro-capacitor is determined by its regnant system of instincts (which is itself imposed through the sustaining institutions of the age or people in question), the economy of the macro-capacitor is determined either by an "enlightened" lawgiver or, more usually, by chance. In the rare cases of dynastic empires, which preserve the structural link between institutions and instincts over the course of centuries, resolute lawgivers may dare to model their householding on the will to power itself, which Nietzsche describes as "a household without expenses or losses" (WP 1067). "Until today," he believes, one could glimpse such hyperopic lawgiving only in the design of the Roman Empire: "This organization was firm enough to withstand bad emperors: the accident of persons may not have had anything to do with such matters – *first* principle of all grand architecture" (AC 58).

Through its sustaining mores and institutions, a people or an age imposes a uniform principle of organization onto the invisible bodies of individuals agents, providing them with the instincts they need to flourish as micro-capacitors. Just as corporeal vessels require regular exercise to maintain (or enhance) their constrictive power, so must the soul be fortified through the forcible imposition of instinctual regimes: "The beauty of a race or family, their grace and graciousness in all gestures, is won by work: like genius, it is the end result of the accumulated work of generations" (TI 9:47). Owing to their training and cultivation, individuals not only inherit the instincts legislated and reinforced by previous generations, but also contribute to the enhanced vitality of successor generations. A healthy people or age both reproduces itself in its constituent individuals and provides each succeeding generation with the opportunity to eclipse the accomplishments of its predecessors. The vast diversity of the cultures that have appeared throughout world history thus attests, or so Nietzsche believes, to the plasticity of the human soul and the adaptable nature of the human animal.

Bearing the imprint of the age or people that spawned them, these micro-capacitors reflect the relative vitality of the macro-capacitor as a whole. The vital range of volitional activity, within which one may attain an enhanced feeling of power, is a function not of a "free will" resident within the individual, but of the capacity of one's invisible body to propagate the quanta of force at the disposal of the macro-capacitor. Great human beings, like Napoleon and Goethe, can do no more than manage and direct the involuntary expression of the general vitality of the people or age as a whole; they can neither defy nor improve the general condition of the macro-capacitors they represent. By virtue of his postulated analogy between souls and peoples, Nietzsche thus incorporates into his political thinking the anti-voluntarism and fatalism that characterize his post-Zarathustran writings.

The Economic Cycle of Growth and Decay

As macro-capacitors, peoples and ages observe economic laws that govern the reserve and discharge of their vital resources. Although Nietzsche nowhere explicitly expounds these laws as such, their operation and regularity implictly contour the critical project of his post-Zarathustran period. While these laws also govern the economic regulation of micro-capacitors, their operation and necessity are more clearly evident in the case of a people or an age. Like Socrates in the *Republic*, Nietzsche turns to political philosophy to gain a microscopic view of the soul.

The Law of Inevitable Decay

First and foremost, Nietzsche insists that the eventual decay of all macro-capacitors is inevitable. More so than any other of his insights, the discovery of this law reflects the "realism" for which he congratulates himself in his post-Zarathustran writings. While some exceptionally healthy peoples have brazenly staked their claims to everlasting vitality, all such claims are ultimately interesting to Nietzsche only as symptoms of the underlying health of the peoples in question. A healthy age or people may appear (especially to itself) to squander itself without penalty or depletion, but subsequent generations must eventually pay for the luxury of these profligate expenditures. In a note from 1888, he thus insists that

> the phenomenon of decadence is as necessary as any increase and advance of life: one is in no position to abolish it . . . A society is not free to remain young. And even at the height of its strength it has to form refuse and waste materials.

The more energetically and boldly it advances, the richer it will be in failures and deformities, the closer to decline. (WP 40)

At some point in the natural development of every people, continued expenditures of vitality will weaken, rather than fortify, the macro-capacitor itself. Beyond such a point, as the regnant instincts decay, successive generations must counteract their creeping anemia by consuming the squandered vitality of their predecessors.

Peoples and ages cannot indefinitely afford the sumptuary excesses associated with the model of general economy, and some successor generation must eventually compensate for the profligacy of its prodigal predecessors.[2] All macro-capacitors thus partake of the model of restricted economy, for their measured, calculated expenditures of vitality are regulated in accordance with externally imposed conditions of scarcity and finitude. Nietzsche consequently interprets Western history in terms of a renewable cycle of inexorable growth and decay. He apparently views this cycle as natural and its laws as immutable. Declining ages inevitably succeed healthy ages; strong peoples naturally degenerate into weak peoples.[3] Indeed, the attainment of flourishing health is a sure sign to the attentive symptomatologist of impending decay: "The danger that lies in great men and ages is extraordinary; exhaustion of every kind, sterility, follow in their wake. The great human being is a finale; the great age – the Renaissance, for example – is a finale" (TI 9:44).

Notwithstanding occasional lapses into the sort of moralizing he expressly condemns, Nietzsche thus intends *decadence* as a purely descriptive, morally neutral diagnostic term. While the palpable decay of a formerly noble people may certainly offend his aesthetic sensibilities, he is generally careful not to overlay this offense with a moral judgment. A people or an age is not responsible for the decadence it enacts, and it can do nothing to prevent its inevitable exhaustion and collapse.

The Law of Necessary Regulation

Second, Nietzsche maintains that each macro-capacitor must observe a regimen of internal regulation in order to control the influx and expenditures of its restricted economy. Appealing once again to the economic destiny that links individuals with the people or age they represent, he reminds his readers that "in the end, no one can expend [*ausgeben*] more than he has: that is true of an individual, it is true of a people" (TI 8:4).

Through the directed expression of the collective vitality of its constituent members, however, a people can both postpone and pre-emptively compensate for the eventual decay of its regnant system of instincts. While the determination of this internal regimen is usually left to chance, enlightened lawgivers occasionally emerge who design political regimes that artificially extend the vitality of the epoch in question. Nietzsche consequently applauds Manu for creating institutions designed to impose fructifying discipline onto individual souls: "To set up a code of laws after the manner of Manu means to give a people the chance henceforth to become master, to become perfect – to aspire to the highest art of life" (AC 57). The political regime of a people or an age thus contributes – either positively or negatively – to the inevitable expenditure of its limited fund of vital forces.

Although Nietzsche occasionally suggests that particular peoples and ages might legitimately aspire to grander forms of political organization, this suggestion is almost always rhetorical rather than sincerely prescriptive in nature. For the most part, political regimes accurately reflect the native vitality of the peoples and ages that legislate them:

> The newspaper reader says: this party destroys itself by making such a mistake. My *higher* politics says: a party which makes such mistakes has reached its end; it has lost its sureness of instinct. Every mistake in every sense is the effect of the degeneration of instinct, of the disintegration of the will: one could almost define what is bad in this way. (TI 6:2))

Aristocracy is certainly preferable to democracy as an expression of the excess vitality of a healthy people, but it is not a preferable form of political regime for those declining peoples that can afford only democracy. Nietzsche does slip here occasionally, confusing his own anachronistic preferences with what modernity can in fact afford, but for the most part he does not recommend the installation of political regimes that are simply incompatible with the depleted resources of late modernity.

Because a people can neither reserve more than it contains nor expend more than it reserves, it must bear without forgiveness the opportunity cost of its expenditures. "Culture and the state," Nietzsche insists, "are antagonists" (TI 8:4), for their respective demands upon the restricted economy of a people cannot simultaneously be met.[4] Although "the new Germany" appears to command a (relative) surplus of expendable vitality, its enthusiasm for Bismarck's *Reich* signifies to Nietzsche the continued decline of German culture:

> If one spends oneself for power, for power politics, for economics, world trade, parliamentarianism, and military interests – if one spends in *this* direction the quantum of understanding, seriousness, will, and self-overcoming that one represents, then it will be lacking for the other direction. (TI 8:4)

The new Germany is destined for cultural ruin because its choice to consolidate political and military power is really no choice at all. The institution of the *Reich* is not the cause of decay, but its latest effect and "necessary consequence" (TI 9:37). Rather than initiate the descensional trajectory of the new Germany, Bismarck merely establishes the current nadir in a protracted, inexorable process of irreversible decline.

The Law of Self-Overcoming

The implosive, self-destructive nature of decadence suggests to Nietzsche a third basic law that governs the cycle of growth and decay: "All great things bring about their own destruction through an act of self-overcoming [*Selbstaufhebung*]: thus the law of Life will have it, the law of the necessity of 'self-overcoming' [*'Selbstüberwindung'*] in the nature of Life" (GM III:27). As Nietzsche's formulation of this "law" suggests, "self-overcoming" represents a natural, irresistible event in the life of any age or people. Indeed, the very conditions of creative self-expression that launched the ascensional trajectory of a people or age must eventually initiate its descensional trajectory as well. As a people or age begins to wane, it can no longer afford to sustain the institutions, wars, festivals, and other externalized forms of self-expression that memorialize its vitality. Crushed under the accumulated weight (and prestige) of its own externalized vitality, a declining people or age must invariably attempt to preserve itself by disowning its greatest, defining accomplishments.

As Socrates reminded his accusers (and Nietzsche his Socrates), decadent peoples are therefore mistaken to fear (or blame) external enemies as the causes of their decline. It is the destiny of each people to overcome itself, to precipitate and provoke its own demise. Aroused by the unmistakable stench of a dying foe, barbarians appear at the gate only, as it were, by invitation. The apparent "victory" of external enemies is not the cause of a people's decline, but its most obvious (and hermeneutically intractable) effect: "The church and morality say: 'A generation, a people, are destroyed by license and luxury.' My recovered reason says: when a people approaches destruction, when it degenerates physiologically, then license and luxury follow from this" (TI 6:2). Because a decadent people cannot *afford* to expend itself in creative expression, it will require external stimulants – such as war, xenophobia, chauvinism, paranoia, and mass hysteria – to do so, much as a decaying body will require stimulants of ever-increasing potency in order to withstand the expenditure of its own reserve vitality (TI 6:2). Such expenditure is always mortal in consequence, for it results in irreparable structural damage to the macro-capacitor itself.

The inexorable advance of decay eventually renders the macro-capacitor fully distended, at which point it can no longer regulate the propagation and expenditure of the vital forces that flow through it. At the conclusion of each cycle of growth and decay, a declining people or age involuntarily capitulates to its besetting decadence, resorting exclusively to self-destructive expressions of its dwindling vitality. Decadent peoples eventually exhaust themselves in what Nietzsche calls the "will to nothingness," the will never to will again (GM III:28). At this nadir in the cycle of growth and decay, an age or epoch invests its remaining energies in the willful destruction of itself as a macro-capacitor, thereby providing the purgative precondition for the nascent people or age that must invariably follow.

Charting the Cycle of Growth and Decay

These simple laws of growth and decay convince Nietzsche that all macro-capacitors must belong to one of two basic types: *healthy* peoples and ages, which express themselves through the expenditure of a continually replenished store of vital forces; and *declining* peoples and ages, which express themselves through the expenditure of a continually diminished store of vital forces. Both types manifest their native vitality by engaging in creative endeavors – only an exhausted people no longer expresses itself in outward manifestations – but these creative endeavors issue, respectively, either from a surfeit or a deficiency of vital resources.

Healthy peoples and ages, like healthy souls, are characterized by their excess, overflowing vitality. The commitment to tradition, of which the aristocratic regimes that Nietzsche admires are products, is therefore possible only for those peoples that can afford both to regulate themselves and to project their creative legislations into the future. He thus determines the relative health of a people by measuring the magnitude of its signature expenditures:

> Supreme rule of conduct: before oneself too, one must not "let oneself go." The good things are immeasurably costly; and the law always holds that those who *have* them are different from those who *acquire* them. All that is good is inherited: whatever is not inherited is imperfect, is a mere beginning. (TI 9:47)

Traditions and institutions often outlive the ascensional trajectory of the people that creates them, for they represent objectified structures of excess vitality upon which declining generations will cannibalistically draw for their sustenance. Through the spontaneous creation of traditions and institutions, a people thus (unwittingly) provides for its posterity, even through its period of inevitable decline, thereby extending the duration of its vitality and influence. A political constitution, for example, may originally serve its people not as a carefully redacted basis for positive law, but as an emphatic, outward expression of its swaggering autonomy and power; later, when a people can no longer afford the luxury of resolute judgments and spontaneous legislations, it may come to revere its constitution as a source of externalized, objectified wisdom; finally, when a flagging people can no longer live up to the ideals and accomplishments of its greatest exemplars, it may either disown its constitution or retire it to a heritage museum.

Declining peoples and ages cannot afford to inaugurate traditions and institutions, and they can at best only cherish those they inherit. The cultural variegation that Nietzsche associates with decadent peoples and ages, which corresponds in the macrosphere to the "instinctual disarray" of the microsphere, thus derives not from some misguided choice or wrong turn, but from their epigonic situation in the natural cycle of growth and decay: "In an age of disintegration that mixes races indiscriminately, human beings have in their bodies the heritage of multiple origins, that is, opposite, and not merely opposite, drives and value standards that fight each other and rarely permit each other any rest" (BGE 200). A declining people inherits fragments of traditions and institutions from various predecessor stages in its development, and it must cobble these atavisms into a motley *bricolage* of its own design.[5] To urge declining peoples to invest their residual vitality in the inauguration or restoration of traditions is folly; if they could afford to nurture incipient traditions, they would already have them.

The lawgivers who preside over declining peoples and epochs are not the mythical creators of new values, but crafty *bricoleurs* of depleted, recyled, and abandoned political resources.[6] If ruled wisely, declining peoples can continue to thrive, through a strategic inhabitation of the traditions and institutions founded (and externalized) by their predecessors. But they can neither found new institutions and traditions of their own nor contribute to the objectified vitality of those they inherit. The resourceful innovations of a plucky *bricoleur* may not be as impressive as the founding labors of a legislator of new values, but decadent peoples and ages simply cannot afford the luxury of a Promethean lawgiver.[7]

Nietzsche's interpretation of peoples and ages as souls writ large thus suggests two models of creative expression: A macro-capacitor expends its creative, vital resources either as a "squandering" or as a "sacrifice."[8] A healthy people creates, and thus expends, from strength or overfulness; its expenditures take the form of squanderings. A declining people creates from deprivation or exhaustion; its expenditures take the form of sacrifices. Any creation issuing from need or lack constitutes a sacrifice of vital forces, whereas any creation emanating from surfeit or nimiety constitutes a squandering of vital forces. Nietzsche thus insists:

> In its measure of strength every age also possesses a measure for what virtues are permitted and forbidden to it. Either it has the virtues of *ascending* life: then it will resist from the profoundest depths the virtues of declining life. Or the age itself represents declining life: then it also requires the virtues of decline, then it hates everything that justifies itself solely out of abundance, out of the overflowing riches of strength. (CW E)

At a critical juncture in the inevitable decline of any people or age, the squandered vitality of past generations is fully consumed, and the sustaining institutions and traditions begin to disintegrate. Continued creative self-expression now requires the expenditure of those vital forces that have been held in reserve to sustain the macro-capacitor itself. At this juncture, a people or age becomes genuinely decadent as it relies ever more exclusively on displays of self-destruction to enact its dwindling vitality. Let us not be confused, then, by the tumultuous death throes of "mellow old cultures whose last vitality was even then flaring up in splendid fireworks of spirit and corruption" (BGE 257). A decadent people or age can survive only at the expense of its own future (GM P6), for every expression of vitality further cripples the capacitor itself. Nietzsche thus characterizes decadence – in both individuals and peoples – as the habitual, instinctual attraction to everything that is disadvantageous for themselves: "That is how far decadence has advanced in the value-instincts of our politicians, of our political parties: *instinctively* they prefer what disintegrates, what hastens the end" (TI 9:39).[9]

In the case of a people or age, decadence manifests itself as the failure of the cognizant institutions to impose the necessary discipline and order onto the invisible bodies of individual agents. Just as decadent souls are those bereft of an effective system of instinctual regulation, so decadent peoples are those whose guiding institutions can no longer provide and enforce the system of acculturation that ensures a "well-constructed and happy commonwealth." As in the case of decadent souls, a formerly well-constructed and happy commonwealth falls under anarchic or ochlocratic political regimes, which sanction the ongoing clash between rival instinct systems. Once a people's regnant instinct system begins to disintegrate, the vital link between micro- and macro-capacitor is finally dissolved. Nietzsche thus laments: "The whole of the West no longer possesses the instincts out of which institutions grow, out of which a *future* grows. . . . One lives for the day, one lives very fast, one lives very irresponsibly: precisely this is called 'freedom'" (TI 9:39).

In the *Genealogy,* he attributes the integrity of a regnant instinct system to the stability of a people's circulatory network of customs, mores, rituals, and folkways. A stable circulatory network ensures the continued validity and justification of an instinct system by presenting desirable patterns of instinctive behavior as the honorable legacy of a people's revered ancestors. In a healthy tribe, then, fear of the ancestor preserves the integrity of the regnant instinct system:

> The *fear* of the ancestor and his power, the consciousness of indebtedness to him, increases, according to this kind of logic, in exactly the same measure as the power of the tribe itself increases, as the tribe itself grows ever more

victorious, independent, honored and feared. By no means the other way around! Every step toward the decline of a tribe, every misfortune, every sign of degeneration, of coming disintegration, always *diminishes* fear of the spirit of its founder and produces a meaner impression of his cunning, foresight, and present power. (GM II:19)

In order to honor its debts to its predecessors, each rising generation must reproduce in faithful detail its people's ancestral rituals and customs, thereby ensuring (albeit unwittingly) the continued cultivation of the people's signature instincts. In fact, Nietzsche claims to detect an inverse relationship between the health of a tribe and its reliance on priests to preside over sacred rituals. The accession to power of a priestly class thus indicates that the tribe in question has already begun its inevitable decline (GM II:19).

Although Nietzsche is explicitly concerned here with the tribal, or premoral, stage in the development of a people, his analysis is also pertinent to the post-tribal, or moral, stage of a people's history. He understands the basic institutions of civil society as atavistic outgrowths of a people's circulatory network of customs, mores, rituals, and folkways. The moral stage of a people's history does not so much replace the premoral stage as carry it forward in a sublated, "civilized" form. The basic moral code of a healthy people may not explicitly cultivate a primal fear of the ancestor, but it nevertheless serves a similar social function, insofar as it ensures the continued integrity of the people's regnant system of instincts.

A declining people, conversely, is characterized by an irreversible deterioration of the bond between morality and instinct. As a people declines from the heights marked by its past greatness, its fear of the ancestor (or any analogous moral commitment to tradition and duty) wanes accordingly, until that people no longer recognizes an obligation to honor and cherish tradition. As self-congratulatory deviations from venerable traditions, the social trends that Nietzsche treats as emblematic of modernity – trends toward secularism, enlightenment, liberalism, democracy, universal suffrage, and so on – thus appear as signs of advanced decline: "But this is the simile of every style of *decadence:* every time, the anarchy of atoms, disgregation of the will, 'freedom of the individual,' to use moral terms – expanded into a political theory, '*equal* rights for all'" (CW 7). Only an irrecuperably decadent people would happily spurn the social and political resources made available to it by tradition, for only an irrecuperably decadent people would mistake its past glories for the primitive fumblings of a dark nonage. Nietzsche nowhere proposes, however, that decadent peoples should (or even could) attend more respectfully to their heritage and traditions. If "ought" implies "can," then decadent peoples cannot help but rush headlong toward exhaustion. To paraphrase Nietzsche: One does not choose to be "progressive" in one's disdain for tradition; one must be sick enough for it.

In addition to this basic dichotomy between types of peoples, Nietzsche also identifies substages within the development of each type. His compact, five-stage "history of Israel," which culminates in the degeneration of Judaism into its antipode, Christianity, is essentially a survey of the natural growth and decay of the people of Israel (AC 25). He refers to this cycle of growth and decay as "the typical history of the denaturing of natural values," thereby linking the spread of decadence to the retreat from naturalism (AC 25). He identifies other such ages and peoples that can no longer afford to squander themselves, for whom any expenditure necessarily entails sacrifice. Late modernity in Europe is one such epigonic epoch, as was the "sunset," post-Socratic age of Epicurus.[10]

Symptomatology and/as Cultural Criticism

The interpretation of entire peoples and ages is a tricky business, however, for any single policy or practice might signify either strength or weakness, health or decay. In order to gain a critical purchase on any particular people or age, Nietzsche consequently directs his attention to the relative health displayed by its representative exemplars.

Nietzsche believes, for example, that a people might suspend punishment of its enemies either because it can withstand and accommodate such transgressions (and can thus afford not to punish its enemies) (GM II:10) or because it cannot afford the expenditure necessary to mete out a just punishment (BGE 201). Hence it is insufficient for philosophers simply to observe cultural practices; they must also interpret these practices as symptomatic of their invisible preconditions. Furthermore, the vitality of a people or age is not easily measured – notwithstanding Nietzsche's enthusiasm for the dynamometer – for it is neither constant nor consistently distributed across the individuals who express it. "The sickness of the will is spread unevenly over Europe," he explains: "It appears strongest and most manifold where culture has been at home longest" (BGE 208).

As a solution to this interpretive problem, he restricts his focus to those representative exemplars who "stand for" an age as a whole.[11] That is, the position of an epoch within the cycle of growth and decay is determined only with respect to the superlative achievements of its exemplary specimens. Because "ages must be measured by their positive strength" (TI 9:37), the pathologist of culture must attend to those individuals who embody the apotheosis of the age, those capable of the (relatively) greatest expenditures of vital forces. If we focus on the "average" exemplar, then all ages and peoples will assume a similar aspect, for the average exemplars of all ages reserve and discharge a similar capacity of volitional resources. Ages vary most obviously with respect to the heights respectively achieved by their representative exemplars. When Nietzsche observes that we are now "weary of man," he means that modernity has failed for the most part to produce those "lucky strikes" on the part of the species who could refresh our "belief in man" (GM I:12).

If we measure ages by "their positive strength" and attend exclusively to their representive exemplars, then "that lavishly squandering and fatal age of the Renaissance appears as the last *great* age; and we moderns . . . appear as a *weak* age" (TI 9:37). Nietzsche exposes the moral progress of modernity, of which his contemporaries are evidently quite proud, as simply "the decrease in instincts which are hostile and arouse mistrust." This decline of the "manly" instincts in turn "represents but one of the consequences attending the general decrease in *vitality*. . . . Hence each helps the other; hence everyone is to a certain extent sick, and everyone is a nurse for the sick. And that is called 'virtue'" (TI 9:37).

Every age and people produces a signature measure of nobility, but the representative exemplars of healthier ages and peoples command relatively greater stores of vital resources. The Italian Renaissance marked the last great age in European culture. The exemplary individuals of each subsequent age have manifested a perceptible decline from the exotic, overflowing health of Cesare Borgia (TI 9:37). In decadent epochs like our own, only a relatively insignificant distance separates exemplary human beings from "average" ones. As Zarathustra laments, "Naked I saw both the greatest and the smallest man: they are still all-too-similar to each other. Verily, even the greatest I found all-too-human" (Z I:7).

Nietzsche's vitalism thus underlies the peculiar form of historicism to which he cleaves: ideas, standards, mores, and values are all relative to the epoch whose native vitality they express.[12] Any attempt to assess the creative accomplishments of one age by appealing to the immanent standards of another will invariably invite a potentially egregious category mistake. His experiment with vitalism thus explains why the art and law that are characteristic of one epoch may be unintelligible to observers and critics whose respective ages occupy different stages of development.

Nietzsche draws his most poignant examples of this disparity between ages and their corresponding states of the soul from his own checkered career. Just as his anachronistic call for a rebirth of tragic culture betrays a misunderstanding of Attic tragedy, so he insists that the true audience for *Zarathustra* will not emerge for decades. In both cases he explains that a work of art that expresses a degree of vitality that is presently unattainable will surely be misunderstood. As an expression of (relatively) overflowing vitality, *Zarathustra* is virtually impossible for Nietzsche's enervated contemporaries to appreciate, or so he claims. Its true readers are likely to emerge only after the demise of modernity itself. While accounting for the inscrutability of *Zarathustra*, he thus observes that "ultimately, nobody can get more out of things, including books, than he already knows. For what one lacks access to from experience one will have no ear" (EH:gb 1). In a moment of remarkable candor, induced perhaps by the "offensively Hegelian" stench of his earlier account of Greek tragedy (EH:bt 1), Nietzsche acknowledges the limitations of his own formative experiences: "Let us finally own it to ourselves: what we men of the 'historical sense' find most difficult to grasp . . . is precisely the perfection and ultimate maturity of every culture and art, that which is really noble in a work or a human being" (BGE 224).

In order to appreciate and judge creative expressions whose physiological preconditions are unfamiliar to him, and thus compensate for the asymmetry between the economic stages respectively expressed by tragic Greece and nineteenth-century Europe, Nietzsche accedes to the "objective" standpoint of the physician of culture.[13] As a symptomatologist, he supposedly can evaluate even those cultural events and artifacts whose vital preconditions outstrip his own capacities. This move to symptomatology is crucial to the success of his revised critical project, for he can otherwise gain no access to states of the soul that exceed his own; his post-Zarathustran return to the problem of tragedy, for example, would have been otherwise impossible. He consequently attributes his "wisdom" to his experience with opposing perspectives and to his mastery of the art of reversing perspectives (EH:wise 1). Although unable to extricate himself from the decadence of late modernity, he is adequately versed in the reversal of perspectives to appreciate and pass judgment on expressions of vitality that excel his own.

In the end, the political extension of Nietzsche's theory of decadence is as dubious as it is beguiling. His critical appraisal of macro-capacitors inherits all of the interpretive problems that plague his symptomatology of the invisible body. He is characteristically vague, for example, with respect to the vital "stuff" reserved and discharged by macro-capacitors, referring alternately to the strength, health, vitality, spirituality, and creativity that peoples and ages husband and expend. As in his treatment of micro-capacitors, moreover, his diagnoses of peoples and epochs strain the scientific, naturalistic grounding he claims for his symptomatology. Indeed, his turn to symptomatology is no more successful in the political macrosphere, for he offers no empirical means of evaluating the merit of his ensuing diagnoses. In lieu of universal access to his trusty dynamometer, one either "sees" the internal disarray of declining peoples or one does not. His postulated analogy between souls and peoples furthermore bears an inordinate share of the philosophical weight; if this analogy is not legitimate, then very little of his post-Zarathustran political thinking survives intact.

The Twilight of the Idols

Nietzsche's favorite image for the late epoch in which he toils is the "twilight of the idols." The idols in question are the dominant values and sustaining ideals of modernity as a whole. The "twilight" of these idols signifies an advanced stage of decay, such that the age can express itself only in a self-destructive retreat from, and betrayal of, its founding ideals and values. The twilight of the idols thus characterizes late modernity, the epigonic epoch in which modernity attains its debilitating self-consciousness.

Reluctantly posted in this crepuscular epoch, Nietzsche both sees and foresees the failure of the grand experiments in liberalism and democracy, as well as the self-overcoming of Christian morality. Suggesting a "simile" for "every style of decadence," he observes that "the whole no longer lives at all: it is composite, calculated, artificial, and artifact" (CW 7). As this simile indicates, late modernity may still resemble its predecessor epochs in certain formal respects, but the traditions and institutions it claims to uphold have been reduced to hollow shells and flimsy facades of their former incarnations. Like Wagner, whom Nietzsche summons as representative of the age as a whole, late modernity "is admirable and gracious only in the invention of what is smallest, in spinning out the details" (CW 7). We late moderns continue to inhabit these lifeless shells, cherishing their grand ideals in diminishing miniature, obscuring behind platitudinous rhetoric our inexorable march toward the vanishing point of modernity. Having consumed the objectified vitality of the Renaissance, and of Napoleon and Goethe, late modernity must soon consume itself in a final, cataclysmic explosion of its residual vitality.

The exhaustion of modernity as a macro-capacitor is reproduced in the enervation of its constituent micro-capacitors, those individual human beings who must enact the waning vitality of the epoch as a whole: "The past of every form and way of life, of cultures that formerly lay right next to each other or one on top of the other, now flows into us 'modern souls,' thanks to this mixture; our instincts now run back everywhere; we ourselves are a kind of chaos" (BGE 224). As we have seen, the clash of instincts manifests itself as a crippling *akrasia*. "Today," Nietzsche observes, "nothing is as timely as weakness of the will" (BGE 212). The expenditures required to sustain the threshold level of affective engagement, which in turn produces a feeling of power, have become increasingly prohibitive. Viable goals for the will grow ever more scarce, ever more exotic and bizarre, and ever more decadent. At some point, bereft of alternatives for affective engagement, the decaying micro-capacitor must secure this feeling of power by willing its own destruction. Of the human beings who reside in late ages and represent dying peoples, Nietzsche says, "Their most profound desire is that the war they *are* should come to an end" (BGE 200).

The pronounced weakness of the will that afflicts agents in late modernity reflects the growing disparity between the cognitive and volitional resources at their disposal. Cleaving faithfully to his strict naturalism, Nietzsche traces this pandemic weakness of will to an organic dysfunction that besets the epoch as a whole: "Biologically, modern man represents a *contradiction of values*; he sits between two chairs, he says Yes and No in the same breath" (CW E).[14] Life in a decadent epoch proceeds tentatively under the growing shadow of the *absurdum practicum* in which decadence manifests itself. Individuals can no longer afford to appeal to the values and ideals that have presided over the constitution of their identity. The goals and practices that have (supposedly) justified their existence now lie well beyond their reach, and they are either too proud or too tired to transfer their allegiances to low-vitality, substitute ideals.

Like the townspeople whom the Madman angrily confronts (GS 125), we late moderns are free neither to renounce our belief in the idols of modernity nor to create the values whereby we might reconstitute our lives in the gloaming. Unable any longer to muster a resolute belief in God, we have killed him – not as a Zarathustran declaration of our strength and independence, as Nietzsche's "existentialist" champions would have it, but, following the ignoble lead of Socrates' judges, to eliminate a nagging reminder of our irremediable weakness. While revealing himself to Zarathustra as the "murderer of God," the Ugliest Man confesses similar motives at work:

> His pity knew no shame: he crawled into my dirtiest nooks. This most curious, overobtrusive, overpitying one had to die. He always saw me: on such a witness I wanted to have revenge or not live myself. The god who saw everthing, *even man* – this god had to die! Man cannot bear it that such a witness should live. (Z IV:7)

Like the Ugliest Man, however, we late moderns have failed to liberate ourselves, for we still crave the redemption that only God could provide. Rather than inter the rotting corpse of the fallen deity, we continue to worship it even as it putrifies before us. Because we cannot afford to own this potentially *übermenschlich* act of deicide, it remains "more distant from [us] than the most distant stars" (GS 125). The Madman's soliloquy thus suggests (though not necessarily to him) that the death of God is not the cause of our decay and enervation, but a predictable expression (or effect) of our inevitable decline.[15]

The crisis that besets modernity thus lies not in its reigning idols, but in us. Volitionally incapable of investing resolute belief in the superlative values that have sustained past generations, we suddenly now object to their "shabby" human origins.[16] Unwittingly conserving our dwindling fund of vitality – an involuntary practice related to Nietzsche's own preservatory fatalism (EH:wise 6) – we earnestly vow to reserve our convictions only for the highest values, those that originate *causa sui* (TI 3:4). Although Nietzsche suggests in a gravid notebook entry from 1887 that *"the highest values devaluate themselves"* (WP 2), we might better understand the crisis of modernity in terms of a self-contemptuous campaign to debase our highest values to a level commensurate with our own decline.

Zarathustra may (initially) understand the death of God, like Feuerbach, as a sign of the imminent maturation of humankind, of its repudiation of the metaphysical bogeys of its nonage, but Nietzsche himself is far less charitable to his modern and late modern readers. The death of God signals an irrecuperable level of depletion in the fund of expendable vital resources. When interpreted within the context of his vitalism, the death of God stands as a symbol for that critical moment in the devolution of any age, Christian or otherwise, at which a people becomes conscious not merely of itself, but also of the *absurdum practicum* it is destined to play out.

At this critical juncture in the natural development of a people, any additional display of creative self-expression will necessarily compromise the structural integrity of the macro-capacitor itself. From this critical point downward, the people or epoch in question expresses itself only in creative bursts of self-abnegation. In the twilight of the idols, individuals are increasingly aware not only of the dissipation of their native vitality and of the disintegration of their sustaining institutions, but also of their sheer inability to retard or reverse the process of decay. This *absurdum practicum* will eventually culminate, Nietzsche believes, in the "will to nothingness" (GM III:28), which secures for decadent peoples their final and permanent release from the torment of existence.

The self-induced paroxysms of guilt that ensue from the death of God are undeniably overwhelming, but this unprecedented regimen of self-flagellation ensures our continued (albeit self-destructive) vitality as a people. Having failed to excite the anemic will of modernity in the pursuit of time-honored, conventional goals, we now must derive meaning and direction from our "duty" to impose a just punishment onto the cold-blooded murderers of our loving God:

> In this psychic cruelty there resides a madness of will which is absolutely unexampled: the *will* of man to find himself guilty and reprehensible to a degree that can never be atoned for; his *will* to think himself punished without any possibility of the punishment becoming equal to his guilt. (GM II:22)

Cultural practices that may seem barbaric to civilized obervers assume a strictly natural aspect when refracted through the lens of Nietzschean symptomatology. Just as a trapped predator might gnaw off a leg in order to escape a binding snare, so the human animal will lacerate its own soul in order to sustain a threshold level of affective investment in its own continued vitality. Only a desperately enervated people would sacrifice its own god(s), the guarantor(s) of its value, in order to galvanize its remaining volitional resources in a self-consuming quest for revenge and retribution. According to Nietzsche, however, all peoples and epochs naturally and inevitably reach this final stage of devolution.

The Miscarriage of *The Birth of Tragedy:* A Postpartum Postmortem

We can gain a sense of the larger political implications of Nietzsche's vitalism by comparing the later critique of modernity in *Twilight of the Idols* with the earlier critique in *The Birth of Tragedy.* Here we see that he no longer invests any hope whatsoever in his ability to orchestrate the redemption of modernity. The postmodern, tragic culture for which he longs cannot commence until the decadence of modernity has run its inexorable, purgative course.

Upon returning to *The Birth of Tragedy* in 1886, in order to draft a new preface for the new edition, Nietzsche surveys the distance his peripatetic muse has traveled in fourteen years:

> Today I find it an impossible book: I consider it badly written, ponderous, embarrassing, image-mad and image-confused, sentimental, in places saccharine to the point of effeminacy, uneven in tempo, without the will to logical cleanliness, very convinced and therefore disdainful of proof, . . . an arrogant and rhapsodic book that sought to exclude right from the start the *profanum vulgus* of "the educated" even more than "the mass" or "folk." (BT P3)

This exacting appraisal of his beloved "firstborn" by no means represents an isolated exercise in self-castigation. In yet another review, he allows that *The Birth of Tragedy* now "smells offensively Hegelian" to him (EH:bt 1), complaining that his artless recourse to dialectics further obscures the wondrous union of Dionysus and Apollo. Indeed, his post-Zarathustran writings collectively essay a startling confession: Despite the many insights conveyed by *The Birth of Tragedy,* its youthful author failed to understand Greek tragedy.[17]

This failure to understand the Greeks, we now understand, devolved from Nietzsche's prior mismeasure of modernity as an age allegedly ripe for rebirth and revitalization. This mismeasure of modernity is most clearly expressed in his grandiose presumption that he (and Wagner) might effect a reversal of fortune on behalf of their declining age. From the warped vantage point of the self-appointed savior of modernity, the "birth and death of tragedy" thus appears as a simplistic morality play in which the ruthless Socrates (abetted by his unwitting stooge, Euripides) murders the spirit of music and consigns the tragic age of the Greeks to a premature extinction. Encouraged by the apparent capitulation of the "music-practicing" Socrates, Nietzsche consequently resolved to arrange a different fate for his age, unctuously urging Wagner to assume a role of political (as well as aesthetic) leadership in modernity.

As the 1886 preface to *The Birth of Tragedy* confirms, however, the "solution" Nietzsche originally proposed to the "problem" of modernity is in fact complicit with the crisis he hubristically presumed to treat. In his zeal to disclose hopeful historical precedents for the crisis of his own age, he shamelessly distorted the birth and death of tragedy, forcibly imposing upon the tragic Greeks the cramped frame of modernity:

> I now regret . . . that I *spoiled* the grandiose *Greek problem*, as it had arisen before my eyes, by introducing the most modern problems! That I appended hopes where there was no ground for hope, where everything all too plainly pointed to an end! That on the basis of the latest German music I began to rave about "the German spirit" as if that were in the process even then of discovering and finding itself again – at a time when the German spirit, which not long before had still the will to dominate Europe and the strength to lead Europe, was just making its testament and *abdicating* forever, making its transition, under the pompous pretense of founding a *Reich*, to a leveling mediocrity, democracy, and "modern ideas!" (BT P6)

In a parlance foreign to *The Birth of Tragedy* but native to his later writings, Nietzsche subsequently interprets Attic tragedy as symptomatic of a degree of vitality that is unattainable (and therefore inexpressible) by late modernity. The tragic hero is not an autonomous, causally efficient agent – though his belief in himself as such may contribute to his spectacular fall – but a receptive conduit for the trans-individual agency that animates all mortal beings. To affirm the hero's inevitable demise is to affirm the unquenchable vitality of Life, of will to power, which eventually destroys even the greatest of the embodied media through which it amorally propagates itself.

In order to correct for his earlier misunderstanding of Greek tragedy, he thus revises his account of the tragic psyche:

> The psychology of the orgiastic as an overflowing feeling of life and strength, where even pain still has the effect of a stimulus, gave me the key to the concept of *tragic* feeling, which had been misunderstood both by Aristotle and, quite especially, by our modern pessimists. (TI 10:5)

As this self-referential dig at "modern pessimists" confirms, Nietzsche now realizes that the source of his attraction to Greek tragedy also places "the spirit of music" beyond the volitional horizon of late modernity. Although Wagner can produce art that formally resembles Greek tragedy, he cannot reproduce the surfeit of vitality that Greek tragedy involuntarily signified – hence his "inevitable" embrace of Christianity in *Parsifal*. Like all decadent artists, Wagner expresses himself creatively only as a miniaturist (CW 7). Unable to create original tragic forms, he borrows old ones – shamelessly blending Christian and pagan myths – and embroiders them with new details.

What Nietzsche originally identified as the "death" of tragedy, at the hands of the villainous tag team of Socrates and Euripides, he now interprets as the natural, inevitable onset of decadence. In the original *Birth of Tragedy*, that is, he unwittingly disclosed a critical moment of fragmentation within the defining ethos of the tragic Greeks, as this formerly noble and sublime people began its slow, gradual decline from the pinnacle of its vitality, as immortalized in the tragedies of Aeschylus and Sophocles.[18] Nietzsche's original suspicions of Socrates and Euripides were in fact well founded (even if his original indictment was not), for their common expression of optimism attests to the perceptible decline not only of Attic tragedy, but also of the Greeks as a people.

Having literally stumbled upon this untimely discovery, however, the young Nietzsche was ill-equipped to convey his extraordinary findings to his readers:

> What spoke here – as was admitted, not without suspicion – was something like a mystical, almost maenadic soul that stammered with difficulty, a feat of the will, as in a strange tongue, almost undecided whether it should communicate or conceal itself. It should have *sung*, this "new soul" – and not spoken! (BT P3)

Rather than mount an "archaeological" investigation of the triumphant apex and inevitable decline of the tragic age of the Greeks, this callow initiate instead produced a clumsy pastiche of dialectical legerdemain and romantic intrigue, for which he was justly ridiculed by Wilamowitz-Möllendorff and others.

In his post-Zarathustran writings, he consequently attempts to recuperate the failings of his original account of tragedy. Like all examples of aesthetic creation, Attic tragedy reflects the relative vitality of the people or epoch that produces it, by virtue of the response it enacts to the tragic meaninglessness of human suffering. He most admires the response expressed in the tragic pessimism of Aeschylus and Sophocles, which affirms the demise of the tragic hero as a necessary moment within the boundless economy of Life itself. He least admires the response expressed in the Socratic optimism of Euripides, which affirms the tragic condition of humankind only by first interposing saving fictions, from which one might derive a "metaphysical comfort." Tragic pessimism thus signifies the overflowing vitality of the Greeks, while Socratic optimism betrays the advancing decadence of this formerly vital people. Drawing on this revised, symptomatological interpretation of tragedy, he now insists that the unified dramatic form of Attic tragedy actually spans a decisive watershed in the culture of the tragic Greeks, expressing both the pinnacle *and* subsequent decline of the people who created it. As we shall see, the very possibility of this insight into the decay of the tragic age implies a similar condition for modernity as well, for only decadent epochs can undertake an investigation of decadence.[19]

As Nietzsche leads us to suspect of any philosopher, his mismeasures of modernity and antiquity invariably trade on the "great error" involved in "confusing cause and effect" (TI 6:1). This confusion in turn betrays a failure to embrace the sort of vitalism that informs his post-Zarathustran writings, as well as the critique of agency it enables. Indeed, any attempt to infuse modernity (or any other declining age) with the tragic experience it "lacks" rests on a basic confusion of cause and effect. Tragedy was not the cause of the overflowing vitality of the Greeks, but an effect or sign of their abiding "health." Superlative cultural achievements, such as Attic tragedy, arise only as spontaneous expressions of superfluous vitality and never in response to a perceived lack or deficiency.

Had the Greeks *needed* tragedy (as Nietzsche formerly believed was true of modernity), they never would have been in a position to produce it.[20] That Socrates and Euripides "triumphed" in Athens proves neither that they caused the demise of tragic culture nor that Wagner might resuscitate it, but only that tragedy had already perished of natural causes. Similarly, Nietzsche and Wagner cannot induce a rebirth of tragic culture; that modernity needs tragedy means that it cannot afford to sustain it. Owing to this confusion of cause and effect, in fact, Nietzsche's youthful interpretation of Hamlet's "doctrine" has it precisely backwards (BT 7). Knowledge does not kill action; the futility of action in decadent epochs artificially inflates the importance of knowledge – and of the philosophers who purvey it.

Nietzsche's scorn for Cornaro's diet, which he presents as an example of this confusion of cause and effect (TI 6:1), thus applies as well to his own critique of modernity in *The Birth of Tragedy*. Like Cornaro, who mistook his own sluggish metabolism for a judicious dietary regimen, the young Nietzsche erroneously conceived of tragic pessimism as a viable option equally available to moderns as to ancients, which modernity hitherto had simply failed to elect. He thus confused the effect (or symptom) of the overflowing Hellenic will with its cause or precondition. The Greeks did not *choose* pessimism, for they did not choose the "strength" their pessimism signified; similarly, we late moderns choose neither the vapid optimism that defines us nor the besetting anemia our optimism involuntarily reflects. That we perceive the need to display a "pessimism of strength," in fact, is sufficient evidence that we shall never muster it.

In addition to the philological foolishness it wrought, Nietzsche's confusion of cause and effect furthermore compromised the political aims of *The Birth of Tragedy*. Indeed, the curative measures he prescribes therein – a steady diet of Schopenhauerian pessimism and Wagnerian opera – are thoroughly infected with the decadence they are meant to reverse. A politically orchestrated "rebirth" of tragic culture represents an economic impossibility for late modernity, which has expended its vital resources beyond the point of replenishment (TI 9:39).[21] That an unpolitical, unheroic university professor presumed to preside over the political rejuvenation of his entire age stands as compelling evidence that modernity is destined to suffer a fragmentation similar to that displayed in Nietzsche's own, pathetic life.

Nietzsche's romantic desire to redeem modernity, based on his appeal to the Greeks as a trans-historical standard of cultural "health," thus betrays his failure to understand the dark divinity to whom he had presumptuously attached himself.[22] The figure of Dionysus represents a celebration not of Life as we might (romantically) imagine it to be or have been, but of Life as it is, in its painful, amoral immanence:

> Saying Yes to Life even in its strangest and hardest problems, the will to Life rejoicing over its own inexhaustability even in the very sacrifice of its highest types – *that* is what I called Dionysian, *that* is what I guessed to be the bridge to the psychology of the *tragic* poet. (TI 10:5)

The original *Birth of Tragedy* thus enacts a stunning anachronism – the consequence, perhaps, of the romantic pessimism its author contracted from Wagner. By virtue of its resounding failure to affirm Life in late modernity, *The Birth of Tragedy* confirms that its author was no more fit for initiation into the mysteries of Dionysus than modernity was prepared to reproduce the overflowing vitality of Attic tragedy. The young Nietzsche had not only mistaken the cause of Attic tragedy for its effects, but also confused the Teutonic gravity with which he approached his craft with the "pessimism of strength" expressed by the tragic Greeks. In his "Attempt at a Self-Criticism," he consequently ridicules his youthful call for a rebirth of tragic culture, along with the romantic idealization of the Greeks that it presupposes:

> My dear sir, what in the world is romantic if *your* book is not? Can deep hatred against "the Now," against "reality" and "modern ideas" be pushed further than you pushed it in your artists' metaphysics? . . . Isn't this the typical creed of the romantic of 1830, masked by the pessimism of 1850? Even the usual romantic finale is sounded – break, breakdown, return and collapse before an old faith, before *the* old God. (BT P7)

The Problem of Socrates Revisited

As we have seen, Nietzsche's failure to understand antiquity can be traced to his antecedent mismeasure of modernity, which furnished the impetus for his misbegotten return to tragedy. His retrospective account of his "first-born" thus reflects his revised critique of modernity as a whole, within the context of which he confidently revisits "the problem of Socrates."

In his later critique of modernity, as rehearsed in *Twilight of the Idols*, Nietzsche renounces his "Cornarism," attempting to correct for the confusion of cause and effect that faulted his earlier writings. Indeed, the most obvious difference here from the critique of modernity outlined in *The Birth of Tragedy* is his discovery of the "invisible" body, the subsystem of drives and impulses that functions as an amoral capacitor. The problem of modernity, as he now understands it, is ultimately "physiological" in nature: "In times like these, abandonment to one's instincts is one calamity more. Our instincts contradict, disturb, destroy each other; I have already defined what is *modern* as physiological self-contradiction" (TI 9:41). By "physiological self-contradiction," he means not only that human agents in modernity observe competing and often incompatible instinctual systems, but also that some of these instincts actually threaten the continued function of modernity as a macro-capacitor. This dominance of life-threatening instincts is therefore symptomatic of decay. He even defines *decadence* as the "instinctive preference" for "what disintegrates, what hastens the end" (TI 9:39). Evoking an image of the hemlock-quaffing, death-bound Socrates, he observes, "The instincts are weakened. What one ought to shun is found attractive. One puts to one's lips what drives one yet faster into the abyss" (CW 5).

Twilight of the Idols thus offers no real hope for an antidote to the instinctual disarray to which Nietzsche now traces the problem of modernity. Although he generally recommends the instincts as competent and trustworthy guides (TI 6:2), he suspends this recommendation (and most others) in the event of advanced decadence. In a vaguely political vein, he opines that "rationality in education would require that under iron pressure at least one of these instinct systems be paralyzed to permit another to gain in power, to become strong, to become master" (TI 9:41). Yet the "iron pressure" needed to "paralyze" an entire "instinct system" is virtually unthinkable without the sort of institutional support that he maintains is no longer possible. Because "the whole of the West no longer possesses the instincts out of which institutions grow, out of which a future grows" (TI 9:39), modernity is powerless to prevent the continued disintegration of the instincts.

Nietzsche concludes his revised critique of modernity by calmly observing that we cannot reverse our decadence, though we can certainly and disastrously fool ourselves into believing otherwise: "Nothing avails: one *must* go forward – step by step further into decadence (that is *my* definition of modern 'progress'). One can *check* this development and thus dam up degeneration, gather it and make it more vehement and *sudden*: one can do no more" (TI 9:43). His discussion of "great individuals" in *Twilight*, which is reminiscent in form of both *The Birth of Tragedy* and *Schopenhauer as Educator*, only reinforces the political impotence of late modernity. Great individuals are "squanderers" who "cannot be put to any public use" (TI 9:50).

In *Twilight,* Nietzsche once again summons Socrates to stand for modernity, whose decadence he prefigured. But in place of the "music-practicing Socrates" valorized in *The Birth of Tragedy,* whose deathbed conversion hinted at a dialectical hope for modernity, at a glimmer of health for those attuned to the romantic strains of Wagnerian opera (BT 15), Nietzsche now presents the life-weary Socrates, who gratefully offered a cock to Asclepius in exchange for a healing draught of hemlock (TI 2:12). No longer vilified as the calculating, cold-blooded murderer of tragedy and diabolical patron of Alexandrian science, Socrates appears in *Twilight* as a toothless ironist in search of a deep, dreamless sleep. Nietzsche no longer holds Socrates accountable for the decadence of post-tragic Greece; he is merely an expression of that decadence, an unwitting "instrument of the Greek dissolution" (TI 2:2).

Having submitted his revised diagnosis of Socrates, Nietzsche washes his hands of his erstwhile rival. Laboring all these years under a confusion of cause and effect, he has consistently misidentified Socrates as an enemy – as *the* enemy – to be battled and bested. As it turns out, however, neither Socrates nor Plato is ultimately worthy of Nietzsche's enmity and invective; they are merely the typical symptoms of the irreversible decline of a once-noble people. Fully apprised of the inevitability of the decay of postwar Athens, he now takes Socrates at his own, unironic word: " 'Socrates is no physician,' he said softly to himself; 'here death alone is the physician. Socrates himself has merely been sick a long time' " (TI 2:12). Having finally gained a definitive insight into the condition of his former rival, he summons Socrates one last time, but only to dismiss him as a harmless decadent.[23] Announcing a dramatic shift in allegiance and focus, he suggests in *Twilight* that his genuine influences (and enemies) emanate not from Athens, but from Rome (TI 10:2). As we shall see, his true rival in the battle for control of the future of humankind is none other than St. Paul.

Nietzsche's vitalism thus accounts for his anachronistic practice of enlisting the death-bound Socrates to stand for modernity as a whole. In orchestrating his own trial, conviction, and execution, Socrates manifests a stage in the decay of the Greeks that is similar to that expressed by Nietzsche and the other representative exemplars of nineteenth-century European cultures.[24] The death-bound Socrates thus represents modernity neither in its ascendancy nor in its renascence, but in the throes of its demise and capitulation. Nietzsche's enduring fascination with Socrates is thus attributable to the common economic destiny he believes they share; indeed, the desperate straits they separately negotiate would amplify any victory Nietzsche might score over his rival. This common economic destiny furthermore enables him to deliver a similar prognosis for both epochs. Indeed, Socrates too was a symptomatologist – which itself attests to the advanced decay of which he partakes – for "he saw through" the faded masks of nobility worn by his fellow Athenians (TI 2:9). Nietzsche even attributes to Socrates a diagnosis of postwar Athens that echoes his own diagnosis of late modernity: "Everywhere the instincts were in anarchy; everywhere one was within five paces of excess: *monstrum in animo* was the general danger" (TI 2:9).

If we extend this analogy, then the pronounced decadence of Epicurus, who was constitutionally ill-disposed to endure pain or suffering of any kind, bears an isomorphic resemblance to that of the nodding, blinking "last man" whom Zarathustra foresees (Z P5).[25] Like the post-Socratic epoch of Epicurean Greece, which Nietzsche describes as "merely the afterglow of the sunset" (BT P1), late modernity awaits the advent of its final will, the "will to nothingness," which promises to complete the cycle of growth and decay and inaugurate the successor age.

While Nietzsche's revised critique of modernity may appear overly pessimistic, especially when compared with the Socratic optimism of *The Birth of Tragedy*, it in fact reflects the principled realism and cool detachment of the symptomatologist. His project of critique is still viable in the post-Zarathustran writings, but it leads to no general prescriptions for political reform. By the time he writes *Twilight*, he has discerned the immutable laws that regulate the economy of decadence, and he realizes that nothing can be done to reverse or arrest the decline of modernity: "All our political theories and constitutions – and the 'German *Reich*' is by no means an exception – are consequences, necessary consequences, of decline" (TI 9:37).

Although his contempt for the German *Reich* is unmistakable, he nowhere indicates that a viable alternative is either available or attainable; indeed, any political reaction or response to the *Reich* would be equally expressive of the besetting decadence of modernity. While he unabashedly admires the republican ideals and *virtù* that he associates with the Italian Renaissance, he nowhere suggests that any such ideals would be appropriate for late modernity.[26] On the contrary, he consistently argues that he and his contemporaries cannot legitimately aspire to the vitality of which such ideals are indicative: "What is certain is that we may not place ourselves in Renaissance conditions, not even by an act of thought: our nerves would not endure that reality, not to speak of our muscles" (TI 9:37). Notwithstanding his enduring fascination with the Greek polis as a sublime enactment of the Homeric *agon*, he no longer indulges his fantasies of a similarly revivifying political contestation for late modernity.[27]

Indeed, he criticizes the various political schemes of late modernity not because he is fundamentally apolitical, but because they all trade on a common confusion of the causes and effects of cultural "reform." These bankrupt redemptive schemes – including his own youthful call for a rebirth of tragic culture – all presuppose a fund of vital resources that is simply incompatible with the decadence of modernity:

> To say it briefly (for a long time people will still keep silent about it): What will not be built any more henceforth, and *cannot* be built any more, is – a society [*Gesellschaft*] in the old sense of that word; to build that, everything is lacking, above all the material. *All of us are no longer material for a society.* (GS 356)

It is folly to recommend political measures that presuppose a capacity for squandering if continued sacrifice alone is possible. To advocate political forms that are incompatible with the native vitality of the people or age in question is not only inefficient, but also cruel.[28]

Nietzsche consequently exposes the folly of all moral and political schemes designed to reverse or "cure" the decadence of an age or epoch. A decadent age must move inexorably toward the exhaustion of its vital resources, and any attempt to defy this economic law threatens instead to accelerate this process:

> It is a self-deception on the part of philosophers and moralists if they believe that they are extricating themselves from decadence when they merely wage war against it. Extrication lies beyond their strength . . . they change its expression, but they do not get rid of decadence itself. (TI 2:11)[29]

Although liberal democracy is symptomatic of decay (BGE 203), Nietzsche concedes that we late moderns can legitimately aspire to nothing greater. To claim otherwise, that we have chosen liberal democracy as an expression of our highest virtue, is to reprise the signature calumny of slave morality. Indeed, his unrelenting ridicule of liberal democracy tends to obscure his observation that democratic regimes are particularly well suited to the depleted vitality of late modernity. It is entirely consistent with his critique of modernity, in fact, that twentieth-century Nietzscheans sincerely (and nostalgically) lament the deterioration of nineteenth-century democracies into ever more amorphous political regimes.

This is not to say, however, that late modernity is simply a stagnant, lifeless epoch. The age itself may be dying, but its besetting decay constitutes a thriving form (rather than an abject negation) of Life. As the age sputters toward exhaustion, bridges will continue to be built and burned, technological wonders introduced and worshipped, treaties signed and broken, personal fortunes gained and lost. Nietzsche believes, in fact, that he ushers in a period of "great politics," which will replace the "petty politics" with which modernity has busied itself (EH:destiny 1).

The "great wars" that ensue will invariably be interpreted as signs of renascent vitality, but they will in fact mark the spasmodic reflexes of a dying epoch. In the throes of death, modernity will apparently become more interesting, if not more vital and important, than ever before:

> We shall have upheavals, a convulsion of earthquakes, a moving of mountains and valleys, the life of which has never been dreamed of. The concept of politics will have merged entirely with a war of spirits; all power structures of the old society will have been exploded – all of them are based on lies: there will be wars the like of which have never been seen on earth. (EH:destiny 1)

In the face of the escalating chaos that Nietzsche forecasts for the remainder of the epoch, one thing remains certain: The decadence that attends the twilight of the idols must run its inexorable course. Modernity will not be redeemed from within. As Heidegger would conclude nearly a century later, only a god can save us now[30] – but only, Nietzsche would add, if the god in question is Dionysus.

Nietzsche's experiment with vitalism thus frees his critique of modernity, and his political thinking in general, from the confusion of cause and effect that had previously plagued it. No mortal can legislate against the economic destiny of his age as a whole. The emergence of a lawgiver who creates new values does not cause a new epoch to begin, but instead signals that the career of a new epoch is already underway. As a decadent, post-tragic age, late modernity has no choice but to enact its decadence, to choose instinctively what is disadvantageous for it, and to destroy itself in a cataclysm of instinctual disarray.[31]

Nietzsche's inventory of the political resources available to late modernity strikes many readers as both thin and uninspiring. Some critics, especially those who champion some version of a liberal political project, maintain that he prematurely pronounces the failure of the democratic reforms and liberal ideals of modernity.[32] Blinded perhaps by his romantic attachments to bygone epochs, he underestimates the political alternatives available to agents in late modernity.[33] In this critical light, his diagnosis of modernity appears as a self-fulfilling prophecy: Anticipating the imminent exhaustion of his age, he is content simply to administer its last rites. Still other critics actually bemoan his successful *completion* of the logic of Enlightenment, proposing his embrace of will to power as the necessary, self-reflexive culmination of the career of instrumental reason.[34] Despite his fulminations against all things modern, he has nevertheless failed to identify and pursue the most promising ramifications of the political legacy bequeathed to him.

These wide-ranging criticisms helpfully illuminate the extent to which Nietzsche's post-Zarathustran political thinking presupposes his diagnosis of modernity as a decadent age. Those readers who do not accept his "realistic" critique of modernity are not likely to endorse his gloomy diagnosis of the troubled contemporary incarnations of liberal democracy.[35]

This is not to say, however, that his critics have succeeded in discrediting his diagnosis of modernity. For the most part, he is simply pronounced wrong by virtue of a misundertanding of modernity that is supposedly as obvious as it is egregious.[36]

Nietzsche's critics are fond of exposing the indefensible prejudices that inform his "realism," thereby closing the circle of self-reference, but they are not so quick to confer a similar epistemic status upon their own alternatives. His rhetorical weapons are easily turned against him, but the resulting stalemate is rarely palatable or even admissable to his critics.[37] To adopt his strategy of reducing convictions to prejudices, if only for the sake of argument, is to surrender one's own claim to a defensibly superior account of modernity. Indeed, if his critique of modernity is to be exposed as a genuinely fraudulent mismeasure of the age – as opposed, say, to an unpopular, curmudgeonly assessment of our collective failures – then his critics are eventually obliged to produce actual (as opposed to theoretical) counterexamples to the descensional trajectory he purports to chart.[38] Whether this productive task lies within the purview of contemporary philosophy remains to be seen.

As modernity descends to embrace its apocalyptic "will to nothingness," Nietzsche scrambles to gather momentum for the postmodern, anti-Christian epoch that he hopes will follow. As we shall see in the next chapter, the twilight of the idols affords him the unique opportunity – despite his own decadence – to found communities of resistance within the political microsphere.

Notes

1   I am indebted here to Eric Blondel's account of a similar analogy between the body and culture, in *Nietzsche: The Body and Culture*, trans. Seán Hand (Stanford, CA: Stanford University Press, 1991), especially chapters 3 and 10. While I find Blondel's "genealogical" thesis intriguing, Nietzsche's writings offer little evidence of the precise analogy he proposes. Nietzsche consistently extends his symptomatology to treat ages and epochs – rather than "cultures" – as the macrostructures corresponding to individual bodies. Within the context of Nietzsche's vitalism, culture itself is "merely" an expression of the native vitality of the age or people in question; genealogical analysis must therefore focus on the historically specific vitality that a culture reflects.

2   This distinction between general and restricted economies is developed by Georges Bataille, in *Inner Experience,* trans. Leslie Anne Boldt (Albany: State University of New York Press, 1988); and "The Notion of Expenditure," in *Visions of Excess,* ed. Allan Stoekl, trans. Allan Stoekl, Carl R. Lovitt, and Donald M. Leslie, Jr. (Minneapolis: University of Minnesota Press, 1985), pp. 116–129. A general economy is bounded by no external conditions imposed on its internal regulation of influx and expenditure, and it consequently squanders itself in the generation of excess. By way of contrast, a restricted economy must

govern its internal regulation in accordance with externally imposed conditions or restrictions; the calculated, measured expenditures of a restricted economy are therefore incompatible with the generation of genuine sumptuary excess. My interpretation of Bataille is indebted to Jacques Derrida's essay "From Restricted to General Economy: A Hegelianism Without Reserve," in *Writing and Difference*, trans. Alan Bass (Chicago: University of Chicago Press, 1978), pp. 251–277.

3   Bernard Yack suggests that we distinguish between Nietzsche and Oswald Spengler on this point, since "when [Nietzsche] warns of modern decadence, he is speaking of the decadence of man, not of the degeneration that occurs at the end of a culture's life cycle" [*The Longing for Total Revolution* (Princeton, NJ: Princeton University Press, 1986), pp. 343–344]. Nietzsche explicitly rejects this interpretation of decadence (EH:destiny 7), and his own account of "modern decadence" is remarkably similar to the interpretation Yack attributes to Spengler. Witness Spengler's diagnosis of modernity: "For Western existence the distinction [between culture, which is vital, and civilization, which is mummified] lies at about 1800 – on the one side of the frontier life in fullness and sureness of itself, formed by growth from within, in one great uninterrupted evolution from gothic childhood to Goethe and Napoleon, and on the other the autumnal, artificial, rootless life of our great cities under forms fashioned by the intellect" [*The Decline of the West*, trans. Charles Francis Atkinson, 2 volumes (New York: Knopf, 1926 and 1928), p. 353].

4   Spengler draws a similar distinction between "culture and civilization," which he then likens, respectively, to "the living body of a soul and the mummy of it" (*The Decline of the West*, p. 353).

5   By dint of the "disquieting suggestion" he advances (*After Virtue*, pp. 1–5), Alastair MacIntyre masterfully exposes the moral discourse of modernity as just such a decadent *bricolage*.

6   This image of the decadent lawgiver as a *bricoleur* is drawn from Claude Lévi-Strauss, *The Savage Mind* (Chicago: University of Chicago Press, 1966). According to Lévi-Strauss, "The 'bricoleur' is adept at performing a large number of diverse tasks; but, unlike the engineer, he does not subordinate each of them to the availability of raw materials and tools conceived and procured for the purpose of the project. His universe of instruments is closed and the rules of his game are always to make do with 'whatever is at hand,' that is to say with a set of tools and materials which is always finite and is also heterogeneous because what it contains bears no relation to the current project, or indeed to any particular project, but is the contingent result of all the occasions there have been to renew or enrich the stock or to maintain it with the remains of previous constructions or destructions" (p. 17).

7   It is not often noted that Martin Heidegger too, for all of his preoccupation with preparing himself for a new gift of Being, recommends a project of ethical husbandry. In his 1947 "Letter on Humanism," he thus maintains: "The greatest care must be fostered upon the ethical bond at a time when technological man, delivered over to mass society, can be kept reliably on call only by gathering and ordering all his plans and activities in a way that corresponds to technology. Who can disregard our predicament? Should we not safeguard and secure

the existing bonds even if they hold human beings together ever so tenuously and merely for the present? Certainly. But does this need ever release thought from the task of thinking what still remains principally to be thought and, as Being prior to all beings, is their guarantor and their truth?" [*Basic Writings*, ed. David Farrell Krell (New York: Harper & Row, 1977), pp. 231–232].

8 Bataille's influential distinction between "general" and "restricted" economies roughly reprises Nietzsche's own distinction between the economies of "squandering" and "sacrifice," which in turn provides the basis for Nietzsche's general distinction between "health" and "decadence."

9 This account of decadence recalls, for example, Socrates' admonition that his fellow Athenians could no longer distinguish adequately between their benefactors and malefactors (*Apology*, 38c–e).

10 Nietzsche likens "modern men" to Epicureans in GS 375.

11 Nietzsche's notion of "great men" as standing for or representing their respective peoples and ages is probably attributable to the influence of Emerson. See, e.g., *Representative Men: Seven Lectures*, in *The Collected Works of Ralph Waldo Emerson*, Volume 4, ed. Wallace E. Williams and Douglas Emory Wilson (Cambridge, MA: Harvard University Press, 1987). My appreciation for Nietzsche's Emersonian legacy is indebted to Stanley Cavell's stimulating essay "Aversive Thinking: Emersonian Representations in Heidegger and Nietzsche," collected in *Conditions Handsome and Unhandsome: The Constitution of Emersonian Perfectionism* (Chicago: University of Chicago Press, 1990), pp. 33–63.

12 Robert B. Pippin argues that Nietzsche's complicated historicism represents the most formidable challenge to the Hegelian project of taking the measure of an entire age [*Modernism as a Philosophical Problem: On the Dissatisfactions of European High Culture* (Cambridge, MA: Basil Blackwell, 1991)]. As I have suggested, however, Nietzsche's own historicism may not be so "pure" and anti-Hegelian as Pippin's argument suggests.

13 Daniel Ahern provides a careful reconstruction of Nietzsche's activities as a physician of culture, in *Nietzsche as Cultural Physician* (University Park: Pennsylvania State University Press, 1995), especially chapters 2–3.

14 Bernd Magnus advances a "therapeutic" interpretation of Nietzsche's philosophy in "The Deification of the Commonplace: *Twilight of the Idols*," in *Reading Nietzsche*, ed. Robert C. Solomon and Kathleen M. Higgins (New York: Oxford University Press, 1988), pp. 152–181. Because Nietzsche locates the crisis o modernity not in a pathology of cognition – we *know*, after all, that God is dead – but in a failure of volition, in a weakness of the will, the "therapy" that Magnu claims to derive from Nietzsche can at best afford us only a more penetratin; insight into the nature of our complicity in the besetting decadence of moder nity. The example Magnus cites of his own Zarathustran desire for a redemptivε *Übermensch* indicates that the goal of this therapy is to "become aware of hov deeply" one's pathology "dominate[s] the structure of [one's] life and thought' (p. 176). As Magnus realizes, no amount of "becoming aware" will "cure" us oɪ the volitional deficiencies that are the destiny of agents in late modernity.

15 This point is lost on the Madman as well. His angry, disappointed response tc his obtuse interlocutors conveys his conviction that they might (or should) havε responded otherwise!

16 Nietzsche's famous characterization of the "meaning of nihilism" as "the devaluation of our highest values" is somewhat misleading, for it locates the decay of modernity in these values themselves rather than in us. But the superlative values of modernity have not changed, and they are in fact still available for our belief. We, however, are no longer volitionally disposed to invest in them the wholehearted and resolute belief mustered by earlier generations.

17 Here he is in good company, for Goethe too failed to understand the Greeks (TI 10:4)!

18 *The Birth of Tragedy* thus comprises a rudimentary version of the method of inquiry that Foucault would later call "archaeology." See, e.g., Michel Foucault, *The Archaeology of Knowledge*, trans. Alan M. Sheridan Smith (New York: Harper Colophon, 1972). According to Foucault, the "archaeologist of knowledge" attempts to identify historical periods of epistemic convergence across a cluster of sciences and disciplines, as well as to chart the transformation and eventual disintegration of epistemic coherence within the discursive practices of science.

19 As Foucault realized (and as Nietzsche eventually came to understand), an "archaeology of knowledge" is possible only in an epoch of epistemic disintegration. Independent of the truth of the historical theses advanced in *The Birth of Tragedy*, then, the very possibility of such a project speaks unequivocally to the decadence of the epoch in which it is undertaken.

20 On two separate occasions in Section Three of *The Birth of Tragedy*, Nietzsche explains the Greeks' invention of the Olympian gods as a response to a basic, existential need: "What terrific need [*ungeheure Bedürfniss*] was it that could produce such an illustrious company of Olympian beings?" [*Sämtliche Werke, Kritische Studienausgabe* in 15 Bänden, ed. G. Colli and M. Montinari (Berlin: deGruyter/Deutscher Taschenbuch Verlag, 1980), Vol. 1, p. 34]; and "It was in order to be able to live that the Greeks had to create these gods from a most profound need [*aus tiefster Nöthigung*]" (ibid., p. 36).

21 A similar confusion compromises Bataille's attempt, avowed in *On Nietzsche*, trans. Bruce Boone (New York, Paragon, 1992), to live the experimental life that Nietzsche outlines for himself, to reproduce Nietzsche's fragmentation and, if necessary, his madness (pp. xix–xxxiv). The disgregation of Nietzsche's soul was not the cause of the excesses that Bataille admires, but the effect of his besetting decadence. That Bataille needs the excesses he associates with Nietzsche is sufficient evidence that he cannot afford them.

22 On Nietzsche's idealization of the Greeks, see Staten, *Nietzsche's Voice*, p. 46.

23 Both Werner Dannhauser, in *Nietzsche's View of Socrates* (Ithaca, NY: Cornell University Press, 1974), and Nehamas, in *Nietzsche*, draw attention to Nietzsche's "quarrel" with Socrates, and both agree that this quarrel never reaches a definitive conclusion in triumph for either party. Dannhauser maintains, for example, that "for Nietzsche, the quarrel with Socrates is part of a vast historical drama which he recounts and which features Socrates as the first villain and Nietzsche as the final hero" (p. 272). In both studies, however, the centrality and endurance of Nietzsche's quarrel with Socrates strike me as overstated, especially with respect to the post-Zarathustran writings. While it may be the case, as Dannhauser and Nehamas both maintain, that Nietzsche has no right to claim victory over Socrates, the symptomatological reduction of Socrates in

Twilight – from calculating villain to unwitting symptom – would appear to signal the end of their quarrel. Indeed, both Dannhauser and Nehamas downplay Nietzsche's subsequent quarrel with a new, more dangerous "villain," St. Paul.

24 After describing the "dialectician's clarity *par excellence*" found in *Daybreak*, Nietzsche explains, "My readers know perhaps in what way I consider dialectic as a symptom of decadence; for example, in the most famous case, the case of Socrates" (EH:wise 1). Unlike Socrates, however, Nietzsche recovered from his own debilitating malady to exploit and resist his decadence: "Now I know how, have the know-how, to *reverse perspectives*: the first reason why a 'revaluation of values' is perhaps possible for me alone" (EH:wise 1).

25 Nietzsche suggests that we understand "the Epicureans' resolve *against* pessimism" as "a mere precaution of the afflicted" (BT P1).

26 For an ingenious interpretation of Nietzsche as a champion of *virtù*, while disentangling *virtù* from the particular political context favored by Machiavelli, see Bonnie Honig, *Political Theory and the Displacement of Politics* (Ithaca, NY: Cornell University Press, 1993), chapter 3, especially pp. 66–69. Linking Deleuze's praise for Nietzsche's deterritorializing activities with Nehamas's account of Nietzsche's aestheticism, Honig maintains that "Nietzsche . . . does not share Machiavelli's enthusiasm for politics. *Virtù* in his view is an individual excellence in the service, not of founding a republic, but of the strategic disruption of the impositional orderings of the herd and of the alternative construction of the self as a work of art" (p. 69). While Honig astutely acknowledges Nietzsche's likely resistance to the naivete, nostalgia, and resentment that inform the republican project she attributes to Machiavelli (p. 73), she does not entertain the possibility that Nietzsche's own "recovery of responsibility" – or her own Arendtesque reconstruction of this recovery – might incite a similar resistance by Nietzscheans committed to "strategic disruption." Indeed, despite her titular interest in "the displacement of politics" – a phenomenon she mysteriously labels "mysterious" (p. 2) – Honig does not seriously consider Nietzsche's diagnosis of late modernity as an epoch incapable of sustaining the "agonistic conflict" she wishes to defend. If Nietzsche is right, then those theorists whose respective "displacements of politics" threaten to "close down" the *agon* may simply be involuntary expressions of an anemic, post-agonistic epoch. In late modernity, that is, the robust contestations that Honig celebrates may be possible only in abstraction, conducted perhaps between sequestered intellectuals via remote internet access. In this light, her explicit concern with the project of political theory (p. 2), as opposed, say, to the project of politics itself, may be more Nietzschean than she realizes.

27 Despite Nietzsche's consistent observation throughout the post-Zarathustran period of his career that the depleted vitality of modernity is simply incompatible with the aristocratic political regimes he favors, readers often assume that he means to revive modernity and resurrect a premodern, Greek model of politics. Keith Ansell-Pearson maintains, for example, that "Nietzsche's aristocratism seeks to revive an older conception of politics, one which he locates in the Greek *agon*" [*An Introduction to Nietzsche as a Political Thinker: The Perfect Nihilist* (Cambridge: Cambridge University Press, 1994), p. 34]. Expanding

upon this point, Ansell-Pearson explains that "in its social and political aspects, Nietzsche's thinking concerns itself with how the sentiments and passions of a noble morality, resting on a superabundance of health, can be cultivated again in the modern age" (p. 162). While Nietzsche certainly hoped at one time in his career to contribute to the resuscitation of modernity, expressions of this hope are virtually absent from his post-Zarathustran writings, especially those from 1888. The tendency to attribute such hopes to the post-Zarathustran Nietzsche is perhaps responsible in part for Ansell-Pearson's conclusion that Nietzsche's political thinking is riddled with paradox and contradiction.

28   Ansell-Pearson, for example, insists that Nietzsche's "politics of force" not only conflicts with the nonmetaphysical ethical teachings of Zarathustra, but also overestimates the volitional resources at the disposal of modernity [*Nietzsche contra Rousseau* (Cambridge: Cambridge University Press, 1991), pp. 223–224]. If Nietzsche were involved in promoting the "politics of transfiguration" that Ansell-Pearson attributes to him, then Ansell-Pearson would certainly be right to confront him with his own claim that "modern liberal societies" lack the resources "to cultivate such individuals" (p. 224). At least in his post-Zarathustran writings, however, Nietzsche does not imagine that modern liberal societies could ever produce, as a matter of design, the exemplary human beings he envisions for the postmodern, tragic age to come. As he makes clear in his 1886 preface to *The Birth of Tragedy*, for example, he is well aware that his enthusiasm for great men, tragic culture, and political aristocracy is simply incompatible with the decadence that defines his historical situation (BT P6). In light of Nietzsche's post-Zarathustran turn to self-criticism, Ansell-Pearson's attention to the alleged naivete of his political thinking may be misplaced.

29   A persistent theme of Nietzsche's notes from 1888 is the belief that philosophers, moralists, and statesmen regularly mistake the consequences of decadence for its causes (cf. WP 38–48). Hence the failure of all prescriptive measures for "treating" decadence: "But the supposed remedies of degeneration are also mere palliatives against some of its effects: the 'cured' are merely one type of the degenerates" (WP 42).

30   "Nur noch ein Gott kann uns retten," Der Spiegel, No. 23, 1976, pp. 193–219.

31   Tracy Strong has long maintained that Nietzsche's preoccupation with a "politics of transfiguration" vitiates his thought. Strong thus insists that "at the end of Nietzsche's life . . . [he] comes to despair of the possibility of ever accomplishing such a transfiguration" ["Nietzsche's Political Aesthetics," in *Nietzsche's New Seas*, ed. Tracy Strong and Michael Gillespie (Chicago: University of Chicago Press, 1988), pp. 13–14]. By the "end of Nietzsche's life," however, he had long since acknowledged the decadence of his youthful longings for a redemption of modernity. Strong thus chronicles the "despair" of a Nietzsche whom Nietzsche himself had already subjected to a withering self-criticism. Wallowing in this despair, Strong's Nietzsche continues to yearn for the Greek polis and ultimately has nothing to say to modernity about politics. As I have tried to show, however, the post-Zarathustran writings of Nietzsche's career are political, and precisely to the extent that they transcend the despair that paralyzes Strong's Nietzsche.

32   See, e.g., Ansell-Pearson, *An Introduction to Nietzsche*, especially chapters 3 and 4.

33 For a bristling riposte to Nietzsche's critique of modernity, see Jürgen Habermas, *The Philosophical Discourse of Modernity: Twelve Lectures*, trans. Frederick G. Lawrence (Cambridge, MA: MIT Press, 1987), pp. 83–105. Habermas accuses Nietzsche of mismeasuring the resources of modernity, especially those resident within the dialectic of enlightenment: "Like all who leap out of the dialectic of enlightenment, Nietzsche undertakes a conspicuous leveling. Modernity loses its singular status; it constitutes only a a last epoch in the far-reaching history of a rationalization initiated by the dissolution of archaic life and the collapse of myth" (p. 87).

34 MacIntyre thus argues that "the concept of the Nietzschean 'great man' is also a pseudo-concept . . . It represents individualism's final attempt to escape from its own consequences" *(After Virtue*, p. 259).

35 According to Ansell-Pearson, for example, Nietzsche "seem[s] blind to the virtues of a democratic polity" *(An Introduction to Nietzsche*, p. 79). Ansell-Pearson later explains that "[Nietzsche's] final position remains overly culturalist and aestheticist, and rests on a devaluation of the political realm as an arena which provides a space for the practice of democratic citizenship" (p. 95). Ansell-Pearson admirably supports the thesis that Nietzsche abjured the liberatory promise of contemporary democratic societies, but in claiming that he did so unjustly (or erroneously or prematurely) Ansell-Pearson appeals more readily to the current enthusiasm for liberal democracy than to a direct refutation of Nietzsche's diagnosis of modernity.

36 For example, Warren eloquently points out that Nietzsche "failed" to understand the peculiar political conditions of modernity because "he lacked the categories of analysis appropriate to contemporary social organizations, especially those organized as markets and bureaucracies" *(Nietzsche and Political Thought*, p. 209). While Warren is surely correct to remind us of Nietzsche's limitations as a social theorist, he does not adequately demonstrate why such "categories of analysis" might (or should) lead Nietzsche to revise his diagnosis of modernity. Is it not possible that "markets and bureaucracies" are merely additional (and perhaps redundant) signs of the decay of contemporary societies?

37 Relying heavily on the destructive power of Nietzsche's own critique of the Enlightment, MacIntyre poses the pithy (and exclusive) disjunction of Aristotle versus Nietzsche. According to MacIntyre, "The defensibility of the Nietzschean position turns in the end on the answer to the question: was it right in the first place to reject Aristotle? For if Aristotle's position in ethics and politics – or something like it – could be sustained, the whole Nietzschean enterprise would be pointless" *(After Virtue*, p. 117). MacIntyre later declares Nietzsche the loser in this battle royale (p. 257), assuring his readers that "the Aristotelian tradition can be restated in a way that restores intelligibility and rationality to our moral and social attitudes and commitments" (p. 259). While I suspect that the "victory" of Aristotle is more clearly promised than demonstrated, I am more concerned with the very nature of the reconstructive project that MacIntyre proposes to undertake. What would constitute sufficient evidence that the historical rejection of Aristotle was a *mistake*? And why would he believe that the recognition of this mistake might motivate Western civilization to "return" to

Aristotle? Furthermore, if "[Nietzsche] does not win" (p. 257), then why does MacIntyre feel compelled to defend Aristotle against him? Finally, is it not typically modern (and therefore myopic) of MacIntyre to suggest that the entire history of Western ethical and political thought can be reduced to a zero-sum contest between two thinkers?

38   For an admirably balanced and philosophically measured appraisal of Nietzsche's critique of modernity, see David Owen, *Nietzsche, Politics and Modernity: A Critique of Liberal Reason* (London: Sage, 1995), chapters 3 and 4.

4

ET TU, NIETZSCHE?

Nietzsche's . . . task lies elsewhere: beyond all the codes of past, present, and future, to transmit something that does not and will not allow itself to be codified. To transmit it to a new body, to invent a body that can receive it and spill it forth; a body that would be our own, the earth's, or even something written.
   Gilles Deleuze, "Nomad Thought."[1]

Around the hero everything turns into a tragedy; around the demi-god, into a satyr-play [*Satyrspiel*]; and around God – what? perhaps into "world?"   (BGE 150)

Nietzsche's critique of modernity raises more questions than it adequately answers, and perhaps none is more vexing than the question of self-reference. Any claim to expertise in matters of decadence must, by its very nature, call itself into question, for only decadent philosophers formulate theories of decadence. That Nietzsche has an account of decadence thus stands as sufficient confirmation of its self-referential ambit and application.

As we have seen, however, Nietzsche himself is not unduly disturbed by his complicity in the besetting decay of modernity. He openly pronounces his decadence, attributing his superlative critical standpoint to his "*dual series of experiences*" with decadence and health, which have granted him "access to apparently separate worlds" (EH:wise 3). While it is undeniable that his exceeding "wisdom" affords him a unique critical perspective on his age, I am more concerned here to investigate the ways in which he unwittingly corroborates his own general theory of decadence. Toward this end, I devote this chapter to an exploration of the self-referential implications of Nietzsche's critique of modernity.

The Moralization of Decadence

Nietzsche's scorn for philosophers is well known. Although he praises the mythical "philosophers and the past" and the amorphous "philosophers of the future" as "commanders and legislators" (BGE 211), one need look no further than to his own writings for a definitive inventory of the cowards, frauds, shills, valets, charlatans, demagogues, invalids, decadents, and buffoons who are characteristically accorded the title of "philosopher." While his criticisms of philosophers are both varied and diverse, his post-Zarathustran writings distill these criticisms into a definitive, summary objection: Philosophers characteristically serve declining peoples and ages as teachers of decadence, as prophets of doom and apocalypse.

Nietzsche proposes the emergence of philosophers as an unmistakable symptom of the inevitable decay of a people or age. Offering a symptomatological revision of the history of philosophy, he heretically insists that "the great sages are types of decline" (TI 2:2). As a rule, philosophers gain credence and authority only as a people's spontaneous self-expressions become labored and indirect, as a creeping weakness of will paralyzes its resident heroes and lawgivers. The importance of philosophical knowledge is therefore inversely related to the degree of efficacy a people or age attributes to its legitimate range of agency. With the exception of those mysterious commanders and lawgivers of the future, to whom Nietzsche hopefully defers, philosophers always arrive late in the cycle of growth and decay, furnishing reasons and justifications, ex post facto, for values and practices that heretofore have required none.

As cultural epigones, philosophers both embody and perpetuate the confusion of cause and effect that is symptomatic of decay. They involuntarily slip "doers" behind "deeds," and they instinctively yoke the creative expressions of a people to the demand for theoretical justification.[2] Nietzsche thus endorses Hegel's dictum that a people or age attains self-knowledge only when its store of volitional resources has been nearly exhausted. The emergence of philosophers who track the crepuscular flight of the owl of Minerva thus announces the irreversible decline of the people or age they represent.

Nietzsche himself is no exception to this law. The cycle of growth and decay becomes discernible only when a sufficient degree of degeneration illuminates the distance that separates the apex of a people's development from its current state of decline. His "discovery" of this cycle, coupled with his inability to prescribe meaningful curative measures, thus confirms his own decadence, as well as that of modernity as a whole. Like Plato and

Socrates before him, he "appears on earth as a raven, inspired by a little whiff of carrion" (TI 2:1).

Noble ages and peoples are defined simply by their capacity to squander their vital resources in the creation and preservation of externalized forms of order. They consequently neither seek nor require a philosophical justification for their outward expressions of vitality. A decadent age or people, by contrast, must husband its resources and cannot afford to squander itself in creative expression. Because its expenditure necessarily takes the form of a sacrifice, a decadent people generally requires "good reasons" to justify its creative expressions. As previously spontaneous actions become increasingly tentative, the perceived need for additional theorizing intensifies to the point that philosophers and priests begin to command authority where they formerly had none. With respect to the post-tragic Greeks in particular, and to all decadent peoples in general, Nietzsche wonders:

> Could it be possible that, in spite of all "modern ideas" and the prejudices of a democratic taste, the triumph of *optimism*, the gradual prevalence of *rationality*, practical and theoretical *utilitarianism* . . . might all have been symptoms of a decline of strength, or impending old age, and of physiological weariness? (BT P4)

He thus treats utilitarian calculations, and consequentialism in general, as symptomatic of the decline of a formerly noble epoch, which can now afford only "reasonable" expenditures of its vital resources.[3]

From the "realistic" perspective of a healthy people, which has no need for theories or justifications of its signature practices, philosophers invariably appear pathetic and foolish:

> Before Socrates, dialectic manners were repudiated in good society: they were considered bad manners, they were compromising . . . Wherever authority still forms part of good bearing, where one does not give reasons but commands, the dialectician is a kind of buffoon: one laughs at him, one does not take him seriously. (TI 2:5)

Only in a decadent epoch do a people's signature creative expressions fall under suspicion, such that the philosopher's demands for justification gain widespread credence. Nietzsche thus describes Socrates as "the buffoon who *got himself taken seriously*" (TI 2:5).

Yet it is not simply a justification that philosophers habitually demand of the peoples and epochs they represent, for even the most decadent of peoples can concoct good reasons for their signature ideals and practices. Philosophers tend to acknowledge only those standards of justification that transcend time and place, such that any people or age might confirm the legitimacy of the practice or policy in question. Socrates manifests his decadence, for example, by inviting the *stranger* to stand in judgment of the traditional, "instinctual" practices of his fellow Athenians.[4] This demand not only is impossible to fulfill – since cultural practices stand logically prior to the discursive justifications that philosophers demand – but also hastens the incipient disintegration of the instincts. As an involuntary expression of decay, the philosopher's betrayal of his people and traditions can be mitigated, if at all, only through the purgative measures agreed upon by Socrates and his judges.

When an age or people comes to self-consciousness in the "bad conscience" of its resident philosophers, it also invariably misunderstands itself as having failed to realize, or even to articulate coherently, its avowed aims. Upon attaining self-consciousness, a people or age thus becomes a problem for itself.[5] This self-misunderstanding in turn yields a *moralization of decadence*, whereby philosophers prematurely bemoan the end of the age or people they involuntarily represent. Whereas Nietzsche urges his readers to interpret the signature self-expression of a people or age in terms of the natural, amoral outpouring of superfluous vitality, philosophers characteristically tame these bursts of creative self-externalization by superimposing upon them the cramped frame of intentionality. Because philosophers habitually confuse cause and effect, they tend to interpret the past glories of an age or people as the intended consequences of a well-devised plan, as if the age or people in question had consciously set for itself the task of attaining these precise goals. This confusion of cause and effect, with respect to the agency propagated by both micro- and macro-capacitors, thus represents a prime symptom of decadence. Estranged from the vitality we reserve and discharge, we come to view ourselves as its efficient (albeit derelict) cause – hence the irreverence and hubris of philosophers.

In their warped accounts of the onset of decadence, philosophers typically overlay the natural, amoral self-expression of a people with moralizations of its various external by-products, which are then hailed as representative of a bygone "golden age." Moralizations of decadence typically take the form of summary judgments: Because our intended ends cannot be adequately defended, much less attained, we will henceforth produce nothing of value. Although a decadent age or people will continue to express itself in creative externalizations of its (dwindling) vitality, this mode of self-expression is customarily judged by resident philosophers to fall unacceptably short of past achievements. The degeneration of a once vital people is consequently deemed to be total and complete, incapable of sheltering the unintended successes that genealogists like Nietzsche claim to discover.

As symptoms of decline, philosophers are thus responsible not only for the emerging historical consciousness of the peoples and ages they represent, but also for the damning self-denigrations that invariably ensue. The attainment of self-consciousness on the part of an age or people is thus accompanied by an immediate, involuntary moralization of its besetting decadence, as if the age or people in question could somehow have avoided or altered its destiny. Because the resources of a dying age are insufficient to reverse its degeneration, they are deemed insufficient *simpliciter* – thus speaks the decadent philosopher. Thus moralized, decadence becomes a definitive objection to an age or people, rather than an unavoidable, morally neutral stage in its natural development. The moralization of decadence thus displaces decay from its proper situation within the economy of Life, transforming it into the opposite or negation of Life itself.

Nietzsche occasionally attributes the moralization of decadence to the ascetic priest, in whom he detects a strong family resemblance to the (decadent) philosopher (GM III:10). With the blessing of the ascetic priest, "the ascetic treats life as a wrong road on which one must finally walk back to the point where it begins, or as a mistake that is put right by deeds – that we *ought* to put right" (GM III:11). The ascetic priest ingeniously interprets suffering as an undiscovered country, within which human beings might experiment with novel, potentially empowering configurations of agency, only to present his own guidance as a non-negotiable condition of exploring this undiscovered country. Having freed his weary charges from the thrall of "suicidal nihilism," he promptly enslaves them to his own, self-serving account of suffering as a punishment they deserve for unspecified crimes in the past.

Nietzsche's genealogy of morals detects a similarly fiendish modus operandi in the signature labors of the philosopher. Unable to rule real cities or to influence the course of world history, philosophers must instead found "cities in speech" and devise sweeping narratives that enforce a discursive mastery of history. In all such speculative endeavors, philosophers betray the twisted genius of their priestly heritage: Their discursive mythcraft discloses previously unknown faculties and powers, but only as an enticing prelude to the moralizations of decadence that invariably follow. Philosophers characteristically reveal exciting new routes to the future of humankind, only to ambush unwary pilgrims with unanticipated trials and hazards, which effectively transform these once-promising passages into dead ends and blind alleys.[6]

The enduring drawback of a moralization of decadence is that it effectively negates the value of the descensional trajectory described by any age or people. Moralizations of decadence typically maintain that decadent epochs are simply spent, their contributions to the future of humankind exhausted. The moralization of decadence thus functions as a self-fulfilling prophecy, imposing a (pessimistic) conclusion onto a story that is in fact not yet finished. As long as a people or age continues to function at all as a macro-capacitor of vitality, Nietzsche believes, it serves as a medium through which the will to power might express itself in novel, unprecedented modalities. Zarathustra's morbid maxim – "Die at the right time!" (Z I:21) –

is not only equally applicable to macro-capacitors, but also equally difficult for them to embrace.

Even the self-destructive gyrations of a dying epoch might serve to illuminate the full range and depth of human agency. From the "realistic" perspective Nietzsche presumes to command, how an age dies is no less important than how it lives.[7] As he explains in the *Genealogy*, for example, the ascetic priest always succeeds in revealing unknown faculties resident within the human soul, even as he preaches the futility of Life itself. The ascetic priest thus unwittingly subverts his own moralization of decadence, for the suffering he inflicts in the process contributes to the production of constellations of agency that are uniquely possible only for decadent agents. According to Nietzsche, then, the ascetic ideal only appears to negate the value of Life; it is in fact "an artifice for the *preservation* of Life" (GM III:13).

Here, too, with respect to the moralization of decadence, Nietzsche himself is no exception to the general rule. Although he sincerely intends to present a morally neutral treatment of decadence, treating it as a natural, unavoidable stage in the development of any people or age, he cannot actually realize this intention. Despite his understanding of the dangers involved in the moralization of decadence, he is not immune to its thrall. Although he aims to deliver a realistic appraisal of the volitional resources available to late modernity and thereby reclaim the decadence of modernity as an undiscovered country, he cannot abide prospective explorers who dispute the authority of his own cartography. Like the ascetic priest, he too essays a totalizing narrative, which both reveals and prematurely discounts decadence as the historical condition of novel configurations of agency. He too treats decadence as an objection to modernity as a whole, if not to Life itself.

Nietzsche's vaunted historicism, which several postmodern champions have seized as their own, actually trades on his more basic appeal to the trans-historical cycle of growth and decay.[8] As a consequence, the truth of his historicism is not itself historical, for it devolves from his account of the immutable laws that regulate the vitality of every epoch.[9] His account of the cycle of growth and decay consequently lies outside the purview of his celebrated historicism, and it in fact serves as the philosophical foundation on which his historicism rests.[10] He furthermore presents this account as the product not of his humble, limited, infra-objective perspective, but of his glimpse of the *truth*. His frequent (and confident) appeals to truth throughout the writings from 1888 suggest, in fact, that his "perspectivism," regardless of what this "position" may ultimately involve and entail, does not preclude his access to the truth.[11]

That he anchors his own theory of decadence in a metanarrative account of Western history, despite his understanding that all such accounts are epistemically bankrupt, thus stands as compelling evidence of his own decay. While he certainly "knows better" than to traffic in trans-historical verities of this sort – hence the insistent claims by some scholars of his innocence or irony – his decadence implicates him in the weakness of will that besets all of modernity. Nietzsche may not always be equal to his own best insights,[12] but his diagnosis of modernity accurately predicts the precise weakness for metanarrative justification that his post-Zarathustran writings manifest.

Nietzsche offers his readers no general solutions to the problem of modernity. Even his celebrated teachings of affirmation, with which he exhibits a disturbing lack of familiarity, are reserved for the stolid commanders and lawgivers who will someday found the successor epoch to modernity. The cognitive triumph supplied by his insight into the trans-historical cycle of growth and decay promises no recuperation whatsoever of the volitional crisis of modernity. He can understand decadence and resist it perhaps, but he cannot arrest its inexorable advance. While (allegedly) superior in volitional resources to his anemic contemporaries, he cannot extricate himself from the decadence that defines his age.

Active and Passive Nihilism

As a "child of his time" (CW P), Nietzsche is in no position to redeem anyone, let alone modernity as a whole. He consequently situates himself squarely within the ongoing crisis of modernity, presenting himself as a decadent who discerns – but cannot alter – the inexorable cycle of growth and decay.[13] As his own diagnosis would predict of him, he is much more a thinker than a doer; his insight into the peculiar conditions of late modernity far outstrips his ability to amend them.[14]

According to Nietzsche, however, his own decadence does not precisely mirror that of late modernity as a whole. He distinguishes himself from (most of) his contemporaries in several respects. First of all, his signal insight into the trans-historical cycle of growth and decay marks him as a *nihilist;* as it turns out, moreover, he is an "active" nihilist to boot. Second, his own decadence is accidental rather than constitutive, and it afflicts him only periodically. Third, his underlying condition of "health" enables him to resist his decay, apparently to good effect. Although he is a reliable judge neither of the nature of his condition nor of its effects, his account of his resistance to decadence sheds clarifying light on the (relatively modest) political goals of his post-Zarathustran writings.

While it is customary for Nietzsche's readers to equate decadence with nihilism or to conflate the two phenomena, it may be more accurate to conceive of nihilism as a particular cognitive modality of decadence. All nihilists are also decadents, but not all decadents are nihilists. The advent of nihilism thus stands as an unmistakable symptom of advanced decay; in fact,

Nietzsche would insist, most philosophers are practicing nihilists, regardless of the nature of their official teachings and public pronouncements.

In perhaps his most famous account of nihilism, contained in a note from 1886, he explains: "What does nihilism mean? *That the highest values devaluate themselves.* The aim is lacking; 'why?' finds no answer" (WP 2).[15] Nietzsche's response to his own query reveals an important and often overlooked aspect of his understanding of nihilism. The devaluation of our highest values accounts for the meaning of nihilism, but not for its cause.[16] That we are currently in a condition of "aimlessness" simply means that our highest values, which were hitherto responsible for postponing the onset of this condition, have devaluated themselves.[17] He consequently exposes the error involved in equating the experience of decadence with the cause of nihilism: "It is an error to consider 'social distress' or 'physiological degeneration' or, worse, corruption, as the *cause* of nihilism" (WP 1).

Nietzsche's published writings refer only infrequently to the phenomenon of nihilism, but all of the relevant passages support an interpretation of nihilism as a historically specific insight into the economy of decadence.[18] On two occasions in the *Genealogy,* for example, he refers to nihilism as the experience that attends his own insight into the inexorable decay of modernity. He describes his historical situation as verging upon a "European Buddhism" (GM P:5), and he notes that we have grown "weary of man" (GM I:12). On two other occasions, he links nihilism to the advent of a "will to nothingness" (GM II:24; III:14), which constitutes the final will of any dying epoch or people.

In his notes from the period, he similarly refers to nihilism as the "psychological state" that accompanies (but does not cause) the exhaustion, erethism, pessimism, and dissipation of will that he presents as symptoms of advanced decay (WP 12). These notebook entries thus confirm that Nietzsche understands nihilism as a cognitive modality of decadence, as a moment of insight and recognition:

> Nihilism, then, is the *recognition* of the long *waste* of strength, the agony of the "in vain," insecurity, the lack of any opportunity to recover and to regain composure – being ashamed in front of oneself, as if one had *deceived* oneself all too long. (WP 12, emphasis added)

As this passage suggests, he views nihilism as the recognition of irreversible decay; we should therefore take quite seriously his frequent associations of nihilism with "sickness" or "disease."[19]

A nihilist is therefore a particular type of decadent, one who knows that all expressions of strength and vitality, even those that have been accorded a permanent, supernatural status, must eventually decay. Nihilists understand not only that the ages and peoples they represent lack the vitality needed to sustain themselves, but also that this depleted vitality is the natural, amoral result of the ways in which these ages and peoples have expressed themselves in the past. As a nihilist, Nietzsche knows that nothing endures permanently, that even the greatest human creations must eventually fall, that no antecedent moral order ensures the happiness – or even the survival – of humankind. The world beheld by the nihilist is none other than the "world viewed from inside" (BGE 36), the world as will to power, which Nietzsche describes as a chaotic, indifferent, amoral "monster of energy" (WP 1067). He consequently acknowledges the utter lack of supernatural or metaphysical warrant for the superlative values from which modernity (or any age) has heretofore derived meaning and vitality.[20] Like his peripatetic twin "sons," the Madman and Zarathustra, Nietzsche divines the "death of God" and conveys this obituary to an obtuse, unbelieving audience.[21]

Nietzsche also distinguishes in his notes between "active" and "passive" modes of nihilism, implying that he and his "friends" partake of the former mode, while virtually everyone else partakes of the latter. Nihilism is "ambiguous," he explains, because it can signify either "increased power of the spirit, as *active* nihilism," or "decline and recession of the power of the spirit, as *passive* nihilism" (WP 22; cf. WP 23).[22] While both forms of nihilism share a common insight into the economy of decay, they differ with respect to the volitional response that is engendered by this insight. Active nihilists are able to affirm the entire cycle of growth and decay, despite the inevitable destruction of themselves as "individual" agents. Passive nihilists characteristically (and involuntarily) generalize from their own decay, projecting it onto humankind and history as a whole; their own crippled agency proves to them that agency per se is nearly defunct. Active nihilists consequently see decadence as a necesary ingredient of Life, whose rich economy includes, but is not reducible to, their own careers as individual agents. Passive nihilists, by contrast, cannot help but see decadence as the opposite or negation of Life itself.[23]

Active nihilists welcome the inevitable decay of cultural idols as a determinate negation, as the necessary precondition of a future renascence. Decadence thus performs an indispensable purgative function at the conclusion of every cycle of growth and decay; Nietzsche consequently locates the enduring value of "everything modern" in its emetic service to successor epochs (GM III:19).[24] Passive nihilists, conversely, view the decay of an epigonic people or age as final and apocalyptic, as an indeterminate negation, and they consequently assign no positive value to decadence itself.

Whereas active nihilists can afford to behold the world in its painful, amoral immanence, passive nihilists must first interpose saving, metaphysical fictions between themselves and the world. Indeed, the moralization of decadence is itself a result, or by-product, of the attempt by passive nihilists to invest their otherwise meaningless existence with *some* purpose, no matter how perverse. In his notes, Nietzsche occasionally employs the term *in-*

complete nihilism to describe the plight of those passive nihilists who can neither create lasting illusions nor abjure their reliance on them.[25]

The most enduring illusion to which passive nihilists cling is the fiction of *individual agency*. Rather than rethink their guiding prejudices in light of the growing disparity between the cognitive and volitional resources available to them, passive nihilists (involuntarily) insist to the end that they are causally efficient agents, albeit failed ones. Passive nihilists cling tenaciously to the naive voluntarism of folk psychology, despite their realization that it has culminated in the *absurdum practicum* that now defines their agency. Passive nihilists thus view decadence as the product not of one's unalterable destiny, but of one's voluntary elections gone awry. Indeed, moralizations of decadence typically attribute the advent of decay to some tragic, misguided choice on the part of oneself or one's ancestors, such that more promising paths of development were temporarily obnubilated and permanently forfeited. The familiar doctrine of original sin represents a typical instance of the moralization of decadence, for it locates within individual agency a powerful impulse toward a predestined self-destruction. Passive nihilists thus believe that decadence, though intrinsically worthless in and of itself, performs an invaluable moral service to successor ages and peoples. Decadent ages and individuals stand to posterity as negative exemplars, whose damning mistakes should – and can – be avoided.

Active nihilism is the exclusive province of those exemplary individuals who boast some minimal capacity for squandering their remaining volitional resources. Passive nihilism is the lot of those individuals whose insight into the economy of decadence regrettably coincides with the sheer exhaustion of their native vitality. While active nihilists are enabled as squanderers by their insight into the trans-historical cycle of growth and decay, passive nihilists respond by surrendering to decadence, by expending all remaining vitality in the pursuit of self-abnegation. According to passive nihilists, the death of God spells the end not of our crippling guilt, but of all hope that our indebtedness might someday be redeemed. Most philosophers and priests are passive nihilists, for they treat decay as the definitive objection to existence itself (GM III:11).

Whereas passive nihilists declare their contribution to the enhancement of humankind to be complete, locating their own "perfection" in their timely demise and extinction, active nihilists seek to continue their explorations of the human soul, even (or especially) in the twilight of the idols. Active nihilists thus pursue heretofore unknown possibilities for human enhancement, in the face of a self-fulfilling prophecy that proclaims the future course of humankind to be already determined. The volitional resources available to a crepuscular epoch may pale in comparison to those squandered by predecessor epochs, but this disparity alone does not warrant the moralization that passive nihilists typically attach to it. In an unusually detailed sketch of the active nihilist, Nietzsche explains:

> With a single glance he sees what, given a favorable accumulation and increase of forces and tasks, might yet *be made of man;* he knows with all the knowledge of his conscience . . . how often the type "man" has already confronted enigmatic decisions and new paths. . . . Anyone who has thought through this possibility to the end knows one kind of nausea that other men don't know – but perhaps also a new *task!* (BGE 203)

For active nihilists, the *absurdum practicum* associated with decadence presents an unprecedented opportunity to rethink the notion of agency, to philosophize outside the constraints of traditional categories and frameworks, to investigate decadent forms of Life, and to experiment with untested constellations of human faculties. At their realistic best, active nihilists conceive of decadence as delivering them a novel (rather than an empty) slate of potentialities, which they might then explore and enact.

The opportunity to investigate unknown forms of Life arises only when the advance of decadence exposes the fiction of individual agency and the limitations of individual "subjects." Freed from the tarnished cage of their own individual agency, active nihilists might better appreciate their situation within the overlapping economies of Life, Nature, and will to power. By continuing their explorations of the human soul, even throughout the twilight of the idols, active nihilists will succeed neither in defying the transhistorical cycle of growth and decay, nor in developing a cure or treatment for decadence. But they may nevertheless bequeath to the founders of the successor epoch an unprecedented insight into the nature and limitations of human agency.

As it withers and dies, a decadent people or age enacts a unique sequence of involuntary paroxysms, all of which potentially contribute to our understanding of Life. Even in the twilight of the idols, human beings remain "incomplete" animals, "pregnant with a future" that remains to some extent unknown (GM II:16). While this "pregnancy" may seem destined for miscarriage, active nihilists vow to continue their maieutic efforts and bring this troubled pregnancy to term. In their ongoing efforts to say "yes to Life even in its strangest and hardest problems" (TI 10:5), active nihilists explore the possibilities afforded them even by their imminent demise.

Nietzsche's hypothesis of the will to power, which displaces the causal agency that is popularly attributed to individual subjects, is an example of the sort of experiment that is possible only within a decadent epoch. (Of course, the fatalistic cast he imparts to this experiment, whereby he reduces individual "agents" to passive conduits of a trans-individual, amoral, hylozoic agency, faithfully attests to the difficulties involved in resisting the moralization of decadence.)[26] As this hypothesis suggests, the continued exploration of the human soul may involve constituting oneself and one's agency in modes that the (now-defunct) model of individual agency had previously ruled out as unambiguous instances of imperfection.

Indeed, it may be fruitful to regard the enigmatic *Übermensch* in terms of the possibilities that arise when the traditional notion of agency is placed in question, when decadence itself is treated as a potentially productive context for reconstituting the human soul. The familiar, Zarathustran model of the *Übermensch* as an asocial monster or world-historical conqueror may be misleadingly narrow (and moralistic) in its construal of the historical conditions under which such exemplars typically emerge. As unprecedented embodiments of human perfection, *Übermenschen* may appear in various forms and aspects – some of them entirely unimaginable to Nietzsche and Zarathustra – depending on the resources available to the historical period in question. Indeed, although Nietzsche and Zarathustra tend to think of the *Übermensch* on the familiar model of individual agency, it is entirely possible that other, potentially grotesque constellations of agency might also constitute *Übermenschlichkeit*, especially within the context of a dying people or epoch.[27]

Nietzsche's favorite example of a passive nihilist is Socrates, who, upon realizing the failure of his desperate gamble on rationality, cheerfully committed suicide (TI 2:12). Unable to reorganize his constituent drives and impulses under a dominant system of instincts, he declared them to be irremediably chaotic and utterly resistant to human design. Having failed to "master" his convulsive appetites, he concluded that they are therefore intractable. One's only hope for mastering one's appetites thus lies in extirpation, a strategy that requires, in its extreme form, the healing properties of hemlock.

Socrates' logic here is typical of passive nihilism, whose representatives characteristically present life as a "trial," "sentence," or "punishment" and who cherish death as a welcome release. According to Nietzsche, however, the only "truth" of such doctrines lies in the besetting decay of their teachers: "Castration, extirpation . . . is instinctively chosen by those who are too weak-willed, too degenerate, to be able to impose moderation on themselves. . . . Radical means are indispensable only for the degenerate" (TI 5:2).

Our best example of an active nihilist is Nietzsche himself.[28] His complicity with the decadence of modernity is mitigated by his standing as an exemplary specimen of his age. Accounting for his "wonderful life," he explains that "for the task of a *revaluation of all values* more capacities may have been needed than have ever dwelt together in a single individual – above all, even contrary capacities that had to be kept from disturbing, destroying one another" (EH:clever 9). Although he regularly exaggerates his capacity for the propagation of vitality, the reservoir of expendable affect at his disposal far surpasses that of his contemporaries; as we shall see later, he is also ignorant of the precise nature of the excesses over which he presides. Nietzsche offers no extra-genealogical explanation for his exemplary standing, referring to it simply as his "fate" or "destiny," and we should resist the temptation to overlay this amoral destiny with a moral intrepretation. We might admire (or despise) him for having turned out well, but he does not deserve our approbation (or blame) for having done so.

Throughout most of his career, Nietzsche mightily resisted his destiny, presenting himself instead as the herald of someone greater. As miserable as he is, however, he stands among the most "noble" exemplars of his age. Where passive nihilists see only a darkened horizon, Nietzsche spies an "open sea" onto which he might dispatch his intrepid navigators (GS 343). What priests and moralists depict as a cruel joke perpetrated by a malicious deity, he reclaims as a novel opportunity to limn the unexplored reaches of the human soul. Despite his self-loathing, then, and his resentment of an age that spawns no one greater, he finally accepts the mantle of the lawgiver for late modernity. He is, in short, "at the same time a *decadent* and a *beginning*" (EH:wise 1).

Ecce Homo functions, in large part, to document Nietzsche's legislative credentials. "Great men," we know, are "explosives," and he finally introduces himself as "dynamite" (EH:destiny 1). Reflecting on an earlier attempt at hagiography, he confirms his readers' suspicions about his third *Untimely Meditation*: "It is admittedly not 'Schopenhauer as Educator' that speaks here, but his opposite, 'Nietzsche as Educator'" (EH:um 3). His "formula for greatness in a human being" is *amor fati* (EH:clever 10), which he also describes as his "inmost nature" (EH:cw 4). He consequently presents himself not simply as a representative exemplar of late modernity, but as a world-historical figure for humankind as a whole: "It is my fate that I have to be the first *decent* human being; that I know myself to stand in opposition to the mendaciousness of millennia" (EH:destiny 1).[29]

Evaluating himself in contradistinction to his contemporaries, he proclaims himself "the bad conscience of his time" (CW P), thereby announcing himself as one of the "furtherers of humankind [*Förderer des Menschen*]" whom he had earlier lauded (BGE 212). This ordinal rank he shares with other exemplary products of modernity, such as Goethe, whom he ordains as the apotheosis of eighteenth-century European culture. Although Nietzsche and Goethe each establishes the apex of his respective epoch, these epochs occupy successive stages in the decline of modernity. The resources at Nietzsche's disposal are therefore considerably diminished, especially in comparison to those available to Goethe. As a pioneer in the investigation of the unique possibilities afforded humankind by advanced decay, Nietzsche himself may very well be an *Übermensch* of sorts. As we shall see, however, his greatest contributions to the exploration of decadence are almost certainly unknown to him.

In any event, Nietzsche intends the difference between active and passive nihilism to yield important political consequences. He thus advertises his "revaluation of all values" as a marked improvement upon Socrates' timid farewell. According to Nietzsche, Socrates had embarked upon a doomed campaign to cure the decadence of his age, much as Nietzsche himself had once vowed to orchestrate the redemption of modernity. Convinced finally that his prescription of rationality had yielded only an alternative expression of decadence, Socrates concluded that continued resistance would be pointless. Rather than exacerbate further the decadence of his friends and fellow Athenians, Socrates contrived to pay Asclepius in advance: "Socrates *wanted* to die . . . he forced Athens to sentence him. 'Socrates is no physician,' he said softly to himself; 'here death alone is the physician. Socrates himself has merely been sick a long time'" (TI 2:12).[30]

The imputation of suicide suggests that Socrates may have prematurely exhausted his meager reserve of volitional resources. Socrates mistakenly reasoned, or so Nietzsche would have us believe, that because he could neither reverse nor arrest the decay of Athenian culture, political resistance was therefore futile. While Socrates had no choice but to express the decadence of his age, Nietzsche surmises, he might have exploited his comparative advantage in volitional resources to contribute to the fashioning of the successor epoch.[31] Hoping to avoid a similarly premature farewell, Nietzsche squanders his remaining volitional resources in an "explosion" that will supposedly steer modernity toward a timely death.

Despite his bravado, Nietzsche despairs that the last laugh may still fall to Socrates. Does his scheme to guide modernity to a timely end constitute a genuine alternative to Socrates' farewell, or does it indicate that his decadence now outstrips that of the dying Socrates? Is it possible that Socrates is the superior pathologist of culture, that he successfully orchestrated for himself the timely death that Nietzsche covets for himself and his age?[32] In that event, rather than exploit a political alternative unknown (or unavailable) to Socrates, he would merely rehearse the post-Socratic decadence of Epicurus.[33] If Socrates was right to offer a cock to Asclepius, then Nietzsche's plan to impress his signature onto the postmodern age belongs in comedy – or, as we shall see shortly, in a satyr play.[34]

Opposing Decadence: Toward a Politics of Resistance

While Nietzsche can do very little to influence the course of world history, by 1888 he has also significantly deflated the role he reserves for himself in realizing the political agenda for which he is now famous. His will is not so robust that it can deliver him from the decadence of modernity, but its relative "health" enables the *resistance* to decadence that now comprises the whole of his personal political response to the problem of modernity.

Nietzsche apparently believes that whereas some people are born to decadence, others have decadence thrust upon them. He consequently insists that although he is a decadent, he is "also the opposite [*Gegenstück*]" of a decadent, an opposition to which he attributes his copious "wisdom" (EH:wise 2). He similarly associates his capacity to "resist" decadence to the salutary residence of "the philosopher in [him]" (CW P1). His own decadence is "periodic" rather than constitutive, signifying an underlying condition – as "*summa summarum*" – of health (EH:wise 2).[35] Because he participates in the decay of modernity only "as an angle, as a speciality," his decadence is something he can *use* as "an energetic *stimulus* for life, for living *more*" (EH:wise 2). Indeed, if he is "strong enough to turn even what is most questionable and dangerous to [his] advantage" (EH:clever 6), then he can turn even his own decadence against itself. An active nihilist is not free to divest himself of the decadence of his age, but he may exploit his decadence for his own ends. This is the extent of Nietzsche's comparative political advantage in the twilight of the idols.

To Nietzsche and those like him, the twilight of the idols constitutes an *entr'acte* in which the resistance of decadence can perhaps effect indirect political change. As the cultures of late modern Europe sputter inexorably toward exhaustion, the formative power of cultural institutions wanes accordingly. While this burgeoning freedom is meaningless to most agents, whose own volitional resources are nearly spent as well, active nihilists find that relative to their epoch as a whole, they now command a comparative advantage in the endowment of volitional resources. He thus insists that "the relationship between a genius and his age is like that between strong and weak, or between old and young: the age is relatively always much younger, thinner, more immature, less assured, more childish" (TI 9:44). Because Nietzsche's volitional resources excel those of "average" individuals, the twilight of the idols affords him a modest window of opportunity within which he might act to exert an influence on the disposition of the successor epoch. Indeed, he is an active nihilist because his insight into the economy of decadence frees him to squander – rather than sacrifice – his remaining volitional resources. His own (relative) greatness and "explosive" capacity increase as this window of opportunity closes. Taking advantage of the limited sphere of influence he commands as a representative exemplar of late modernity, he expresses his own decadence in the form of a resistance to decadence.

As a representative exemplar of late modernity, Nietzsche enjoys some measure of control over the direction of his expenditures of vitality – herein lies his capacity for resistance. As we have seen, he likens the "directing force" of agency to a match, and the "driving force" of agency to a "ton of gunpowder" (GS 360). This simile helps to clarify his melodramatic accounts of great human beings as explosives (and of himself as dynamite), for he apparently means to suggest here that a strategic disposition of one's residual vitality can touch off an explosion of dammed-up forces. His command of the relatively insignificant "directing force" of agency is therefore sufficient to steer the "driving force" that he and his age involuntarily enact. Although he holds only a single "match," a timely strike could ignite the epochal conflagration that will reduce modernity to ashes. Reprising the brazen impiety of Prometheus, Nietzsche bestows divine fire upon a dying race, in the full knowledge that both he and his recipients will pay dearly for the transfer of this ambiguous gift.

Nietzsche's post-Zarathustran writings consistently depict this window of opportunity as open only to him and those like him.[36] As we have seen, active and passive nihilism do not represent voluntary options, which anyone might alternately elect or decline at will. Advanced decadence is the inescapable destiny of late modernity; one is free neither to reverse one's decay nor to alter one's reserve of residual vitality. Nietzsche's revised critique of modernity is consequently aesthetic, rather than moral in nature. When at his "realistic" best, he issues no prescriptive teachings either to active nihilists or to their passive counterparts; he proclaims no general or universal "ought" to be fulfilled by strong and weak alike. Those who can afford to treat the twilight of the idols as an *entr'acte,* as a field of unexplored possibilities, will do so as a matter of course, independent of Nietzsche's misplaced exhortations. Those who cannot live in the navel of the age, where its own self-understanding refluxes and implodes, also cannot see the twilight of the idols as a window of opportunity.

No prescriptive, normative distance separates Nietzsche's mobilization of his depleted resources from its illuminative effect on like-minded readers. They will immediately do likewise, not simply because they can do so, but also because they cannot help but do so. After asking himself why he has embraced the "strange and insane task" that guides his life, Nietzsche simply reiterates that "it is a *task,*" as if no further justification were either necessary or possible (BGE 230). To those who are not like-minded, however, his preoccupation with the timely death of modernity is likely to seem cruel, perverse, and morbid.

Bending the Bow

Although the economy of decadence will brook no permanent deviations from its general laws, it is nevertheless sensitive to transient, local interruptions: "Nothing avails: one *must* go forward – step by step further into decadence (that is *my* definition of modern 'progress'). One can *check* this development and thus dam up degeneration, gather it and make it more vehement and *sudden*: one can do no more" (TI 9:43).[37]

The possibility of some such strategic disruption in the economy of decadence serves as the backdrop for Nietzsche's attempt to steer modernity toward a timely end. As this passage suggests, he might exploit his comparative advantage in volitional resources to arrange for a "more vehement and sudden" explosion of the residual vitality of the epoch. He elsewhere associates active nihilism with "a violent force of destruction" (WP 23), and he apparently intends to harness this violent force in an attempt to accelerate the decay of the senescent cultural institutions against which he regularly inveighs.[38] His attempt to orchestrate an explosion of dammed-up forces is thus continuous with his desire to auscultate the bloated idols of late modernity, whose collective dead weight needlessly postpones the eventual renascence of humankind. Indeed, he explicitly links "the greatest of all tasks, the attempt to raise humanity higher," with "the relentless destruction of everything that [is] degenerating and parasitical" (EH:bt 4).

The image of Nietzsche managing the decadence of modernity recalls the familiar motif of a gathering and explosion, which he occasionally employs to convey his interpretation of his own destiny. Rallying support for his "fight against the Christian-ecclesiastical pressures of millennia," for example, he appeals hopefully to "a magnificent tension of the spirit the like of which had never yet existed on earth: with so tense a bow we can now shoot for the most distant goals" (BGE P). The focus of this "magnificent tension," he decides in 1888, now resides in him. It is his destiny to release the straining bowstring of the human spirit, dispatching his successors like arrows toward the distant target of the postmodern epoch. He similarly describes the "fate" of himself and his fellow Hyperboreans in terms of "the abundance, the tension, the damming of strength" (AC 1). If Nietzsche is dynamite, then he is certainly the last weapon remaining in the plundered armory of late modernity; the timing of his explosion must therefore be perfect.[39]

In point of fact, however, even this modest account of Nietzsche's window of opportunity may be misleadingly voluntaristic. Despite his various concessions to the diminished vitality of late modernity, he continues to misrepresent the volitional resources at his own disposal. Although he employs a host of concussive images to convey a sense of his unique destiny, his primary contribution to the founding of the successor epoch lies in his uniquely *cognitive* triumph. By virtue of his immersion in the decadence of late modernity, he sees more clearly than others the peculiar ethos (and subsequent disintegration) of his age.[40] In touching off his vaunted explosion, he realistically aspires not so much to destruction and devastation, as to revelation and illumination. While he certainly prefers the muscular image of the archer flexing his bow, his own humble quiver contains only signal flares and warning arrows; the strength to dispatch more lethal ordnance lies beyond his diminished capacities.

Nietzsche can do nothing to reverse or arrest the decay of modernity as a whole, but he believes that he can exert an indirect influence on the founding of the successor epoch by bequeathing his insights to those who can translate them into active legislation. If his diagnosis of late modernity is correct, then some such politics of resistance represents the sole alternative available to him – and to us. The intended target of his explosion is Christian morality, whose deleterious influence he hopes to expose before the advent of the successor age. The explosion to which he alludes is none other than his "revaluation of all values," which he understands as a precondition of the creation of new values in the tragic age to come.

The flashpoint of this explosion will bathe Christian morality in the cold, unflinching glare of genealogy, exposing the Pauline priests as pathogenic agents and teachers of decline. His revaluation will thus bequeath to his successors, the creators of new values, a truthful assessment of the legacy of Christianity. Although he personally cannot purge modernity of its prevailing Christian influences, he is confident that his revaluation of all values will prompt the legislators of the future to consign Christian morality to the history books.

Nietzsche thus pursues a political agenda that he believes is fully consistent with the critique he advances of modernity.[41] He neither advocates a return to bygone standards of nobility and civility nor fatuously anticipates the redemption of his age. Simply waiting, whether in monkish repose or in preparing oneself to receive the gift of releasement, is as unacceptable to him as hastily implementing a half-baked scheme to revive an anemic epoch.[42] He neither promises to free his readers from the chains of decadence, nor advises them to learn to love their chains, nor offers to render these chains legitimate. Hoping to set a political course that is consistent with the depleted vitality of modernity, he promises simply to "dance in his chains" (BGE 226). Nietzsche's bizarre chorea – a St. Vitus's dance for a dying epoch – will invariably dramatize the decay of modernity, but it may also succeed in influencing the founding of the successor epoch.

Nietzsche's *Entr'acte:* The Satyr Play of Late Modernity

Nietzsche's understanding of late modernity as an *entr'acte* leaves him little room to maneuvre. In light of the cramped corner into which he has painted himself, it is perhaps appropriate that the *satyr play* emerges in his post-Zarathustran writings as a compelling figure for the political legacy of late modernity. Indeed, the figure of the satyr play not only conveys his recognition (and strategic embrace) of the political impotence of late modernity, but also reveals the extent of his involuntary participation in the epilogue farce he purports to chronicle. His complex performance on the stage of late modernity thus comprises his final, pathetic attempt to influence the founding of the successor epoch, which in turn provides indirect corroboration of his diagnosis of modernity. Nietzsche's desperate wish to distance himself somehow from the satyr play of his epigonic epoch thus contributes – albeit unwittingly – to our greater appreciation of the fractured ethos of late modernity.

While lamenting Wagner's "deathbed" conversion to Christianity, Nietzsche remarks that self-parody alone constitutes a suitable farewell for a great tragedian: "A great tragedian . . . like every artist, arrives at the ultimate pinnacle of his greatness only when he comes to see himself and his art *beneath* him – when he knows how to *laugh* at himself" (GM III:3). Venting his distaste for the smug self-assurance of Wagner's *Parsifal* (reminiscent here of the "Socratic optimism" expressed by Euripides), Nietzsche explicitly links the lusty, self-directed laughter of the tragedian to the production of a satyr play:

> One might be tempted [*versucht*] to suppose . . . that the Wagnerian *Parsifal* was intended as a joke, as a kind of epilogue and satyr play [*Satyrdrama*] with which the tragedian Wagner wanted to take leave of us, also of himself, above all of *tragedy* in a fitting manner worthy of himself, namely with an extravagance of wanton parody of the tragic itself, of the whole gruesome earthly seriousness and misery of his previous works, of the *crudest form*, overcome at long last, of the anti-nature of the ascetic ideal. (GM III:3)

In a remark that effectively links Wagner's "supposed" farewell to that of modernity as a whole, Nietzsche announces, "I estimate the value of men, of races, according to the necessity by which they cannot conceive the god apart from the satyr" (EH:clever 4).

Nietzsche's allusion to the satyr play may be anachronistic, but it accurately conveys his enduring admiration for Wagner's prodigious gifts. The notion that Wagner might have bid farewell to tragedy by composing a satyr play sympathetically associates him with such eminent tragedians as Aeschylus and Sophocles. More important, Nietzsche's anachronism serves to corroborate his diagnosis of late modernity as an anemic epoch incapable of producing genuine tragedy. Indeed, if Wagner could not resist taking himself seriously, yielding in the end to the "metaphysical comfort" of Christian redemption, then who will compose the satyr play that concludes the tragic cycle of modernity?[43]

Since Nietzsche had come to view Wagner as his antipode, we might interpret his lament as a vow not to repeat the Master's embarrassing *faux pas*. Indeed, his wishful revision of Wagner's farewell perhaps suggests a blueprint for his own final testament. Confirming his belief that self-parody

alone marks a fitting conclusion to the career of a worthy artist, he explains
that

> the martyrdom of the philosopher, his "sacrifice for the sake of truth," forces
> into the light whatever of the agitator and actor lurks within him . . . It is
> necessary . . . to be clear *what* spectacle one will see in any case – merely a satyr
> play [*Satyrspiel*], merely an epilogue farce, merely the continued proof that the
> long, real tragedy *is at an end*, assuming that every philosophy was in its genesis
> a long tragedy. (BGE 25)

This passage is patently autobiographical, and it leads us to suspect that
Nietzsche too has bequeathed to us a satyr play. This passage furthermore
implies that the philosopher's production of a satyr play (as opposed to the
tragedian's) need be neither conscious nor deliberate. In that event, we may
confidently set aside all questions of Nietzsche's own authorial intentions,
for his satyr play is performed on a stage to which he enjoys no immediate
cognitive access.[44]

Throughout the fifth century B.C.E. in Athens, playwrights who entered
the dramatic competition of the Dionysia were obliged to submit sets of four
plays (or tetralogies) consisting of three tragedies (a trilogy) followed by a
relatively short epilogue farce. This epilogue farce was known as a satyr play,
for it customarily introduced a displaced band of satyrs, often led by Silenus,
into the familiar heroic landscape of Homeric mythology.[45] The satyr play
was apparently introduced into Athens midway through the sixth century
B.C.E., probably by Pratinas, a Dorian from the Peloponnese.[46] The popularity of this imported dramatic form steadily increased in Athens, culminat-
ing in the official incorporation of the satyr play into the competition of the
Dionysia. Throughout the fifth century B.C.E., the satyr play occupied the
final position in each contestant's tetralogy, and it held this privileged place
well into the next century[47] – despite the apparent protests of Euripides.[48]
Of the entire body of satyr plays written for presentation at the festival of the
Dionysia, only one, Euripides' *Cyclops*, has descended to us in its entirety.

As a burlesque appendage to the tragic cycle, the satyr play was apparently intended as an ephemeron, as a trifle that would not endure. It was
created solely for the moment, for festival and parody, and it was not judged
by the standards applied to the tragic trilogy that preceded it – if, in fact, it
was judged at all. The satyr play was a celebration simultaneously of the
moment and of the momentary, and it served to consecrate the secular, the
quotidian, the ordinary, and the all-too-human.[49] It constituted a transient
moment of foolishness and buffoonery within an otherwise serious dramatic
competition.

Late modernity is similarly a moment of transient decadence, which seals
the tragic cycle of modernity. To judge late modernity a failure leads only to
the will to nothingness and to suicidal nihilism. If a twilight epoch is to be

judged at all, then it must be judged on its own satyric terms, as a transient moment falling outside the grim continuum of time itself.[50] If only for the brief, festive moment commemorated in the satyr play, time's relentless arrow is frozen in midflight, allowing late modern agents to frolic outside the oppressive, moralizing frame of ascetic consequentialism. As the carnivalesque reversals of the satyr play suggest, such moments might afford us the unprecedented luxury of laughing at our collective foibles, of ridiculing our all-too-human penchant for gravity and severity.

The satyr play immediately preceded the judgment on the tetralogy as a whole, and it consequently stood in judgment of the tragic trilogy that preceded it. Although the satyr play had no direct bearing on the merit of the preceding trilogy, a popular satyr play could nevertheless sway public opinion, which might in turn indirectly influence the opinions of the judges. To submit a satyr play, then, was to request a final, definitive judgment of one's imperfect labors. This is a compelling image for late modernity, since calling for a summary judgment – and thereby signally a finale – is precisely the task that epigonic epochs find most difficult to execute.

Nietzsche's insistence on the finality of his anemic epoch bears further scrutiny, however, for it betrays his own unique moralization of decadence. His distinctly Apollinian reverence for the dramatic form of the tragic cycle animates the clarifying image of late modernity as a satyr play, but it also suggests that the besetting decadence of his epoch is tolerable only as a brief interlude between successive tragic cycles. He can affirm decadence as a morally neutral ingredient of Life, but only under the condition that it will soon yield to the renascent health prefigured in his own labors of resistance.

Nietzsche consequently fails to investigate decadence itself, on its own terms, requiring instead the saving illusion provided by his pre-philosophical faith in the formal integrity of the tragic cycle. Indeed, he never dared dream that late modernity itself might spawn subsequent satyr plays *ad infinitum* or that his satyr play, the "final" epoch of the modern age, might continue indefinitely, indifferent to his destiny as the focal node of history. As Nietzsche frequently remarks, it is characteristic of decadents to misjudge themselves and their times, often under the influence of delusions of grandeur.

The satyr play properly belonged neither to the genre of tragedy nor to that of comedy. It was instead a grotesque marriage of the two forms, and it thus occupied a shadowy, liminal position within the typology of the dramatic arts. In aesthetic terms, then, the satyr play was a monstrosity, much like the hybrid goat-men it celebrated and thrust into positions of unlikely heroism. As an *entr'acte,* late modernity occupies a similarly ill-defined position between modernity and the successor epoch. Agents in late modernity boast sufficient insight into the disintegrating ethos of modernity to plot a reasonable course for its successor age, but they lack the volitional resources needed to found a new epoch. Representative exemplars of late modernity are, in short, too wise to be modern and too weak to be extra-modern.

In itself, the genre of the satyr play was neither revolutionary nor subversive. Its contributions to social and political reform were strictly revelatory, and they only indirectly achieved fruition. Excused from the formal constraints of tragedy, the playwright liberally rearranged and reversed established social orders, often with the result that he exposed these social orders in an unconventional light. Although a cleverly designed satyr play could eventually lead to the indirect formulation of new values, it offered nothing new in itself. The figure of the satyr play thus captures the volitional crisis that besets a twilight epoch. Just as the playwright was obliged in his satyr play merely to derange and pervert popular Homeric myths (rather than introduce new dramatic forms), so the representative exemplars of a decadent age are powerless to create new values. Their creative, form-giving activity is restricted exclusively to the revaluation of existing values, which Nietzsche claims as his own signal triumph.

The figure of the satyr play thus conveys the aggravated imbalance that obtains between the cognitive and volitional resources at his disposal, and it furthermore expresses the weakness of will that cripples his recuperatory efforts. Rather than bid a concussive farewell to his age, by virtue of some titanic act of will, he concludes the tragic cycle of modernity by revealing (and attempting to direct) its valedictory satyr play. Of course, every triumph of cognition always carries a residual volitional charge. It is this volitional residue of his account of late modernity that Nietzsche hopes will exert an indirect political influence on the disposition of the successor epoch.

As shadows of the tragedies they followed, satyr plays were only indirectly creative and regenerative. While the sexual and scatological motifs of the satyr play perhaps suggest a prima facie link with the celebration of fertility rites, satyric humor is actually far tamer than the bawdy ribaldry of Attic comedy.[51] Stranded midway between two productive genres, the satyr play gave birth to no new myths or tragic situations. In its reversal of existing social forms, however, the satyr play may have exerted an indirect influence on the creative labors of future playwrights. So too with the representative exemplars of a twilight epoch: Their revaluation of existing values does not create new values, but it may contribute indirectly to the founding of new values in the successor epoch.

This final act of dissemination may be infertile, but it is often illuminating and perhaps indirectly regenerative.[52] By virtue of his involuntary role in the satyr play of late modernity, in fact, Nietzsche may yet record his most enduring triumph:

Perhaps this is where we shall still discover the realm of our *invention,* that realm in which we, too, can still be original, say, as parodists of world history and God's buffoons – perhaps, even if nothing else today has any future, our *laughter* may yet have a future. (BGE 223)

What he does not say, of course, and perhaps could not fully acknowledge in his own case, is that any laughter that "may yet have a future" must be self-directed, if not self-consuming. While his parodies of world history are certainly entertaining, only his unintended *self*-parodies will contribute further to our understanding of the fragmented ethos of modernity.

While it was widely held in antiquity that no single playwright could produce both gripping tragedies and exquisite comedies, contestants in the festival of the Dionysia were nevertheless required to engage in these para-comic exercises in self-parody. The requirement of the satyr play therefore served both to exhibit and to lampoon the artistic limitations of the competing tragedians. Self-parody thus emerged as the governing trope of the genre of the satyr play. Although the tragedian's exercise in self-parody invited a painful, public self-examination, it may also have afforded him considerable latitude in delivering veiled criticisms of the prevailing social orders. While the political functions and ramifications of the dramatic festival are not well known, it is possible that the oblique political criticism essayed in the satyr play may have anticipated the social reversals that Bakhtin has catalogued under the rubric of the "carnivalesque."[53]

Nietzsche similarly prizes self-parody, for it minimizes the risk that a decadent philosopher will be received as an unchallenged authority or priest. Philosophers invariably create the world in their own image, presenting themselves as the guardians of superlative truths. Self-parody thus represents the most effective means whereby philosophers might arrange for a pre-emptive neutralization of their own residual priestly authority. Self-parody is especially salutary for those philosophers who labor in twilight epochs, those who cannot resist the temptation to issue gloomy moralizations of decadence. The terminal seriousness of philosophy must be turned against itself, and the self-reflexive gesture of self-parody represents the full extent of the volitional range available to the decadent philosopher.

As the example of *Zarathustra* suggests, however, the philosopher's self-parody is not restricted to these displays of intentional self-erasure. While strategic self-parody is a commendable course for any philosopher to pursue, Nietzsche is more interested in the political value of the *unintended* self-parody that all philosophers invariably enact. Unlike the great tragedians, who intentionally complied with the established conventions of the Dionysia, philosophers unwittingly enact the satyr play of the age they represent. Their involuntary performance of a satyr play thus contributes to *our* understanding of the epoch they represent, though not necessarily to their own.

The figure of the satyr play consequently furnishes an *infra-tragic* context for heroism. Although satyrs were not ordinarily considered heroic, they were sympathetically identified by their common plight with the familiar heroes of the Homeric myths.[54] In *Cyclops,* for example, the unlikely alliance of satyrs and heroes generates most of the buffoonery of the satyr play, as Odysseus and his shipmates are forced to cooperate with (or at least tolerate) their unlikely comrades. But this alliance also endows the satyrs with a measure of heroism of their own; they become "heroes for a day." The satyrs sustained their residual heroism only as long as the burlesque reversal was maintained; once the satyr play concluded, the hero departed and the satyrs returned to their customary social roles. But an enduring link was nevertheless forged between the hero and the satyr. This unprecedented coalition produced a more naturalistic portrait of the noble hero, who was not usually known for his all-too-human ribaldry and humor, and a less cartoonish portrait of the goatish satyrs, who were usually not associated with the serious pursuits of gods and heroes. The hero's virtues were thus shown to be contextual, mirrored imperfectly in his unlikely mates, whereas the satyrs were revealed to possess noble qualities that were not ordinarily associated with them. Their residual heroism faded quickly, to be sure, but perhaps not completely.

Self-parody falls far short of the greatness signified by an impassioned profession of *amor fati* (EH:destiny 10), but it may nevertheless constitute a "lower" ideal of greatness that is commensurate with the depleted volitional resources of late modernity. Just as one would not urge satyrs to aspire regularly to the heroism of Odysseus, so Nietzsche attempts not to measure modern agents against the unrealistic standards established by the representative exemplars of great peoples and bygone ages. His own "explosive" performance in the satyr play of late modernity certainly pales in comparison to the heroic self-creation he attributes to Goethe (TI 9:49–50), but then Goethe was spared the hardship of laboring in the twilight of the idols.

In fact, Nietzsche indirectly alludes to a historical precedent for the self-parody he enacts. "In the age of Socrates," he explains, "among men of fatigued instincts . . . *irony* may have been required for greatness of soul" (BGE 212). Since Nietzsche often enlists Socrates to stand (anachronistically) for modernity as a whole, and since modernity too is populated by "men of fatigued instincts," we might conclude that some species of irony – the self-parody of the satyr play, perhaps – constitutes the highest ideal of heroism to which we late moderns might legitimately aspire.

Nietzsche strikes a similar chord when recommending "another ideal" that still "runs ahead of us." The mysterious hero whom he envisions will apparently conclude the satyr play of late modernity, thereby renewing the tragic cycle, insofar as he confronts all earthly seriousness so far, all solemnity in gesture, word, tone, eye, morality, and task so far, as if it were their most incarnate and involuntary parody – and in spite of all this, it is perhaps only with him that *great seriousness* really begins, that the real question mark is posed for the first time, that the destiny of the soul changes, the hand moves forward, the tragedy *begins*. (GS 382)

While "the tragedy *begins*" is an obvious reference to the title of GS 342, *Incipit tragoedia,* Nietzsche complicates this reference in his 1886 preface to the second edition of *The Gay Science*: "'*Incipit tragoedia*' we read at the end of this awesomely aweless book. Beware! Something downright wicked and malicious is announced here: *incipit parodia,* no doubt" (GS P1). By mocking his own earlier aspirations to tragedy, he believes that he might yet play some limited, indirect role in the inauguration of the "*great seriousness,*" which alone can initiate the tragic age he foresees. Although the "ideal" he envisions "runs ahead of us," he nevertheless insists upon reserving for himself some modest role in its eventual realization. As we shall see, Nietzsche's attempt to parody his youthful pretensions to tragedy is continuous with his general plan to assume (limited) control of the satyr play of late modernity.

In order to appreciate the extent of Nietzsche's reliance on the satyr play as a figure for politics in the *entr'acte* of late modernity, we might turn briefly to survey his post-Zarathustran writings. On at least six occasions he describes his own political situation in terms that call to mind the satyr play.

1. Part IV of *Thus Spoke Zarathustra.* In this burlesque farce, Nietzsche documents the confederacy of the bumbling "higher men," who, in response to Zarathustra's invitation, congregate at the entrance to his cave. In Zarathustra's brief absence, the higher men inaugurate a secular festival, centering on their reverent worship of an omni-affirmative ass (Z IV:17.2).[55] Although briefly disheartened by the recidivistic piety of his new satyr friends, the "hero" Zarathustra soon joins them in their celebration, asking them always to consecrate this pagan holiday in honor of his memory (Z IV:18.3). Later, in a satyric reversal that propels Part IV toward its ambiguous, unsatisfying conclusion, the ugliest man unexpectedly ejaculates the teaching of eternal recurrence (Z IV:19.1), which Zarathustra himself has struggled to affirm and impart throughout the book. In his correspondence, Nietzsche describes Part IV of *Zarathustra* as both a "blasphemy of the gods with the whim of a buffoon [*Hanswurst*]"[56] and an *entr'acte* (*Zwischenakt*).[57]

2. The retrospective prefaces of 1886, which undertake a project of strategic self-criticism. These prefaces galvanize interest in the author of the post-Zarathustran writings, but only at the expense of the authority of the

pre-Zarathustran writings. As in the tradition of the Dionysia, Nietzsche's deliberate exercise in strategic self-parody bears public witness to his vitality and strength of soul.

3. Essay III of *On the Genealogy of Morals*. Here Nietzsche announces in passing that the only "real enemies" of the ascetic ideal, those who "arouse mistrust" of it, are the "comedians of the ascetic ideal" (GM III:27). He volunteers no examples of these comedians at work, nor of their triumphs, but we have good reason to suspect that the *Genealogy* itself (unwittingly) comprises some such "comedy."[58] His burlesque marriage of "comedy" and "asceticism" furthermore evokes the hybrid monstrosity that constitutes the genre of the satyr play. Moreover, the subversive power of these "comedians" is apparently cognitive rather than volitional in nature: They illuminate but cannot resolve the internal tensions and contradictions of the ascetic ideal.

4. Intended and unintended doublings of St. Paul in *The Antichrist(ian)*. In exposing the resentment and cruelty of the Pauline priests, Nietzsche unwittingly exemplifies the priestly mischief against which he regularly fulminates. To the extent that he is successful in discrediting the authority of the priests, he is also successful in discrediting the residual priestly authority he reserves for himself. In electing the strategy of the *Doppelgänger*, he becomes, ironically, more successful than he realizes in his campaign to expose the mendaciousness of the Christian priesthood.

5. Images of self-presentation in *Ecce Homo*. In the preface to this dubious "autobiography," the author implores his readers "*not to mistake [him] for someone else*," only to identify himself promptly as *der und der* – a literal, if not figurative, plurality (EH:P1). Throughout the text of *Ecce Homo*, Nietzsche returns regularly to the theme of his duplicity, alternately referring to himself as a buffoon (*Hanswurst*), a satyr, a mummer, and a *Doppelgänger*.

6. *The Dionysus–Dithyrambs*, dedicated on 1 January 1889 to Catulle Mendès, the librettist of *Isoline*.[59] Under the signature of Dionysus, Nietzsche praises Mendès in this dedication as the "first and greatest satyr alive today – and not only today."[60] Is it not possible that the *Dithyrambs* represent Nietzsche's final attempt to consecrate a discipleship of Dionysus and to convoke a brotherhood of satyrs?[61]

As these examples demonstrate, Nietzsche's reliance on the figure of the satyr play is not always intentional.[62] Indeed, his unwitting role in enacting the death throes of late modernity suggests that the figure of the satyr play may be more appropriate to his destiny than he ever dreamed. It is no accident, in fact, that his peculiar recourse to the figure of the satyr play actually serves to obscure the crucial differences that obtain between the tragedian and the philosopher. Whereas the tragedian intentionally engaged in self-parody as a public demonstration of his artistic command, the epigonic philosopher has no choice but to enact the satyr play that will deliver his dying epoch to a post-tragic conclusion. As Nietzsche himself observes in a moment of remarkable candor,

> let us not doubt that we moderns, with our thickly padded humanity . . . would have provided Cesare Borgia's contemporaries with a comedy at which they could have laughed themselves to death. Indeed, we are unwittingly funny beyond all measure with our modern "virtues." (TI 9:37)

As Nietzsche's general theory of decadence would predict, however, he characteristically exempts himself from the company of this unwittingly funny "we." Despite acknowledging his decadence, he strives to the end of his sanity to stake out some measure of power or nobility that might distinguish him from his somnambulant contemporaries. His appeal to the figure of the satyr play presents no exception to this general strategy of self-exclusion. Here he pretends to usurp the creative role of the great trage-dian, albeit in a diminished capacity, attempting to impose his will onto history as a buffoon (*Hanswurst*) or jokester.[63] In a pre-emptive strike against his ineluctable destiny, he resolves to bombard posterity with the "bad jokes" that his contemporaries will unwittingly rehearse at their own expense.[64] He desperately attempts, that is, to choose the role that fate will impose upon him in any event, hoping thereby to distance himself ever so slightly from the pathetic scarecrows who must join him on stage.

Even here, however, as his general critique of modernity faithfully pre-dicts, Nietzsche fails to master his historical destiny. His unprecedented insight into the economy of decadence does not excuse him from the burlesque farce unfolding around him. In fact, his hubristic efforts to influ-ence the staging of the satyr play of late modernity (which recall the Stoics' futile attempts to "master" their ineluctable fate) are largely an expression of his own resentment of modernity itself. Independent of his intended efforts at buffoonery, and even of the unintended buffoonery that he occa-sionally (if vaguely) acknowledges, he must also become a Parsifal figure, whose ignorance of his folly contributes to the reversals enacted in the satyr play.

It is this unwitting role in the satyr play of late modernity that Nietzsche predicted, but could neither own nor abide, and that thus constitutes the grand lacuna in his account of his age. Yet even this lapse may yield produc-tive results. Although he does not succeed entirely in securing his preferred role in the satyr play of late modernity, this failure may eventually produce other, unimagined successes that remain unknown to him. As Nietzsche himself puts it, though undoubtedly with no intended reference to the specific details of his own historical situation:

But on the day that we can say with all our hearts, "Onwards! our own morality too is part *of the comedy!*" we shall have discovered a new complication and possibility for the Dionysian drama of "The Destiny of the Soul" – and one can wager that the grand old eternal comic poet of our existence will be quick to make use of it! (GM P7)

The Case of Nietzsche

Nietzsche's scheme for managing the demise of modernity may be ingenious, but it is also the brainchild of a decadent philosopher. If we take seriously his decadence, subsuming it under his own general diagnosis and explanation, then his political intentions and aspirations are ultimately irrelevant to the fragmented agency he enacts. What he says about modernity and the possible configurations of its successor epoch holds value primarily as a symptom of his own decay. His discursive critique of modernity consequently tells us a great deal about him and his besetting illness, but virtually nothing about "modernity" itself.

Nietzsche is entitled to claim, perhaps, that a dying epoch ought to settle its accounts and to prepare itself for a timely and orderly demise. He is not entitled to claim, however, though he often does, that his strategic "explosion" will positively influence the founding of the postmodern age. The farewell configuration of a decadent epoch may be entirely irrelevant to the founding labors of the successor epoch, which may or may not recognize (much less value) the (dis)order furnished it by its predecessor. Although it is difficult for Nietzsche to accept, the difference between his best and worst efforts may be utterly insignificant to the "philosophers of the future." The eventual disposition of the successor epoch may very well be determined independently of what the death of late modernity does or does not accomplish.

While he reserves for himself a partial exemption from his general account of decadence – claiming, for example, to be "a bearer of glad tidings like no one before [him]" (EH:destiny 1) – he has already exposed this precise gambit as a typical symptom of advanced decay. He too participates in the moralization of decadence, spicing his "objective" inventory of modernity's resources with dismissive appraisals and unflattering comparisons. He too attributes the onset of decadence to a wayward agency, alternately identified in his various etiologies as slave morality, the ascetic priest, or St. Paul. In fact, if we subject Nietzsche's critique of modernity to the rigors of his own account of decadence, then we must conclude that he has taken the measure not of his age, but only of the illness he apparently shares with it. His discursive critique of modernity continues to attract sympathetic readers, but its enduring appeal may simply attest to the pervasiveness of the decay it manifests. Indeed, his own lapses testify to the enormous difficulties involved in resisting the moralization of decadence.

Nietzsche's unintended contributions to the moralization of decadence are most obviously displayed in the *Genealogy*, a book in which he both documents and exemplifies the twisted psychology of the slave revolt in morality. In fact, virtually everything he says about the ascetic priest applies equally well to himself as a genealogist of morals.[65] Like the ascetic priest, he "alters the direction of *ressentiment*," exciting in his readers an affective enmity for the institutions of slave morality. Like the ascetic priest, he aims to assuage the *horror vacui* of the human will by providing an interpretive context in which suffering is justified. Toward this end, he fashions a genea-logical narrative that catapults the reader back to a point of historical rup-ture, the consequences of which define our current plight. His "genealogy of morals" thus attributes our experience of decadence to the mischief of a dimly historical figure, the ascetic priest, who similarly locates the source of our current suffering in "a piece of our past" (GM III:20).

Most important, Nietzsche figures the ascetic priest as an *agent*, thus availing himself of the intentionalist categories and vocabulary that the *Genealogy* ostensibly seeks to discredit. The victory of slave morality, he ex-plains, is predicated on the currency of its enabling account of moral agency – namely, its successful transformation of sufferers into sinners. Inspired to creative genius by his consuming *ressentiment*, the ascetic priest presides over the birth of the will, a metaphysical construct to which the slaves appeal in order to blame the nobles for their besetting nobility. In a similar fashion, Nietzsche cleverly exhorts his readers to blame the ascetic priest for their current misery and to hold him responsible for the victory of slave morality.[66] Nietzsche may concede, officially, that the ascetic priest only appears to be an "enemy of Life" (GM III:13), but he otherwise casts his rival as the consummate villain, whose assault on Life has very real consequences.

Throughout his account of the genesis and ascendancy of the ascetic ideal, he unwittingly presents himself as a *Doppelgänger* of the ascetic priest. The *Genealogy* thus becomes its author's own priestly weapon, for it repro-duces and exemplifies the precise interpretive strategy that he imputes to the ascetic priest. As a consequence of his own complicity in the moraliza-tion of decadence, Nietzsche's reckoning of the genealogy of morals is simultaneously an instance of the phenomenon he seeks to chronicle. He recapitulates the logic of the slave revolt even as he documents it.

While it might be tempting to attribute this doubling to the successful prosecution of Nietzsche's complex textual strategies in the *Genealogy*, this account would fail to convey the whole truth of the matter. He is an ascetic priest of sorts, and his priestly mischief, though rhetorically amplified, is genuine. He does not speak from the privileged, external perspective of the physician of culture, but from within slave morality itself. He too is a creature of *ressentiment*, and he quite openly resents the apparent victory of slave morality.[67]

It is not as if the *Genealogy* were immaculately conceived, free of all moral prejudices – despite what Nietzsche might think of it. Witness the shameless affectation of scientific objectivity, whereby he dignifies his complicated brand of anti-Semitism (GM I:7), or the suspiciously oblique trajectory he describes in his preface in order to score an academic victory over Paul Rée, a former rival for the affections of Lou Salomé (GM P:4,7). The *Genealogy*, in short, not only identifies the unmistakable stench of *ressentiment* (GM I:14), but emits it as well.

The *Genealogy* consequently fails to realize its avowed ends, for it cannot ultimately account for the irreducibly dual role of the genealogist of morals. Nietzsche not only chronicles the history of morality, but contributes to it as well, and this latter role forever eludes the compass of the former. The self-referential failures of the *Genealogy* furthermore presage the limitations of Nietzsche's critique of modernity as a whole. He not only diagnoses the decadence of modernity, but partakes of it as well. He goes so far as to claim that it is precisely his immersion in the decadence of his age that provides him with his immanent critical standpoint (EH:wise 2). As such, his critique of modernity can never recuperate the besetting decadence of the critical standpoint from which it arises.

But Nietzsche's full critique of modernity is not contained within the discursive confines of his account of the economy of decadence – even if he thinks it so. When situated within the interpretive frame of his own general account of decadence, his discursive critique of modernity in fact reveals itself to be a red herring of sorts, as a symptom of his own decay. As we shall see more clearly in Chapter 7, his full critique of modernity is essayed by his unwitting enactment of the tensions and contradictions that define his age as a whole. In order to interpret and assay this critique of modernity, Nietzsche's readers must dare to turn against him the symptomatological method he teaches.

Notes

1   Gilles Deleuze, "Nomad Thought," trans. David B. Allison, collected in *The New Nietzsche: Contemporary Styles of Interpretation*, ed. David B. Allison (New York: Delta, 1977), p. 142.

2   According to Nietzsche, an instructive example of this methodological error is found in the work of C. A. Lobeck, who "gave us to understand that all these [Dionysian] curiosities really did not amount to anything" (TI 10:4). Lobeck accounts for the genesis of Dionysian festivals by conjecturing that an initially

meaningless experience was retrospectively invested with meaning by those who sought reasons for these seemingly pointless Dionysian rites. Although the "original" Dionysian enthusiasts had no reasons for their actions – had Lobeck dared to pursue this idea, he might have been onto something – he assumes that reasons alone enable historical explanation. He thus imports the distortions of his own (decadent) epoch by granting priority and causal efficacy to reasons and justifications, of which the original Dionysiacs had none. Owing to this confusion of cause and effect, Lobeck must consequently posit a contingent of intermediate reason-seeking and reason-finding enthusiasts.

3   On the relations of utility and sacrifice, see Georges Bataille, "The Notion of Expenditure," collected in *Visions of Excess: Selected Writings, 1927–1939*, ed. Allan Stoekl, trans. Allan Stoekl, Carl R. Lovitt, and Donald M. Leslie, Jr. (Minneapolis: University of Minnesota Press, 1985), pp. 116–129.

4   On the importance of this invitation for the formation (and deformation) of community, see Alphonso Lingis, *The Community of Those Who Have Nothing in Common* (Bloomington: Indiana University Press, 1994), especially chapter 1.

5   Foucault is similarly interested in the emerging self-consciousness of an age or epoch, for this "problematization" of a disintegrating *episteme* constitutes the unique space within which he labors. For a succinct account of Foucault's own impressions of his unique method of philosophical critique, see the interviews entitled "On the Genealogy of Ethics: An Overview of Work in Progress" and "Polemics, Politics, and Problematizations," both collected in *The Foucault Reader*, ed. Paul Rabinow (New York: Pantheon, 1984) pp. 340–372; 381–390. Nietzsche's theory of decadence thus provides a framework or background for Foucault's work that Foucault refuses to give (i.e., a genetic account of the possibility or impossibility of problematization). If Nietzsche is right, then Foucault does not simply choose to chronicle problematizations; he has no other options for his attempts at philosophical critique. On the ethical (though non-normative) ramifications of Foucault's "problematizations," see Charles Scott, *The Question of Ethics: Nietzsche, Foucault, Heidegger* (Bloomington: Indiana University Press, 1990), pp. 53–58.

6   Deleuze and Guattari chart a similar double gesture at work in the "satisfaction" of repressed desire within the schizoid framework of advanced industrial capitalism, in *Anti-Oedipus: Capitalism and Schizophrenia*, trans. Robert Hurley, Mark Seem, and Helen R. Lane (Minneapolis: University of Minnesota Press, 1983), especially chapter 4, sections 4–5. Deleuze and Guattari insist that the "deterritorialization" of the social machine, which capitalism both promises and delivers, is immediately followed (and largely negated) by the "reterritorialization" of the social machine. Capitalism surreptitiously contours the freedoms and opportunities it delivers, that is, in order to accommodate the schizoid demands of repressed desire: "Everything in the system is insane: this is because the capitalist machine thrives on decoded and deterritorialized flows; it decodes and deterritorializes them still more, but while causing them to pass into an axiomatic apparatus that combines them, and at the points of combination produces pseudo codes and artificial reterritorializations. It is in this sense that the capitalist axiomatic cannot but give rise to new territorialities and revive a new despotic *Urstaat*. The great mutant flow of capital is pure deterritorializa-

tion, but it performs an equivalent reterritorialization when converted into a reflux of means of payment" (p. 374).

7   Foucault similarly maintains that an "archaeology of knowledge" is possible only when an *episteme* begins to disintegrate, as the clustered sciences and disciplines become conscious of the nature – and limitations – of the common epistemic framework they share. At the conclusion of an *episteme*, the archaeologist is able to detect the internal incoherencies, which, when hidden, enabled the epistemic convergence of discursive practices in the first place. Like Nietzsche, Foucault celebrates the unique critical standpoint afforded him by the ongoing disintegration of the *episteme* governing the "age of man." For a representative example of Foucault's practice of archeology, see *The Order of Things: An Archaeology of the Human Sciences* (New York: Vintage, 1973), especially chapters 9–10.

8   Mark Warren applauds Nietzsche's historicism as a welcome, "postmodern" alternative to metaphysics, in *Nietzsche and Political Thought* (Cambridge, MA: MIT Press, 1987). Warren correctly notes that Nietzsche conceives of agency, subjectivity, and selfhood not as static, ahistorical data, but as historically constituted possibilities for power (see especially pp. 8–12). In attempting to salvage Nietzsche's historicism from his pernicious metaphysical entanglements, however, Warren fails to see that Nietzsche's historicism itself derives from his more basic, extra-historicist commitment to vitalism, which Warren would presumably judge to be irrecuperably metaphysical. While Warren apparently means to recommend a version of Nietzschean historicism that is not derived from any extra-historicist principles of explanation, the validity of such a position remains elusive, if not unintelligible.

9   Nietzsche's historicism thus partakes of a trans-historical logic for which it (qua historicism) cannot adequately account on its own terms. In his writings from 1888, he regularly refers to the trans-historical warrant that he claims for his historicism. As a symptomatologist, he has discerned the "laws" that govern the succession of historical epochs – hence his "scientific" diagnosis of modernity as an epoch beset by advanced decay.

10 The case of Nietzsche's "historicism" would appear to support the anti-historicist thesis advanced by Leo Strauss in *Natural Right and History* (Chicago: University of Chicago Press, 1953), especially chapter 1. According to Strauss, champions of "radical" historicism can offer no consistent historicist account of the thesis they advance: "The final and irrevocable insight into the historical character of all thought would transcend history only if that insight were accessible to man as man and hence, in principle, at all times; but it does not transcend history if it essentially belongs to a specific historic situation. It belongs to a specific historic situation: that situation is not merely the condition of the historicist insight but its source" (pp. 27–28). Nietzsche himself might add, though perhaps not with specific reference to his own "historicism," that the attraction to historicism as a philosophical position is itself symptomatic of decadence. For Nietzsche, then, historicism is of no particular interest in itself as a potentially explanatory theory, but only as a symptom of decay.

11 Maudemarie Clark persuasively argues that Nietzsche "overcomes his denial of truth" in the books of the post-Zarathustran period, in *Nietzsche on Truth and Philosophy* (Cambridge: Cambridge University Press, 1990), pp. 109–117. Clark

also astutely points out that Nietzsche's "perspectivism" makes little sense as a reductionist version of anti-foundationalism (pp. 150–158).

12 Warren argues in *Nietzsche and Political Thought* that "Nietzsche's own politics . . . violates the intellectual integrity of his philosophical project" (p. 208). Had Nietzsche better understood "contemporary markets and bureaucracies," he might have remained true to the "philosophy of agency" that Warren believes is consistent with Nietzsche's critique of metaphysics. Like Nietzsche, Warren is willing to shuffle the cards in the ontological deck and experiment with novel conceptions of agency. Unlike Nietzsche, however, Warren refuses to deal a new hand. Rather than offer an example of a "post-metaphysical" political theory, he instead lists four "values" that such a theory would presumably incorporate: "individuation, communal intersubjectivity, egalitarianism, and pluralism" (p. 247). In light of Nietzsche's own failure to resist the allure of "metaphysics," Warren's reluctance here is certainly understandable. As it stands, however, Warren "avoids" metaphysics only insofar as he refuses to advance a thicker political theory. Were he to venture any further toward the articulation of an actual political theory, he might very well expose the residual metaphysical presuppositions that guide his enthusiasm for these four "values."

13 Stanley Rosen suggests that Nietzsche's account of decadence itself contributes to an esoteric strategy designed to accelerate the decay of modernity, in "Nietzsche's Revolution," collected in *The Ancients and the Moderns* (New Haven, CT: Yale University Press, 1989), pp. 191–198.

14 Only in the writings of late 1888 and in those letters inspired by incipient madness does Nietzsche lay claim to any world-historical political designs. For an account of the emergence of politics – thereby eclipsing aesthetics – as the "master trope" of Nietzsche's thought, see Tracy B. Strong, "Nietzsche's Political Aesthetics," in *Nietzsche's New Seas*, ed. Michael Allen Gillespie and Tracy B. Strong (Chicago: University of Chicago Press, 1988), pp. 153–174. Turning in "desperation to politics" (p. 168), Nietzsche "at the end of his life . . . thinks that a political act is necessary to make the aesthetic experience possible," which would in turn make "the recognition of self and other and thus politics possible" (p. 169).

15 Nietzsche asks a similar question of meaning in Essay III of the *Genealogy: Was bedeuten asketische Ideale?* Nietzsche's interest in the meaning of nihilism thus links this note thematically to the third essay of the *Genealogy*, which is devoted to the meaning of the ascetic ideal. Later in the *Genealogy*, he explains his hermeneutic focus: "It is my purpose here to bring to light, not what this [ascetic] ideal has *done*, but simply what it *means*; what it indicates; what lies hidden behind it, beneath it, within it; of what it is the provisional, indistinct expression, overlaid with question marks and misunderstandings" (GM III:23).

16 Here I depart from the account of nihilism advanced by Michael Alan Gillespie in his excellent study *Nihilism Before Nietzsche* (Chicago: University of Chicago Press, 1995). Apparently conflating the meaning of nihilism with its source or cause, Gillespie observes that "nihilism, according to Nietzsche, is the *consequence* of the fact that God and all eternal truths and standards become unbelievable. The highest values devaluate themselves" (p. xi, emphasis added). Reprising this account later in his study, Gillespie explains that "nihilism for

Nietzsche is the *result* of the fact that the highest values devaluate themselves, that God and reason and all of the supposed eternal truths become unbelievable" (p. 174, emphasis added). Gillespie's tendency to conflate the meaning of nihilism with its cause may partially explain why he ultimately finds Nietzsche's notion of nihilism to be insufficient.

17 Heidegger takes up the question of Nietzsche's nihilism in "The Word of Nietzsche: God is Dead," in *The Question Concerning Technology and Other Essays*, trans. and ed. William Lovitt (New York: Harper & Row, 1977), pp. 53–112. While Heidegger rightly concludes that "Nietzsche cannot think the essence [*Wesen*] of nihilism" (p. 93), Nietzsche's actual interest lies elsewhere, in determining the *meaning* of nihilism. Heidegger's guiding concern with the essence of nihilism thus marks a significant deviation from Nietzsche's own strategy.

18 Gillespie persuasively demonstrates in *Nihilism Before Nietzsche* that "nihilism is not the central teaching of Nietzsche's thought" (p. 178).

19 While explaining why we must concentrate on Nietzsche's notebooks rather than on his published works, Martin Heidegger describes "the two final years 1887 and 1888" as "a time of utter lucidity and keen insight" [*Nietzsche IV: Nihilism*, trans. and ed. David F. Krell (San Francisco: Harper & Row, 1982), p. 13]. Even if we grant Heidegger's assessment of the period 1887–88, we might wonder why the published works of this period are not of greater value to him. Although Nietzsche's published books from this period say very little about nihilism itself, the account of decadence they collectively essay suggests that he wisely suspended his plans for the envisioned *Hauptwerk*.

20 Nietzsche knows that nothing endures, but he usually presents the truth of this insight as itself enduring. As we have already seen, the truth of his historicism is not itself historical. Heidegger's famous criticism is therefore accurate, for Nietzsche hypostatizes the *nihil* of nihilism, transforming it into a thing or being in its own right: "Yet for Nietzsche nihilism is not in any way simply a phenomenon of decay; rather nihilism is, as the fundamental event of Western history, simultaneously and above all the intrinsic law of that history. . . . Nietzsche thinks nihilism as the 'inner logic' of Western history" ("The Word of Nietzsche: God is Dead," p. 67). Heidegger is not so perspicacious, however, with respect to his own complicity in the history of nihilism. If it is true that the question of Being is illuminated only for decadents, and if decadents cannot help but ultimately reduce Being to a being, then Heidegger's criticism of Nietzsche will also apply self-referentially.

21 In Book V of *The Gay Science*, which he added to the 1886 edition, Nietzsche returns to the theme of the "death of God" (GS 343). Reprising the imagery of the Madman passage (GS 125), he now implicates himself in the ignorance of the townspeople who are "responsible" for the death of God. He too has overestimated his ability to digest the meaning of this unprecedented event.

22 The distinction between active and passive nihilism is related, though by no means identical, to the distinction he draws in his published writings between realism and idealism. See TI 10:2; EH:clever 10.

23 On the necessity of decadence within the economy of whole, and Nietzsche's wavering allegiance to active nihilism, see Staten, *Nietzsche's Voice*, p. 22.

24 On the productive, purgative functions of nihilism, see Maurice Blanchot, *The*

Infinite Conversation, trans. Susan Hanson (Minneapolis: University of Minnesota Press, 1993), pp. 136–151. The active nihilist, Blanchot insists, is distinguished by an insight into the transience of the experience of negation that accompanies nihilism: "Nihilism is the impossibility of being done with it and of finding a way out even in that end that is nothingness. It says the impotence of nothingness, the false brilliance of its victories; it tells us that when we think nothingness we are still thinking being . . . Nihilism thus tells us its final and rather grim truth: it tells of the impossibility of nihilism" (p. 149).

25 In a note in which he introduces the term "incomplete nihilism," Nietzsche explains, "Attempts to escape nihilism without revaluating our values so far: they produce the opposite, make the problem more acute" (WP 28).

26 Referring explicitly to the hypothesis of will to power, Karl Jaspers thus concludes that "Nietzsche's thoughts about the world" undergo "self-destruction," in *Nietzsche: An Introduction to the Understanding of His Philosophical Activity,* trans. Charles F. Wallraff and Frederick J. Schmitz (South Bend, IN: Regnery/Gateway, 1965), pp. 329–330. According to Jaspers, "What, in Nietzsche's meditations on truth, was an expressive circle constantly giving rise to new movements of thought, finally becomes, in his thoughts about the world, an annulment of metaphysics now become dogmatic: that of the will to power, as a militant exegesis temporarily believed. Here the contradictions become incapacitating, for there is a dead finality about them that prevents them from giving rise to anything new" (p. 330).

27 Gianni Vattimo addresses this point in *The Adventure of Difference: Philosophy After Nietzsche and Heidegger* (Baltimore: Johns Hopkins University Press, 1993). As Vattimo points out in his Marxish critique of Nietzsche, "The discovery that the protagonist of history is not the individual but the class is just the first step on the way to the discovery, practical and theoretical at once, of a new and more authentic mode of human existence. For the time being it can be seen only in occasional and tantalizingly ambiguous glimmerings" (pp. 57–58).

28 In his notes, Nietzsche announces himself (in the third person) as "the first perfect nihilist of Europe, who, however, has even now lived through the whole of nihilism, to the end, leaving it behind, outside himself" (WP P3). Returning to this theme, he intimates, "That I have hitherto been a thorough-going nihilist, I have admitted to myself only recently: the energy and radicalism with which I advanced as a nihilist deceived me about this basic fact" (WP 25).

29 Indeed, virtually the entire section of *Ecce Homo* entitled "Why I Am a Destiny" is an exercise in epochal self-presentation. Hoping perhaps to drum up enthusiasm for his forthcoming statement of revaluation in *The Antichrist(ian),* Nietzsche portrays himself in this section as the conqueror and destroyer of Christian morality.

30 Nietzsche elsewhere reiterates the idea that Socrates had become apprised of his decadence, proposing the "ruse" of dialectics as Socrates' "secret," as his ownmost "irony" (BT P1).

31 Nietzsche's idiosyncratic interpretation of Socrates' ironic farewell instructively raises the question of Plato's irony. While Nietzsche may be right about Socrates' failure to explore this political option, Plato – another decadent Athenian – nevertheless attempted to correct for his teacher's error of omis-

sion. Plato's epochal presentation of Socrates did not rescue Athens from its inevitable decay and capitulation, but it did (and does) influence the configuration of successor cultures and ages. On the political importance of Plato's irony, see John Seery, *Political Returns* (Boulder, CO: Westview, 1990).

32 Werner J. Dannhauser pursues a similar line of inquiry in his seminal study *Nietzsche's View of Socrates* (Ithaca, NY: Cornell University Press, 1974), pp. 271–274. According to Dannhauser, the quarrel between Nietzsche and Socrates "can scarcely be said to issue in a clear victory for Nietzsche" (p. 272). Indeed, if their quarrel "is viewed as a personal contest, an *agon,* as Nietzsche occasionally hints it should be viewed, it is again doubtful whether Nietzsche achieves victory. When all is said and done, Socrates emerges as the fuller, more profound, and more enduring figure. . . . One would be hard put to it to make a list of desirable traits or characteristics present in Nietzsche and absent in Socrates" (p. 273).

33 The identification with Epicurus would be especially unfortunate, for Nietzsche maintains that Epicurus fought to exterminate the fledgling cult of Christianity. "And Epicurus would have won," he furthermore predicts, had Paul not appeared on the scene (AC 58).

34 For an analysis of the undertones of despair in Nietzsche's "voice," see Staten, *Nietzsche's Voice,* p. 34.

35 While recounting his own convalescence, Nietzsche refers to "periods of decadence" in which he was obliged to forbid himself all feelings of *ressentiment* (EH:wise 6). With the passing of such periods, such feelings were not so much harmful to him as simply beneath him.

36 In an attempt to explain why he remains largely unknown, Nietzsche points to "the disproportion between the greatness of [his] task and the *smallness* of [his] contemporaries" (EH P1).

37 Drawing on this imagery of a gathering and explosion, Nietzsche predicts that Russia would soon emerge as a concussive force in world politics: "There the strength to will has long been accumulated and stored up, there the will – uncertain whether as a will to negate or a will to affirm – is waiting menacingly to be discharged, to borrow a pet phrase of our physicists today" (BGE 208).

38 I am indebted here to the thesis of Rosen's stimulating essay, "Nietzsche's Revolution."

39 The ambiguity of Nietzsche's scheme is conveyed by his own account of the psychology of asceticism, which similarly involves a strategic gathering and explosion: "For an ascetic life is a self-contradiction . . . here an attempt is made to employ force to block up the wells of force" (GM III:11).

40 Spengler similarly recommends in *Decline of the West* the cognitive triumph to be achieved by the representative exemplars of declining ages: "We cannot help it if we are born as men of the early winter of full Civilization, instead of on the golden summit of a ripe Culture, in a Phidias or a Mozart time. Everything depends on our seeing our own position, our *destiny* clearly, on our realizing that though we may lie to ourselves about it we cannot evade it. He who does not acknowledge this in his heart, ceases to be counted a man of his generation, and remains either a simpleton, a charlatan, or a pedant" (p. 44).

41 Advancing an alternative thesis, Mark Warren maintains in *Nietzsche and Political*

Thought that Nietzsche's political thinking is inconsistent with the "post-modern theory of power" that Warren attributes to him. Owing to this inconsistency, Warren argues, "Nietzsche as a political philosopher must be rejected" (p. 210). The normative force of Warren's "must" apparently derives in part from his belief "that at least some aspects of [Nietzsche's] political vision are distinctly fascist" (p. 211).

42 Gianni Vattimo maintains in *The Adventure of Difference* that, in the end, Nietzsche's critique of modernity implicates him in the preparatory thinking (allegedly) practiced by Heidegger: "Nietzsche's point here is analogous to Heidegger's stress on the fact that the new epoch of Being cannot depend on one of our decisions. The most we can do is wait for it, and prepare for its coming (though how we do this is unclear)" (p. 55). While I am sympathetic to Vattimo's deflation of Nietzsche's own political moment – indeed, Nietzsche perhaps should have drawn some such conclusion – I nevertheless insist that Nietzsche's own attempts to influence the founding of the successor epoch merit further study, even (or especially) if they are doomed to failure.

43 Claudia Crawford suggests that Nietzsche may have had in mind *Isoline,* an operetta written by Catulle Mendès, as the antipode of (and antidote to) Wagner's *Parsifal* [*To Nietzsche: Dionysus, I Love You! Ariadne* (Albany: State University of New York Press, 1995), pp. 275–287].

44 My attention to Nietzsche's unintended contributions to the satyr play of late modernity is indebted to Peter Sloterdijk's fine study *Thinker on Stage: Nietzsche's Materialism,* trans. Jamie Owen Daniel (Minneapolis: University of Minnesota Press, 1989), especially chapter 2. According to Sloterdijk, "Nietzsche has set in motion an unprecedented intellectual psychodrama. Through his audacious game with the double mask of the deities, he has made of himself a genius of self-knowledge as of self-accusation. He has become a psychologist spontaneously – he has become the first philosopher to be a psychologist as philosopher; his antiquating role playing has set him on this path" (p. 31).

45 Here I paraphrase from Dana F. Sutton, *The Greek Satyr Play* (Meisenheim am Glan: Verlag Anton Hain, 1980), p. ix. For the following account of the history and nature of the satyr play, I have also relied on William Arrowsmith, "Introduction to 'Cyclops,'" collected in *Satyrspiel,* ed. Bernd Seidensticker (Darmstadt: Wissenschaftliche Buchgesellschaft, 1989), pp. 179–187; and Frank Brommer, *Satyrspiele* (Berlin: deGruyter, 1959).

46 See Katherine Lever, *The Art of Greek Comedy* (London: Methuen, 1956), p. 41. See also Sutton, *The Greek Satyr Play,* chapter 1.

47 See J. Michael Walton, *The Greek Sense of Theatre* (London: Methuen, 1984), p. 149.

48 In an apparent attempt to protest, or perhaps experiment with, the conventions of the Dionysia, Euripides once presented *Alcestis,* which is clearly not a satyr play in the fourth place of his tetralogy. See Sutton, *The Greek Satyr Play,* pp. 183–184.

49 This redirection of focus onto the quotidian plane of the all-too-human is discussed by Mikhail Bakhtin in his influential study *Rabelais and His World,* trans. Helene Iswolsky (Cambridge, MA: MIT Press, 1968). Although Bakhtin is primarily interested in the perspectival reversals depicted in the literature of

the medieval world, he explicitly links the grotesque realism of the "popular-festive travesties of carnival" to the "satyric drama" (p. 28). Tracing a direct lineage of descent from the Attic satyr play to the "grotesqueries" of Rabelais, Bakhtin thus maintains, "It can be said that medieval culture of humor which accompanied the feasts was a 'satyric' drama, a fourth drama, after the 'tragic trilogy' of official Christian cult and theology to which it corresponded but was at the same time in opposition. Like the antique 'satyric' drama, so also the medieval culture of laughter was the drama of bodily life (copulation, birth, growth, eating, drinking, defecation)" (p. 88).

50   Bakhtin persuasively argues in ibid. that the satyr play may function to free its viewers momentarily from the gravity and consequentialism of "eschatological" time: "Let us stress in this prophetic picture the complete destruction of the established hierarchy, social, political and domestic. It is a picture of utter catastrophe threatening the world. . . . The basic artistic purpose of the par-odied and travestied prophecies and riddles is to uncrown gloomy eschatologi-cal time, that is, the medieval concept of the world. The parodies renew time on the material bodily level, transforming it into a propitious and merry notion" (pp. 237–238).

51   See Sutton, *The Greek Satyr Play*, pp. 160–179.

52   Bakhtin thus points in *Rabelais and His World* to the aesthetic reorientation achieved by some who partake of the riddles and reversals of the satyr play: "Instead of being gloomy and terrifying, the world's mystery and the future finally appear as something gay and carefree. This, of course, is not philosophi-cal affirmation; it is an expression of the artistic and ideological tendency of the time, seeking to hear the sounds of the world in a new key, to approach it not as a somber mystery play but as a satyrical drama" (p. 233).

53   Bakhtin thus maintains in ibid. that the apparent cruelty involved in (self-) par-ody is eventually redeemed by the laughter elicited by the parodist: "There is no pure abstract negation in the popular-festive system of images; it tends to em-brace both poles of becoming in their contradiction and unity. The one who is thrashed or slaughtered is decorated. The beating itself has a gay character; it is introduced and concluded with laughter" (p. 203).

54   Sutton thus explains in *The Greek Satyr Play* the temporary sympathetic alliance that forms between satyrs in bondage and recognized Homeric heroes: "Many satyr plays were written about the defeat of some villain, ogre, or monster by a hero, often in more or less agonic circumstances, and it is thought that the satyrs would routinely be cast as slaves to the villain, as in Euripides' *Cyclops* and *Sciron.* Thus, as in *Cyclops,* the satyrs were commonly presented as sharing the lot of the sympathetic central character, and so appeared as sympathetic them-selves; part of the happy endings of such plays would be the liberation of the satyrs, who would be free to rejoin their proper master Dionysus" (p. 138).

55   For an interpretation of Part 4 of *Zarathustra* in the light of Nietzsche's debts to Menippean satire, see Kathleen Marie Higgins, *Nietzsche's Zarathustra* (Phila-delphia: Temple University Press, 1987), pp. 206–232. On Part 4 of *Zarathustra* as a satyr play, see Crawford, *To Nietzsche*, pp. 289–296.

56   See Nietzsche's letter to Köselitz on 14 February 1885 (*Sämtliche Briefe*, Vol. 7, No. 573, p. 12).

57   See Nietzsche's letter to Carl Fuchs on 29 July 1888 (*Sämtliche Briefe,* Vol. 8, No. 1075, p. 374).

58   I pursue this thesis at some length in my essay "Comedians of the Ascetic Ideal: The Performance of Genealogy," in *The Politics of Irony: Essays in Self-Betrayal,* ed. Daniel W. Conway and John E. Seery (New York: St. Martin's, 1992), pp. 73–95.

59   Friedrich Nietzsche, *Dithyrambs of Dionysus,* trans. R. J. Hollingdale (Redding Ridge, CT: Black Swan, 1984), pp. 18–19.

60   *Sämtliche Briefe,* Vol. 8, No. 1235, p. 571. Nietzsche confirms his high opinion of Mendès (under the signature of Dionysos) in a letter to Paul Deussen on 4 January 1889 (*Sämtliche Briefe,* Vol. 8, No. 1246, p. 574).

61   Here I am indebted to Crawford, who, in *To Nietzsche,* characterizes the *Dithyrambs* as "a story of Nietzsche's actual performance of a dancing, singing, satyrical 'madness' and ecstasy" (p. 290).

62   On Nietzsche's unintended performances on stage, see Sloterdijk, *Thinker on Stage,* pp. 38–49; see also Staten, *Nietzsche's Voice,* chapter 2.

63   In a letter to Ferdinand Avenarius on 10 December 1888, Nietzsche alludes to the role he arrogates to himself in staging the satyr play of late modernity: "In these years, in which a monstrous task, the revaluation of all values, lies upon me, and I literally must carry the destiny of humankind, it belongs to my proofs of strength to be able to be a clown, satyr, or, if you will, a *feuilletonist* – to be able to be, as I have been in *Der Fall Wagner.* That the profoundest spirit must also be the most frivolous is almost the formula for my philosophy: it could be that I have already completely cheered myself up in an improbable way over and above all other 'great ones' " (*Sämtliche Briefe,* Vol. 8, No. 1183, pp. 516–517). Nietzsche reprises this image of himself as a *feuilletonist* or *Hanswurst* in his letters of 3 January 1889 to Cosima Wagner (*Sämtliche Briefe,* Vol. 8, No. 1240, p. 572) and 6 January 1889 to Jacob Burckhardt (*Sämtliche Briefe,* Vol. 8, No. 1256, pp. 577–579). For a provocative interpretation of Nietzsche's buffoonery, see Crawford, *To Nietzsche,* pp. 279–281.

64   In his final performance, a letter to Burckhardt on 6 January 1889, Nietzsche explains, "Since I am predestined to entertain the next eternity with bad jokes [*schlechte Witze*], I have a writing business here that really leaves nothing to be desired, very fine and not at all strenuous. The post office is five steps away; I post the letters there myself, in order to play the part of the great *feuilletonist* of the *grande monde*" (*Sämtliche Briefe,* Vol. 8, No. 1256, pp. 577–579). He proceeds to entertain Burckhardt in this letter with his "first two bad jokes."

65   Note how accurately the following sketch of the ascetic priest also describes its suspiciously well-informed author: "The ascetic priest is the incarnate desire to be different, to be in a different place, and indeed this desire at its greatest extreme, its distinctive fervor and passion; but precisely this power of his desire is the chain that holds him captive so that he becomes a tool for the creation of more favorable conditions for being here and being man . . . the ascetic priest, this apparent enemy of Life, this *denier* – precisely he is among the greatest *conserving* and yes-creating forces of life" (GM III:13).

66   Just as the ascetic priest blames the sick for their own bad conscience, so Nietzsche blames the ascetic priest for his moral interpretation of the bad conscience. According to Nietzsche, the suffering associated with the bad con-

science is simply the price we pay for having renounced our natural instincts. Although no one is responsible for the existential suffering of the bad conscience, the ascetic priest is responsible for the surplus suffering engendered by his moral interpretation of the bad conscience. Nietzsche feels that his interpretation of the suffering of the bad conscience (as meaningless) is preferable to the more familiar, guilt-based interpretation of the ascetic priest; neither eliminates the pain of the bad conscience, but Nietzsche's would presumably eliminate the surplus suffering of guilt.

67   Robert C. Solomon carefully documents the complexity of Nietzsche's own attitude to resentment in "One Hundred Years of Resentment: Nietzsche's *Genealogy of Morals*," collected in *Nietzsche, Genealogy, Morality: Essays on Nietzsche's "On the Genealogy of Morals*," ed. Richard Schacht (Berkeley: University of California Press, 1994), pp. 95–126.

5

PARASTRATEGESIS: ESOTERICISM FOR DECADENTS

Every profound spirit needs a mask: even more, around every profound
spirit a mask is growing continually, owing to the constantly false, namely
shallow, interpretation of every word, every step, every sign of life he gives.
(BGE 40)

The truth speaks out of me. – But my truth is *terrible;* for so far one has
called *lies* truth.   (EH:destiny 1)

Nietzsche's post-Zarathustran writings are not innocent of the grandiose
political ambitions for which he is infamous. In fact, his strategic aims
generally survive the disruptions introduced by his complicity in the decadence of modernity. He consequently targets for elimination the greatest
obstacle to the founding of a postmodern, tragic age: Christian morality.
The successful prosecution of his rebellion against Christianity, he believes,
will enable the "philosophers of the future" to legislate against the anti-
affective animus of Christian morality and to install a naturalistic alternative
to the ascetic ideal.

Owing to his own decadence, however, as well as that of modernity as a
whole, he must revise the terms of his contribution to the attainment of this
goal. His depleted strategic resources are not sufficient on their own to
ensure the success of his ambitious campaign against Christian morality. In
order for him to be "born posthumously" as the Antichrist, he will require
the assistance of readers who can extend his influence into the next millennium, at which time his "untimely" teachings might descend upon receptive

ears. He will certainly not preside over the redemption of modernity, but he may indirectly influence the founding of a post-nihilistic epoch.

Not-So-Great Politics

While Nietzsche would like nothing better than to add his own distinctive scrawl to the palimpsest of world history, he realizes that his political influence is simply too meager to prosecute on his own a successful campaign against Christian morality. As a decadent in his own right, he serves primarily, if not exclusively, as a vessel or medium for the teachings he erratically promulgates. He is, consequently, not equal to the tragic wisdom that he is destined to dispense. Unlike his anchoritic "son," Zarathustra, who supposedly can afford to forsake humanity and repair to his cave, Nietzsche needs the assistance of others.[1] He is dependent upon his readers not merely to continue the work he begins, but also to bring it to fruition.

Rather than renounce the grandiose political ambitions of his youth, Nietzsche seeks to satisfy them indirectly. His ultimate goal, his "destiny," remains the founding of a tragic age in which a thoroughgoing naturalism would supplant the anti-affective animus of Christian morality: "I promise a tragic age: the highest art in saying Yes to Life, tragedy, will be reborn when humanity has weathered the consciousness of the hardest but most necessary wars *without suffering from it*" (EH:bt 4). Yet his perceived contribution to this founding is far more oblique, and his causal influence far more attenuated, than he originally believed. His pronouncement of his own decadence thus signals an important shift in political strategy. He must beget a generation of Nietzscheans who will protect and disseminate his teachings throughout the interregnum that separates him from his rightful audience. Devising a plan that is consistent with his own decadence, he resolves to accomplish through his readers and disciples what he could not accomplish on his own.

Powerless to redeem modernity as a whole, he turns instead to the creation of underground communities that might convey his teachings into the next millennium. In a letter to Franz Overbeck on 24 March 1887, he alludes to the burgeoning "subterranean" influence he now commands: "In all radical parties (Socialists, Nihilists, anti-Semites, Orthodox Christians, Wagnerians) I enjoy a wondrous and almost mysterious respect."[2] His goal is not merely to cultivate for himself a readership, but, through the careful training of these readers, to convene a gathering of those unknown friends who can similarly afford to resist the decadence of modernity. He aims neither to rally the sick and infirm to greatness, nor to incite in would-be warriors a Dionysian frenzy – all such schemes presuppose a strength of will that late modernity lacks – but simply to announce himself to those in whom the will is similarly strong: "Such men alone are my readers, my right readers, my predestined readers: what matter the *rest?* The rest – that is merely humankind" (AC P).

Nietzsche founds these communities of resistance not by means of conscription or conversion, but solely by means of self-annunciation. In order to attract the attention of these unknown friends and comrades, he transforms himself into a sign of the residual vitality he commands. He intends this sign only for a select and self-selected audience of fellow travelers, all of whom similarly command a comparative advantage in volitional resources. At the same time, however, he displays himself for all to see, confident that most of his readers either will not acknowledge this sign or cannot respond to it. The prescriptive dimension of his response to decadence thus extends no further than his explosive act of revaluation; he issues no "ought" that his rightful successors have not already legislated for themselves (GS 382).[3] His writings from the period 1885–88 thus serve to announce his presence to kindred spirits who labor in the twilight of the idols, offering them succor and companionship for the duration of the ebbing epoch.

The point of founding these communities is neither to reverse nor retard the decadence of modernity, which must inexorably run its course (TI 9:43), but to gather political momentum for the successor epoch to modernity. Nietzsche believes that these communities represent his best opportunity to exert an anti-Christian influence on the founding of a postmodern, tragic age. While these communities are destined to succumb to the decadence that afflicts all of modernity, their guerilla resistance may help to ensure that Christian morality expires along with the rest of modernity. In that event, Nietzsche would have (indirectly) inscribed his signature onto the postmodern age, and he would be "born posthumously" as its architect.

Nietzsche's "children" and their children will wage the war he declares on Christian morality, hoping finally to bequeath his "untimely" teachings to a tragic age that is innocent of the anti-naturalism against which he inveighs. As we shall see, however, this trans-generational chain of command is weakened considerably by the decadence that he involuntarily transmits to his children. Because he does not trust his readers to convey his teachings intact, he attempts to defy the crippling effects of his decadence, hoping to invest in his teachings a degree of vitality that he simply does not possess. Not content to serve merely as a sign of his times – nor to observe the constraints of his own historicism – he aspires to illuminate the remainder of modernity and extend his formative influence into the next millennium.

Nietzsche thus aspires to accede to the station of the Antichrist. He consequently promises to "break history in two" and to reset the calendar to commemorate his world-historical "revaluation of all values."[4] In order that the successor epoch to modernity might successfully proscribe the practice of Christian morality, he arms himself as an "explosive" device that will destroy the residual authority of the Christian priesthood. If successful in transforming the rubble of Christianity into the foundation for a new tragic age, this revaluation of all values would constitute an enhancement of humankind as a whole. It is his fate, he immodestly believes, to be born posthumously as the Antichrist through the consummatory efforts of those intrepid followers who will transport his teachings across the threshold of the postmodern epoch.

In order to muster the candlepower needed to become the millennial Antichrist, however, as opposed to an influential anti-Christian of late modernity, he must harness as expenditure stores of vitality whose effects on his children are unknown to him. In particular, he must tap and vent an unacknowledged reservoir of priestly affect, which in turn inflects the reception and transmission of his teachings. Unbeknownst to Nietzsche, his children in turn must seize and wield the priestly weapons they eventually aim to retire. The ensuing assault on Christian morality may be successful, but only in ways unimaginable to Nietzsche himself.

Crumbling Masks: Decadence and Esotericism

In order to compensate for the weakness of will that periodically afflicts him, Nietzsche resolves to modify his practice of esotericism. His most significant concession to his own decadence is to exchange the impenetrable masks of his early and middle periods for a family of less complicated personae. In his writings from 1888, he dons the unfamiliar mask of the champion par excellence of truth.

Rather than risk losing our way in the labyrinth of Nietzsche's *Auseinandersetzung* with Plato, we might tarry fruitfully over his "final" word on the subject. As far as Nietzsche is concerned, Alfred North Whitehead may keep his precious "European philosophical tradition," footnotes and all: "For heaven's sake, do not throw Plato at me. I am a complete skeptic about Plato, and I have never been able to join in the admiration for the *artist* Plato which is customary among scholars. . . . Plato is boring" (TI 10:2). Verging upon philosophical heresy, Nietzsche furthermore calls into question the traditional reception of Plato as a rhetorical master: "Plato, it seems to me, throws all stylistic forms together and is thus a first-rate decadent in style" (TI 10:2). How, Nietzsche asks, could the Platonic dialogue – "this horribly self-satisfied and childish kind of dialectic" (TI 10:2) – possibly shelter anything resembling the Dionysian wisdom needed to redeem the folly and accident that define the human condition?

Nietzsche's skepticism of Platonic *poiesis* is directed particularly toward the celebrated esotericism it ostensibly serves. Plato's elusive "secret teachings," he suspects, amount to little more than rhetorical legerdemain, designed to bewitch disciples of similarly weak character:

In the end my mistrust of Plato goes deep: he represents such an aberration from all the basic instincts of the Hellene, is so moralistic, so pre-existently Christian . . . that for the whole phenomenon Plato I would sooner use the harsh phrase "higher swindle," or, if it sounds better, "idealism," than any other. (TI 10:2)

With respect to the venerable guardian of Plato's secret teachings, who alone grants entry to the inner sanctum of the unmasked master, Nietzsche is equally disrespectful. Plato may have been "the most beautiful growth of antiquity" (BGE P), but he was corrupted by the "plebeian" influence of Socrates (TI 9:2), who, Nietzsche believes, both deserved and desired the harsh sentence handed down by his Athenian judges. The wily Socrates somehow convinced Plato to employ his unmatched repertoire of masks and personae – "the greatest strength that any philosopher so far has had at his disposal" (BGE 191) – in the service of decadence. Socratic irony, the chief vehicle of Platonic esotericism, thus amounts to nothing more than an enticing smokescreen, for the meaning of life does lie, after all, in a healing draught of hemlock.

Although Nietzsche nowhere claims to have infiltrated the inner circle of Platonic esotericism, he repeatedly insists that his indirect method of access, via symptomatology, justifies his profound mistrust. The secret teachings that Plato might have dispensed to his favorites, encrypted in the motley dramatic forms of the aporetic dialogues, could only be teachings of decadence and decline, continuous perhaps with Socrates' explicit teaching in the *Phaedo*.[5] For this iconoclastic appraisal of Plato and Socrates, Nietzsche claims full credit:

> This irreverent thought that the great sages are *types of decline* first occurred to me precisely in a case where it is most strongly opposed by both scholarly and un-scholarly prejudice: I recognized Socrates and Plato to be symptoms of degeneration, tools of the Greek dissolution, pseudo-Greek, anti-Greek. (TI 2:2)

Closing the book on Plato, Nietzsche directs our attention and contemplation to the last book closed by Plato himself:

> Nothing . . . has caused me to meditate more on *Plato's* secrecy and sphinx nature than the happily preserved *petit fait* that under the pillow of his deathbed there was found no "Bible," nor anything Egyptian, Pythagorean, or Platonic – but a volume of Aristophanes. How could even Plato have endured life – a Greek life he repudiated – without an Aristophanes? (BGE 28)

Nietzsche's diagnosis of Plato and Socrates may shed only diffuse light on the nature of their secret teachings, but it is absolutely invaluable as a guide to his own experiments with esotericism. Nietzsche too loved masks, and he apparently delighted in confounding his readers: "My triumph," he boasts, "is precisely the opposite of Schopenhauer's: I say *non legor, non legar*" (EH:gb 1). Moreover, since Nietzsche also describes himself as a decadent philosopher, his diagnosis of Plato and Socrates should prove instrumental in untangling the unruly ramifications of his own rhetorical strategies.

Nietzsche takes Plato and Socrates to task not for their decadence itself, but for their failure to accommodate their decadence in the development of their signature esoteric strategies. Hoping to avoid the rhetorical chaos he discerns in the Platonic dialogues, he sets out to tailor his own esotericism to the dwindling fund of resources at his disposal. He consequently tempers his familiar claim to rhetorical mastery, for he cannot enforce an effective distinction between esoteric and exoteric teachings. The distinguishing mark of rhetorical mastery is the strategic deployment of rhetorical devices in the service of larger political ends. The rhetorical master succeeds not only in assembling an elite cadre of esoteric readers, but also in persuading his exoteric readers of the wisdom and justice of his political vision; these latter readers need not be exposed to the master's esoteric wisdom in order to serve his covert political ends.

While the esoteric teaching dispensed by the rhetorical master is designed to enlighten or transfigure its recipients, the exoteric teaching does not and need not effect a change in the souls of its recipients. The exoteric teaching consequently brings about the intended political consequence, while excluding its recipients from the esoteric teaching it serves to reinforce. In order to attain rhetorical mastery, teachers of esoteric wisdom must assume the double aspect of Janus, the divine patron of all gatekeepers and guardians of the truth. Each mask displayed by the rhetorical master functions as a selective portal, simultaneously granting admission to the elite cognoscenti while turning away the unwashed hoi polloi. In an apparently autobiographical aphorism published in 1880, Nietzsche acknowledges and presumably accepts the personal demands of rhetorical mastery:

> *Stylistic caution.* – A: But if *everyone* knew this, most would be harmed by it. You yourself call these opinions dangerous for those exposed to danger, and yet you express them in public? B: I write in such a way that neither the mob, nor the *populi*, nor the parties of any kind want to read me. Consequently, these opinions of mine will never become public. A: But how do you write, then? B: Neither usefully nor pleasantly – to the trio I have named. (H II:71)

Nietzsche's enmity for the reading "mob" never wanes, but by 1888 his confidence in his own rhetorical skills has faded appreciably. He may "have a 'second' face in addition to the first, *and* perhaps also a third" (EH:wise 3), but his besetting decadence prevents him from manipulating these masks in the continued service of esotericism. Indeed, whatever degree of facility he might once have possessed in the art of masquerade has largely vanished. By

1888, his masks have become increasingly unstable and fragile, compromising the integrity of his esoteric teachings while encouraging in his exoteric readers an untoward familiarity.[6] Unable to safeguard his esoteric teachings from the taint of decadence, he cannot realistically hope to persuade his exoteric readers to further unwittingly his political ends. He attempts to compensate for the corruption of his rhetorical strategies, displacing himself behind his "most multifarious art of style" (EH:gb 4), but his Silenian elusiveness largely backfires.[7] Indeed, despite his best rhetorical efforts, Nietzsche has become a philosopher "for all and none," embraced by Christians, liberals, feminists, postmodernists, anti-Semites, democrats, anarchists, and virtually every other community or constituency that he expressly condemned.[8]

Nietzsche's impassioned pleas for *his* readers, to whom he might dispense his unvarnished esoteric wisdom, are popularly dismissed as quaint, charming anachronisms. *We* are his legitimate heirs, or so the story goes, for we have cracked his code, confounded his writerly snares, plumbed the depths of his myriad neuroses, charted his textbook Oedipal drama, disarmed his "explosives," deconstructed his logocentrism, exhumed his inner child, and exposed his unwitting complicity with oppressive regimes of phallocratic power. We late moderns, who must either become or beget the nodding, blinking "last men," have taken the measure of Nietzsche.

To his credit, Nietzsche anticipated the indignity of his reception by his late modern readers: "I have a terrible fear that one day I will be pronounced *holy*" (EH:destiny 1). Indeed, a significant manifestation of his decadence is his growing despair that he might never cultivate the homologous readership that would continue his work.[9] In sharp contrast to the bravado of his public persona, he privately fears, like Zarathustra, that he has failed as a teacher of esoteric wisdom.[10] He thus lands, or so he believes, in the rhetorical quandary faced by Plato, Socrates, and all other decadent philosophers. Any audience that falls within the shrinking sphere of his rhetorical mastery would be too feeble to fulfill his political agenda, while any readership capable of furthering his ends would also be strong enough to distort his teachings beyond recognition. He must either trust his diminished rhetorical powers and continue his dubious esoteric strategies or discard (some of) his masks and expose his teachings to an unworthy audience. In either case the risk is virtually prohibitive: On the one hand, he may fail to dispense his secret teachings; on the other hand, he may inadvertently bequeath them to vulgarians.

Nietzsche's decadence may land him in the rhetorical quandary that paralyzed Plato and Socrates, but his recognition of his decadence signals a way out. "We have discovered happiness," he proclaims of himself and his fellow Hyperboreans; "we know the way, we have found the exit out of the labyrinth of thousands of years" (AC 1). It is no coincidence that his books from the year 1888 also proclaim him the champion par excellence of truth. As we shall see more clearly in Chapter 6, Nietzsche conceives of his revaluation of all values as an explosion of truth, as a grand exposé of Christian morality. Telling the truth about Christian morality, he believes, is his only means of contributing to the founding of a tragic epoch; it is in any event a gambit he has not vigorously pursued heretofore.

Upon acceding to the station of epochal truth teller, Nietzsche ostensibly retires the masks and personae that have served his esotericism. He now disseminates his teachings indiscriminately to all readers: "The pathos of poses does *not* belong to greatness; whoever needs poses is *false*. – Beware of all picturesque men!" (EH:clever 10).[11] This departure from esotericism, he continues, occasions the world-historical confrontation that is his destiny: "For when truth enters into a fight with the lies of millennia, we shall have upheavals, a convulsion of earthquakes, a moving of mountains and valleys, the like of which has never been dreamed of" (EH:destiny 1). He consequently begins his "autobiography" with an unprecedented gesture of self-disclosure:

> Seeing that before long I must confront humanity with the most difficult demand ever made of it, it seems indispensable to me to say *who I am* . . . I have a duty against which my habits, even more the pride of my instincts, revolt at bottom – namely, to say: *Hear me! For I am such and such a person* [*Ich bin der und der*]. *Above all, do not mistake me for someone else.* (EH P1)

Readers schooled in suspicion will certainly object here that Nietzsche's self-disclosure itself functions as a mask, which his correspondence from 1888 perhaps confirms.[12] Indeed, it is unlikely that he could ever shed all his masks, thereby exposing the authentic core of his being, even if he were so inclined. He is a notoriously "interested" reader of his own motives, and he is admittedly not "a man of knowledge" with respect to himself (GM P1). He may be the world's foremost authority on decadence, but he habitually misinterprets the symptoms of his own decay. We may safely conclude, in fact, that he is neither willing nor able to disclose the full, unvarnished truth about Herr Nietzsche.

Although some degree of suspicion is certainly warranted of "the truthful Nietzsche," who continues to dissemble with respect to the purity of his motives, his advocacy of truth nevertheless signals an important concession to his own decadence and that of his readers. In fact, the ensuing modification of his practice of esotericism constitutes the most significant of the disruptions introduced by his acknowledgment of his own decay. Nietzsche is determined to tell (more of) the truth in his writings from 1888, and he conceives of his revaluation of all values as a grand disclosure of the truth of Christian morality. We should be wary, however, of attributing this determination to a burgeoning sense of altruism on his part. Like all symptoms of decadence and decline, Nietzsche's eleventh-hour embrace of the truth is both involuntary and "instinctual."

The two gestures of self-disclosure that mark his writings from 1888, the self-diagnosis of decadence and the advocacy of truth, are thus related, and they collectively announce an important modification of his rhetorical method. On the one hand, the mask of the truth teller is his last resort, a sign not of his rhetorical mastery, but of his failure as rhetorical master. It represents the most ambitious rhetorical persona that the decadent Nietzsche can sustain. The time may have come for him to dispense the truth, but only because he can no longer shelter it adequately behind his buckling screen of exoteric teachings. On the other hand, the very historical conditions that disrupt his practice of esotericism also render it otiose. Because no one (including Nietzsche himself) is sufficiently "healthy" to understand his signature teachings, a certain degree of esotericism is imposed from without by the decadence of late modernity.[13] Like Poe's purloined letter, Nietzsche's teachings may be openly displayed for all to see, their "secrecy" ensured by the obtuseness of their likely recipients.[14]

These teachings are "secret" not in the sense that he hides them from us, as Zarathustra jealously guards his teaching of eternal recurrence, but in the sense that we do not (and cannot) know what to make of them. The successful reception of these teachings presupposes a degree of health, strength, and vitality of which "modern men," including Nietzsche, can only dream. In the hands of decadent disciples, these explosive teachings are as dangerous as Promethean fire in the hands of mortal hominids; they are intended for beings greater than ourselves, and Nietzsche must be careful when bequeathing them to us. As the morbid Soothsayer warns Zarathustra about his own secret teaching of eternal recurrence (Z II:19), Nietzsche's "untimely" teachings may become for us doctrines of death and apocalypse.[15] Yet he can no longer afford, or so he believes, to indulge his love of masks, for he needs us to convey his teachings into the next millennium.

Responding to these twin threats to his practice of esotericism, Nietzsche retires (many of) his favorite masks.[16] First of all, he is no longer fit to serve as the guardian of esoteric wisdom, for his decadence renders him incapable of distinguishing friend from foe. Second, he can no longer afford to veil his teachings, for he needs to bequeath them to those successors who can guarantee their delivery to the audiences of a distant posterity. He entrusts these successors neither to interpret nor to promulgate his secret teachings, but simply to convey them safely to their rightful heirs. He is fully aware, however, that the appropriation and interpretation of his teachings will prove irresistible to the late modern readers whom he recruits. The (relative) strength of will that enables them to shepherd his teachings for the duration of the epoch also emboldens them, despite his cautions, to usurp the station reserved for his intended audience. They consequently presume not merely to safeguard his teachings for successor generations, but also to provide expert interpretation and commentary. He thus gambles that the distortions introduced by his children and their children will not disfigure his teachings beyond recognition.

Despite his unchallenged authority in matters of decadence, Nietzsche is blind to the precise nature and effects of his own decay. He understands that his decadence weakens his will, rendering him incapable of disseminating his teachings without the help of successor generations of unknown co-conspirators. He consequently contrives to compensate for his weakness of will, deploying experimental rhetorical devices that might attract complementary readers. But his decadence is not restricted to his periodic weakness of will; he also overestimates the urgency of his situation, as well as the vital reserves at his disposal. An additional, undetected manifestation of his decadence thus issues from his grandiose plan to become a sign not merely for his time, but for the remainder of the millennium. He consequently fails to grasp the extent of his corrupting influence on his recruits, who, unbeknownst to him, inherit the sickness and resentment that he cannot abide in himself.

Nietzsche thus mistakenly concludes that he can neutralize, or compensate for, his decadence, if not for that of his late modern readers. It is perhaps crucial to the success of his anti-Christian rebellion that he cannot see that he has the readers he deserves, created in his decadent image and likeness. Having inherited his peculiar blindness, much as he inherited his father's congenital ills, his true children are born similarly ignorant of the nature and effects of their own decadence.

Parastrategesis

Through his experiments with parastrategesis, Nietzsche attempts to attract the sort of readers who will detect and correct for his own complicity in the decadence of modernity. He realizes that the timely dissemination of his teachings depends crucially on the success of these readers in resisting the sort of discipleship that he cannot help but cultivate in them. In creating readers who will eventually presume to take his measure, however, he risks contributing to the distortion of his own teachings. His willingness to assume such a risk conveys the sense of desperation that pervades his post-Zarathustran philosophy. If he cannot persuade his readers to convey his teachings across the threshold of the coming millennium, then humankind is destined for further depradations at the hands of the Christian priests.

In order to found the communities of resistance that would indirectly continue his work, Nietzsche experiments with various rhetorical forms that might insulate his "ideal" readers from his own decay. Toward this end, he develops the experimental rhetorical method that I call *parastrategesis*. In the parastrategic dimension of his philosophy, he cultivates the type of reader who might resist the formative influence of his decadence. By means of his experiment with parastrategesis, he deliberately trains readers who will venture beyond the sphere of his influence. Such readers must eventually declare their independence from him, but he gambles that the teachings he bequeaths to them will survive the tumult of their apostasy.

The term *parastrategesis* is not Nietzsche's, but my own. I intend the term to designate those rhetorical strategies that he intentionally crafts to exceed the sphere of his own authorial control. The term *parastrategesis* thus marks off the dimension of his thought that lies neither fully within nor fully without the legitimate jurisdiction of his strategic design. The constructions that arise and develop within the parastrategic dimension are, consequently, neither fully strategic nor purely accidental. Although he no longer lays claim to rhetorical mastery, he is loathe to relinquish the diminished privilege of authorial intention, which finds a modest home within the confines of his parastrategesis.

The prefix *para-* is thus intended to elicit the double sense of a philosophical operation that not only functions alongside familiar rhetorical strategies, but also exceeds the known boundaries of the strategic. On a topographical map of the rhetorical devices employed by Nietzsche over the course of his career, we might situate the parastrategic dimension within that gray interstitial space that separates the towering peaks of rhetorical mastery from the lowlands of reader-response fetishism.

The strategic dimension of Nietzsche's philosophy is familiar enough, for it comprises, even in his post-Zarathustran writings, his various attempts to persuade his "perfect" readers to take up the banner of his crusade against Christian morality. He consequently invites the readers of *Ecce Homo* to join him on the threshold of the coming millennium:

> Let us look ahead a century; let us suppose that my attempt to assassinate two millennia of antinature and desecration of man were to succeed. That new party of Life which would tackle the greatest of all tasks, the attempt to raise humanity higher . . . would again make possible that excess of Life on earth from which the Dionysian state, too, would have to awaken again. (EH:bt 4)

As we have seen, however, his decadence compromises his stratagems, such that the only readers who follow him are not equal to the task for which they were recruited. He thus inherits the dilemma that stymied the pedagogical efforts of Zarathustra. Rather than abandon his grandiose political aims, he experiments instead with parastrategesis, which he believes may offset the crippling effect of his decadence. The deployment of such devices both presupposes and produces the type of reader who will reject Nietzsche in the name of Nietzsche. Like Zarathustra, who in Part IV abandons the strategy of *Untergang* and takes up his fishing pole, Nietzsche arranges for the selection of those readers who can resist the blandishments of discipleship. Yet the recursive, self-reflexive moment embedded within his parastrategesis is neither accidental nor arbitrary. He builds into his parastrategesis a mechanism for self-overcoming, such that the logical unfolding of his stratagems leads to the subversion of the rhetorical mastery in which they originate.

Nietzsche's parastrategesis originates in his strategic disclosure of his own decadence, but its natural development in the hands of his most independent readers soon outstrips his authorial designs.[17] He sets the parastrategesis in motion, but he cannot control its eventual direction or form.[18] Parastrategesis is therefore dependent upon, but by no means reducible to, his strategic experiment with self-criticism and self-disclosure. It is neither intelligible independent of his diminished rhetorical mastery nor exclusively attributable to it. He furnishes the concatenation of psychological and historical insights from which parastrategesis will arise, but his readers must forge the final, self-referential link that applies these insights to him. Although he nowhere explicitly resigns his claim to rhetorical mastery, his readers' forcible divestiture of this privilege would be inconceivable without the critical tools he furnishes them. Hence the division of labor that informs Nietzsche's nascent rebellion against Christian morality: He makes the parastrategic dimension possible, whereas his readers make it actual.[19]

Nietzsche's experiment with parastrategesis thus affords him an opportunity to persuade his readers to visit upon him a severity that he is too weak to visit upon himself. In order to render a full disclosure of the truth of Christian morality, he must recruit assistants who will disclose the full truth about him, especially about his subtle, unintended complicities with the Christian priesthood. The parastrategic dimension thus constitutes an arena of dialectical contest within which the decadent Nietzsche is forced to confront his most independent readers. Although his claim to rhetorical mastery will be discredited, his teachings will also be disseminated in the process.

The decadent Nietzsche will inevitably be cast aside as yet another traitor to the founding of a new tragic age, but only by those readers in whom his esoteric teachings have been indelibly encoded; they may ruthlessly trample him, but they do so only in his image and likeness. As a result of this parastrategic contest, the formative influence of his decadence is exposed and perhaps neutralized. As his readers fashion themselves into an audience critical of Nietzschean discipleship, they may unwittingly participate in his posthumous birth as the Antichrist.

The construction of the parastrategic dimension thus requires a collaborative venture between Nietzsche and his readers.[20] He supplies the necessary psychological insights, diagnoses, and interpretive strategies, which his readers in turn deploy in a critical engagement with their master.

The parastrategic Nietzsche is therefore a hybrid production, a bastard son born to him and his readers. In his "Attempt at a Self-Criticism" (*Versuch einer Selbstkritik*), for example, which he appended to the 1886 edition of *The Birth of Tragedy*, he provides his readers with an example of how a parastrategic criticism of Nietzsche might proceed. In this new preface, he contributes only an attempt at self-criticism, leaving it to his readers to complete the task he has begun. In light of this division of labor, it is important to note here that *Versuch* could evoke the sense of an "experiment" or "temptation" as well as that of an "attempt."[21] If his readers are trained properly, then they are not likely to show him the kindness he involuntarily shows himself. They will yield to his "temptation" and bring his "experiment" to its logical, self-referential conclusion.

The precise contours of the parastrategic dimension will vary from reader to reader, depending upon the extent to which each can afford to subject Nietzsche to the sort of critical scrutiny that he reserves for his most hated foes. We might think of the strategic dimension of his thought as a cramped anteroom or vestibule, and of the parastrategic dimension as an adjoining chamber of varying proportions. While Nietzsche himself fashions the strategic anteroom, he relies on his readers to construct the parastrategic chamber that artificially expands the domain of his rhetorical jurisdiction. For those readers who idolize Nietzsche and cannot afford to subject him to his own critical insights, the parastrategic dimension will remain unexplored and undeveloped. For other readers, the parastrategic dimension will extend outward, but not so far as to jeopardize the project of rehabilitating Nietzsche or of locating in his thought a precursor of their own. These two types of reader will honor his claim to rhetorical mastery, but they will lack the critical skills needed to resist the thrall of Nietzschean discipleship. They may wish to participate in his grand exposé of Christian morality, but not at the expense of learning and disclosing the truth about their master. Despite his occasional lapses into self-deception, Nietzsche does not trust such readers to transport his teachings into the next millennium.

He consequently stakes the future of his anti-Christian rebellion on the parastrategesis practiced by his perfect reader, whom he describes as "a monster of courage and curiosity," as "a born adventurer and discoverer," and, echoing Zarathustra, as a fearless quester (*Versucher*) who "embarks with cunning sails on terrible seas" (EH:gb 3). Such perfect readers would, in short, forcibly apply to him the philosophical and psychological insights that he applies to others, interpreting his philosophy as "the personal confession of its author and a kind of involuntary and unconscious memoir" (BGE 6). Just as Dionysus Zagreus initiates and intoxicates the band of enthusiasts who will eventually rend and dismember him, so Nietzsche cultivates a readership who will eventually show him as little kindness as he shows orthodox metaphysicians. If successful, this parastrategic collaboration will transform Nietzsche into the Antichrist and his perfect readers into the anti-Christian vanguard of the millennium. Indeed, he can become the Antichrist only if his readers contribute to his posthumous birth, which in turn requires that they forcibly revoke his claim to rhetorical mastery.

Here the elusive identity of Nietzsche's favored readers – the mysterious "we" that figures so prominently in his post-Zarathustran writings – receives a definitive determination. He apparently believes that the contest he stages will consecrate a knightly vanguard of warrior-genealogists.[22] The Nietzschean "we" thus comprises those select readers who are strong enough to contest the master on his own terms. The communities of resistance he founds thrive, or so he supposes, not through conversion, but through agonistic attraction.[23] The readers that Nietzsche wants, like the warriors that Wisdom wants (Z I:7), are not fawning disciples, and they do with him as they please. Such readers interpret any apparent benevolence on his part as an ever more formidable obstacle to their own progress. Even the "invitation" to join him as a warrior and to win the favor of Wisdom doubles as a throw of the rhetorical gauntlet.

Nietzsche's parastrategesis thus legislates, or so he believes, a heroic, manly *agon*, wherein worthy successors are molded through mutually empowering contests with their master.[24] Within the terms of this *agon*, warriors who begin as rivals or enemies become the fastest of friends: "How much reverence has a noble man for his enemies! – and such reverence is a bridge to love" (GM I:10). Nietzsche thus imagines his perfect readers as fearless warrior-genealogists who honor his legacy even as they snatch his wilted wreath.[25]

In order to train this vanguard, Nietzsche must actively cultivate readers who see through his stratagems and falsehoods, who treat him as irreverently as he treats his own philosophical predecessors. These readers, in turn, must be sufficiently resistant to the thrall of discipleship to ignore the distractions and misdirections served up by Nietzsche himself. Rather than accept at face value his account of his "wisdom," "cleverness," "good books," and "destiny," such readers will survey his life with the cool, objective eye of the symptomatologist. Rather than simply rehearse his own account of his "virtues" – his nobility, magnanimity, *amor fati*, freedom from *ressentiment*, and so forth – these readers will undertake an independent appraisal of his philosophy. Most important, these readers must be strong enough to set aside his discursive account of modernity and attend instead to the account he involuntarily embodies as a representative exemplar of his age.

Nietzsche acknowledges the dangers involved in cultivating readers more powerful than himself, but he is apparently confident that he can train these readers to protect his teachings as fiercely as they claim their independence from him. In the spirit of creating this vanguard of intrepid readers, he places his own motto in the mouth of Zarathustra: "Now I bid you lose me and find yourselves; and only when you have denied me will I return to you" (Z I:22).[26]

Textual evidence confirms that Nietzsche longed for an audience strong enough to contest him on his own terms. His desire for intrepid readers, however, is overruled in the end by his own decadent needs. He is not free to train the warrior-genealogists he has in mind, for he simply lacks the *virtù* he hopes to instill in them. The "noble warrior" motif that informs the *Genealogy*, as well as *Zarathustra* and other writings, is little more than a decadent romance, which expresses succinctly his resentment of modernity.[27] Indeed, the occasional intrusion of this warrior romance into the text of the *Genealogy*, especially in his less inhibited metaphorical jags, confirms his blindness to the forms in which his decadence typically manifests itself.[28]

Nietzsche can sustain this romance only so long as he denies the formative influence of his decadence on his readers. He tends, consequently, not to think of his readers as the products of a decadent philosopher, believing instead that he can contain his decadence and neutralize its effects. While introducing himself in the course of his faux autobiography, for example, he attributes his copious "wisdom" to the "dual series of experiences" he has inherited from his father and mother (EH:wise 1–2). Rather than deny his decadence, he instead identifies decay as belonging exclusively to his patriarchal legacy, which no longer influences his vitality: "I am . . . already dead as my father, while as my mother I am still living and becoming old" (EH:wise 1). Like his father, he commands a unique, immanent perspective on sickness and decay; unlike his father, he survives to deploy this perspective in the service of life. He is both a moribund German and a newborn Pole, "at the same time a *decadent* and a *beginning*" (EH:wise 1). Just as his mother's indomitable health delivered him from the regrettable fate of his weakling father, so he bequeaths to his children the health that will enable them to endure (and exploit) the decadence he also imparts. His presumptive desire to serve as a male mother to his children perhaps reflects the delusional content of this masculinist romance.

His parastrategesis does initiate a contest with his readers, but it is not the noble, manly *agon* of his fantasies. The atavistic warriors whom he yearns to train would be prohibitively overmatched in any blood sport with their master, for they would stand heroically defenseless against the duplicitous strategies he deploys. Noble virtues are not nearly so helpful in a *battle royale* with Nietzsche as those simulacra of noble virtues that shelter resentment and revenge.

The Teaching of Eternal Recurrence

The esoteric wisdom hidden behind Nietzsche's crumbling masks is expressed in the gnomic teachings of eternal recurrence, *amor fati*, and the innocence of Becoming.[29] These are the transfigurative doctrines he hopes to impart to the founders of the post-nihilistic epoch, and he reveals them in the same book, *Ecce Homo*, in which he claims to shed his masks.

The teaching of eternal recurrence has proved to be the most beguiling of Nietzsche's "positive" teachings, and his readers often treat it as an amalgam or apotheosis of the full complement of his affirmative doctrines. Some readers have gone so far as to insist that the teaching of eternal recurrence might somehow provide the impetus for secular redemption, cultural reform, and even political revolution.

What exactly do we know about this celebrated "teaching?" We know from *Ecce Homo* that the idea of eternal recurrence originally descended upon Nietzsche in August 1881, as he "walk[ed] through the woods along the lake of Silvaplana" (EH:z 1). We know from his notebooks that he attempted to integrate the idea of eternal recurrence into the physics of the day, hoping to derive some sort of unifying cosmological principle.[30] He of course failed in this endeavor, and he realized as much.[31] We know that he eventually proclaimed himself "the teacher of eternal recurrence" (TI 10:5), although he nowhere promotes in any detail an identifiable teaching of eternal recurrence. He helpfully remarks that Heraclitus may already have promulgated this elusive teaching (EH:bt 3), but he unhelpfully neglects to direct our attention to the relevant fragment(s) left behind by his obscure predecessor.

We know from the handful of scattered passages that suggest an account of eternal recurrence that Nietzsche never articulates this teaching in a voice recognizably his own.[32] In the most famous passage, we are introduced to the eternal recurrence not by Nietzsche, but by a demon, and the crucial questions with which the passage ends are left unanswered (GS 341). For "a bringer of glad tidings like no other before [him]" (EH:destiny 1), he furnishes alarmingly few details concerning his signature teaching of affirmation. Despite his entreaties not to be "misheard" or "mistaken for someone else" (EH P1), he virtually ensures the failure of his readers to understand him as the teacher of eternal recurrence. Calling to mind Nietzsche's own figure of Christ, the *idiot* who is too weak to contradict any interpretation of his "glad tidings" (AC 29), the "teacher" of eternal recurrence is remarkably unprepared to deflect wayward interpretations of his own consummatory teaching.

In fact, it is not clear that we are justified even in assuming that Nietzsche promotes a single, discrete teaching of eternal recurrence.[33] There may be several related teachings, or a single teaching that evolves over the course of his career, or no such teaching at all.[34] While it is perhaps understandable that he regarded the eternal recurrence as "the highest formula of affirmation," what would incline anyone else to share this grandiose opinion? Do we have anything but his own dubious word on the matter?

Nor is Nietzsche's "son" any more successful in promulgating this revolutionary new gospel. Zarathustra summarily dismisses the interpretations of eternal recurrence advanced by the soothsayer (Z II:19), the spirit of gravity (Z III:2), his animals (Z III:13), the pre-literate, omni-affirmative ass (Z IV:17), and the ugliest man (Z IV:19), but he never adequately distinguishes his "untimely" teaching from the tired, hackneyed refrains to which he opposes it. Although his animals confidently proclaim his destiny as "*the teacher of the eternal recurrence*," he never explicitly confirms their pronouncement, ignoring them in order to "converse with his soul" (Z III:13.2). Further distancing himself from his animals' pronouncement, he later confesses that he seeks the solitude of mountain peaks because he can "speak more freely" there than in the presence of his "domestic animals" (Z IV:1).

Even if Nietzsche is sincere in advertising "the idea of eternal recurrence" as "the fundamental conception of [*Zarathustra*]" (EH:z 1) – again, without elaboration or examples – his immodest predictions of the book's untimely reception militate against the likelihood of our attunement to "this highest formula of affirmation that is at all attainable" (EH:z 1). Recounting the bewilderment of a friend, Heinrich von Stein, he boasts:

> Having understood six sentences from [*Zarathustra*] – that is, to have really experienced them – would raise one to a higher level of existence than "modern" men could attain. Given this feeling of distance, how could I wish to be read by those "moderns" whom I know! (EH:gb 1)

As this passage confirms, the central teachings of *Zarathustra* (and, a fortiori, its "fundamental conception") are not intended for Nietzsche's epigonic readers. If *Zarathustra* harbors an identifiable teaching of eternal recurrence, then it either falls embarrassingly short of the untimely status that Nietzsche smugly confers upon it or it remains undiscovered to this day.

This dearth of textual evidence uniquely qualifies the eternal recurrence as a teaching of affirmation. Never stated directly or promulgated as such by Nietzsche himself, the teaching of eternal recurrence remains mysterious, occult, oblique – and therefore full of promise.[35] The eternal recurrence is so often hailed as sheltering his esoteric wisdom not because of any properties or elements deemed essential to this vague doctrine, but because nothing else in his corpus stands out as a likely candidate for a "final teaching" befitting him.[36] The eternal recurrence thus occupies, *in absentia*, a privileged place within the economy of his thought.

Because Nietzsche says virtually nothing about this teaching, we cannot rule out the possibility that it encapsulates his elusive last word. The teaching of eternal recurrence thus serves as a shimmering, pan-receptive screen onto which his readers might violently project their ownmost anxieties and hopes, all the while shunting ownership of these haunting emanations onto him. Indeed, the enduring attraction of this empty teaching is symptomatic of our own decay, of our perceived need for the redemption it dishonestly promises. Nietzsche himself whets his readers' appetite for a redemptive teaching, hinting salaciously at the epiphanies that await his rightful audience.

As Nietzsche might have predicted, twentieth-century readers have collectively advanced a plethora of ingenious interpretations of this gnomic teaching. Even a brief survey of the secondary literature yields a stunning array of diverse interpretations: the eternal recurrence as an approximation ˉetween being and becoming (Simmel); as a pedagogical-regulative idea (Ewald); as a muddled, inconsequential distraction from the doctrine of the *Übermensch* (Bäumler); as the repetition of classical antiquity at the pinnacle of modernity (Löwith); as a (failed) attempt to overcome subjectivistic metaphysics (Heidegger); as a heuristic Utopian fiction (Vaihinger); as an existential statement of the overcoming of nothingness (Jaspers); as a thought experiment for measuring the meaning of the moment (Arendt); as a form of cosmic therapy (E. Heller); as a differential centrifuge that expels all reactive forces (Deleuze); as an empirical cosmology (Danto); as a neurological hallucination (Klossowski); as a pagan alternative to the Christian conceptions of history and time (Kaufmann); as a model of Dionysian excess and disintegration (Bataille); as a model of Apollinian integration and self-control (Nehamas); as a bankrupt formula for political transfiguration (Strong); as an appropriate attitude toward existence (Stambaugh); as a selectively transformative, high-intensity phantasm (Lingis); as a figure for the unbearable lightness of being (Kundera); as a sign heralding the end of the historical dominion of difference (Vattimo); as a mode of attunement to the historicity of human agency (Warren); as a self-consuming existential imperative (Magnus); as a matricidal wish never to have been born of a female other (Irigaray); as an unexplored alternative to the ascetic ideal and will to truth (Clark); as a trans-discursive call to retnink the concepts of presence and absence (Shapiro); and as the founding doctrine of a post-esoteric "immanentism" (Lampert). This inventory list would be longer still if it were to include the various ingenious attempts to figure eternal recurrence on the model of an inexhaustible male orgasm.[37]

While this wealth of imaginative interpretations may attest to the fecundity of the teaching of eternal recurrence, it may also betray Nietzsche's failure to invest his "final word" with any discernible content or meaning. Indeed, the ingenuity of these interpretations is matched only by the reluctance of their authors to acknowledge their own impressive contributions to the construction of a teaching of eternal recurrence. As uncredited coauthors of a teaching they attribute to Nietzsche alone, these interpreters thus resemble the "pale criminal" whom Zarathustra describes (Z I:6), for they refuse to own, much less to celebrate, the constructive violence they visit upon Nietzsche's underdeveloped thinking.

These elaborate teachings are all attributed with a great deal of confidence and certitude to Nietzsche – despite his refusal to say very much of anything about eternal recurrence. From the time of his epiphanic experience at Silvaplana in 1881, he prepared some nine books for publication, often at considerable expense to himself. His cumulative remarks on eternal recurrence in these books, including Zarathustra's laconic contributions, would fill only a few pages. While his experience of eternal recurrence in 1881 is clearly important to the development of his philosophy, he may have concluded (and justifiably so) that this experience simply defies discursive communication. His readers, it would seem, display a substantially greater interest in divining the teaching of eternal recurrence than he ever did.[38]

Critics and champions alike generally agree that some teaching of eternal recurrence resides within the body of Nietzsche's writings, and that we have access – however limited – to this teaching through him. Any interpretation (and, a fortiori, any critique) of Nietzsche's teaching of eternal recurrence thus rests on two basic presuppositions: first, that he has successfully conveyed a sense of this teaching to some of his readers, perhaps in spite of his own limitations; and second, that some of his readers have successfully received this teaching from him, despite his reliance on masks, personae, analogies, allegories, and other forms of indirection.

While this latter presupposition may appear more problematic, insofar as it blatantly contradicts Nietzsche's own appraisal of his late modern readers, I am more concerned here with the plausibility of the former presupposition. Nietzsche's account of decadence suggests that despite his protestations to the contrary, he too may be unworthy of the affirmative teachings he supposedly harbors. If his decadence prevents him from attaining the rarefied state of soul – "6000 feet beyond man and time" (EH:z 1) – that is commensurate with the adventitious experience of eternal recurrence, then his "secret" teachings may be largely unknown to him as well. Indeed, we have little evidence that his blinding epiphany in August 1881 survived the halcyonic moment it suffused and even less evidence that this experience admits of incorporation into a communicable teaching.[39] Like his pompous "son," Nietzsche may be little more than a flawed mouthpiece for a prophecy he cannot divine, a champion of Life and affirmation who unwittingly precipitates death and destruction.

If we take seriously Nietzsche's own decadence, then we should expect him neither to understand nor to enact the untimely teaching he has been called to disseminate. He may stand as far removed from the teaching of eternal recurrence as his enervated readers stand from Zarathustra. He can certainly mouth the "untimely" teachings of eternal recurrence, amor fati, and the innocence of Becoming, but, again like Zarathustra, he does so only within the timely metaphysical context of revenge and redemption. His destiny, like that of the readers he recruits, may simply be to safeguard the teaching of eternal recurrence until it can be delivered to those audiences of a distant posterity whose experiences are commensurate with it. So although Nietzsche does not articulate a teaching of eternal recurrence that constitutes for modern readers "the highest formula of affirmation," he does provide an account of why neither he nor we should be considered equal to such a teaching. That he may not have intended this account to apply to himself as a teacher of eternal recurrence is, in the end, irrelevant.

There is, in short, no teaching of eternal recurrence that is both faithfully conveyed by Nietzsche (or Zarathustra) and grasped in its entirety by twentieth-century readers. There is only the presence of the absence of a consummatory teaching, only the nagging pain that issues from the gaping wound that this teaching would finally heal. We recognize the superlative fructifying role that eternal recurrence is supposed to play, and we understand that the possession of this teaching would transform us forever (GS 341). All we now need from Nietzsche or his scions is the transfigurative teaching itself.

Nietzsche's doctrine of *amor fati*, which readers often associate closely with eternal recurrence, confirms the distance that separates him from his own teachings of affirmation. Following the Stoics, from whom he borrows this doctrine (EH:bt 3), Nietzsche proposes *amor fati* as emblematic of human greatness. In his account of the conditions of *amor fati*, however, he implies that its attainment would outstrip the volitional resources available to modern agents:

> My formula for greatness in a human being is *amor fati:* that one wants nothing to be different, not forward, not backward, not in all eternity. Not merely bear what is necessary, still less conceal it – all idealism is mendaciousness in the face of what is necessary – but *love* it. (EH:clever 10)

If "greatness in a human being" involves "wanting nothing to be different," then it would appear that no one in late modernity, including Nietzsche himself, approaches greatness. He may claim *amor fati* as his "inmost nature" (EH:cw 4), but his partners in parastrategesis know better.[40] Furthermore, if *amor fati* requires an unconditional love of eternity, then it is not clear that any representatives of late modernity actually aspire (however foolishly) to its achievement. The noblest among us may occasionally desire to bear the necessity of evil, loss, accident, and tragedy, but no one, including Nietzsche, aspires with any constancy to an *amor fati* constitutive of "human greatness."[41] Indeed, only in rare, adventitious moments can Nietzsche affirm his own fate as part of the natural cycle of growth and decay, as ingredient to the brute immanence of Life itself. This conclusion further corroborates his account of modernity as a decadent epoch: Greatness is neither possible nor desirable for modern agents to attain.[42]

In light of Nietzsche's own decadence, we might profitably interpret his teaching of eternal recurrence as an exercise in parastrategesis. Unable to deduce on his own the founding doctrines of the coming tragic age, he attempts to establish the formal specifications for the teaching of eternal recurrence. He then bequeaths to his readers the task of conveying this teaching to the "philosophers of the future," who will in turn invest it with its proper content and meaning. The teaching of eternal recurrence, he ordains, should express a love of life as it is, in its painful, amoral immanence; it should convey a parsimonious naturalism, in contrast to the metaphysical spectralities that have haunted philosophy thus far; it should promote a respect of the earth as a singular, closed system for which humankind is solely and uniquely responsible; it should champion the perfection of the human soul and sanction the project of self-overcoming; it should halt the protracted adolescence of the species and invite the highest humans to accede to full maturity; it should oversee the evolution of the species and bring to term the "pregnancy" of the bad conscience; and it should enshrine an unflinching *amor fati* as the highest expression of human flourishing.

It is no accident that Nietzsche and Zarathustra restrict their teaching of eternal recurrence to the promulgation of these inspirational slogans. While anyone can rehearse the formal specifications of this teaching, only the representatives of a healthy epoch or people command the requisite strength of soul to enact this teaching and invest it with meaning. As Nietzsche knows from the failures of the tripartite *Zarathustra,* any attempt to connect this teaching with the impoverished experiences of modern agents will result only in caricature and distortion. Zarathustra and Nietzsche may in fact be bona fide teachers of eternal recurrence, but it is impossible for their modern and late modern readers to see them as anything but dangerous mutations of the ascetic priest. As the gloomy Soothsayer accurately predicted, this teaching would spell disaster for those cripples and invalids to whom Zarathustra considers entrusting its dissemination (Z II:20).

Here we encounter once again the inherent danger of parastrategesis. The only readers who are strong enough to shoulder the burden of Nietzsche's secret teaching are also strong enough to countermand his admonitions concerning its proper audience. Recruited solely to disseminate his teachings, these perfect readers cannot help but interpret them as well and to present their interpretations as faithful to their master's legacy. This presumption on their part is inextricably tied, moreover, to their ability to transmit his teachings, so it is not a matter of simply finding less imperious readers. Only those who would also dare to sip from this forbidden grail are able to bear its weight. The ensuing distortions of the eternal recurrence may eventually disfigure Nietzsche's teaching beyond recognition, but this is the risk he must accept in order to project his influence into the next millennium.

The Dangerous Game

Although Nietzsche willingly accepts the uncertainties involved in his plan to recruit imperfect readers, he generally underestimates the risks involved in parastrategesis. His own decadence not only compounds the danger that his teachings will be distorted, but also contributes an additional element of recklessness to which he remains blind. Owing to his unacknowledged need for recognition and companionship, Nietzsche actually plays a game that is far more dangerous than he imagines.

Nietzsche's brave insights into the decadence of late modernity and the "active" nihilism they enable are the source of great pride on his part. In his principled iconoclasm, he comes to constitute his own image of the "genuine philosopher":

> And if a man is praised today for living "wisely" or "as a philosopher," it hardly means more than "prudently and apart." Wisdom – seems to the rabble a kind of escape, a means and trick for getting well out of a dangerous game. But the genuine philosopher – as it seems to *us*, my friends? – lives "unphilosophically" and "unwisely," above all *imprudently*, and feels the burden and the duty of a hundred attempts [*Versuchen*] and temptations [*Versuchungen*] of life – he risks *himself* constantly, he plays *the* dangerous game. (BGE 205)

Nietzsche's account of the dangerous game thus establishes its continuity with his project of self-annunciation. In order for his "experiments" to become "temptations," he must transform himself into a sign. To those readers who are aroused by this temptation, his experiments signify a (residually) healthy will. As we have seen, his rendition of the dangerous game comprises his various "attempts" at parastrategesis, in which he risks the integrity of his esoteric teachings in order to transport them into the next millennium.

While it is true that Nietzsche possesses an impressive appetite (and stomach) for risk, it is also true that he characteristically underestimates the dangers involved in parastrategesis. The perceived risks of his dangerous game are amplified considerably by his own decadence, which actually compels him to *invite* the distortion of his signature teachings. After all, if Nietzsche's modern readers are as hopelessly obtuse as he suggests, then why does he repeatedly attempt to reach them? Why does he not simply "pass them by" (Z III:7), as Zarathustra prudently (if hypocritically) recommends? His experiment with parastrategesis obviously requires his intercourse with imperfect readers, but his preoccupation with his contemporaries is not entirely explained by their instrumental role in the dissemination of his teachings. As it turns out, he also depends on them for recognition and devotion – precisely as his account of decadence would lead us to expect of any twilight philosopher.

Nietzsche may publicly lament that he has no readers or that his actual readers are unworthy of the teachings he imparts to them, but the truth is that his readers lie well beyond the domain of his authorial control. His experiments with parastrategesis are far more dangerous and far more desperate than he is willing to allow. His scheme to influence indirectly the founding of the postmodern epoch would be equally well served by sealing cryptic letters in envelopes that bear neither postage nor address.[43] The chances that his teachings will land safely in the right hands, much less that such hands will ever exist, are mind-bogglingly slim. It is ironic that only here, in his moment of last resort and greatest desperation, does Nietzsche participate in the divine "dice throw" that he claims to revere. And although his reckless dissemination of his teachings may suggest the squandering, careless economy of Dionysus, Nietzsche himself can ill afford the luxury of such profligacy.

This inestimable degree of risk is only exacerbated by Nietzsche's decadence, whose effects he characteristically underestimates. Like most decadents, he apparently believes that he can anticipate and compensate for his periodic lapses. Indeed, he specifically designs his experiments with parastrategesis to insulate his readers and his teachings from his own weakness of will. As Nietzsche himself would lead one to expect, however, he largely fails in his self-neutralizing endeavors. As a decadent in his own right, he sincerely wants for his readers to be strong, but he instinctively needs for them to be weak.[44] In his attempt to muster a vanguard of select readers, he paradoxically desires that which he could neither tolerate nor acknowledge: readers who can afford to take his measure. This divergence between intention and execution, between instinct and well-being, is emblematic of the decadence that besets late modernity.

Decadence and Parastrategesis

The extent of Nietzsche's decadence is nowhere more evident than in his persistent refusal to confront his actual "children." He readily blames his obtuse readers, or modernity as a whole, for his chronic failure to cultivate an audience of "perfect readers," but never himself: "Perhaps I know how to fish as well as anyone? – If nothing was caught, I am not to blame. *There were no fish*" (EH:bge 1). Unlike his contemporaries, he is afflicted only by "periods" of decadence, which ultimately signify an underlying instinct for health. He thus exempts himself from the moral lesson imparted by

Zarathustra's chronic pedagogical failures, accepting no responsibility whatsoever for the perceived inadequacies of his reception as an author.

This familiar dodge allows Nietzsche to postpone indefinitely the question of his rightful audience, but only at the expense of his credibility and authority as a philosopher.[45] As long as he projects the emergence of his rightful readers into the distant future, he refuses to investigate – and to acknowledge – his own contribution to the cultivation of the "unworthy" readers who gravitate so readily toward him. The self-knowledge he supposedly craves is consequently restricted by his refusal to own his role in the creation of children whom he loathes. Just as Oedipus exempts himself from the general solution he proposes to the riddle of the Sphinx, so Nietzsche exempts himself from the psychological profile he sketches of the priestly type. While the priests bait their hooks with poisonous invertebrates and fiendish lures, sickening their prey in order to land them, Nietzsche, we are supposed to believe, *has caught nothing?*

It is ironic that the only child whom Nietzsche acknowledges, Zarathustra, fully inherits the sins of his father. Zarathustra too is quick to attribute his pedagogical frustrations entirely to the limitations of his auditors. Experimenting with various styles of parabolic address, he struggles to tailor his teachings to the infirmities of the rubes and dimwits who typically gather to hear him speak. Like Nietzsche, Zarathustra refuses to acknowledge his real children, reserving his secret teaching and final *Untergang* for those mysterious cherubs whose propinquity is supposedly announced by the appearance of the swarm of doves and the laughing lion (Z IV:20). Of course, he characteristically misinterprets these signs, summarily banishing the "higher men," whose presence, for all he knows and cares, may actually fulfill the prophecy he claims to honor.

Throughout Parts I–III, in fact, Zarathustra is surrounded by his *real* children, all of whom embody the relationship of dependency that he has unwittingly cultivated in them: the dutiful "flock" of disciples who present their "shepherd" with a staff (Z I:22); the child whose mirror reflects Zarathustra's face as the devil's visage (Z II:1); the disciple who renders a self-serving, Zarathustraesque interpretation of the chilling nightmare (Z II:19); the hunchback who calls attention to Zarathustra's duplicitous esoteric teachings (Z II:20); the ersatz Zarathustra who "apes" the hollow teachings of his master (Z III:7); and so on. They are embodied reproaches, living refutations of Zarathustra's self-presentation.

Rather than acknowledge his own contribution to the creation of these "fragments and cripples," however, Zarathustra habitually interprets their challenges to his authority as confirmations of his wisdom and goodness. He consequently disowns his real children, transforming them into signs of his progress toward the progeny for which he yearns. Like his "father," Zarathustra cannot bear to acknowledge the decadence reflected back to him by his real children. Despite his insight into the treachery perpetrated by all priests and moralists, he cannot implicate himself in it. Preserving his family resemblance to Nietzsche (and so to Oedipus), he exempts his own teachings from the cruel truths he dispenses about all teachings. Zarathustra is no priest, or so he claims, even though he cannot explain why. Nor can he distinguish his opposition to the priesthood from the signature mischief of the anti-priest, whom he reveals to his auditors as an especially dangerous species of priest.

Although Nietzsche summarily disowns his real readers, pointing instead to his subterranean influence over "radical parties and factions,"[46] he actually provides us with a compelling portrait of the children he is likely to beget. His account of the oafish "higher men" in Part IV of *Zarathustra* serves as a model for the type of community that is likely to be founded by a decadent philosopher in the twilight of the idols. The designation and portrayal of the higher men are parodic, to be sure, but, especially if we situate Part IV of *Zarathustra* in late modernity, they are also accurate. Like Zarathustra, Nietzsche longs for heroic followers to whom he can confidently entrust his teachings. But his real readers, like the higher men who are drawn to Zarathustra, faithfully reflect the depleted vitality of the age. Rather than the chivalric throwbacks who populate his fantasies, Nietzsche attracts misfits, fools, buffoons, brigands, rascals, miscreants, and sociopaths – the higher men, that is, of late modernity.

While Nietzsche would undoubtedly covet Zarathustra's mountain retreat and the attendant freedom to dissolve all imperfect communities that might arise there, his own final *Untergang* blunted his strategy of endless deferral. Although he mistrusts his partners in parastrategesis, stopping just short of Zarathustra's outright repudiation of the higher men (Z IV:20), the future of his teachings rests in their grubby hands. He cannot afford the luxury of the indefinite postponement practiced by Zarathustra, and he can no longer disown the real children who labor in his name.

Nietzsche's obsession with his contemporary readers, whom he can neither resolutely acknowledge nor finally ignore, is perhaps the single most obvious symptom of his failure to contain his own decadence. While he clearly wants to conserve himself for those homologous readers of the future who will incorporate his untimely teachings into the founding of a tragic age, he also needs to exert an influence over his contemporary Europeans – who, he realizes, cannot help but distort his teachings. This need to pander to decadent readers distracts him from his epochal task, diverting precious vitality from the site of his planned "explosion." Unable to fix his gaze firmly on the future, he attempts instead to straddle two millennia, contriving anxiously to preview the posthumous birth he foresees for himself. He consequently arrogates to himself a title – the Antichrist – that he has not yet earned (EH:gb 2). In the end, he is simply too decadent to transact the world-historical task he sets for himself; he is not equal to his own destiny. His all-too-human need to become timely muffles the reverberations of his untimely explosion, thus jeopardizing the contribution of his secret teachings to the founding of a postmodern epoch.

Nietzsche's decadence is manifested in his exploitation of the erotic bond that he forges between himself and his readers.[47] He typically ingratiates himself to his readers by exposing frauds and mountebanks, toppling idols, debunking pernicious dogmas, defrocking priests and moralists, while generally encouraging his readers to identify him with their own aspirations to irreverence and iconoclasm. He thus presents himself as the quintessential loose cannon, the patron saint of all rebellious spirits yearning to breathe free. In the eyes of many readers, he is the consummate anti-priest, a powerful ally in virtually any skirmish with established authority. Even unsympathetic readers are often eager to harness his explosive power to serve their own, anti-Nietzschean ends.[48] In this regard, he is not unlike Socrates, who "was also a great *erotic*" precisely because "he discovered a new kind of *agon*," in which even lowly plebs could participate (TI 2:8).

Socrates is not only an erotic, but a decadent as well. He may sincerely intend to serve Athens as a benefactor of divine appointment, just as he may sincerely hope to lead his young interlocutors to autonomy and self-reliance,[49] but his own need for recognition and discipleship compromises the potentially salutary effects of his dialectic. For the most part, Socrates' youthful interlocutors more closely resemble fawning followers than free-thinking philosophers.[50]

Here again, Nietzsche would point to the *Phaedo,* the dialogue whose dramatic setting most clearly illuminates the deleterious effects of Socrates' decadence on his friends. Rather than expose the glaring flaws that vitiate Socrates' shaky argument for the "indestructibility" of the soul, Simmias and Cebes, who are "strangers" to Athens, assure him that he has successfully deflected their most formidable challenges. Phaedo himself, so voluble in his reportage to Echecrates, happily restricts his own participation to the periodic affirmations of an inveterate yes-man. Rather than directly convey his true feelings about the imminent death of his friend and teacher, Crito too dissembles, masking (for the most part) his preoccupation with the quotidian details of burial and mourning. When shamed by Socrates' unflattering comparison to the weeping women whom he had earlier banished from his cell, Crito, Phaedo, and Apollodorus promptly cease their "unseemly" wailing and lamentation (117 c–e).

Having learned from Socrates to comfort the weak and confused with soothing myths and allegories – a gambit he deploys even on his final day – his dutiful disciples now undertake to comfort their dying master by shielding him from the logical flaws that permit him cheerfully to welcome death. If the *Phaedo* is a reliable document of Socrates' genuine influence, then his enduring legacy is constituted not (only) by philosophical fellowship and honest inquiry, but (also) by the discipleship he has cultivated in his dysfunctional friends. It is no wonder that Plato, whose alleged "illness" contrasts sharply with Socrates' own,[51] did not attend this macabre farewell party.

Like Socrates, Nietzsche exacts a usurious fee from those who join the *agon* over which he presides. Like all philosophers, he needs to aggrandize himself at the expense of his audience; he simply cannot separate his talents for debunking from his decadence. His signature rhetorical gambit, of which he is the involuntary master *non pareil*, is to assume the role of the insider outside. He characteristically secures the trust of his readers by divulging the trade secrets of a common foe, such as the priests. Having established this touchstone point of all-too-human solidarity with his readers, he promptly cultivates with them a relationship that precisely reproduces the dependency from which he has supposedly delivered them. Having liberated his readers from the shackles of prejudice, dogma, and ignorance, Nietzsche promptly claps them into irons of his own design and forge. He thus exploits unwittingly the "incomplete nihilism" that characterizes his modern readers. His teaching of eternal recurrence extends the hope of redemption to those who know better, but who cannot help themselves from reaching in vain for the golden ring of eternity.

In order to become posthumously the millennial Antichrist, Nietzsche must therefore cultivate readers who have somehow freed themselves from his decadent influence. This is a freedom that he eagerly promises but cannot deliver. He may know that he is decadent, but he is apparently ignorant of the precise manifestations of his decay. As his general account of decadence would predict, he is not a reliable reader of his own "symptoms." Like any decadent, he cannot consistently distinguish between what is best and worst for him. His pronouncement of his own decay consequently does not ensure that he can prevent it from infecting his attempts to cultivate a select readership. Casting a wide net for the sort of reader who might complete his work, he lands all sorts of odd fish whom he would surely throw back if we were able. But he is not. He needs – and loathes – them all.

This involuntary need for idolatrous readers places his teachings at risk. Rather than safeguard these teachings for delivery to their rightful recipients, those unknown audiences of a distant posterity, Nietzsche uses them to secure the admiration and devotion of his contemporary readers. As a decadent, he can no longer resist the temptation to dangle before us the redemptive teachings of eternal recurrence, *amor fati*, and the innocence of Becoming, despite insisting that such teachings are too lofty for his late modern readers to appreciate and comprehend. Having identified in his contemporaries a pathological craving for redemptive teachings, messianic benedictions, and consummatory pronouncements, he cannot help but let slip that he shelters the foundational teachings of the post-nihilistic epoch, that he seeks brave companions to whom he might entrust the secrets that burden his wearied soul. Although he scrupulously avoids investing these teachings with any positive content, he nevertheless contributes to their eventual distortion by encouraging us to divine their true meaning. Much as Zarathustra dilutes his teaching of the *Übermensch* in the hope of attracting a sympathetic audience (Z P:5–9), so Nietzsche compromises the integrity of his own secret teachings in order to gain the idolatrous readers he needs.

Like Zarathustra, who, for all his misanthropy, cannot resist the thrill of the *Untergang,* Nietzsche is unwittingly dependent on his modern readers for a recognition that he can never accept. Insofar as he panders to his modern readers, his teachings become infected, in his renditions of them, with his besetting decadence. His signature teachings, which he at one time hoped might catalyze a rebirth of tragic culture in Europe, have become bargaining chips in a pathetic scheme to broker the discipleship of his decrepit readers.

Notes

1   As it turns out, Zarathustra is not free to forsake humanity when he wishes. While it is true that he needs others to receive his wisdom, "hands outstretched" (Z P1), this is not the full extent of his reliance on his auditors. Indeed, the drama of *Zarathustra* is fueled largely by the central character's failure to acknowledge the extent of his reliance on the recognition of others.

2   *Friedrich Nietzsche: Sämtliche Briefe, Kritische Studienausgabe in 8 Bänden,* ed. G. Colli and M. Montinari (Berlin: deGruyter/Deutscher Taschenbuch Verlag, 1986), Vol. 8, No. 820, p. 48.

3   Stanley Cavell persuasively makes this point with respect to Emerson in "Aversive Thinking: Emersonian Representations in Heidegger and Nietzsche," collected in *Conditions Handsome and Unhandsome: The Constitution of Emersonian Perfectionism* (Chicago: University of Chicago Press, 1990).

4   The "Decree Against Christianity" (*Gesetz wider das Christenthum*), which both Kaufmann and Hollingdale exclude from their translations of *The Antichrist(ian),* is dated from the first day of this new calendar. The "Decree" is found in the *Kritische Studienausgabe,* Vol. 6, p. 254.

5   The *Phaedo* was the Platonic dialogue with which Nietzsche was most familiar. He lectured on the *Phaedo* several times while at Basel, and his various accounts of Socrates – as reluctant practitioner of music, enigmatic ironist, decadent buffoon, despiser of the body, and grateful debtor to Asclepius – seem to be drawn almost exclusively from the *Phaedo.*

6   In a letter to Nietzsche in December 1888, Strindberg admonishes him to beware of appropriation by the "rabble," reminding him of the need "to guard the esoteric teachings" [Karl Strecker, *Nietzsche und Strindberg* (München: Georg Müller Verlag, 1921), p. 35]. See Claudia Crawford, *To Nietzsche: Dionysus, I Love You! Ariadne* (Albany: State University of New York Press, 1995), p. 144.

7   In *Nietzsche: Life as Literature* (Cambridge, MA: Harvard University Press, 1985),
    Alexander Nehamas attributes to Nietzsche the "effort always to insinuate him-
    self between his readers and the world" (p. 37). "He accomplishes this,"
    Nehamas continues, "by making, through his many styles, his own presence as
    an author impossible to overlook" (p. 38). According to Nehamas, then, Nietz-
    sche's deployment of "the most multifarious art of style" is actually intended to
    mitigate certain rhetorical effects, such that his readers not unwittingly invest in
    him an undue measure of authority. Although ingenious, Nehamas's interpre-
    tation strikes me as overly charitable, both with respect to Nietzsche's rhetorical
    mastery and to his apparently altruistic concern not "to fall back into dogma-
    tism" (p. 40). After all, the decadent Nietzsche readily resorted to
    "dogmatism" – see, for example, the concluding sections of *The Antichrist(ian)* –
    to further his larger political ends. And although Nietzsche praises the "infalli-
    ble instinct" that guides his own reliance on the "most multifarious art of style"
    (EH:gb 4), he also associates the deployment of multiple styles with literary
    decadence. He dismisses "the *artist*" Plato, for example, because Plato "throws
    all stylistic forms together and is thus a first-rate decadent in style" (TI 10:2).

8   Nietzsche supplies a similar list of his own: "The human being who has *become
    free*... spits on the contemptible type of well-being dreamed of by shopkeepers,
    Christians, cows, females, Englishmen, and other democrats" (TI 9:38). On the
    irony of Nietzsche's appropriation by contemporary readers, see Stanley Rosen,
    "Nietzsche's Revolution," collected in *The Ancients and the Moderns* (New Haven:
    Yale University Press, 1989), especially pp. 189–190.

9   In a letter to Reinhard von Seydlitz on 12 February 1888, Nietzsche writes, "I am
    now alone, absurdly alone; and in my unrelenting and underground battle
    against everything heretofore revered and loved by humankind (– my formula
    for this is 'revaluation of all values'), I have become, unbeknownst to me, a kind
    of cave – something hidden, which no one finds, even those who set out in
    search of it" (*Sämtliche Briefe*, Vol. 8, No. 989, p. 248).

10 In his published writings from 1888, Nietzsche tends to mask this despair by
    celebrating his "untimely" status: "It would contradict my character entirely if I
    expected ears and hands for my truths today: that today one does not hear me
    and does not accept my ideas is not only understandable, it even seems right to
    me" (EH:gb 1). He thus deflects all responsibility for his failures onto his
    woefully inadequate contemporaries. In his review of *Beyond Good and Evil*, for
    example, he remarks, "From this moment forward all my writings are fish
    hooks: perhaps I know how to fish as well as anyone? – If nothing was caught, I
    am not to blame. *There were no fish*" (EH:bge 1).

11 Laurence Lampert attributes Nietzsche's post-Zarathustran embrace of truth to
    the unique historical conditions of his enterprise, in *Nietzsche and Modern Times:
    A Study of Bacon, Descartes and Nietzsche* (New Haven, CT: Yale University Press,
    1993). According to Lampert, Nietzsche follows in the esoteric tradition of
    Bacon and Descartes, daring to translate the success of his predecessors into a
    bold departure from their own practice of esotericism: "Nietzsche aims to bring
    philosophy out from behind its shelters and to construct a new accord between
    philosophy and the public. Nietzsche's openness, his rashness, his betrayal of
    Platonic sheltering, forces a confrontation with perhaps the most profound and

problematic of all the issues of Nietzsche's thought, his true radicality: Can a human community be built on the deadly truths known to philosophy?" (pp. 277–278).

12   In his letter to Köselitz on 30 October 1988, Nietzsche accounts for the "audacity" of *Ecce Homo:* "Not only did I want to present myself *before* the entirely uncanny solitary act of *revaluation,* – I would also like to *test* what risks I can take with the German ideas of freedom of speech. My suspicion is that the first book of the revaluation will be confiscated on the spot – legally and in all justice." The appearance of *Ecce Homo,* he hopes, will "make the question [of revaluation] so intensely serious, and such an object of curiosity" that the cognizant authorities might be discouraged from confiscating *The Antichrist(ian).* In order to galvanize public sentiment in his favor, Nietzsche consequently informs *Ecce Homo* with an array of psychological snares: "To be sure, I talk about myself with all possible psychological 'cunning' and cheerfulness [*Heiterkeit*] – I do not want to present myself to people as a prophet, savage beast, or moral monster. In this sense, too, the book could be salutary: it will perhaps prevent people from confusing me with my opposite" (*Sämtliche Briefe,* Vol. 8, No. 1137, p. 462).

13   Lampert's account of "modern times" in *Nietzsche and Modern Times* suggests a more positive, optimistic fate for Nietzsche's positive teachings, but this fate is difficult to reconcile with Nietzsche's critique of modernity and his pronouncement of his own decadence: "Nietzsche lived in times dominated by public science and hence by 'the youngest virtue,' honesty or intellectual probity. Nietzschean esotericism does not consist in some masking process of noble lying. It consists, first, of insight into the distance separating perspectives, a distance of rank; and second, of communicating that insight in such a way as to elevate to the high, to school in the esoteric . . . One of the tasks of Nietzschean esotericism is to school in the unavoidability of esotericism, to demonstrate a fact unwelcome to a democratic age: philosophers like Plato, Bacon, and Descartes are so sovereign that they could presume to become educators of humankind – and succeed" (p. 277).

14   For provocative remarks on Poe's literary aims in "The Purloined Letter," see Jacques Derrida, *The Post Card: From Socrates to Freud and Beyond,* trans. Alan Bass (Chicago: University of Chicago Press, 1987), especially "Du Tout," his inverview/conversation with René Major, pp. 500–521. See also Jacques Lacan, "Seminar on 'The Purloined Letter,'" trans. Jeffrey Mehlman, in *The Purloined Poe: Lacan, Derrida and Psychoanalytic Reading,* ed. John Muller and William Richardson (Baltimore: Johns Hopkins University Press, 1988), pp. 28–54.

15   Lampert acknowledges in *Nietzsche and Modern Times* that these are "deadly truths" (p. 281), but he is remarkably upbeat about our ability to confront and accommodate them, especially since we have been prepared so thoroughly and helpfully by Nietzsche's Hyperborean approach to the history of philosophy.

16   Here I follow the lead of Lampert, in ibid., who argues that the development of science enables Nietzsche to abandon the esotericism practiced by predecessor lovers of truth (chapter 11). If the time has come to discard the masks of esotericism, however, then perhaps the time has also come to unmask Nietzsche, to separate his potentially revolutionary teachings from his involuntary pathogenic influences. Lampert may be right about Nietzsche's signature

teachings as post-nihilistic and post-foundational, but he is wrong about Nietzsche himself as the appropriate medium or vehicle for these teachings. To be
sure, we late moderns are not equal to these revolutionary teachings; but neither, apparently, is Nietzsche himself!

17 My account of Nietzsche's parastrategesis is indebted to the constellation of
readerly strategies collected under the general umbrella of "deconstruction."
For a representative range of such strategies, see Jacques Derrida, "Otobiographies: The Teaching of Nietzsche and the Politics of the Proper Name," in *The
Ear of the Other*, ed. Christie McDonald (New York: Schocken, 1986), pp. 8–11;
Paul DeMan, *Allegories of Reading* (New Haven, CT: Yale University Press, 1979);
and Henry Staten, *Nietzsche's Voice* (Ithaca, NY: Cornell University Press, 1990).
In attributing the deflation of Nietzsche's textual authority to his own experiment with parastrategesis, however, I suggest a division of deconstructive labor
that signficantly diminishes the role of the literary critic. Nietzsche both anticipates and plots the deconstruction of his parastrategic constructions; the literary critic is needed simply to chart the development of the parastrategesis once
it exceeds the periphery of Nietzsche's sphere of influence.

18 Jacques Derrida thus warns against the belief "that Nietzsche's mastery is infinite, his power impregnable, or his manipulation of the snare impeccable. . . .
To use parody or the similacrum as a weapon in the service of truth or castration
would be in fact to reconstitute religion, as a Nietzsche cult for example, in the
interest of a priesthood of parody interpreters . . . Nietzsche might well be a
little lost in the web of his text, lost much as a spider who finds he is unequal to
the web he has spun" [*Spurs/Éperons: Nietzsche's Styles*, trans. Barbara Harlow
(Chicago: University of Chicago Press, 1978), pp. 99–100]. While Derrida's
admonition is apposite, he does not adequately consider the possibility that
Nietzsche has deliberately spun a web in which he is "a little lost" or that his
grand political ambitions require him to spin a web he cannot escape.

19 On the relationship between parastrategesis and the insights that Nietzsche
supplies, see Staten's account in *Nietzsche's Voice* of the "psychodialectic" that
obtains between Nietzsche's "voice" and the libidinal economy of his texts,
especially pp. 34–39. Something like this psychodialectic is transacted in the
parastrategic collaboration of Nietzsche and his trained readers.

20 In this respect, Nietzsche may have been influenced by Sextus Empiricus, who
deployed the skeptical strategy of *peritrope* against his Stoic rivals. For an ex-
tended discussion of this affinity, see Daniel W. Conway and Julie Ward, "Physicians of the Soul: *Peritrope* in Sextus Empiricus and Nietzsche," collected in
Nietzsche und die antike Philosophie, ed. Daniel W. Conway and Rudolf Rehn
(Trier: Wissenschaftlicher Verlag, 1992), pp. 193–223.

21 For a sustained examination of the operation of the *Versuch* motif in Nietzsche's
post-Zarathustran writings, see my *Nietzsche and the Political* (London: Routledge, 1997), chapter 5.

22 Rene Girard helpfully draws attention to the complex situation of Nietzsche's
delusions of grandeur within the economy of his thought, in "Strategies of
Madness – Nietzsche, Wagner, and Dostoevski," collected in *To Double Business
Bound* (Baltimore: Johns Hopkins University Press, 1978), pp. 61–83, especially
pp. 70–72.

23 David Owen offers a masterful defense of Nietzsche's "agonal politics," in *Nietzsche, Politics and Modernity* (London: Sage, 1995), especially chapter 6.

24 For a sympathetic treatment of Nietzsche's "heroic individualism," see Leslie Paul Thiele, *Friedrich Nietzsche and the Politics of the Soul* (Princeton, NJ: Princeton University Press, 1990). Thiele faithfully documents the various obstacles that clutter the path of the aspiring hero, but he uncritically adopts Nietzsche's own (romantic) understanding of himself as a lone, solitary figure struggling against an uncaring, inhospitable world. Like Nietzsche, Thiele tends to attribute the frustrations of "heroic individualism" to the recalcitrance of the external world, rather than to the decadence of the self-styled hero. Although Thiele nowhere allows that Nietzsche's heroic individualism trades on an anachronistic romance, he does helpfully suggest that it would be continuous with Nietzsche's "teaching" to remain wary even of Nietzsche's pet recipes for "soulcraft" (pp. 218–225).

25 William Connolly elicits from Nietzsche's writings the elements of an "agonistic democracy" in *Identity/Difference: Democratic Negotiations of Political Paradox* (Ithaca, NY: Cornell University Press, 1991), especially chapter 6. Although promising as a model for postmodern political organization, Connolly's account of the Nietzschean *agon* fails to accommodate the subversive, destabilizing influences of advanced decadence. In an epoch of diminished macropolitical resources, how can the integrity of the political *agon* be protected from those who would alter its structure and rules in order to gain for themselves a more favorable result? It is the signature gambit of slave morality, after all, to revise the terms of any *agon* in which the slaves are unsuccessfully engaged. How, in short, could Connolly (or anyone else) claim to preserve the continued stability of the social context of rules, customs, habits, and mores, which alone makes possible an "agonistic democracy?" Would the irrecuperable fragility of such a social context not render an agonistic democracy either palpably unjust or unpalatable to its potential participants?

26 Nietzsche also cites this passage as the conclusion of his Preface to *Ecce Homo*. This passage demonstrates, or so Nietzsche believes, that Zarathustra – and, presumably, Nietzsche himself – says "the opposite of everything that any 'sage,' 'saint,' 'world-redeemer,' or any other decadent" (EH P4) would say.

27 The precise origins of Nietzsche's investment in this masculinist romance are difficult to determine, but in a postcard to his mother and sister on 28 November 1884, he alludes to his growing desire to found a "colony" of "sympathetic people" in Nice to whom he might disseminate his philosophy (*Sämtliche Briefe*, Vol. 6, No. 560, pp. 562–563). Was he perhaps inspired by (and/or jealous of) the colonial designs of his future brother-in-law?

28 For a withering critique of the nostalgia and romantic anachronisms that inform Nietzsche's social philosophy, see Alasdair MacIntyre, *After Virtue* (Notre Dame, IN: Notre Dame University Press, 1984), especially pp. 114–129.

29 Lampert helpfully characterizes Nietzsche's teachings in *Nietzsche and Modern Times* as comprising a position of naturalism, or "immanentism" (see especially his chapter 14 and epilogue). While I think Lampert is right about Nietzsche's teachings, I believe he is wrong about Nietzsche himself. That is, the decadent Nietzsche does not resolutely hold the immanentist position that Lampert

attributes to him. In fact, Nietzsche's decadence expresses itself most forcefully in his own contribution to the distortion of his teachings.

30 For a lucid account of the cosmological influences on Nietzsche's musings on eternal recurrence, see George Stack's seminal study *Lange and Nietzsche* (Berlin: deGruyter, 1983), chapter 2.

31 Bernd Magnus has persuasively argued that, in 1888, Nietzsche not only abandoned plans for his proposed *Hauptwerk,* but also instructed his landlord to dispose of some of the materials that he had once intended for incorporation into *The Will to Power.* See *Nietzsche's Case: Philosophy as/and Literature,* with Stanley Stewart and Jean-Pierre Miller (New York: Routledge, 1993), pp. 35–46. If Magnus is right, then a perusal of the notebooks is unlikely to help us in reconstructing Nietzsche's idea of eternal recurrence, though it may prove interesting in its own right.

32 Gary Shapiro goes still further, observing that *"the thought* [of eternal recurrence] *is never spoken by a human voice,"* in *Alcyone: Nietzsche on Gifts, Noise, and Women* (Albany: State University of New York Press, 1991) p. 95.

33 Karl Jaspers succinctly states this objection in *Nietzsche:* "Hence we must not overlook the wavering in [Nietzsche's] idea of recurrence. It may appear as a precise doctrine with a definite content, only to become an indeterminate symbol of faith; or it may first be presented as scientifically demonstrable, only to reappear as something giving non-cognitive meaning to *Existenz*" (p. 353).

34 On the unstable and fragmentary nature of this teaching, see Gary Shapiro, *Nietzschean Narratives* (Bloomington: Indiana University Press, 1989), p. 37.

35 This enthusiasm for an unknown teaching calls to mind Nietzsche's critique of agnosticism within science: "'There is no knowledge: *consequently* – there is a God': what a new *elegantia syllogismi!* what a *triumph* for the ascetic ideal" (GM III:25).

36 For example, Clark allows in *Nietzsche on Truth and Philosophy* that she "can find only two serious candidates for the counterideal Zarathustra teaches [cf. EH:gm]: the *Übermensch* and the ideal of affirming eternal recurrence" (p. 253). Having ruled out the *Übermensch* as "still too closely tied to the ascetic ideal," Clark concludes that "the affirmation of eternal recurrence [is] Nietzsche's proposed solution to the problem of nihilism" (p. 253).

37 Luce Irigiray delivers a powerful exposé of the latent (and not-so-latent) gynophobia of Nietzsche's teaching of eternal recurrence in *Marine Lover of Friedrich Nietzsche,* trans. Gillian C. Gill (New York: Columbia University Press, 1991), pp. 20–28. Irigaray traces Nietzsche's masculinist prejudices to his self-absorbed narcissism, which itself bespeaks a besetting fear of the maternal body (pp. 77–94). Irigaray thus concludes, on behalf of Ariadne, that Nietzsche/Dionysus loves only himself (albeit in an abstract, matricidal idealization); he consequently cannot love Ariadne without similarly idealizing (and so detroying) her. For a comprehensive investigation of Nietzsche's masculinist and misogynist prejudices (and of these prejudices unwittingly reproduced by Nietzsche's postmodern scions), see Kelly Oliver's excellent study *Womanizing Nietzsche: Philosophy's Relation to the "Feminine"* (New York: Routledge, 1994), especially chapters 1 and 4.

38 Of course, the paucity of overt textual references to a teaching of eternal

recurrence is also perfectly consistent with the promulgation of an esoteric doctrine, and many commentators have defended some such teaching by pointing to Nietzsche's conspicuous silence on such an allegedly important topic.

39 Shapiro persuasively suggests in *Alcyone* that human beings may not yet be prepared to communicate discursively the thought of eternal recurrence: "To give voice to this thought as if one were now explaining what was really and truly present, as opposed to all of those false candidates for presence in the metaphysical and theological traditions, would be to betray the thought" (p. 96).

40 In a postscript added the next day to a letter dated 14 October 1888, Nietzsche thanks his friend Heinrich Köselitz for the thoughtful birthday letter he received that morning, on which occasion he also composed the interleaf epigraph to *Ecce Homo*. On the same day on which Nietzsche professed his boundless gratitude to his life, he also mentioned to Köselitz that he had received no other birthday greetings (*Sämtliche Briefe*, Vol. 8, No. 1130, p. 451).

41 Magnus describes the teaching of eternal recurrence as a "self-consuming concept," most recently in *Nietzsche's Case*, pp. 21–34. According to Magnus, "Self-consuming concepts [are] notions whose very articulation simultaneously invites and refuses meaning and coherence . . . They purchase their sense, their plausibility, and their force, at the expense of reinscribing the very contrasts they wish to set aside" (pp. 22–23). Although Magnus intends this notion to bear a great deal of explanatory weight (p. 34), the precise nature and logic of these "self-consuming concepts" remains unclear. He introduces the process of "self-consumption" as a logical operation pertaining to the internal economy of the concepts in question (p. 22), but he quickly expands his definition of "self-consumption" to incorporate the subjective experiences and mental states of those (modern) agents who entertain the concepts in question (pp. 23–29). While this expansion of the notion of self-consumption is harmless in itself, it leads Magnus to treat the experiences and mental states of modern agents as relevant to the nature of the teaching of eternal recurrence. He never explains, however, why *our* experiences should be summoned to measure the teaching itself. That we cannot embrace the thought of eternal recurrence or muster the all-encompassing affirmation it enjoins tells us a great deal about us and our diminished reserves of volitional resources, but virtually nothing about eternal recurrence itself. While it may be true that our best renditions of eternal recurrence amount to (or trade on) self-consuming concepts, Magnus's appeal to the subjective experiences of modern agents need bear no relevance whatsoever for the teaching itself. Indeed, here Magnus seems to misplace the "perspectivism" that he is ordinarily pleased to have inherited from Nietzsche. We have no evidence that the teaching of eternal recurrence, or the concept conveyed by the teaching, consumes itself; we have evidence, at best, that our feeble attempts to grapple with this teaching consume themselves. And this conclusion is continuous with Nietzsche's familiar critique of his modern and late modern readers.

42 Magnus thus concludes in ibid. that only an *Übermensch* (another self-consuming concept) could affirm unconditionally the teaching of eternal recurrence, for only an *Übermensch* is "willing to eternalize each moment" (p. 30).

While I have my doubts about Magnus's interpretation of the *Übermensch* – how does he explain, for example, the discussion in AC 4? – I certainly agree that eternal recurrence presents a formula of affirmation that is inhospitable to a familiar range of human sensibility. But why should we (or Magnus) be surprised by the failure of modern and late modern agents to embrace this teaching – especially in light of Nietzsche's later critique of modernity? Is it not clear from everything Nietzsche says about his readers (cf. EH:gb 1) that his signature teachings are neither intended for us nor suited to our enfeebled faculties of discernment?

43 My attention to the compound dangers of parastrategesis is indebted to Derrida's elliptical explorations of indirect, anonymous, and apostrophic forms of address in *The Post Card*. While Derrida's psychoanalytic orientation and faux epistolary style in *The Post Card* prevent him from taking up the distinctly political issues that I have raised here on Nietzsche's behalf, his analysis of the postal card strikes me as both apposite and readily adapted to the complex political project Nietzsche sets for himself.

44 Such paradoxes and "double investments" are artfully illuminated by Staten in *Nietzsche's Voice*, especially chapters 2 and 5.

45 Gary Shapiro recommends in *Alcyone* the term "hysteria" for Nietzsche's practice of continually announcing "pregnancies" that never come to term (p. 136).

46 Letter to Franz Overbeck on 24 March 1887 (*Sämtliche Briefe*, Vol. 8, No. 820, p. 48).

47 In a letter to Overbeck on 31 March 1885, Nietzsche confirms the dangers associated with his attempt to cultivate a sympathetic readership: "My longing for pupils and heirs makes me impatient now and then, and it has even, it seems, made me commit during recent years follies that were mortally dangerous" (*Sämtliche Briefe*, Vol. 7, No. 589, p. 34).

48 MacIntyre is happy to allow Nietzsche to destroy the Enlightenment thinkers who stand in the way of an Aristotelian renascence. MacIntyre mysteriously insists, however, that Nietzsche's destructive power is ineffectual against the Aristotelian alternative MacIntyre recommends. See especially chapter 9 of *After Virtue*.

49 For a sympathetic defense of Socrates as an ironic teacher of autonomy, see Gregory Vlastos, *Socrates: Ironist and Moral Philosopher* (Ithaca, NY: Cornell University Press, 1991). Vlastos's interpretation centers more on the putative intentions and possible results of Socratic irony than on its actual effects on Socrates' interlocutors in the dialogues. While Socrates may serve some (modern) readers as a teacher of autonomy, we have little evidence that his interlocutors and fellow Athenians similarly partook of this service.

50 Allan Bloom makes a presuasive case for the moral education of Glaucon, in whom Socrates cultivates the virtues of a guardian, in the "Interpretive Essay" he appends to his translation of the *Republic*, in *The Republic of Plato*, 2d edition, ed. and trans. Allan Bloom, (New York: Basic, 1991), pp. 325–344.

51 At *Phaedo* 59b, the title character explains to Echecrates that Plato, apparently stricken with illness, was not present on Socrates' final day.

6

SKIRMISHES OF AN UNTIMELY MAN: NIETZSCHE'S REVALUATION OF ALL VALUES

But one misunderstands great human beings if one views them from the miserable perspective of some public use. That one cannot put them to any use, that in itself may belong to greatness. (TI 9:50)

I am no man, I am dynamite. . . . It is only beginning with me that the earth knows *great politics.* (EH:destiny 1)

Introduction

By virtually all accounts except Nietzsche's own, *The Antichrist(ian)* is a disappointment, even something of an embarrassment. His self-appointed executors prudently withheld the book from print, eventually publishing it in a selectively edited form. Once safely, if incompletely, in print, *The Antichrist(ian)* was summarily denounced as a product of its author's incipient madness.

Unlike many of Nietzsche's other "untimely" books, *The Antichrist(ian)* has not yet attracted a belated readership of serious scholars. Even Nietzsche's sympathetic readers have largely ignored (or apologized for) *The Antichrist(ian),* treating his critique of Christianity as an inessential (and perhaps malignant) outgrowth of his more promising philosophical insights. Apparently concluding that a domestication of Nietzsche's thought is a fair (and perhaps desirable) price to pay for his newly accorded status as a respectable philosopher, his contemporary champions have gently nudged this angry book into a shadowy, liminal position on the periphery of his

178

oeuvre.[1] The resulting vector of silence, indifference, and faint praise has effectively called into question the status of the book, which may, sympathetic readers are apparently willing to concede, bespeak the advent of madness.[2] Indeed, if *The Antichrist(ian)* is an important statement of Nietzsche's philosophy, then why is it not even mentioned in the summary review of his "good books" in *Ecce Homo*?[3]

The standard scholarly reception of *The Antichrist(ian)* stands in marked contrast to Nietzsche's own immodest opinion of the book. He viewed *The Antichrist(ian)* as his most important book (other than *Zarathustra*), and he described it prior to its publication as "the most independent book" ever presented to humankind (TI 9:51). In his letter of 4 October 1888 to Malwida von Meysenbug, he refers to *The Antichrist(ian)* as "the greatest philosophical event of all time, with which the history of humankind will be broken into two opposing halves."[4] Two months later, he boasts that *The Antichrist(ian)* is "actually a judgment on the world [*Weltgericht*]," in part because it "pronounces a death sentence of a kind [*Art*] that is perfectly *übermenschlich*."[5]

Nietzsche's general sense of his accomplishment in *The Antichrist(ian)* is conveyed most clearly in its companion book and "prelude," *Ecce Homo*.[6] He begins *Ecce Homo* by explaining his motive for introducing himself: "Seeing that before long I must confront humanity with the most difficult demand ever made of it, it seems indispensable to me to say *who I am*" (EH P1). He does not elaborate further on the "demand" to which he alludes, but it is clearly related somehow to the concussive book that he plans "before long" to release. Indeed, he most likely has in mind *The Antichrist(ian)* when he claims that "One day my name will be associated with the memory of something tremendous – a crisis without equal on earth, the most profound collision of conscience, a decision that was conjured up *against* everything that had been believed, demanded, hallowed so far" (EH:destiny 1). These passages, along with others like them in *Ecce Homo,* convey Nietzsche's perception of the need to prepare his readers for something "tremendous" soon to come. In fact, he evidently intended *Ecce Homo* to provide curious readers with a favorable account of the philosopher who would soon render the terrible, antinomian "decision" to which he alludes.[7] "I am one thing," he insists in this tactical autobiography; "my writings are another matter" (EH:gb 1).[8]

The checkered production history of these two books further attests to the grandiosity of Nietzsche's claims for *The Antichrist(ian)*. Upon completing the First Book of *The Revaluation of All Values* on 30 September 1888,[9] he promptly shelved his "explosive" manuscript, turning instead to begin work on the "autobiographical" project that would become *Ecce Homo*. In light of the world-historical significance that he attached to *The Antichrist(ian)*, as well as his persistent attention to the timely production of all his books, his decision to postpone the publication of *The Antichrist(ian)* is indeed extraordinary.[10] Although it is true that he conceived of *The Revaluation of All Values* in quadrapartite form until very late in the year, he had decided early on that its four proposed installments should be published separately.[11] If Nietzsche, who had grown accustomed to rushing his evolving ideas into print, often at his own expense, voluntarily withheld from publication a completed installment of his proposed *Hauptwerk*, then his ambitions and designs must have been grand indeed!

Nietzsche's correspondence from the Autumn of 1888 confirms his ulterior motives in turning with such urgency to this strange autobiography.[12] Concerned that *The Antichrist(ian)* might be proscribed in Germany if he were perceived as a madman or rabble-rouser, he attempts in *Ecce Homo* to distance himself from the obloquy that perfuses *The Antichrist(ian):* "There is nothing in me of a founder of a religion – religions are affairs of the rabble" (EH:destiny 1). He consequently presents his myriad trials and triumphs as necessary steps along the way to the unqualified affirmation expressed in the interleaf epigraph to *Ecce Homo*. No loose ends compromise the tidy, totalizing narrative he spins; no event falls, unexplained, outside the genealogical frame he imposes on his life. Turning to his advantage the virtual anonymity under which he has labored hitherto, he liberally embellishes the "facts" of his life, delivering in the end a highly idealized (and highly strategic) self-portrait.

The author of *Ecce Homo* claims to be content with his mastery of the "little things" in life, with his own quaint brand of miniaturism (EH:clever 10). Immersed in the wondrous details of nutrition, place, climate, and recreation, he no longer steals sidelong glances at the glories of bygone ages, in comparison to which his own achievements must seem puny and insignificant. This is a book in which he proclaims himself "dynamite," while attending instead to picayune issues of diet and cuisine. This is a book in which the self-styled Antichrist speaks urgently not of the redemption of modernity, nor of "breeding" exemplary human specimens, but of his minor triumphs as a pianist and composer. The philosopher who once dared to reawaken the tragic muse is now content with the sweet grapes reserved for him by respectful Turinese costermongers.

According to the serene author of *Ecce Homo*, the willful author of *The Antichrist(ian)* is undeniably possessed of strong passions, but he too is also ultimately in control of himself. Despite what he says, he need not be feared: "I do not want to be a holy man; sooner even a buffoon – Perhaps I am a buffoon" (EH:destiny 1). *Ecce Homo* thus presents Nietzsche to his readers as a civilized, self-possessed gentleman, untroubled by the untoward excesses that riddle *The Antichrist(ian)*.[13] Although he explicitly announces himself as "the most terrible human being that has existed thus far" (EH:destiny 2), the Apollinian rhetoric of his self-presentation simultaneously disarms his readers and piques their interest in the "destruction" he promises to visit upon them.[14] Hence the irony surrounding the current reception of Nietzsche's writings (and the tacit agreement to forgive him for producing *The Antichrist(ian)*) in the Anglophone world: Those who would willfully domesticate this dangerous thinker follow in a tradition that actually began with the hagiography strategically essayed in *Ecce Homo*.

Insofar as he intended *Ecce Homo* as a safeguard against the confiscation of *The Antichrist(ian)*, Nietzsche sheds some clarifying light on the relative importance he attaches to these two books. Whereas the value of *Ecce Homo* is largely – though by no means exclusively – instrumental, as a pre-emptive deflection of the threat of censorship, *The Antichrist(ian)* comprises the culmination of his philosophy, which he immodestly calls the "revaluation of all values [*Umwerthung aller Werthe*]." *Ecce Homo* is thus supposed to furnish his readers with a sympathetic introduction to the self-appointed executor of the revaluation of all values.[15] *The Antichrist(ian)* is so "explosive" and so momentous that he must hurriedly issue *Ecce Homo* as a hedge against censorship, reinventing himself in the process as a thoughtful, measured lover of truth. Because he intends *Ecce Homo* as a prelude and introduction to *The Antichrist(ian)*, he cannot include in the former book a review of the latter. Of course, his breakdown in January 1889 thwarted these elaborate strategies for outwitting the German censors and cultivating a readership conducive to his project of revaluation.[16] *The Antichrist(ian)* was first published in modified form in 1895, and *Ecce Homo* finally appeared in print in 1908.

A Hundredfold Declaration of War

As Nietzsche's complex scheme suggests, his lofty expectations for *The Antichrist(ian)* are directly related to the "revaluation of all values" rehearsed therein. It is precisely with respect to this revaluation of all values, however, that his epochal self-presentation throughout *The Antichrist(ian)* strikes his readers as hopelessly grandiose and perhaps as symptomatic of incipient madness.

Nietzsche begins *The Antichrist(ian)* by announcing that he and his fellow Hyperboreans "have found the exit out of the labyrinth of entire millennia" (AC 1). He trades here on the Thesean imagery familiar to his readers, and the "labyrinth" he has in mind is apparently the anti-naturalism of Western Christianity. While this announcement strikes an optimistic chord in sympathetic readers,[17] it nevertheless remains obscure: If Nietzsche has discovered an exit from the labyrinth, then why does he continue to wander the maze with the rest of us? If he has broken Western history in two (EH:destiny 8), then why does the "new" epoch so closely resemble its decadent predecessor? If the calendar is now reckoned from the "last day" of Christianity (AC 62), then why does everyone, including Nietzsche, continue to observe the intercalary conventions of historical Christendom? If Nietzsche's celebrated revaluation of all values is supposed to have vanquished Christian morality, then perhaps *The Antichrist(ian)* signals the onset of madness after all.

While Nietzsche's ambitions in *The Antichrist(ian)* are undeniably grandiose, they are neither as fantastic nor as futile as is commonly suggested. Indeed, his revaluation of all values is often misunderstood, especially when conflated with his earlier teachings and pronouncements. To some extent, this misunderstanding is perfectly understandable, for both Nietzsche and Zarathustra have led us to expect this revaluation to accomplish nothing short of the redemption of modernity, the rebirth of tragedy, the terrible reign of the *Übermensch,* the annihilation of reactive forces, the restoration of noble morality, the overcoming of nihilism, or some such cataclysm of unprecedented proportions.

Much of the confusion surrounding Nietzsche's *Umwerthung aller Werthe* may be traced to the ambiguity of the prefix *Um-,* which supports equally well a number of translations (and corresponding interpretations). Both *revaluation* and *transvaluation,* for example, are acceptable renderings of *Umwerthung,* though particular translators may have good reason to prefer one to the other. The question thus remains: What complex operation(s) did Nietzsche intend to convey by his use of the term *Umwerthung?* While the textual evidence is simply too diffuse to support definitively any single interpretation of this difficult concept, some important clues stand out. For example, if *The Birth of Tragedy* constitutes Nietzsche's "first *Umwerthung* of all values" (TI 10:5), then he cannot sincerely mean to convey that this *Umwerthung* involves either a creation of new values or a radical rethinking of the very nature and place of value. Similarly, the magnitude of any *Umwerthung* that "has become flesh and genius in [him]" (EH:destiny 1) must pale in comparison with the transfigurative labors of those "philosophers of the future" who will found the successor epoch to modernity. Perhaps we should take advantage of the ambiguity of *Umwerthung* and employ the term *revaluation* to describe any reversal of existing values, while reserving the term *transvaluation* for the originary act of creating new values.[18] In this light, any *Umwerthung* accomplished by Nietzsche himself must therefore constitute a revaluation of all values.

Thus we see that Nietzsche's revaluation of all values does not (and could not) involve the creation *ex nihilo* of new values, which might directly contribute to the founding of a post-Christian epoch. Nietzsche apparently believes that "new" values arise either from an originary act of creation or from a reversal of existing values. The former, "active" mode of evaluation is available only to healthy peoples and ages, whereas the latter, "reactive" mode of evaluation characteristically falls to decadents, invalids, slaves, and anyone else who cannot afford the luxury of spontaneous self-expression. In the *Genealogy*, for example, he exposes the revaluation of all values as the handiwork of the priests, whereby the creative forces of *ressentiment* indirectly produce a mutant "deed" (GM I:11).

Nietzsche's pronouncement of his own decadence thus situates his revaluation of all values squarely within the familiar tradition of reactive evaluation as practiced and perfected throughout the evolution of "slave morality."[19] A revaluation of values is all that is possible in the twilight epoch of any age or people. Unlike the philosophers of the future, whom he identifies as "legislators of new values" (BGE 44), he can do no more than challenge and perhaps reverse the reigning values of his age. He is neither a "new beginning," nor a "self-propelled wheel," nor a "dancing star," nor the fully transfigured "child" prophesied by Zarathustra.[20] To advertise himself as the active creator of new values would be to perpetuate the precise confusion of cause and effect that he himself exposes. Moreover, since the successor age will create new values of its own design, the direct effects of revaluation are at best transient; only its indirect influence on the founders of the successor age is meant to be lasting.

Although Nietzsche may at one time have equated the revaluation of all values with the willful creation of new values – while personally disowning both tasks – he gradually comes to see the former task both as his own and as the necessary precondition of the latter task. It is his destiny to clear the rubble of modernity in order that the philosophers of the future might raise the successor epoch on a smooth, level surface. Although "Christianity finds no civilization as yet," he nevertheless believes that "under certain circumstances it might lay the foundation for one" (AC 22).

Indeed, by the time he writes *The Antichrist(ian)*, he clearly conceives of the revaluation as making possible, rather than actual, the "tragic age" whose advent he envisions. The revaluation he announces in 1888 should therefore not be confused with the willful founding of a postmodern, post-ascetic, post-Christian, or post-nihilistic age; this Promethean labor he explicitly reserves for the philosophers of the future, for whom he anxiously prepares.[21] That *The Antichrist(ian)* has thus far occasioned embarrassment and oblivion, rather than the decisive discontinuities that he and Zarathustra have led us to expect, does not in itself seal the failure of Nietzsche's revaluation.

Nor does he suppose in 1888, as he may have before, that his act of revaluation signals an actual victory over the anti-affective animus of Christian morality. While he speaks with equal intensity of both a revaluation of all values and a protracted campaign against the anti-naturalism of Christian morality, he does not strictly equate the two.[22] As he suggests in his letter of 18 October 1888 to Overbeck, the revaluation enacted in *The Antichrist(ian)* is best understood as a declaration of war on Christian morality:

This time – as an old artilleryman – I bring out my heavy guns: I fear that I will shoot the history of mankind into two halves . . . [*The Antichrist(ian)*] is already a hundredfold declaration of war, with a distant thunder in the mountains; in the foreground, much "merriment," of the sort related to me.[23]

As a "hundredfold declaration of war," *The Antichrist(ian)* initiates a rebellion that Nietzsche cannot realistically expect to finish on his own. He must rely on generations of Nietzscheans to come, and he can only hope that he has provided for their proper training and instruction.[24]

In this light, we need not (yet) attribute his announcement in *The Antichrist(ian)* of a revaluation of all values to delusions of grandeur, for he is not under the impression that he has somehow abolished the formative influence of Christian morality. Having announced the death of God, he cautions that "given the ways of men, there may still be caves for thousands of years in which his shadow will be shown" (GS 108). That Christian morality has (thus far) survived the publication of *The Antichrist(ian)* therefore does not in itself constitute a refutation of his claims to revaluation. Even at his most self-serving, he boasts "merely" of having fired the first salvo in what he imagines as a bitter, bloody battle to determine the future of humankind. *The Antichrist(ian)* limns an exit from the labyrinth of Western Christianity, but it is not an exit of which the decadent Nietzsche can avail himself. He and his "subterranean" followers, whom he has taught to "tunnel and mine and undermine" (D P1), must content themselves with the task of excavating this exit, which others will eventually use to escape the labyrinth.[25]

Although Nietzsche may originally have conceived of the revaluation of all values on the model of an epochal, macro-political event, legislated perhaps by a world-historical redeemer, or *Übermensch,* his writings from 1888 consistently refer to the revaluation as something that he enacts, something that becomes incarnate in him. He describes "great men" as "explosives" (TI 9:44), and he subsequently introduces himself as "dynamite" (EH:destiny 1). He acknowledges only "five or six moments in history" as exceptions to the rule of "anti-nature," and he then ordains himself as yet another (EH:destiny 7). He refers to *The Birth of Tragedy* as his "first revaluation of all values" (TI 10:5), and he defines "revaluation of all values" as "my formula for an act of supreme self-examination on the part of humanity become flesh and genius in me" (EH:destiny 1). He furthermore advertises himself as "the man of calamity," the champion of truth as it "enters into a fight with the lies of millennia" (EH:destiny 1). He even speculates that a revaluation of values is "perhaps possible for [him] alone" (EH:wise 1).[26] Finally, in a letter to Reinhard von Seydlitz on 12 February 1888, he explicitly identifies the revaluation of all values with his own self-imposed regimen of solitude and isolation.[27]

By "revaluation of all values," he does not mean the protracted anti-

Christian campaign that will conclude in the installation of an alternative to the ascetic ideal. He means instead the embodied act of declaring war on the anti-affective animus of Christian morality: "Let us not underestimate this: *we ourselves*, we free spirits, are nothing less than a 'revalution of values,' an *incarnate* [*leibhafte*] declaration of war and triumph over all the ancient conceptions of 'true' and 'untrue' " (AC 13). Nietzsche thus believes that he has successfully completed his revaluation of all values. In writing *The Antichrist(ian)*, he not only issues a declaration of war on Christian morality, but also transforms himself into a declaration of war.[28]

We will return shortly to consider this wondrous act of self-transformation. Let us note for now that in Nietzsche's eyes at least, his political task is complete. He claims to have executed his revaluation of all values, in its entirety, in the body of *The Antichrist(ian)* itself.[29] Perhaps because he has postponed so consistently the political moment of his thought, timidly deferring to Wagner, Zarathustra, the free spirits, the philosophers of the future, and virtually anyone else for whom he might serve as a prelude, it is generally overlooked that in October 1888 he finally accepts the mantle of the political lawgiver.[30] No further experimentation, investigation, research, or determination is necessary. The "*critique* of moral values," which he "demanded" in 1887 (GM P6), is apparently now complete. Satisfied with the tension he has forcibly restored to the human spirit (BGE P), he now releases the bowstring, launching his arrows in an unknown trajectory toward an uncertain future.

This strange little book thus commands our full attention, as the political event, the "explosion," toward which Nietzsche has been pointing all along.[31] Summoning the residual volitional resources at his disposal, he pronounces a summary curse (*Fluch*) on Christianity: "With this I am at the end and I pronounce my judgment. I *condemn* Christianity. I raise against the Christian church the most terrible of all accusations that any accuser ever uttered. It is to me the highest of all conceivable corruptions" (AC 62). So much for the liberal humanism, Christian charity, puckish playfulness, altruistic self-erasure, Whiggish progressivism, antiquarian modesty, and pluralistic tolerance that Nietzsche's Anglophone readers currently attribute to him! Here he decrees categorically that the anti-naturalism of Christian morality shall not be permitted to taint the founding of the successor epoch to modernity.[32]

Nietzsche's confrontation with Christian morality is primarily political in its nature and focus.[33] Although his philosophical differences with Christian theologians are profound, the curse he pronounces on Christian morality is directed toward its unchecked corruption of political regimes and institutions. By 1888, in fact, he has virtually distilled his general critique of modernity into a critique of Christian morality. As the remaining vestiges of noble culture recede into the gloaming, Christian morality reveals itself as the governing trope of modernity as a whole: "The Christian church has left nothing untouched by its corruption; it has turned every value into an un-value, every integrity into a vileness of the soul" (AC 62).

Notwithstanding the smug, self-congratulatory atheism that pervades modernity, its liberal ideals and democratic institutions bear witness to the thoroughly Christian ethos of this supposedly secular epoch. Reproducing the twisted logic perfected by the Christian priests, modernity attempts to moralize its own demise, fatuously reinterpreting decadence as a virtue and claiming to prefer pandemic mediocrity to the cruel nobility of bygone ages. In the twilight of late modernity, however, this elaborate myth of secularization has been rudely shattered. The nausea and pity that Nietzsche everywhere detects are simply naked manifestations of the self-contempt that lies at the heart of slave morality: "The sight of man now makes us weary – what is nihilism today if it is not *that*? – We are weary of *man*" (GM I:12). For Nietzsche, then, modernity is little more than Christian morality writ large, a self-consuming explosion of *ressentiment*.[34] Of course, the precondition of slave morality is the existence of a "hostile external world," whose rampant "evil" alone secures the bogus "goodness" of the slaves (GM I:10). As Christian morality approaches unconditional victory over late modernity, the "triumphant" slaves are threatened with the capitulation of the hostile external world from which they have parasitically drawn their borrowed vitality. Enter the "will to nothingness," which effectively merges goodness with evil and thereby sanctions the glorious self-annihilation of slave morality. Modernity, it thus follows, achieves its apex and destiny only in the purgative exercise of self-destruction.

It is not immediately clear, however, that this revised account of Nietzsche's aims in *The Antichrist(ian)* will or should allay the concerns of skeptical readers. Is it not similarly grandiose of him to imagine his little pamphlet as a "hundredfold declaration of war" on Christianity? He is neither the first nor the most influential critic to call for the end of Christian morality. What possible reason could he have for ascribing such world-historical importance to his own erratic scribblings?

The Pathogenesis of Pity

Nietzsche directs his "hundredfold declaration of war" not at the entire colossus of Western Christianity, but at the priestly class that stands at its head. At the center of his critique of Christian morality lies the charge that the priests are teachers of decadence. Through the teaching and practice of pity, Christian priests have spread their constitutive sickness to humankind as a whole.

As we have seen, Nietzsche believes that the decadence of individual

agents and peoples is either constitutive, as in the case of priests, or acquired, as in his own case (EH:wise 2). But what of humanity as a whole,
independent of its ingredient souls and peoples? Rather than conclude
from his diagnosis of modernity that humankind is by nature decadent,
which would summarily foreclose any prospect of mounting a political response, Nietzsche hypothesizes instead that humankind does not know any
better. He conceives of decadence as an acquired "second nature," which
has been foisted upon humankind by its sick teachers:

> This would still leave open the possibility that it is not humanity that is
> degenerating [*in Entartung*], but only that parasitical type of man – that of the
> *priest* – which has used morality to raise itself mendaciously to the position of
> determining human values – finding in Christian morality the means to come
> to *power*. – Indeed, this is *my* insight: the teachers, the leaders of humanity,
> theologians all of them, were also, all of them, decadents: *hence* the [original]
> revaluation of all values into hostility to life, *hence* morality. (EH:destiny 7)[35]

In a startling reversal of his (and Zarathustra's) earlier pronouncements,
Nietzsche thus suggests that the perceived degeneration of humankind as a
whole is only temporary. The sickness that presently besets humanity, like
Nietzsche's own decadence, is only "periodic" in nature, acquired from the
cumulative efforts of the Christian priests. Although he wisely stops short of
declaring humankind to be indestructible, he nevertheless believes that
humanity can perhaps withstand the worst depradations that the priests can
muster. Clarifying his post-Zarathustran political aims, he explains:

> The problem I thus pose is not what shall succeed mankind in the sequence of
> living beings (man is an *end*), but what type of man shall be *bred*, shall be *willed*,
> for being higher in value, worthier of life, more certain of a future. Even in the
> past this higher type has appeared often – but as a fortunate accident, as an
> exception, never as something *willed*. (AC 3)[36]

Only the priests, then, are incurably decadent.[37] Humankind as a whole is
essentially healthy and will survive this transient wave of sickness.[38] While
only Life itself genuinely partakes of the model of a general economy,
Nietzsche attributes to humankind a degree of resiliency that is simply
unattainable within the restricted economies of souls and peoples.

Rather than mark the negation or the eclipse of humankind as a whole,
decadence represents a natural, inevitable stage in its cyclical development.
Like Nietzsche's own decadence, which "periodically" confounds his otherwise healthy instincts, the decadence of modernity temporarily disturbs the
advance of humankind. If humanity can survive the death of tragedy, the fall
of the Roman Empire, and the miscarriage of the Renaissance, then it can
certainly withstand the demise of Western Christianity. Indeed, if the "bad
conscience" has impregnated humankind with a future (GM II:19), then

the decadence of modernity may be nothing more than an expected – and perfectly natural – bout with morning sickness.

If humankind as a whole is not degenerating, then the spread of decadence can, in principle, be temporarily contained.[39] While the eventual degeneration of any age is inevitable, decay need not spread so quickly and pervasively as in those peoples that allow the priestly class to usurp political power. Nietzsche here suggests that the political containment of Christian morality could temporarily stem – though never arrest or reverse – the advancing tide of decadence. His reference to the priests as "parasites" hopefully suggests that some "host organism" stands to be rescued if this pernicious infestation can be eradicated. Despite two thousand years of practice in the disciplines of decadence, then, humankind is still amenable to a culture predicated on naturalistic disciplines. Indeed, if the advanced decay of Western European cultures is attributable to the self-aggrandizement of their priestly classes, then an elimination of these classes may enable a rehabilitation of those "healthy" values and institutions that were trampled in the priests' rush to power.[40] Most importantly, the anti-naturalism that pervades a decadent epoch like late modernity need not taint the founding of successor epochs.

Here, of course, we must beware of confusing cause and effect, especially on Nietzsche's behalf. The accession to power of a priestly class is not the cause of decadence, but its effect or symptom. That the priests freely disseminate their anti-natural teachings is a sign not of their active triumph (which is inconceivable), but of the inevitable decline of the people or age in question. The flourishing of the priestly class means that the highest types now seek recognition (and affirmation) from lower types, for the priests initially gain political power only as intermediaries between social strata (GM III:15). Announcing the imminent collapse of the pathos of distance that sustains a healthy people, this interdependence of social strata (marked by the corollary rise of the priests to power) signifies the irreversible advance of decadence.

Nietzsche consequently aims to contain the political influence of the priests, but not in order to effect a reversal of the decadence that afflicts modernity. He aims instead to introduce into the economy of decadence a transient endogenous disturbance, in order that he might expose momentarily the truth of Christian morality. He cannot prevent the priests from continuing to infect others with their constitutive sickness, but he can catch them in the act and document their pathogenesis for posterity. This moment of truth, he surmises, will be sufficient to encourage the founders of the successor epoch to expend additional prophylactic resources in the prevention and eradication of priestly power: "The time will come, I promise, when the priest will be considered the lowest type, our Chandala, the most mendacious, the most indecent kind of human being" (AC 45). Nietzsche's primary political aim in *The Antichrist(ian)* is not to rid modernity of all vestiges of Christian morality (which lies well beyond his power to accomplish), but to ensure that nothing like it is allowed to arise ever again.

Nietzsche's critique of Christian morality thus turns on a more basic critique of the purveyors of this morality, who are responsible for its forcible imposition onto those who have no need for it. All priests, he believes, are motivated by the natural impulse to amass and wield power over others. Yet the sole expression of power available to the priests is both indirect and "reactive," requiring them first to sicken those over whom they eventually hope to prevail (GM III:15). Priests aggrandize themselves at the expense of others, exacerbating the suffering of Christian "sinners" and preventing the development of a "European Buddhism" that might provide the sick with a modicum of peace and tranquillity (AC 23). Nietzsche consequently defines *prophets* and *founders of religions* as "gruesome hybrids of sickness and will to power" (EH P:4), a description that aptly captures the priestly type in general. If he is to contribute to the eventual proscription of Christian morality, then he must expose and illuminate the (twisted) will to power that guides the priests.

Nietzsche harbors no ill will toward Christian communities in their "original" or "pure" form, and he reminds us of their many contributions to the development of Western civilization:

> What we have to thank them for is inestimable; and who could be rich enough in gratitude not to be impoverished in view of all that the "spiritual men" of Christianity, for example, have so far done for Europe! . . . they gave comfort to sufferers, courage to the oppressed and despairing, a staff and support to the dependent, and lured away from society into monasteries and penitentiaries for the soul those who had been destroyed inwardly and who had become savage. (BGE 62)

Indeed, Christian morality is perfectly suited to those whose only prospects for peace lie in unearned love and equality, an assurance of undeserved salvation, and an exemption from the imperative to improve their character.

While Nietzsche occasionally registers his aesthetic distaste for the sufferers and invalids who constitute these pure communities, he directs his political criticism only toward that historical mutation of Christianity that aggrandizes the power of the priests at the expense of the sick. Only when disseminated by the priests to the sick and healthy alike, as universally binding, does Christian morality present a danger to a people or epoch as a whole. Nietzsche thus trains his critical focus on the political moment at which Christian morality exceeds its "natural" boundaries and insinuates itself into the lives of those who might otherwise have endured the suffering and meaninglessness of their existence.

From their own experience, the priests understand that human beings repudiate only meaningless suffering. "Meaningful" suffering is not only tolerated, but passionately courted (GM III:27). The priests consequently invest the suffering of the sick and infirm with meaning, situating them within an interpretive context in which their misery achieves a peculiar justification. Emboldened by their guilt to pass judgment on the whole, these sufferers confidently echo the signature refrain of their teachers:

> Instead of saying naively, "*I* am no longer worth anything," the moral lie in the mouth of the decadent says, "Nothing is worth anything, life is not worth anything." Such a judgment always remains very dangerous, it is contagious: throughout the morbid soil of society it soon proliferates into a tropical vegetation of concepts – now as a religion (Christianity), now as a philosophy (Schopenhauerism). (TI 9:35)[41]

The priests invent the metaphysical will for the sole purpose of casting sufferers as sinners, to whom they subsequently offer their services as dispensers of penance and forgiveness. Under the tutelage of the priests, sinners learn to generalize from their own suffering, projecting it not only onto humankind as a whole, but onto Life as well.

Although it might appear, especially to the "sinners" in question, that the priest is a genuine physician of the soul, nothing could be further from the truth:

> [The priest] brings salves and balm with him, no doubt; but before he can act as a physician he first has to wound; when he then stills the pain of the wound *he at the same time infects the wound* – for that is what he knows to do best of all, this sorcerer and animal-tamer, in whose presence everything necessarily grows sick, and everything sick tame. (GM III:15)

The "wound" in question is the existential suffering associated with the *bad conscience* (*schlechtes Gewissen*), which Nietzsche views as the ineliminable opportunity cost of our direct reliance on consciousness (as opposed to instinct) as an organ of regulation (GM II:16). The "infection" in question is the surplus suffering associated with *guilt* (*Schuld*), which the priest cleverly proposes as an interpretation of the otherwise meaningless bad conscience.[42] According to the priest, his sheep suffer *for a reason*, because they *deserve* to suffer, and he anaesthetizes them by convincing them of their guilt (GM III:15). The priest's recourse to metaphysics thus renders meaningful the existential suffering of his sinners, but only by compounding it with the surplus suffering of guilt. He ingeniously discloses *ascesis* as an unexplored field of agency within which sufferers might discover meaning for their lives, but he presents this field to them only under the determinate aspect of the self-serving grid of interpretation that he has superimposed upon it.

The pathogenic power of the Christian priests thus derives from their uniquely *moral* interpretation of human suffering, which in turn trades on a metaphysical account of the human condition. Here as elsewhere, Nietzsche views as "metaphysical" any departure in theory or practice from the strict phenomenalism he champions. He identifies metaphysics with "idealism," which he describes as a "flight from reality" (EH:destiny 3). It is precisely the "metaphysics of the hangman" that he challenges in Christian morality, and his revaluation of values is designed to chart the priest's flight from reality: "We immoralists are trying with all our strength to take the concepts of guilt and punishment out of the world again, and to cleanse psychology, history, nature, and social institutions and sanctions of them" (TI 6:7).

The priestly metaphysics that underlies Christian morality thus constitutes a rejection of the strict phenomenalism that Nietzsche embraces. He acknowledges only the immediate experience of suffering, *simpliciter.* The sick and infirm suffer for no reason whatsoever, and their experience of suffering tells us nothing about human experience in general or the cosmos as a whole:

> Who alone has good reason to lie his way out of reality? He who suffers from it. But to suffer from reality is to be a piece of reality that has come to grief. The preponderance of feelings of displeasure over feelings of pleasure is the cause of this fictitious morality and religion; but such a preponderance provides the very formula for decadence. (AC 15)

Nietzsche thus insists that the existential suffering of the bad conscience is simply meaningless. No further interpretation is either proffered or required: "What alone can *our* teaching be? That . . . no one is responsible for man's being there at all, for his being such-and-such, or for his being in these circumstances or in this environment" (TI 6:8).

Nietzsche furthermore recommends his phenomenalism as the interpretation that is most conducive to a minimization of human suffering. If existential suffering were treated as meaningless, or as natural, then the surplus suffering contributed by guilt would be superfluous. He insists, for example, that the superior palliative value of Indian Buddhism, as "a religion for decadents," lies in its strict adherence to a phenomenalistic account of human suffering (AC 20). No attempt is made to interpret or justify suffering, for all such attempts serve only to exacerbate suffering. He consequently locates his preference for Indian Buddhism over Christianity in the former's embrace and the latter's rejection of phenomenalism:

> Buddhism is a hundred times more realistic than Christianity: posing problems objectively and coolly is part of its inheritance. . . . Buddhism is profoundly distinguished from Christianity by the fact that the self-deception of the moral concepts lies far behind it. In my terms, it stands *beyond* good and evil. (AC 20)

Whereas Christianity anaesthetizes the pain of the bad conscience by compounding it with the surplus suffering of guilt, the Buddha's phenomenalism provides the sick with as much serenity and solace as is possible for them
to have.

Not everyone, however, is currently in a position to accept this strict
phenomenalism as a viable interpretation of the bad conscience. As Nietzsche himself demonstrates in the *Genealogy*, the ascetic ideal owes its ascendancy to the inability of the sick and infirm to accept their existential
suffering as meaningless. The ascetic ideal "saved the will" and prevented
the suicidal nihilism that would otherwise have ensued (GM III:28). The
institutionalization of decadence in Western European cultures has been
accompanied by an institutionalization of guilt as well; both are inscribed
into custom, mores, policy, and law. Once the demise of Christianity is
complete, perhaps, sufferers may find solace and repose in a culturally
sponsored cult of phenomenalism. Perhaps the "philosophers of the future"
will inform the demotic stratum of a hierarchical society with the sort of
"European Buddhism" that might have developed already in the West had
Christianity not intervened. But we must not underestimate the allure of
metaphysics for those who cannot afford to embrace Nietzsche's strict
phenomenalism.

We can achieve even greater precision here, for Nietzsche also identifies
the pathogen whereby the priests infect others with their decadence: pity.
Nietzsche's low regard for pity is well known, and he reserves for it his
harshest judgment:

> Pity stands opposed to the tonic emotions which heighten our vitality. . . . We
> are deprived of strength when we feel pity. . . . Under certain circumstances, it
> may engender a total loss of life and vitality out of all proportion to the
> magnitude of the cause. . . . Pity is the *practice* of nihilism. (AC 7)

While he customarily denounces the practice of pity as despoiling his aesthetic appreciation of the world, as needlessly prolonging the lives of the
botched and the misbegotten, he also believes that pity escalates the suffering of the sick and infirm. He consequently charges the priests with cruelly
prolonging the suffering of all "sinners":

> The physiologist demands *excision* of the degenerating part; he denies all
> solidarity with what degenerates; he is worlds removed from pity for it. But the
> priest desires precisely the degeneration of the whole, of humanity; for that
> reason, he *conserves* what degenerates – at this price he rules. (EH:d 2)

Nietzsche is not the first critic to call attention to the insidious power
relations sheltered within the practice of pity, but he certainly develops this
insight to an unprecedented degree. The practice of pity actually exacerbates the suffering of the sick and infirm, by transforming illness, victimage,
and deformity into the bases for a relationship of strict dependence. Pity not

only reduces sufferers to their respective sins and sicknesses, but also places them in the thrall of those who dispense it. Precious little attention is paid to the humanitarian currents resident within Nietzsche's thought, but he explicitly associates his campaign to eliminate pity with his "love of humanity": "In our whole unhealthy modernity there is nothing more unhealthy than Christian pity. To be physicians *here,* to be inexorable *here,* to wield the scalpel *here –* that is *our* part, that is *our* love of humanity, that is how *we* are philosophers" (AC 7).[43]

Nietzsche's unusual reference to his own philanthropy underscores his concern that pity operates as a pathogen.[44] Pity tends to obfuscate the order of rank among types and thus threatens to extinguish the pathos of distance that sustains the ethical life of any epoch or people. Indeed, it is through their elicitations of pity that the priests spread their own decadence to others:

> Pity makes suffering contagious. . . . It preserves what is ripe for destruction; it defends those who have been disinherited and condemned by life; and by the abundance of the failures of all kinds which it keeps alive, it gives life itself a gloomy and questionable aspect. (AC 7)

Nietzsche's eagerness to wield his healing scalpel will certainly offend some readers, but we must not allow the macabre imagery to obscure his basic point. Pity serves as the metaphysical glue that binds the surplus suffering of guilt to the existential suffering of the bad conscience. Pity thus encourages the sick and infirm to indulge their *ressentiment,* which Nietzsche identifies as both "their specific evil" and "their most natural inclination" (EH:wise 6). As the religion of pity, Christianity does not relieve the suffering of its adherents, but instead compounds it: "To *abolish* any distress ran counter to its deepest advantages: it lived on distress, it *created* distress to eternalize *itself*" (AC 62).

Nietzsche's attention to the pathogenesis of pity thus exposes the currents of cruelty and exploitation roiling beneath the seemingly placid surface of Christian morality: "One should never forget that Christianity has exploited the weakness of the dying for a rape of the conscience; and the manner of death itself, for value judgments about man and the past" (TI 9:36). The disguised misanthropy of the Christian priests is no accident, for it represents the logical external unfolding of priestly *ressentiment.* Slave morality is born of self-contempt (GM I:10), which outwardly expresses itself, especially in its Christian manifestations, as pity:

> Where pity is preached today – and, if you listen closely, this is the only religion preached now – psychologists should keep their ears open: through all the vanity, through all the noise that characterizes these preachers (like all preachers) they will hear a hoarse, groaning, genuine sound of *self-contempt.* (BGE 222)

In order to amass and consolidate political power, the Christian priests must not only exacerbate the self-contempt of the sick and infirm, but also introduce this noxious weed into the redolent gardens of the healthy and noble.

Nietzsche thus discerns a distinctly secular method to the pathological madness of the priests. They preach the practice of pity not primarily to prepare their charges for the afterlife, but to preserve the base of their political power over the sick and infirm (AC 55). These necromancers of the soul transform the suffering of the sick into the realization of their own political designs. Having originally authorized themselves as enemies of sin, they must continually replenish the surplus suffering that they alone can assuage. That this strategy is ultimately self-defeating, that priestly mischief systematically destroys those souls who constitute its limited authority, is simply irrelevant. To paraphrase Nietzsche once again: No one chooses to be a priest; one must be sick enough for it.

Nietzsche hopes to contain the spread of pity by discrediting the authority of its carrier, the priest. In the calamitous transitional period that he envisions for the twentieth and twenty-first centuries, those who cannot endure the meaninglessness of their suffering will no doubt return to the priests for an analgesic dose of guilt. As the priests' authority declines, however, this supplicatory gambit will prove ever less satisfying; the need to exhilarate the will with "artificial" stimulants is inversely related to the power of the priests to provide them. In lieu of any effective treatment for their indebtedness, sufferers may eventually yield to the "suicidal nihilism" from which the moral interpretation of suffering originally saved humankind.

Nietzsche would urge his friends and successors to show these sufferers no pity, but such a requirement may prove to be more demanding than he realized. While he condemns the priests for pitying the weak and infirm, for falsely inflating the hopes of those who should be free to hope no more, he also identifies "great pity for man" as one of the "two worst contagions that may be reserved just for [him and his friends]" (GM III:14). Even Zarathustra, whose refusal of pity constitutes his "real proof of strength" (EH:wise 4), almost succumbs to his pity for the higher men (Z IV:20).[45] Indeed, Nietzsche himself is considerably more vulnerable to pity – especially self-pity – than his heroic self-presentations allow. His weakness for pity reminds us, in fact, that he too must be neutralized if the spread of decay is to be contained.

Nietzsche contra Paul

Nietzsche may skirmish with the Christian priests as a class, but he reserves his heavy artillery for an attack, *mano a mano,* on their founder and political leader. Nietzsche's goal in *The Antichrist(ian)* is no less than to reverse the *original* revaluation of values, which he attributes to St. Paul.[46] Turning the tables on his predecessor, he attempts to reproduce the precise strategy that Paul deployed to unseat the carnal naturalism of the Roman Empire.

In his post-Zarathustran writings, Nietzsche reviles no historical figure more savagely than St. Paul. His references to the saint are not only uniformly disparaging, but also express a complicated anti-Semitism.[47] He describes Paul as the "persecutor of God" (H II 2:85); as a lowly "rug weaver" (GM I:16); as possessing "an evil eye for the passions" (GS 139); as "the Jewish Pascal," a "very unpleasant man who also found himself unpleasant" (D 69); as "the chandala hatred against Rome . . . become flesh, become genius" (AC 58); as "the greatest of all apostles of vengeance" (AC 45); as the "dysangelist" who "nailed [the Redeemer] to his own cross" (AC 42); as the brazen falsifier of Hebrew scripture and tradition (AC 42); and as "the eternal Wandering Jew *par excellence*" (AC 58). Indeed, if we accept Nietzsche's account of Essay I of the *Genealogy* as a chronicle of "the birth of Christianity out of the spirit of *ressentiment*" (EH:gm), then we may confidently finger Paul as the historical model for the villainous ascetic priest.

Nietzsche's enmity for Paul is matched only by his sympathetic identification with the saint.[48] While he eventually manages to reduce his other imagined rivals, including Socrates, to harmless emanations of the epochs they represent, Paul consistently confounds the Procrustean categories of Nietzschean symptomatology.[49] Despite the totalizing scope of his withering critique of individual agency, Nietzsche persists in treating his saintly rival as an *agent*, as commanding sufficient "directing force" to alter the historical disposition of the will to power.[50] Indeed, as decadence consumes the remaining vestiges of Western civilization, all of its representative heroes and villains, save two, recede into the advancing penumbra: either Paul or Nietzsche will render the final legacy and testament of modernity. The "victor" in this millennial contest will determine the future of humankind by influencing the founding of the successor epoch to modernity.

Nietzsche figures Paul as the apotheosis of priestly mischief – that is, as the consummate traitor. Whereas the betrayals of Christ by Judas and Peter partake of the relatively benign logic of denial or contradiction, Paul's betrayal of Christ is far more complex and effective. Judas and Peter may have acted rashly as anti-Christians, but Paul's betrayal identifies him as the Antichrist.[51] His genius lay not simply in falsifying the early history of Christianity, but also in reinventing the history of Israel "so that it might appear as the prehistory of *his* deed" (AC 42). Paul's political revision of early Christian history thus turns on an outright betrayal of his own Jewish heritage, and especially of the Jewish Law.

This attack on the privilege of the priestly class, Nietzsche insists, is not a departure from the hieratic tradition of Israel, but its logical culmination; to secure power through betrayal is the essence of priestly mischief. Paul furthermore embodies the full range of priestly mendaciousness, for in setting himself up as an anti-priest, he effectively exempts himself from his own attack on priestly privilege. Drawing on his prodigious understanding of human psychology, Paul launched an ingenious, two-pronged campaign of treason: His religious opposition to the sanctity of the Jewish Law secured for him sufficient political latitude – as an outsider inside – to implement his secular opposition to the law of the Roman Empire. Nietzsche thus presents the "original" revaluation of values as a grand, unprecedented act of betrayal expertly perpetrated by St. Paul.[52]

Paul's priestly revenge on the priests of Israel serves as an instructive model for Nietzsche's own revaluation of values. He explicitly attributes his own excessive "wisdom," as well as the possibility of his revalution, to his mastery of the art of reversing perspectives (EH:wise 1). Destined to occupy the standpoints of both health and sickness, he now possesses a keen insight into the modus operandi of each type. Obliged to live the reversal that Paul masterminded, he employs his hard-won wisdom in an attempt to overturn the saint's original triumph. Just as Paul betrayed the hieratic tradition of Israel, aggrandizing the fledgling Christ cult at the expense of Judaism as a whole, so Nietzsche sets out to betray his own Christian heritage – including his father and grandfathers, Protestant ministers all.[53] Just as he figures Paul as the *éminence grise* behind the original slave revolt in morality, so he presents himself as the shadowy leader of an incipient counterrevolution, of equal force and opposite polarity.

Nietzsche thus intends to implement a strict logical reversal of the original revaluation, which would (eventually) replace the anti-naturalism of Christian morality with the pagan naturalism it supplanted. It is important to note, however, that the successful execution of this reversal would not return us to the pre-Christian, noble morality that he sketches in the *Genealogy*. His reversal may succeed in legislating only a similacrum of the noble morality; we moderns can only pose as nobles. The renascence of a genuinely noble morality would presumably presuppose a creation of new values, which task lies beyond the scope of Nietzsche's own enfeebled faculties.

In order to reverse the original revaluation, he simply adopts the strategy that proved so successful for his rival. Paul triumphed by harnessing the previously entropic vitality of the early Christian communities:

> What he guessed was how one could use the little sectarian Christian movement apart from Judaism to kindle a "world fire"; how with the symbol of "God on the cross" one could unite all who lay at the bottom . . . Christianity as a formula with which to outbid the subterranean cults of all kinds, those of Osiris, of the Great Mother, of Mithras, for example – *and* to unite them: in this insight lies the genius of Paul. (AC 58)

By transforming this motley assemblage of sufferers, outcasts, and rebels into exemplary sinners, Paul molded the early Christians into a political unit and secured for himself power over them.

Enacting the mirror image of Paul's original slave revolt, Nietzsche vows to found communities of anti-Christians and to nurture this fledgling movement until a macro-political lawgiver – the antipode of Constantine? – emerges to provide institutional support. Just as Paul steered the burgeoning Christ cult into political opposition to Rome, so Nietzsche hopes to galvanize into political units the anti-Christian micro-communities scattered throughout Europe and North America. As evidence of his growing political influence, he proudly recounts the "wondrous and mysterious respect" he enjoys among "radical parties."[54] Like Paul, he will exploit this growing influence to gain support for his attack on the Christian priesthood.[55] He thus envisions his nascent rebellion as the historical counterpart to the Christian "slave revolt," which was fueled by the anti-affective epistles of St. Paul.[56] Simultaneously expressing both distance and kinship, he announces himself as a "bringer of glad tidings like no one before [him]" (EH:destiny 1).

In place of the fictitious dysangelic Christ, around whom Paul reconstructed the early history of Christianity, Nietzsche offers his own fictional hero, Zarathustra, who supposedly preaches the "good news."[57] Just as Paul exploited the otherwise insignificant death of Christ – shamelessly transforming him into the Crucified – so Nietzsche orchestrates the *Untergang* of Zarathustra to awaken a similar pathos in his own readers. His decision to package *Zarathustra* as a Bible of sorts – complete with Lutheresque flourishes, epistolary bombast, and fake scriptural motifs – is parodic, to be sure, but also strategic.[58] The book is to serve as a *vade mecum* for the anti-Christian communities of the next millennium. He even speculated that a few university chairs currently reserved for Biblical scholars might one day be "set aside for the interpretation of *Zarathustra*" (EH:gb 1).

Historical Conditions of the Revaluation

Nietzsche's decision to challenge St. Paul as the high priest of the ascetic ideal is attributable to his wishful belief that they occupy similar stages in the development – and degeneration – of their respective ages. Western Christianity, he believes, evinces a degree of decay similar to that of the Roman Empire at the time of St. Paul. Nietzsche consequently appraises his historical opportunities as comparable to those of his rival, and he hopes to convince his readers (and perhaps himself) that the decay of Western Christianity has already begun.

Like some other proponents of a cyclical view of history, Nietzsche not only assigns great importance to the *fin de siècle,* but also attaches an apocalyptic significance to the turning of the millennium as the point at which the cycle of history will naturally renew itself. "The time for petty politics is over," he writes in 1886; "the very next century will bring the fight for the dominion of the earth – the *compulsion* to large scale politics" (BGE 208). While Nietzsche nowhere explicitly identifies the turning of the millennium as the likely caesura separating modernity from its successor epoch, a good deal of indirect evidence points to his fascination with it. When addressing the fate of his own writings, for example, he often speculates that a worthy audience might arrive shortly after the year 2000.[59] In perhaps his most explicit allusion to the generative and restorative powers of the coming millennium, he writes in 1888:

> Let us look ahead a century; let us suppose that my attempt to assassinate two millennia of antinature and desecration of man were to succeed. That new party of life which would tackle the greatest of all tasks, the attempt to raise humankind higher, including the relentless destruction of everything that was degenerating and parasitical, would again make possible that excess of life on earth from which the Dionysian state, too, would have to awaken again. I promise a tragic age. (EH:bt 4)

As his fascination with the turning of the millennium suggests, Nietzsche believes that his historical situation affords him a comparative advantage similar to that granted to Paul in the first century A.D. by the incipient decline of the Roman Empire.[60] He derives this historical insight from his symptomatological analysis, by means of which he supposedly corrects for the confusion of cause and effect that plagues other scholars. Critics understandably object that he exploits the clarity of hindsight to trace the eventual fall of Rome to the emergence of the fledgling Christ cult. To anyone but a Nietzschean symptomatologist, the Roman Empire of A.D. 1 and the Christian cultures of nineteenth-century Western Europe would most likely appear hale and healthy. Although the actual fall of Rome did not occur for several centuries, he nevertheless detects in the decision to tolerate the emergence of these struggling Christian communities an irrefragable symptom of imperial decline. He is willing to admit that the eventual collapse of Christianity may be as far removed from him as was the fall of Rome from Paul, but in both cases, he believes, the signs of incipient decay are unmistakable.

This sort of symptomatological analysis is absolutely crucial to Nietzsche's project of revaluation, for it serves as the basis for his claim that his own modest influence signifies the decay of Christianity. Throughout 1888, he frequently remarks upon his growing influence throughout Europe (with the exception of Germany) and North America. He reports, for example, "I have readers – nothing but first-rate intellects and proven characters, trained in high positions and duties; I even have real geniuses among my readers. In Vienna, in St. Petersburg, in Stockholm, in Copenhagen, in Paris, in New York" (EH:gb 2). He later repeats this list of cities and identifies his readers as "psychologists" (NCW P). Just as the presence of nascent Christian communities in the first century A.D. signified the incipient decline of the Roman Empire, so the growing influence of Nietzsche as an opponent to Christianity signifies a similar degree of decay within the "Christian Empire" of Western Europe. That the erratic, sectarian cult of Christ was permitted to splinter off from the Jews, who themselves were uneasily tolerated by imperial officials, was a sign that the Empire had already begun to decline – *pace* Gibbon, who confuses cause and effect:

> The great Yes to all things became visible in the *imperium Romanum* . . . And not buried overnight by a natural catastrophe, not trampled down by Teutons and other buffaloes, but ruined by cunning, stealthy, invisible, anemic vampires. Not vanquished – merely drained. (AC 59)

That Nietzsche is able to launch his attack on the Christian institutions of Western culture similarly indicates that Christianity now verges on collapse. Hence the historical significance that he attaches to his revaluation of all values: A "healthy" Christianity would not tolerate his guerilla attacks on its authority. The very appearance of *The Antichrist(ian)* would therefore confirm the truth of its central historical thesis, for the Christian priests would prove themselves unable any longer to distinguish between benefactor and malefactor, friend and foe, mild nuisance and mortal enemy. This symptomatological evidence thus portends for Western Christianity a fate similar to that which befell the Roman Empire. Just as the mighty Empire precipitated its demise at the hands of the early Christians, so the decaying Christian Empire of late modernity will contribute to its own demise at the hands of Nietzsche and his underground communities of anti-Christians. Christian morality not only has produced its other, but also has supplied the weapons that will someday consign it to the museums and history books.

We should not be surprised, then, that Nietzsche "fails" to distinguish himself from the Pauline priests whom he attacks.[61] The similarities between these two rivals, at least as reconstructed by Nietzsche, are indeed striking. He portrays Paul as a kindred active nihilist, possessed of and emboldened by an untimely insight into the incipient decay of the Roman Empire. Only an active nihilist could renounce so decisively the tradition that produced him, as Paul betrays the hieratic tradition of Israel and Nietzsche the Christian priesthood. Only an active nihilist, furthermore, could capitalize on the decadence of an age or people by drawing upon an untapped reservoir of expendable affect. Just as Paul managed to galvanize a defiant sect of heterodox Christians into a political unit, so Nietzsche plans to dispatch nomadic anti-Christians throughout Europe and North America. In fact, the original revaluation that Nietzsche aims to reverse is not so much the historical, political rebellion of Christians against Jews and Romans, but the self-transformation of Saul, the "zealot" of the Law, into Paul, the "destroyer" of the Law (D 68).[62]

As we shall see more clearly in the next chapter, however, Nietzsche's resemblance to St. Paul is not entirely attributable to the strategy of reversal that informs his project of revaluation. Nietzsche is far more closely related to his nemesis than he realizes. Their unacknowledged kinship is furthermore responsible for the mitigated success of his revaluation. Only as an unwitting avatar of St. Paul does he command the influence he needs in order to contribute to the production of the Antichrist.

Temples Razed and Raised

While Nietzsche's expertise in demolition is rarely challenged, his constructive accomplishments are just as rarely applauded.[63] For this reason, perhaps, his readers rarely share his enthusiasm for the momentous "explosion" he claims to touch off. He regularly insists, however, on the logical relation that binds destruction and creation: "If a temple is to be erected *a temple must be destroyed*: that is the law – let anyone who can show me a case in which it is not fulfilled!" (GM II:24).

He consequently presents the creative and destructive components of his revaluation as inextricably linked by the logic of determinate negation: "Negating and destroying are conditions of saying Yes" (EH:destiny 4). As "the annihilator par excellence," he also obeys his "Dionysian nature, which does not know how to separate doing No from saying Yes" (EH:destiny 2). He furthermore explains that his specific task, "the greatest of all tasks, the attempt to raise humanity higher, include[es] the relentless destruction of everything that [is] degenerating and parasitical" (EH:bt 4). Although he undeniably aims to raze the temple of Christianity, he also hopes simultaneously to lay the foundation for the temple of an anti-Christian successor.

Nietzsche's revaluation of all values thus comprises no constructive element that stands independent of its more obvious destructive moment. From within the subversive attack on the Christian priesthood will arise a fellowship of anti-Christians, bound by their common, "hygienic" aversion to the pathogenesis of Christian pity:

> And therefore let us have good company, *our* company! Or solitude, if it must be! But away from the sickening fumes of inner corruption and the hidden rot of disease! . . . So that we may, at least for a while yet, guard ourselves, my friends, against the two worst contagions that may be reserved just for us – against the *great nausea at man*! against *great pity for man*! (GM III:14)

Owing to his reliance on these unknown "friends" to relay his teachings to the audiences of a distant posterity, he is careful to articulate his project of revaluation in terms of the founding of a community:

> The No-saying, *No-doing* part [of my task] . . . included the slow search for those related to me, those who, prompted by strength, would offer me their hands for *destroying*. From this moment forward all my writings are fish hooks: perhaps I know how to fish as well as anyone? (EH:bge 1)

Nietzsche's reference to his books as "fish hooks" – he does not say "bait" – suggests the dual nature of those companions for whom he angles. Because they are "related to Nietzsche," their temptation would be piqued rather than allayed by the fiendishly barbed fish hooks he dangles before them.[64] "Prompted by strength," these unknown friends could afford to squander themselves in the "great war" that he wages against Christianity. His revaluation of all values simultaneously demolishes the tottering institutions of Western Christianity and founds communities of anti-Christian resistance. His "children," those readers who are called to arms by his declaration of war, will appropriate for their own anti-Christian ends the ascetic practices and disciplines developed under the aegis of Christianity.

This constructive element of Nietzsche's revaluation thus sheds light on both the polemical nature and the intended audience of his post-Zarathustran writings. He pens *The Antichrist(ian)* neither to rally the sick and infirm to health, nor to whip aspiring *Übermenschen* into a Dionysian lather – all such schemes presuppose a strength of will that late modernity simply lacks – but to announce himself to those in whom the will is similarly resilient: "Such men alone are my readers, my right readers, my predestined readers: what matter the *rest?* The rest – that is merely humankind" (AC P). *The Antichrist(ian)* thus illuminates the presence of a burgeoning opposition to the dynastic reign of Christendom, and it serves as a rallying call for all those who can afford to join Nietzsche in venting their enmity for the anti-naturalism of Christian morality.

In and of itself, Nietzsche's embodied declaration of war on Christian morality may not amount to a world-historical achievement. But if his "explosion" is reproduced by generations of readers, such that even Nietzsche himself is eventually overcome, then the successor epoch to modernity may successfully install an alternative, anti-Christian disposition of the ascetic ideal. His grandiose self-presentation in *The Antichrist(ian)* is therefore misleading only if we equate it with the immediate revolution or discontinuity that he and Zarathustra have led us to expect. Regardless of what he might have once hoped to accomplish, the post-Zarathustran Nietzsche is committed to clearing the rubble of modernity in order to accommodate the coming founders of a new tragic age (EH:bt 4).

Nietzsche is well aware not only of the enormity of the counterrevolution he inaugurates, but also of the fragility of the communities he founds. The next two centuries, he believes, would be critical for the success of his rebellion, and he prophesies that those centuries would witness an era of "great politics" that begins with him (EH:destiny 1). This interregnum, he hopes, will prove to be as unstable and tumultuous as the period of incipient decay that beset the Roman Empire in the first century A.D. Indeed, the micro-rebellion he foments against Western Christianity has no greater prospects for success than did Paul's surreptitious apostasy from Rome nearly 2000 years ago. His attempt to found communities of resistance within the twilight of the idols is therefore properly viewed as a desperate gamble, as a true squandering of his remaining volitional resources.

The Law of Life and the Logic of Revaluation

As Nietzsche completed his period of "convalescence" from the romantic pessimism he contracted from Wagner, he received an unexpected gift. His ownmost *task*, in the face of which he earlier had wilted and almost died, was unexpectedly returned to him for safekeeping and execution (H II P5). Owing to his improbable recuperative powers (or so he claims both in the retrospective prefaces of 1886 and in *Ecce Homo*), his destiny was reinscribed with the task of orchestrating the demise of Christian morality. His pursuit of this task not only sets the political agenda for the post-Zarathustran period of his career, but also consumes him in the end.

Although Nietzsche has long opposed the formative power and sustaining institutions of Christian morality, he now understands that his destiny demands nothing less from him than "the self-overcoming of morality" (D P4). The self-reflexive inflection of his restored task obliges him to abandon the detached, external critical perspective he has preferred heretofore in order that he might attack Christian morality from within – an attack that must frame Nietzsche himself within its sights. As befits his renascent health, that is, his task is restored to him, but in the difficult, altered aspect of an *immanent* critique of Christian morality.

The self-reflexive compass of this task is no accident. Nothing less than *the law of Life* demands that he abandon the comfortable detachment of his external critique of Christianity and take up an immanent critical standpoint:

> All great things bring about their own destruction through an act of self-overcoming [*Selbstaufhebung*]. . . . In this way Christianity *as a dogma* was destroyed by its own morality; in the same way Christianity *as morality* must now perish, too: we stand on the threshold of *this* event. After Christian truthful-

ness has drawn one inference after another, it must end by drawing its *most striking inference*, its inference *against* itself; this will happen, however, when it poses the question "*what is the meaning of all will to truth?*" (GM III:27)[65]

This passage conveys both the historical warrant for Nietzsche's revaluation and the logic of which it partakes. His restored task fully conforms to the law of Life, which he must now dare to execute and enforce. *He* must instigate a final, self-referential examination on the part of Christian morality. Once it has confronted the untruthful preconditions of its guiding will to truth, Christian morality must necessarily capitulate to its other – whatever that might turn out to be.

Nietzsche thus intends his revaluation of all values to supply the impetus needed to complete the internal logic of Christian morality. By demanding of him an immanent critique of Christianity, however, the law of Life greatly complicates his project of revaluation. Indeed, the full truth of Christian morality lies not in the abstract propositions and formulae essayed by *The Antichrist(ian)*, but in the immanent, embodied practices of living Christians. In order to execute the law of Life, Nietzsche must confront Christian morality not only with a definitive account of itself, but also with its representative exemplars, whose miserable lives corroborate the charges he levels against it. In short, he must essay his critique of Christian morality in "letters" that "even the blind can see" (AC 62).

The self-overcoming of Christian morality is consequently enacted neither in a teaching nor in a syllogism, but in a *living human being*, in whom the signature contradictions of Christian morality have become incarnate. Such a human being would assume the monstrous aspect of a mutant or hybrid, thereby introducing an ambiguous – and ultimately unstable – *tertium quid* into the dialectical logic that governs the law of Life. Such a human being, in fact, would restlessly inhabit the node of historical transformation reserved exclusively for the Antichrist. When forced to confront itself embodied in such a creature, Christian morality must summarily disown its "noble" lineage and repudiate its signature practices. Having involuntarily birthed this horrible changeling, Christian morality must either perish of its own imperatives or overcome itself in the spontaneous enactment of a novel configuration of human agency.[66] As we shall see in the next chapter, however, Nietzsche's precise role in the execution of the law of Life remains unclear. Indeed, his grandiose desire to stand as the Antichrist (rather than, say, as an influential anti-Christian of late modernity) may actually be realized, albeit in ways he never imagined.

According to Nietzsche, the immanent critique he undertakes is unprecedented in the entropic history of Western civilization. On several occasions the law of Life has wrought sickness from health, but it has never before produced the ascendant "other" of decadence. As an example of the magnitude of the logical transformation he hopes to induce, he points to its closest historical parallel, the Italian Renaissance:

> Does one understand at last, does one *want* to understand, what the Renaissance was? *The revaluation of Christian values*, the attempt, undertaken with every means, with every instinct, with all genius, to bring the *counter*-values, the *noble* values, to victory . . . Attacking in the decisive place, in the very seat of Christianity, placing the *noble* values on the throne *here*, I mean, bringing them right into the instincts, into the lower needs and desires of those who sat there! (AC 61)

The overflowing naturalism of the Renaissance renewed the parched landscape of Western European culture, and it nearly succeeded in drowning the anti-affective practices upon which the Christian priesthood had staked its claim to a supernatural authority. Had Luther not rudely intervened to postpone the transaction of the law of Life, this predecessor revaluation might have culminated in the papacy of Cesare Borgia.[67]

The figure of the bawdy Cesare Borgia perched atop the Petrine throne suggests an outright capitulation of Christianity to the naturalism that Nietzsche associates with the Renaissance. Such a carnivalesque papacy would surely have discredited the peculiar supernatural authority of the Christian priests, as the brute carnality of priestly mischief – and of the Pope himself – would be revealed for all to see.[68] The papacy of Cesare Borgia would have precipitated nothing short of a revaluation of the anti-affective values of Christian morality. Having invested its highest authority, the Petrine legacy, in a frightful monstrosity, Christianity would have produced its other, in the person of Pope Cesare Borgia. This papacy would have announced the self-overcoming of Christian morality, for Cesare Borgia would have appropriated the influence and infrastructure of Western Christianity for his own lusty celebration of pagan naturalism. "With that," Nietzsche opines, "Christianity would have been *abolished*" (AC 61).[69]

This fanciful image of a genuinely Babylonian captivity conveys a sense of Nietzsche's aims in *The Antichrist(ian)*. It is his task to introduce Christianity to the Antichrist, a living human being who, like Cesare Borgia, embodies the constitutive tensions and contradictions of Christian morality. Like Cesare Borgia, Nietzsche's Antichrist will assume a monstrous aspect, simultaneously fulfilling and betraying the promise of Christian morality. His body wracked with the surplus suffering of guilt, his instincts scrambled beyond repair, his soul scarred by the invasive disciplines of Christian morality, his life irrevocably estranged from the passion and vitality that might otherwise sustain him, such a person would stand as an embodied sign of the *absurdum practicum* legislated by Christian morality. This grisly portrait, Nietzsche gambles, would be virtually impossible for the philosophers of the future to ignore, and he is eager to affix his signature to it.

When confronted with the monstrosity it has produced as its apotheosis, Christian morality must necessarily overcome itself and capitulate to its other. In order to distance itself from this changeling, Christian morality must undertake a self-transformation so radical that it no longer bears a family resemblance to its monstrous offspring. Just as the papacy of Cesare Borgia would have abolished Christianity, so will the emergence of Nietzsche's Antichrist precipitate the self-overcoming of Christian morality. Indeed, if the emergence of the Antichrist can persuade Christian morality to draw "its *most striking inference*, its inference *against* itself" (GM III:27), then Nietzsche's revaluation will discredit the supernatural authority of the priests as surely as would the papacy of Cesare Borgia.

Cesare Borgia is also important to Nietzsche for what he fails to accomplish. When citing examples of what he means by the *Übermensch,* he often summons Cesare Borgia, but always with important qualifications (EH:gb 1). Had he actually occupied the node of historical transformation that Nietzsche figuratively locates in the papacy, Cesare Borgia would have accomplished the self-overcoming of Christian morality. In consecrating the unholy marriage of Christian asceticism and pagan naturalism, he would have legislated an unprecedented configuration of human agency. Had he gained the Petrine throne, that is, Cesare Borgia would have been an *Übermensch.*

The Antichrist ostensibly will succeed where Cesare Borgia failed, appropriating Christian morality for the founding of the postmodern, tragic epoch. Nietzsche's task, the self-overcoming of morality, thus involves nothing short of the production of an *Übermensch,* a monstrosity that forcibly and permanently deranges the contours of the human soul.[70] Following in the wake of the Antichrist, human beings will finally stand security for their own future, reaping the fruits of autonomy and self-determination from the seeds sown by the priests in the fertile soil of Christian guilt (GM II:2). Duly apprised by the Antichrist of the plasticity of the human soul and the erotogenic power of suffering, the philosophers of the future will incorporate various Christian insights and techniques into their reconstitution of a tragic culture.

The emergence of the Antichrist would thus complete Nietzsche's ambitious critique of modernity, furnishing incarnate confirmation of the crisis to which his diagnosis theoretically points. His contribution to the production of the Antichrist would furthermore unify the disparate themes of his post-Zarathustran philosophy, finally healing the wound inflicted in 1886 by his self-referential turning. It is little wonder, then, that Nietzsche believed himself – albeit with some trepidation – to be "at the end" with the completion of *The Antichrist(ian)* (AC 62). All that remained was for him to make public his statement of revaluation and then to cede his anti-Christian authority to his patient successors. His declaration of war would eventually result, or so he hoped, in the terrible reign of the Antichrist, who would in turn enact the transition from modernity to its successor epoch.

Notes

1   Richard Rorty offers the following sketch of what he calls "his Nietzsche": "'Aw shucks,' one imagines this Nietzsche saying, 'us folks out here beyond good and evil aren't going to make war on anybody; we're too busy actively forgetting, becoming who we are, and all like that. If you're worried about cruelty, it's those busy-body ressenters who you have to watch out for'" ("On Bloom's Nietzsche," *Nietzscheana*, No. 1, May 1989, p. 15).

2   Masterfully dispensing faint praise and muted admiration, Walter Kaufmann recommends *The Antichrist(ian)* as a product of Nietzsche's decline: "Stylistically, the work is, like most of Nietzsche's books, very uneven. The often clipped cadences offer a refreshing contrast to *Zarathustra;* but frequently the rhetoric gets out of hand. Nietzsche is at his best when he manages to restrain himself" [*The Portable Nietzsche* (New York: Viking Penguin, 1982), pp. 567–568].

3   Notable exceptions to this practice of marginalizing *The Antichrist(ian)* include Gary Shapiro, *Nietzschean Narratives* (Bloomington: Indiana University Press, 1989), chapters 5–6; Jörg Salaquarda, "Dionysos gegen den Gekreuzigten: Nietzsches Verständnis des Apostels Paulus," in *Nietzsche,* ed. J. Salaquarda (Darmstadt: Wissenschaftliche Buchgesellschaft, 1980), pp. 288–322; and Weaver Santaniello, *Nietzsche, God, and the Jews: His Critique of Judeo-Christianity in Relation to the Nazi Myth* (Albany: State University of New York Press, 1994), chapter 6.

4   *Friedrich Nietzsche: Sämtliche Briefe, Kritische Studienausgabe in 8 Bänden,* ed. G. Colli and M. Montinari (Berlin: deGruyter/Deutscher Taschenbuch Verlag, 1986), Vol. 8, No. 1126, p. 447.

5   Draft (*Entwurf*) of a letter to Brandes at the beginning of December 1888 (*Sämtliche Briefe,* Vol. 8, No. 1170, pp. 501–502).

6   In a letter to Brandes on 20 November 1888, Nietzsche describes *Ecce Homo* "as the prelude [*Vorspiel*] to the *Revaluation of All Values,* of the work that lies finished before me [namely, *The Antichrist(ian)*]." He also describes the aim of *Ecce Homo* as continuous with (if not identical to) the aim of *The Antichrist(ian):* "The book is called *Ecce Homo,* and it is an unrelenting attack on the Crucified; it ends with thunder and lightning bolts against everything that is Christian or infected by Christianity" (*Sämtliche Briefe,* Vol. 8, No. 1151, p. 482). Finally, in a letter to Köselitz on 9 December 1888, he ascribes to *Ecce Homo* an explosive capacity similar to that of *The Antichrist(ian),* insisting that *Ecce Homo* too "breaks, literally, the history of humankind into two pieces – the highest superlative of dynamite" (*Sämtliche Briefe,* Vol. 8, No. 1181, p. 513).

7   Shapiro's suggestion that *Ecce Homo* "tell[s] us precisely about that unusual moment [from which time is now to be reckoned]" (*Nietzschean Narratives*, p. 147) is perhaps more helpful in understanding the role of the interleaf epigraph to *Ecce Homo* than of the book in its entirety.

8   On Nietzsche's use and abuse of *Ecce Homo,* see Sarah Kofman, *Explosion I: De l' 'Ecce Homo' de Nietzsche* (Paris: Éditions Galilée, 1992).

9 In his preface to *Twilight of the Idols,* Nietzsche dates his signature with the following inscription: "Turin, September 30, 1888, on the day when the first book of the *Revaluation of All Values* was completed" (TI P). In a letter to Overbeck on 18 October 1888, he describes the first book of the *Revaluation* as "ready for press [*druckfertig*]" (*Sämtliche Briefe,* Vol. 8, No. 1132, p. 453).

10 In a draft of a letter to Brandes at the beginning of December 1888, Nietzsche confides, "In three months I will give instructions for the production of a manuscript-edition of [*The Antichrist(ian). Revaluation of All Values*], which remains completely secret" (*Sämtliche Briefe,* Vol. 8, No. 1170, p. 500).

11 In a letter to Overbeck on 18 October 1888, Nietzsche says of *The Revaluation of All Values,* "There will be four books; they will appear individually [*einzeln*]" (*Sämtliche Briefe,* Vol. 8, No. 1132, p. 453).

12 In his letter to Köselitz on 30 October 1888, Nietzsche accounts for the "audacity" of *Ecce Homo:* "Not only did I want to present myself *before* the entirely uncanny solitary act of revaluation, – I would also like to test what risks I can take with the German ideas of freedom of speech. My suspicion is that the first book of the revaluation will be confiscated on the spot – legally and in all justice." The appearance of *Ecce Homo,* he hopes, will "make the question [of revaluation] so intensely serious, and such an object of curiosity" that the cognizant authorities might be discouraged from confiscating *The Antichrist(ian)* (*Sämtliche Briefe,* Vol. 8, No. 1137, p. 462).

13 In order to galvanize public sentiment in his favor, Nietzsche informs *Ecce Homo* with an array of psychological snares. In his letter to Köselitz on 30 October 1888, he intimates, "To be sure, I talk about myself with all possible psychological 'cunning' and cheerfulness [*Heiterkeit*] – I do not want to present myself to people as a prophet, savage beast, or moral monster. In this sense, too, the book could be salutary: it will perhaps prevent people from confusing me with my *opposite*" (*Sämtliche Briefe,* Vol. 8, No. 1137, p. 462).

14 Derrida helpfully reminds us that the Apollinian closure and univocity of *Ecce Homo* are incongruous with Nietzsche's general insight into the multiplicity of the self: "But who has ever said that a person bears a single name? Certainly not Nietzsche. And likewise, who has said or decided that there is something like a Western metaphysics, something which would be capable of being gathered up under this name and this name only? What is it – the oneness of a name, the assembled unity of Western metaphysics? Is it anything more or less than the desire (a word effaced in Heidegger's Nietzsche citation) for a proper name, for a single, unique name and a thinkable genealogy? Next to Kierkegaard, was not Nietzsche one of the few great thinkers who multiplied his names and played with signatures, identities, and masks? Who named himself more than once, with several names? And what if that would be the heart of the matter, the *causa,* the *Streitfall* of his thinking?" [Jacques Derrida, "Interpreting Signatures (Nietzsche/Heidegger): Two Questions," trans. Diane P. Michelfelder and Richard E. Palmer, in *Dialogue and Deconstruction: The Gadamer–Derrida Encounter,* ed. Diane P. Michelfelder and Richard E. Palmer (Albany: State University of New York Press, 1989), p. 67]. Having raised the question of self-reference, however, Derrida promptly backs off, failing to explain why Nietzsche does in fact present himself in *Ecce Homo* under a single name.

15 For a compelling interpretation of *Ecce Homo* as both a preface to Nietzsche's entire corpus and as an epilogue, see Michael Platt, "Behold Nietzsche," in *Nietzsche-Studien*, Vol. 22, 1993, pp. 42–79.

16 While explaining why he is a "destiny," Nietzsche is suspiciously quick to dispel the idea that he is fishing for disciples: "I have a terrible fear that one day I will be pronounced *holy:* you will guess why I publish this book *before;* it shall prevent people from doing mischief with me" (EH:destiny 1). Nietzsche surely means "before" publishing *The Antichrist(ian)*, but we will never know if his elaborate scheme would have prevented the mischief he foresees.

17 Laurence Lampert triumphantly confirms Nietzsche's Hyperborean status, in *Nietzsche and Modern Times* (New Haven, CT: Yale University Press, 1993), especially chapters 12–13. Lampert finds in Nietzsche's naturalism (or "immanentism") the foundation for a philosophy and ethics suited to the peculiar exigencies of "modern times." As I explain later in more detail, I fully share Lampert's enthusiasm for the immanentism he describes, but I do not agree that Nietzsche actually promulgates this precise teaching. Lampert's interpretation lends no credence to Nietzsche's own besetting decadence, which I believe compromises and corrupts his signature teachings.

18 My appeal to this distinction is indebted to conversations with Thomas Brobjer and to his unpublished manuscript *Nietzsche's Ethics of Character.*

19 Robert Solomon takes up this issue in his important essay "A More Severe Morality: Nietzsche's Affirmative Ethics," *Journal of the British Society for Phenomenology*, Vol. 16, No. 3, October 1985, pp. 250–267. Solomon persuasively argues that Nietzsche's rhetoric of creation misstates his own affirmative orientation to ethics. As Solomon astutely notes, Nietzsche's philosophy does not produce a single new value (p. 265), but it does essay a "new" defense of character in an age that has seemingly forgotten virtue (p. 266).

20 Martin Heidegger insists that a genuine revaluation of values must not merely replace "decadent" values with "healthy" ones, but also eliminate the very place of value itself, such that Being is no longer degraded to the status of a value, determined by the (irreducibly subjectivistic) will to power ["The Word of Nietzsche: 'God is Dead,'" collected in *The Question Concerning Technology and Other Essays*, trans. William Lovitt (New York: Harper Torchbooks, 1977), pp. 53–112]. Because Nietzsche never successfully eliminated the residual subjectivism of his thought, Heidegger concludes, "Despite all his overturnings and revaluings of metaphysics, Nietzsche remains in the unbroken line of the metaphysical tradition when he calls that which is established and made fast in the will to power for its own preservation purely and simply Being, or what is in being, or truth" (p. 84). Heidegger is certainly right about Nietzsche's failure to free himself from the thrall of metaphysics, but he does not acknowledge Nietzsche's own prior claim to this insight.

21 Bruce Detwiler, for example, speaks of "the coming revaluation of all values," apparently equating the event with the inauguration of the "new order," in *Nietzsche and the Politics of Aristocratic Radicalism* (Chicago: University of Chicago Press, 1990), p. 134. By relegating Nietzsche to a preparatory role in the installation of an "aristocratic radicalism," however, Detwiler fails to account not only for the urgency of Nietzsche's revaluation of all values, but also for Nietz-

sche's own political activity. By locating Nietzsche's politics in his theoretical contribution to the future reign of an aristocracy of artist-philosophers, Detwiler effectively divorces Nietzsche's politics both from his revaluation of all values and from his declaration of war on Christianity.

22   This confusion is certainly understandable, for Nietzsche often describes his revaluation as if it had brought Christianity to an end. For example, he suggests that we now reckon history not from the first day of Christianity – that "*dies nefastus*": "*Why not rather after its last day? After today?* Revaluation of all values!" (AC 62). He also suggests that he may yet live to see the last Christian.

23   *Sämtliche Briefe*, Vol. 8, No. 1132, p. 453.

24   The martial motifs employed in *The Antichrist(ian)* trade persuasively on the popular mythology of the Antichrist as a human tyrant and warlord (on the model of Caligula or Nero), whose slaughter of God's witnesses (in Jerusalem, on some accounts) prompts the retaliatory strike associated with the Second Coming. See W. Bousset's entry in the *Encyclopaedia of Religion and Ethics*, ed. James Hastings, Volume 1 (New York: Scribner's, 1957), p. 579.

25   While Lampert agrees that Nietzsche's "Hyperboreanism" is essentially a promissory note to be paid by his successors (*Nietzsche and Modern Times*, pp. 279–280), he is also optimistic about the prospects for a timely payment of this note.

26   On the "condensation" and "concretization" of Nietzsche's notion of revaluation, see Shapiro, *Nietzschean Narratives*, pp. 142–147.

27   Nietzsche writes, "I am now alone, absurdly alone; and in my unrelenting and underground battle against everything heretofore revered and loved by humankind (– my formula for this is 'revaluation of all values'), I have become, unbeknownst to me, a kind of cave – something hidden, which no one finds, even those who set out in search of it" (*Sämtliche Briefe*, Vol. 8, No. 989, p. 248).

28   In his preface to *Twilight*, which he dated "*September 30, 1888, on the day when the first book of the* Revaluation of All Values *was completed*," Nietzsche continues his martial theme, claiming of *Twilight* that "this little essay is a great declaration of war" (TI P).

29   He attests to the "first example" of his revaluation of all values as his reversal of the hoary dictum that virtue leads to happiness (TI 6:2).

30   In a letter to Strindberg on 8 December 1888, Nietzsche insists that his *Ecce Homo* "occasionally speaks, in all innoᵣⁿce, the language of the rulers of the world" (*Sämtliche Briefe*, Vol. 8, No. 1176, p. 509).

31   Before congratulating Nietzsche on the political resolve expressed in *The Antichrist(ian)*, however, we must note that he planned even then to postpone its publication for up to a year! In a letter written on 13 November 1888, Nietzsche tells Overbeck that "the first book of the *Revaluation* will appear at the end of the next year" (*Sämtliche Briefe*, Vol. 8, No. 1143, p. 470). Several weeks later, in a draft of a letter to Brandes, he claims that "in three months time" he will authorize the publication of *The Antichrist(ian)* (*Sämtliche Briefe*, Vol. 8, No. 1170, p. 500).

32   The pronouncement of this curse illuminates the point at which Michel Foucault breaks most decisively with Nietzsche, as documented in "Politics and Ethics: An Interview," and "Politics, Polemics, and Problematizations: An Interview," collected in *The Foucault Reader*, ed. Paul Rabinow (New York: Pantheon,

1984), pp. 373–390. Although sympathetic perhaps with Nietzsche's objections to Christian morality, Foucault categorically refuses the mantle of the lawgiver. He is simply not interested in formulating alternative ethical systems or techniques of the self, which might in turn serve as sites for the consolidation of power into structures of domination. He consciously limits himself to an investigation of the historical conditions that sustain the array of subject constitutions available to us. In suspending his subversive genealogical practices, Foucault might say, Nietzsche unwittingly contributes to the formation of regimes of power that are even more dangerous than those manifested within Christian morality. On the topic of Foucault's refusal to serve as a lawgiver, see Charles Scott, *The Question of Ethics: Nietzsche, Foucault, Heidegger* (Bloomington: Indiana University Press, 1990), pp. 53–54.

33   Even scholars who are interested in Nietzsche's contributions to politics tend to ignore his attempt to orchestrate the demise of Christianity, choosing to focus instead on themes such as the *Übermensch*, eternal recurrence, the crisis of European nihilism, the will to power, and so on. While undeniably important to an understanding of Nietzsche's thought, such themes are also eminently safe and abstract, for they may be (and often are) treated as philosophical curiosities that bear no direct or obvious consequences for political life as we know it. Bruce Detwiler, for example, concludes his thoughtful study of Nietzsche's politics by assuring the reader that "the total paradox that Nietzsche represents is best understood not by focusing on his underminings but by appreciating the subtle equipoise between the devaluings and the revaluings, the negations and the assertions. . . . For those who can both delight in Nietzsche's philosophical radicalism and experience horror at where it leads him, the encounter with his thought can be a fruitful one indeed" (*Nietzsche and the Politics of Aristocratic Radicalism*, p. 196). Detwiler does not elaborate on the "fruit" he believes that an encounter with Nietzsche's "total paradox" might bear, but his recommendation of aesthetic detachment – whereby one comes to appreciate "the subtle equipoise" of Nietzsche's thought while simultaneously experiencing the "horror" and "delight" it produces – suggests that he values Nietzsche's "aristocratic radicalism" primarily for its nonpolitical ramifications. In order to take seriously Nietzsche's political thinking, that is, Detwiler must first transplant it into a nonpolitical, aesthetic context, in which it becomes both personally provocative *and* politically harmless.

4   He thus describes "the *democratic* movement [as] the heir to the Christian movement" (BGE 202).

5   Nietzsche similarly maintains that Plato, "the most beautiful growth of antiquity," was corrupted by Socrates, who perhaps "deserved his hemlock" (BGE P).

6   Nietzsche's insistence here that "man is an *end*" (rather than a means to a post- or extrahuman end) stands in stubborn opposition to the thesis of Tracy Strong's pathbreaking book *Friedrich Nietzsche and the Politics of Transfiguration* (Berkeley: University of California Press, 1974). According to Strong, Nietzsche calls for a "politics of transfiguration," which would "require a change in the basic stuff of humanity" (p. 260). Nietzsche of course fails to articulate his vision of a politics of transfiguration, as evidenced by his provocative (but philosophically bankrupt) teaching of eternal recurrence (pp. 287–292).

37 Nietzsche's conclusion here is foreshadowed in the first essay of the *Genealogy*, where he defines the priestly type in terms of its constitutive sickness: "There is from the beginning [*von Anfang*] something *unhealthy* in such priestly aristocracies and in the habits ruling in them which turn them away from action and alternate between brooding and emotional explosions, habits which seem to have as their almost invariable consequence that intestinal morbidity and neurasthenia which has afflicted priests at all times" (GM I:6).

38 A confusion over precisely this point similarly leads Bernard Yack to portray Nietzsche as calling for a radical reconstitution of humanity itself in *The Longing for Total Revolution* (Princeton, NJ: Princeton University Press, 1986). While Yack brilliantly documents the confusions that riddle Nietzsche's pre-Zarathustran forays into political philosophy, his characterization is not so accurate in reckoning the political thinking that informs Nietzsche's post-Zarathustran writings. As Yack himself "supposes," he "relies too heavily" on the pre-Zarathustran writings in also attributing this "longing for total revolution" to the post-Zarathustran Nietzsche (p. 313). Indeed, it is precisely Nietzsche's acknowledgment of the decadence conveyed by his "longing for total revolution" that precipitates the turning described in his post-Zarathustran writings.

39 Nietzsche earlier considered the "danger" and "possibility" that humankind as a whole might be degenerating (BGE 203). While he may have changed his mind about this by the time he writes *Ecce Homo*, I believe that he never settled definitively on either hypothesis.

40 If we take seriously Nietzsche's distinction between "pagan" (i.e., life-affirming) and "decadent" (i.e., life-slandering) priests (AC 55), then it seems reasonable to suppose that the elimination of the Christian priesthood would free the successor epoch to ordain a pagan priesthood.

41 Zarathustra attributes a similar argument to "madness" itself: "Eventually madness preached, 'Everything passes away; therefore everything deserves to pass away. And this too is justice, this law of time that it must devour its children.' Thus preached madness" (Z II:20).

42 My distinction between the "existential suffering" of the bad conscience and the "surplus suffering" of guilt draws on Arthur C. Danto's distinction between "extensional suffering and intensional suffering, where the latter consists of an interpretation of the former" ["Some Remarks on *The Genealogy of Morals*," in *Reading Nietzsche*, ed. Robert C. Solomon and Kathleen M. Higgins (New York: Oxford University Press, 1988), p. 21].

43 A remarkably similar passage is found in the writings of Aldo Leopold, an American naturalist who is not usually associated with Nietzschean cruelty: "I have read many definitions of what is a conservationist, and written not a few myself, but I suspect that the best one is written not with a pen, but with an axe. It is a matter of what a man thinks about while chopping, or while deciding what to chop. A conservationist is one who is humbly aware that with each stroke he is writing his signature on the face of the land" [*Sand County Almanac* (New York: Ballantine, 1970), p. 73].

44 Martha C. Nussbaum investigates Nietzsche's aversion to cruelty in her essay "Pity and Mercy: Nietzsche's Stoicism," collected in *Nietzsche, Genealogy, Morality: Essays on Nietzsche' "On the Genealogy of Morals,"* ed. Richard Schacht (Berkeley:

University of California Press, 1994), pp. 139–167. Although Nussbaum ultimately finds fault with Nietzsche's underestimation of the value of pity (p. 160), she nevertheless detects in his objections to pity "a Stoic argument, one that takes its stand against cruelty and in favor of self-command" (p. 149).

45   The cyclical imagery with which Nietzsche concludes *Zarathustra* furthermore suggests that Zarathustra will encounter the "temptation" of pity again and again.

46   In his seminal essay on *The Antichrist(ian)*, "Dionysos gegen den Gekreutzigten," Salaquarda documents Nietzsche's understanding of Paul as the architect of historical Christianity. Tracing the history of Nietzsche's engagement with Paul, Salaquarda demonstrates how Paul gradually became Nietzsche's arch-nemesis, "the Crucified" (pp. 290–295). As a disciple of Dionysus, Nietzsche assumes his fundamental opposition not to Christ, but to Paul.

47   Notwithstanding Nietzsche's sincere admiration for certain periods in the history of the people of Israel, his critique of their hieratic traditions is tinctured with a peculiar shade of anti-Semitism. In some passages, in fact, his account of the historical legacy of the Jews echoes Paul's. Consider, for example, his account of the origin of Christianity out of Judaism. He attributes to the Jews, whom he calls "the strangest people in world history," the "radical *falsification* of all nature, all naturalness, all reality, of the whole inner world as well as the outer" (AC 24).

48   Nietzsche's "kinship" to Paul is noted first and most influentially by Ernst Bertram in *Nietzsche: Versuch einer Mythologie* (Bonn: H. Bouvier Verlag, 1929), pp. 62–71. Yet Bertram is able to propose such a "kinship" only because he cleaves to a romanticized and un-Nietzschean understanding of St. Paul. See also Salaquarda, "Dionysos gegen den Gekreutzigten," pp. 289–90.

49   Alexander Nehamas identifies Socrates as Nietzsche's primary and enduring historical rival, in *Nietzsche: Life as Literature* (Cambridge, MA: Harvard University Press, 1985). Nehamas locates in Nietzsche's relationship to Socrates the "rage of Caliban," insisting that "Nietzsche . . . is always in direct competition with Socrates" (p. 30). While Nietzsche's rivalry with Socrates is undeniably important, Nehamas's thesis requires him virtually to ignore both *The Antichrist(ian)* and the symptomatological reduction of Socrates in *Twilight*. These exclusions are required in part by Nehamas's apolitical, "aestheticist" interpretation of Nietzsche's philosophy.

50   Paul's unaccountably robust agency provides us with another reason for viewing him as Nietzsche's model for the ascetic priest (EH:gm). Despite Nietzsche's insistence that the ascetic priest *invents* the lie of agency to gain political power over invalids and sufferers, he also consistently treats the ascetic priest as an agent, and not merely as a passive conduit of will to power.

51   See Salaquarda, "Dionysos gegen den Gekreutzigten," pp. 304–309.

52   Nietzsche characterizes Christianity both as "the revaluation of Aryan values" and as "the victory of chandala values" (TI 7:4).

53   Nietzsche attributes his unique "dual descent" and "dual experiences" to the death of his father within him: "I am, to express it in the form of a riddle, already dead as my father, while as my mother I am still living and growing old" (EH:wise 1). Tracy Strong expertly investigates the Oedipal repercussions of

Nietzsche's attack on Christianity in "Oedipus as Hero: Family and Family Metaphors in Nietzsche," *Boundary* 2, Vol. 9, No. 3, and Vol. 10, No. 1, pp. 311–335. See also Jacques Derrida, "Otobiographies: The Teaching of Nietzsche and the Politics of the Proper Name," trans. Avital Ronell, in *The Ear of the Other: Otobiography, Transference, Translation*, ed. Christie McDonald (New York: Schocken, 1985), especially pp. 15–19.

54 In a letter to Franz Overbeck on 24 March 1887, Nietzsche describes the "subterranean" influence he now commands: "In all radical parties (Socialists, Nihilists, anti-Semites, Orthodox Christians, Wagnerians) I enjoy a wondrous and almost mysterious respect" *(Sämtliche Briefe*, Vol. 8, No. 820, p. 48). In 1892, Max Nordau confirms the influence of Nietzsche's "insane ego-mania" on anarchists, freedom-thirsters, and other members of "the generation reared under the Bismarckian system" *[Degeneration* (Lincoln: University of Nebraska Press, 1993), pp. 470–472].

55 Claudia Crawford persuasively identifies the emergence of Nietzsche's "devoted followers" as the "sign" that he might now proceed with his terrible event of revaluation *[To Nietzsche: Dionysus, I Love You! Ariadne* (Albany: State University of New York Press, 1995), pp. 143–161]. In support of her provocative thesis that Nietzsche may have feigned his descent into madness, Crawford points to the importance of a letter Nietzsche received from Strindberg in early December, in which the Swede assures Nietzsche of the need for and possibility of "the mediation of devoted followers in general" (p. 144).

56 Speaking explicitly of Paul (and implicitly, perhaps, of himself), Nietzsche remarks, "To become a founder of a religion one must be psychologically infallible in one's knowledge of a certain average type of souls who have not yet *recognized* that they belong together. It is he that brings them together. The founding of a religion therefore always becomes a long festival of recognition" (GS 353).

57 Although Nietzsche protests (too much) that "there is nothing in [him] of a founder of a religion," he is nevertheless "a bringer of glad tidings like no one before [him]" (EH:destiny 1). He is, after all, the "last disciple of the philosopher Dionysus" (TI 10:5), and the naturalism he recommends could be viewed as contributing to a religion of Dionysus.

58 In his letter to Schmeitzner on 13 February 1883, Nietzsche refers to his *Zarathustra* as a "fifth 'Gospel'" *(Sämtliche Briefe*, Vol. 6, No. 375, p. 327).

59 In a letter to Malwida von Meysenbug on 24 September 1886, Nietzsche parenthetically remarks, with explicit reference to the copy of *Beyond Good and Evil* he earlier had sent her, "Forgive me! Perhaps you should not read it, much less express to me your impressions of it. Let us assume that it will be *permitted* to be read sometime around the year 2000" *(Sämtliche Briefe*, Vol. 7, No. 756, p. 257).

60 See Georges Bataille, "Nietzschean Chronicle," in *Visions of Excess*, pp. 202–203.

61 The case for Nietzsche's "kinship" with Paul is made persuasively by John Bernstein in *Nietzsche's Moral Philosophy* (Cranbury, NJ: Fairleigh Dickinson University Press, 1988). Bernstein intends his thesis to be critical of Nietzsche, as a potentially fatal, self-referential objection to Nietzsche's critique of morality.

62 See Salaquarda, "Dionysos gegen den Gekreutzigten," pp. 303–304.

63 Alasdair MacIntyre's view is typical of the standard reception of Nietzsche's

"positive" contributions: "For it is in his relentlessly serious pursuit of the problem, not in his frivolous solutions that Nietzsche's greatness lies. . . . Nietzsche's problems remain unsolved and his solutions defy reason" [*After Virtue* (Notre Dame, IN: Notre Dame University Press, 1984), p. 114].

64 Jacques Derrida investigates Nietzsche's use of rhetorical barbs in *Spurs: Nietzsche's Styles*, trans. Barbara Harlow (Chicago: University of Chicago Press, 1978), especially pp. 37–47.

65 Nietzsche later suggests that he and Zarathustra have collaborated to induce the self-overcoming of morality: "The name of Zarathustra means in my mouth" the "self-overcoming of morality, out of truthfulness; the self-overcoming of the moralist, into his opposite – into me" (EH:destiny 3).

66 Donna Haraway delivers a compelling feminist interpretation of the "logic of monstrosity" in her essay "A Cyborg Manifesto: Science, Technology, and Socialist-Feminism in the Late Twentieth Century," collected in *Simians, Cyborgs and Women: The Reinvention of Nature* (New York: Routledge, 1991), pp. 149–181.

67 In a letter to Brandes on 20 November 1888, Nietzsche writes, "*Cesare Borgia as Pope* – that would be the *meaning* of the Renaissance, its true symbol" (*Sämtliche Briefe*, Vol. 8, No. 1151, p. 483).

68 An example of the sort of spectacle that Nietzsche has in mind occurs in Part IV of his *Zarathustra*, where the omni-affirmative ass becomes a symbol of this-worldly piety and religiosity (Z IV:17–18).

69 In a typical reversal of Christian eschatology, Nietzsche here turns to his advantage the popular belief, cultivated first by the Franciscans and then by Luther, that the Pope of Rome was either the Antichrist or his predecessor, the *antichristus minor*. See W. Bousset's entry in the *Encyclopaedia of Religion and Ethics*, ed. James Hastings, Volume 1 (New York: Scribner's, 1957), p. 581.

70 Salaquarda remarks that the self-overcoming of Christian morality must comprise an element of preservation, but he does not identify any element of Christian morality that is worthy of preservation ("Dionysos gegen den Gekreutzigten," pp. 306–307). The logic of Nietzsche's revaluation presupposes, I believe, the strategic appropriation of the "techniques of the self" that were developed by the Christian priests. Christian morality has inadvertently made possible the "man of good conscience," who stands security for his own future, who remains a debtor, though only to himself. Such individuals will eventually banish the guilt and bad conscience on which Christian morality characteristically trades.

7

STANDING BETWEEN TWO MILLENNIA: INTIMATIONS OF THE ANTICHRIST

Just between us, it is not impossible that I am the first philosopher of the age – indeed, perhaps even a little more: something decisive and full of destiny, standing between two millennia. For such a rarefied position one continuously atones, through an ever growing, ever icier, and ever sharper seclusion.

> Letter to Reinhardt von Seydlitz on 12 February 1888[1]

Whoever fights monsters should see to it that in the process he does not become a monster. And when you look long into an abyss, the abyss also looks into you. (BGE 146)

One of its heads seemed to have a mortal wound, but its mortal wound was healed, and the whole earth followed the beast with wonder.

> Revelations 13:3

Nietzsche holds *The Antichrist(ian)* in such high regard because it comprises both a statement and a performance of his "revaluation of all values." In *The Antichrist(ian)*, he "detonates" his residual store of vitality, presenting himself as an "incarnate declaration of war" (AC 13). As a squanderer of expendable affect, he not only articulates an alternative to Christian morality, but embodies it as well. As we shall see, however, Nietzsche is not a reliable judge of his own expenditures. His "explosive" performance of revaluation draws upon reservoirs of expendable affect of which he is ignorant, and its public ramifications deviate dramatically from his self-serving accounts of them. Although he may in fact body forth an objection to Christian morality, the precise nature of this objection is known only to those creatures of *ressentiment* whom he has inadvertently schooled in suspicion and symptomatology.

The Explosive Performance of Revaluation

The disagreement between Nietzsche and his readers over the magnitude of his achievement in *The Antichrist(ian)* is not reducible to a simple misunderstanding. Both sides point, whether proudly or piously, to the excesses of the book, and both sides form their judgments accordingly.[2] Walter Kaufmann, who is chiefly responsible for rehabilitating Nietzsche's philosophical reputation in the Anglophone world, is clearly uncomfortable with this shrill and vituperative book, perhaps because it defies so stubbornly his firm editorial hand.[3] Invoking a sumptuary image that Nietzsche himself summons to depict the squanderings of the exemplary human being, Kaufmann opines, "In some passages of *The Antichrist,* Nietzsche's fury breaks all dams."[4]

More so than any of Nietzsche's other books, *The Antichrist(ian)* gives vent to his signature excesses – the crowning achievement, one might suppose, of a born-again disciple of Dionysus (TI 10:5).[5] Indeed, he concludes *Ecce Homo* with what I take to be his most instructive comment on the revolutionary nature of his revaluation of all values: "Have I been understood? – *Dionysus versus the Crucified*" (EH:destiny 9). This pithy opposition is rich in meaning and imagery, much of which has been fruitfully explored by other scholars.[6] For our purposes here, let us note that the opposition suggests two basic approaches to the regulation of the economy of the soul and two corresponding models of expenditure.

Here Nietzsche appeals once again to his familiar, broad-brush distinctions between nimiety and deficiency, excess and privation, profligacy and thrift. Whereas the Crucified partakes of the (restricted) economy of sacrifice, Dionysus partakes of the (general) economy of squandering.[7] In a notebook entry from the Spring of 1888, he explains:

> One will see that the problem is that of the meaning of suffering: whether a Christian meaning or a tragic meaning. In the first case, it is supposed to be the path to a *sacred* existence; in the second case, existence is considered *sacred enough* to justify even a tremendous amount of suffering. . . . The God on the cross is a curse on Life, a pointer to seek redemption from it; Dionysus cut to pieces is a *promise* of Life: it is eternally reborn and comes back from destruction. (WP 1052)

The "Christian" interpretation of suffering falsely generalizes from the sickness and impotence of the "individual" to the worthlessness of Life itself. As we have seen, the popularity of this false generalization is largely attributable to the pathogenesis of the Christian priests, who teach the sick and infirm to seek a reason – any reason – for the suffering that defines them.

The "tragic" interpretation of suffering cleaves a diametrically opposite course. The inevitable fall of the tragic hero, which follows necessarily from his attempt to defy the perceived limitations of the human condition, stands as a testament to the unquenchable powers of self-replenishment that reside within the unbounded plenum of Life itself. As we have seen, neither interpretation of suffering is verifiably true or valid. They are philosophically interesting only as symptoms or signs of the underlying conditions they respectively express.

Like Theseus, Nietzsche relies on Dionysus to limn an exit from the labyrinth. This exit is produced by an explosion of excess vitality, which blasts through the crumbling granite edifice of Christian morality. As a disciple of Dionysus, Nietzsche too squanders himself, and *The Antichrist(ian)* enacts his alternative to the castrative practices of Christian morality. *The Antichrist(ian)* holds nothing in reserve, freely expending its author's accumulated store of vitality in an attack on Christian morality. Like the Cesare Borgia of his fantasies, Nietzsche squanders his vitality in the service of naturalism, ostensibly bodying forth an alternative to the anti-affective animus of Christian morality. Because he squanders himself, or so he believes, his declaration of war actually seals the (eventual) victory of his anti-Christian rebellion, for his act of self-destruction is also an act of creation. As he explains in another instructive clue, "The rightful name of The Antichrist" is none other than *Dionysus* (BT P5). The Antichrist is consequently a monster of excess, an incarnate obliteration of the conventional boundaries of human agency. This monster will eventually be destroyed in the inhuman explosions it enacts, but its "death" confirms the eternal renewal of Life itself.

The Antichrist(ian) is a multivalent, multidimensional work, and its complex economy accurately reflects the internal distance and contradictions that riddle Nietzsche's soul. As a product of excess, the book comprises not only a *statement* of his celebrated revaluation, but also a *performance,* or embodiment, of revaluation.[8] To borrow (and deform) a Wittgensteinian distinction: Whereas the statement of revaluation produces a "saying," a potentially disembodied and abstract doctrine, his performance of revaluation contributes the further, irreducibly Nietzschean dimension of "showing," which bodies forth an example of the perfidy that his statement ostensibly documents. Indeed, if we take seriously his general remarks on symptomatology, then this performative dimension may boast a unique grammar, syntax, and morphology all its own, which clever readers presumably can decipher and interpret.

In his performance of revaluation, Nietzsche involuntarily exhibits the pre-theoretical prejudices that inform and motivate *The Antichrist(ian)*. He consequently does not command full control over the ramifications of the investigations he initiates. His historical and psychological insights invariably double back on him, thereby exposing his own critique of Christian morality as yet another historical unfolding – or performance – of the phenomenon it purports to investigate. At this point, subsumed within his own inquiry, Nietzsche becomes both the subject and the object, both the agent and the patient, of his investigation. His performance of revaluation simultaneously corroborates the conclusions of his historiographical investigations and discredits his own claim to a disinterested, objective authority.

"Every great philosophy so far," he famously reveals, "has been . . . the personal confession of its author and a kind of involuntary and unconscious memoir" (BGE 6). Reading Nietzsche against Nietzsche, we should expect *The Antichrist(ian)* to essay an "involuntary and unconscious memoir" – and the book does not disappoint. His own memoir is written in bile and blood and priestly resentment, its private entries enacted in a public performance of revaluation. Were he an objective chronicler of the historical development of Christian morality, he would inherit the Sisyphean labor of continually revising the final, autobiographical chapter in this chronicle. Suspended in an endlessly recursive loop of self-reference, he would be obliged to record himself recording the history of Christianity, *ad infinitum*.

His performance of revaluation heads off this infinite regress by disclosing the basic, brute prejudices that motivate – and thus vitiate – his critique of Christianity. As his grand exposé intersects his own autobiography, he involuntarily enacts his own complicity in the triumph of Christian morality. His statement of revaluation accomplishes the initial gesture of interrogation, while his performance of revaluation opens (to us, but not necessarily for us) the possibility of extending this interrogation to its implosive, self-referential conclusion. When forcibly turned against Nietzsche, thereby exposing his own ulterior motives and subjective prejudices, his statement of revaluation both consumes its own originary authority and illuminates its previously unacknowledged performative dimension. He intends his statement of revaluation to essay the logos of Christian morality, while his performance of revaluation is supposed to convey the signature pathos of Christianity.

Strictly speaking, the statement and performance of revaluation cannot be said to comprise two distinct dimensions. If Nietzsche is right, then every philosophical statement is always also a performance, every critic a performer. We must therefore beware of conceiving of historical criticism simply as a disembodied theoretical method that one adopts and discards at will. Yet the performative dimension of Nietzsche's revaluation is not accessible to all; some cannot discern it, while others will not. There is obviously a great deal at stake in crossing the threshold of the performative dimension, for those who do so can no longer invest in Nietzsche the same epistemic authority that might have led them to *The Antichrist(ian)* in the first place. Those who would befriend Nietzsche, those who have no choice but to rely on his unchallenged authority, will not acknowlege the performative dimension of his philosophy. They will and must remain content both with his statement of revaluation and with the "objective" knowledge they gain from it. While it is true that he enjoys very little control over the involuntary, performative dimension of his philosophy, it is also true that he is responsible for whatever degree of access his readers have to it, for he has trained them in the methods and techniques of Nietzschean symptomatology.

Nietzsche's statement of revaluation is largely, if not exclusively textual, and it is contained by the artificial boundaries imposed by the logical and rhetorical devices he employs in his discursive prose formulations. This statement conveys his peculiar interpretation of the origin and development of Christianity, as well as the critical appraisal he simultaneously articulates. In principle, his statement of revaluation could be fairly evaluated by friend and foe alike, provided that these evaluations are based solely on the cogency and demonstrability of the arguments advanced. Indeed, when scholars call into question the philological and historical presuppositions of *The Antichrist(ian)*, they generally have in mind the statement of revaluation contained therein.

While this familiar statement of revaluation is neatly contained within the text of *The Antichrist(ian)*, Nietzsche's performance of revaluation exceeds the boundaries of the written word. This performance in turn informs *The Antichrist(ian)* with an unintended dramatic structure, such that Nietzsche's Apollinian statement of revaluation is placed in a relationship of direct, dialogic confrontation with its corresponding Dionysian performance. The internal distance created by this unintended dramatic structure infuses *The Antichrist(ian)* with a reflux of excess that Nietzsche alternately calls "blood," "poison," or "venom." His performance of revaluation thus incorporates into *The Antichrist(ian)* a third dimension of depth, body, or texture that it otherwise would lack.[9] He consequently describes his revaluation as "incarnate" and as having "become flesh." I suspect that many readers of *The Antichrist(ian)* would be willing to overlook the factual and historical errors that vitiate Nietzsche's statement of revaluation if his performance were not so disturbing. Indeed, many criticisms of *The Antichrist(ian)* never venture beyond the level of arguments *ad hominem* to consider the merit of its discursive case against Christian morality. As we shall see, this *ad hominem* response is entirely appropriate on Nietzschean grounds.

While Nietzsche's statement of revaluation is indispensable to his campaign against Christian morality, it is only as a squanderer that he comes to embody a "declaration of war." Indeed, his praise for *The Antichrist(ian)* is usually reserved for his performance of revaluation, which he believes will contribute to the founding of the communities of anti-Christian resistance that will continue his work. As in all cases of the generation of excess, however, the incarnation of Nietzsche's declaration of war exacts a heavy toll from the body of *The Antichrist(ian)* itself. Like the three-dimensional Diony-sian soul on which it is modeled, *The Antichrist(ian)* attains greater internal complexity and difference, but only at the expense of its two-dimensional, Apollinian continence. The reflux infusion of affect and bile compromises the strained economy of the text of *The Antichrist(ian)*, creating sumps and ruptures through which the author's vital humors transude unchecked. The blunt, clumsy words that convey his Apollinian statement of revaluation cannot possibly accommodate the raging affective drama that demands to be enacted.[10] Nietzsche's performance of revaluation consequently exceeds the "private" confines of the text, bleeding into the "public" sphere as an invitation, a gesture of provocation, and, as we have seen, a declaration of war.[11]

Nietzsche's performance of revaluation attains its apotheosis in the "Gesetz wider das Christenthum" (Decree Against Christianity), which he apparently intended to append to the text of *The Antichrist(ian)*.[12] In this "Decree," which Anglophone translators customarily exclude from their editions of *The Antichrist(ian)*, Nietzsche summarizes in seven theses his case against Christianity.[13] Although the discursive themes rehearsed in the "Decree" are familiar enough to readers of *The Antichrist(ian)*, their peculiar performance is decidedly unsettling. First of all, the "Decree" appears neatly framed on a single, free-standing page, which its author may be inviting us to remove and post in a public place. Second, the signatory of the "Decree" is not Friedrich Nietzsche, the avowed author of *The Antichrist(ian)*, but the Antichrist, who now reckons history from "the first day of the first year."[14] Third, the author of the "Decree" declares a "war *to the death* [*Todkrieg*]" against the "depravity" that is Christianity.[15] As the flashpoint of Nietzsche's "explosion," the "Decree" enacts and thus reveals the full measure of his contempt for Christianity.

The message embodied by the "Decree" is clear: Nietzsche's warmonger-ing is not simply metaphorical. He fancies himself a revolutionary, a pam-phleteer perhaps, and he fully intends to perform acts of real violence, as his post-breakdown letters confirm. The fury and hatred vented in the "Decree" thus cast a new light on the grandiosity of his self-presentation in *Ecce Homo:*

> I am by far the most terrible human being that has existed so far; this does not preclude the possibility that I shall be the most beneficial. I know the pleasure of destroying to a degree that accords with my powers to destroy – in both respects I obey my Dionysian nature, which does not know how to separate doing No from saying Yes. I am the first immoralist: that makes me the anni-hilator *par excellence.* (EH:destiny 2)

Hence the wisdom of his "decision" late in 1888 to allow *The Anti-christ(ian)* to stand as the whole of *The Revaluation of All Values:* There could be no additional installments to the envisioned *Hauptwerk,* for he was spent.

When he announced, in the concluding section of *The Antichrist(ian)*, that he was "at the end" (AC 62), he was not necessarily referring only to his recently completed book. As a philosopher and critic of Christianity, Nietzsche was finished. He did manage to dash off two short books before his breakdown – *Ecce Homo* and *Nietzsche contra Wagner* – but he assigned to both a largely instrumental value, as contributing to the cultivation of a sympathetic audience for his strategically postponed revaluation of all values.[16] *The Antichrist(ian)* thus represents his final expenditure of excess vitality. If he has timed his "explosion" correctly and if his readers similarly squander the expendable affect at their disposal, then Christian morality will not survive the demise of modernity as a whole; Dionysus will have vanquished the Crucified. Following his explosive farewell, he assumed his rightful place alongside the rank-and-file decadents of late modernity. His sojourn among them was mercifully brief.

Nietzsche's statement of revaluation has occasionally drawn muted praise from his readers, but his performance of revaluation has prompted nearly uniform revulsion. As if to corroborate his thesis that the Christianized cultures of Western Europe instinctively respond to excess with castrative measures, readers of *The Antichrist(ian)* characteristically recoil in horror. Unsympathetic readers mercilessly denounce the book as a spiteful exercise in megalomania. Even readers who are generally sympathetic to Nietzsche either sanitize the book's excesses, attributing them perhaps to an experimental strategy gone awry,[17] or ignore them altogether.[18] The preoccupation of so many contemporary scholars with his *writerly* excesses suggests a patent evasion of the more disturbing performances of his life and thought. Nietzsche may have "danced with his pen," but he also danced with the devil, and this latter choreography must not be ignored. Nor does his subsequent slide into madness somehow erase, temper, or excuse his bellicose reaction to Christian morality. He may have passed his final decade as a harmless idiot savant, but prior to his breakdown he clearly, if stridently, called for the outright destruction of Christianity.[19]

But the difficulties involved in assessing the merit of *The Antichrist(ian)* are not simply attributable to the recrudescent puritanism that shapes the course of contemporary philosophy. These difficulties lie also, or primarily, in the nature of the drives and impulses that attain excessive proportions in *The Antichrist(ian)*. Nietzsche is not merely exceedingly urbane, or exceedingly erudite, or exceedingly irreverent, or exceedingly iconoclastic; this angry and vituperative book also lends full expression to the "darker" reaches of his tortured soul. Here we encounter, unmeasured by his customary wit and wisdom, the misanthropy, hatred, calumny, and resentment that civilized readers are occasionally willing to tolerate in his earlier books. While the performances staged in *The Antichrist(ian)* are to some degree strategic, designed to reproduce the vitriol spewed by the Pauline priests, the excesses unleashed therein outstrip the ambit of Nietzsche's rhetorical command. The familiar rhythm of his textual strategies, the exquisite balance of gravity and hilarity, the rhetorical measure supplied by his familiar indirection and playfulness – in short, the textual traces that allow us to speak at all of his mastery of strategies and tropes, that encourage us to distinguish between the strategic and the nonstrategic – are all absent from *The Antichrist(ian)*.

As a product of Nietzsche's "raw" excesses, *The Antichrist(ian)* raises anew the stormy moral and political issues that have clouded his reception as a serious philosopher: anti-Semitism, irrational appeals to power and race, revisionist history, threats of public and private violence, incipient madness, intemperate malice, and so on.[20] Much as we moderns might fancy ourselves the untimely readers for whom Nietzsche pined, stationed resolutely "beyond good and evil," we too remain inured to the moral categories of evaluation that define philosophical discourse in late modernity; we are consequently not free to consider Nietzsche's excesses "objectively," independent of moral considerations.

Nietzsche was certainly unaware of the precise nature and consequences of the affects unleashed in *The Antichrist(ian)*. As the foremost authority on the psychology of excess, he astutely observed that any individual consumed in the frenzy of the swollen will is in the worst position possible to survey the ensuing explosions (GS 367).[21] Owing to his breakdown early in 1889, he had neither the opportunity nor the critical distance needed to engage in the sort of reflection that prompted him, in 1885, to pen a fourth, self-parodic installment of *Zarathustra*. We should not be surprised to discover, then, that his appraisal of *The Antichrist(ian)* and its excesses deviates so sharply from our own.

An Explosion of Light and Truth

Although the term *revaluation* (*Umwerthung*) conveys a strongly volitional connotation and although Nietzsche presents himself as a "*force majeure*" (EH:destiny 8), he consistently describes his "explosion" in distinctly cognitive terms as unleashing an excess of insight and understanding. He thus conceives of his revaluation as a revelation of unprecedented scope, and he presents *The Antichrist(ian)* as a manifesto that exposes the anti-natural depradations of Christian morality.

Readers who comb *The Antichrist(ian)* for evidence of a titanic, transfigurative act of will may be looking for the wrong sort of "event." Nietzsche's "revaluation of all values," it turns out, comprises an unprecedented act of truth telling. "It is a painful, horrible spectacle that has dawned on me," he explains, "I have drawn back the curtain from the *corruption* of humankind" (AC 6). In order to "break history in two," that is, he need "merely" reveal the truth of Christianity for all to see, and the self-overcoming of Christian morality will commence as a matter of logical course. He thus describes his "destiny" in terms of a Promethean clarity of vision, which he contrasts with "the faulty vision" of the priests (AC 9). This prodigious gift of vision enables him to present the "perilous nature" of pity "in an even brighter light" (AC 7). He consequently boasts that, in *The Antichrist(ian)*, "the deepest mysteries of human nature suddenly spring out with dreadful clarity."[22]

The motif of Nietzsche's perspicacity is ubiquitous throughout *Ecce Homo* as well. He is excessively "wise" because he has viewed Life from antipodal perspectives (EH:wise 1); his revaluation is an "act of supreme self-examination" (EH:destiny 1); he was "the first to *discover* the truth" (EH:destiny 1); he now commands a height from which he speaks "no longer with words, but with lightning bolts" (EH:um 3); and so on. As evidence of his boundless capacity for confronting and dispensing the truth, he cites his *Zarathustra*, a book "born out of the innermost wealth of truth, an inexhaustible well to which no pail descends without coming up again filled with gold and goodness" (EH P4). Invoking a bizarre image for his own magnanimity, he explains that he cherishes even his enemies, whom he employs as magnifying glasses to "make visible a general but creeping and elusive calamity" (EH:wise 7). He consequently presents himself as a (bastard) child of the Enlightenment, charged with the task of bathing Christian morality in the unflattering light of truth.[23] Nietzsche's vaunted "explosion," in short, is designed to generate more light than heat.[24]

Nietzsche thus conceives of his revaluation of all values as a grand, calamitous exposé of Christianity, and of himself as the teller of truths nonpareil. It is his "destiny," for example, to reverse the "lies of millennia" (EH:destiny 1).[25] Indeed, he alone can afford to entertain the insight into Christian morality that motivates his revaluation: "What defines me, what sets me apart from the whole rest of humanity is that I *uncovered* [*entdeckt*] Christian morality. . . . Blindness to Christianity is the crime *par excellence* – the crime against Life" (EH:destiny 7). He consequently declares war on Christian morality by disclosing, for the first time, its essence and truth: "The uncovering of Christian morality is an event without parallel, a real catastrophe. He that is enlightened about that, is a *force majeure*, a destiny – he breaks the history of humankind in two. One lives before him, or one lives after him" (EH:destiny 8).

Nietzsche's aim in *The Antichrist(ian)* is to distinguish the truth of Christianity from the life of Christ and to expose the former as a willful perversion of the latter.[26] He hopes to show that the supernatural concerns of the priests, from which they ostensibly derive their hieratic authority, derive from the same natural impulses they judge to be "sinful" in others – hence his strategy of collecting and commenting upon several of the "dysangelic" teachings culled from the Gospels (AC 45). Indeed, the castrative measures preached by the priests succeed in producing in them the opposite effect: an excess of expendable hatred and resentment. The priests legislate the extirpation of affect in order to galvanize in themselves the overflowing will they deny to others. According to Nietzsche, then, he need only reveal the "holy witlessness" and "diseased reason" of the priests (TI 6:6), and they will do the rest.

In order to accede to the station of the anti-Christian (and, a fortiori, to that of the Antichrist), Nietzsche must become the perfect Christian, the apotheosis of Christian truthfulness – hence his claim that "most serious Christians have always been favorably disposed to [him]" (EH:wise 7). Rather than oppose Christianity from without, his revaluation actually completes the internal logic of Christian morality. As we have seen, the "law of Life" decrees that Christian morality must precipitate its own demise by giving birth to its "other," which in turn will supplant it. Nietzsche fancies himself this other – witness his equivocal *nom de guerre* – and he consequently sets out to execute the inevitable self-overcoming of Christian morality. Marshaling the remaining volitional resources at his disposal, he attempts to induce Christian morality to undertake an unprecedented – and ultimately fatal – self-examination.[27]

The site of this dialectical transformation is supposed to be constituted by the revaluation of all values, as stated and performed in *The Antichrist(ian)* itself. In the person of Nietzsche, Christian morality ostensibly overcomes itself, by dint of a self-referential exercise of its own will to truth. The project of revaluation thus furnishes the context for his otherwise surprising self-presentation in the writings of 1888 as the champion par excellence of truth.[28]

Nietzsche's service of truth in *The Antichrist(ian)* is not necessarily incompatible with his earlier critique of the will to truth, for he hopes by means of his revaluation to bring the will to truth into conflict with itself. He subsequently advertises himself as the lone defender of truth, proudly claiming to be "the first to discover the truth" and accounting for his "calamitous" destiny by representing himself as "truth enter[ing] into a fight with the lies of millennia" (EH:destiny 1). In light of his political aims, then, a muted celebration of his own will to truth is perfectly understandable. If he is to contribute to the self-overcoming of Christian morality, then it must be the case that he too labors in the service of the will to truth.[29] Indeed, if he is correct in supposing that the will to truth must overcome itself, then we should fully expect the node of logical transformation to be occupied not merely by a suitor of truth, but by her boldest champion.[30]

Nietzsche's faith in truth is furthermore an ingredient of his ineluctable destiny. As he openly admits, he too takes his flame "from the fire ignited by a faith millennia old, the Christian faith, which was also Plato's, that God is truth, that truth is *divine*" (GS 344, cited in GM III:24). We may wish to believe that Nietzsche's interrogation of the will to truth somehow liberates him from its thrall, but the historical situation of his revaluation demonstrates that he is not free to renounce the will to truth – even as he wages war with it.

Although Nietzsche prefers to describe his revaluation in cognitive terms, we must be careful not to misplace its (modest) volitional component. While his insight into the truth of Christianity makes possible his statement of revaluation, it is his performative self-detonation that enacts this statement in an embodied declaration of war. He thus concludes *The Antichrist(ian)* by boasting that "this eternal indictment of Christianity I will write on all walls, wherever there are walls – I have letters to make even the blind see" (AC 62). Nietzsche's graffito is undeniably important as a document of his case against Christianity, but its enduring value lies in its function as an act of resistance, as a sign of a recusant will.[31] His promise to deploy "letters to make even the blind see" refers not to his discursive statement of revaluation, but to his embodied performance, which even "the blind" can appreciate for its sumptuary explosion. As we shall see, however, the volitional component of Nietzsche's revaluation actually belies the Apollinian triumph he claims for himself, reinforcing his kinship with the priests even as he proclaims his distance from them.

Nietzsche's Millennial Anxiety

For all of the confidence that Nietzsche exudes in *The Antichrist(ian)*, he cannot mask his concern that he is not yet ripe for the task thrust upon him. He presents himself as a rival and historical counterpart to St. Paul, but this grandiose self-assessment is not entirely accurate. He stands on the wrong side of the coming millennium, stranded in his decadence by the ebbing tide of late modernity. Hence his greatest, most enduring anxiety of influence: Can *his* revaluation of values possibly reproduce the political success of the original?[32] Or is he more instructively compared to Christ, whose parabolic teachings were distorted and pressed into the service of antithetical ends?

Nietzsche knows that he is "too late" to salvage modernity, and he fears that he is also "too early" – like Zarathustra – to exert any lasting influence on the disposition of the successor age. He fully realizes that the fragile communities that he founds may be obliterated without a trace in the catastrophic upheavals he foresees for the remaining century of the fading millennium. He speaks bravely of squandering himself, but he remains, after all, a decadent from whom expenditure eventually exacts a mortal toll. He pretends to be patient, to be unconcerned that his "fish hooks" have landed no worthy companions, but he despairs of his teachings ever descending upon sympathetic ears. Suspicious of his reception thus far, he does not trust his extant readers to continue the work he has begun.[33] Reluctant to bid his unknown recruits a final farewell, he nervously prolongs *The Case of Wagner* with two postscripts and an epilogue, which were followed several months later by an exceedingly insecure "sequel," *Nietzsche contra Wagner.* Additional "postscripts," madly scribbled in January 1889, promise world-historical deeds that would corroborate the magnitude of his revaluation.

It is this anxiety of influence that fans Nietzsche's burning desire to impress the stamp of the Antichrist onto the successor epoch to modernity. This millennial anxiety in turn engenders the greatest tension within his post-Zarathustran thought, for he strives to extend his influence not only to the end of his century – at which time some of his writings may receive a sensitive hearing[34] – but to the turning of the millennium itself, at which time he will become "timely." He must therefore establish himself as a *fin de siècle* figure not merely once, but twice; only in that event will he muster a serious challenge to the authority of St. Paul.[35] It is perhaps no coincidence that his forecasts for his own reception call for him to become timely on or about the second millennial anniversary of Paul's original revaluation.

In his Preface to *The Revaluation of All Values,* Nietzsche openly acknowledges that he writes for an audience that is not yet born: "How *could* I mistake myself for one of those for whom there are ears even now? Only the day after tomorrow belongs to me. Some are born posthumously" (AC P). The posthumous birth to which Nietzsche refers is not that of the anti-Christian (which transpired prehumously on 15 October 1844), but that of his alter ego, the Antichrist, whose birthday marks the "last day" of Christianity (AC 62).[36] Whether the "birth" prematurely celebrated by Nietzsche in 1888 is actually that of the Antichrist ultimately depends, however, on the fate of the anti-Christian rebellion that his revaluation sets in motion.[37] He will posthumously become the Antichrist (as opposed to an influential anti-Christian) only in the event that future generations are able to trace the commencement of a post-Christian era back to him – which implies, of course, the success of the rebellion he inaugurates. *The Antichrist(ian)* is therefore a pledge across the centuries to an unknown and distant posterity, a promise to be fulfilled only by the posthumous birth of Nietzsche on that fateful day when Christianity finally becomes a harmless curiosity of history.[38]

Hence, it is not enough that Nietzsche fires the first volley in a protracted campaign against Christian morality. The success of this campaign must also survive the caesura of the turning of the millennium such that the "philosophers of the future" trace their anti-Christian lineage back to him. Only in that event will he have succeeded in influencing the disposition of the successor epoch to modernity. The ambiguity of his *nom de guerre* thus reflects the complexity (and the anxiety) of his project in 1888: He is both the anti-Christian buffoon who fancies his pathetic ravings a declaration of war and the Antichrist who is born posthumously on the occasion of the demise of Christianity.[39]

Nietzsche fully understands that he should conform his political ambitions to the historical conditions that circumscribe his destiny, but he is free neither to implement nor to enact this understanding. Rather than deliver the truthful exposé that he promises of Christian morality, he must also and involuntarily grab for the brass ring of the millennium, venting his "darker" excesses in a doomed campaign to catapult himself beyond modernity. Rather than found a modest community of anti-Christians who will continue his work in increments consistent with their depleted volitional resources, he insists on recruiting the shock troops of the next millennium. As a consequence of his besetting decadence, he cannot help but compromise his teachings, placing them in the hands of those who cannot help but profane them.

Nietzsche's slide into madness is perhaps attributable in part to his failed attempt to sustain the distance that separates the polar standpoints of Antichrist and anti-Christian. The strain of attempting to fulfill this divided office may very well have overtaxed the economy of his wearied soul, situating him in the final year of his sanity "with one foot beyond life" (EH:wise 3). As his attempted correspondence from January 1889 suggests, he came to regard himself not simply as the instigator of a nascent rebellion against Christian morality, but as a lawgiver of world-historical consequence.[40] His breakdown thus transports him prematurely to the posthumous standpoint of his own birth as the Antichrist. His inward turning has coiled so tightly that its spiral finally breaks, destroying his soul as a capacitor of vital forces.

Although it would be highly speculative to suggest that the strain generated by Nietzsche's "millennial anxiety" contributed causally to the onset of his madness, the historical proximity of his revaluation and subsequent breakdown may not be purely accidental. In fact, the dissociative pathology that enveloped him early in 1889 may fairly be judged a natural, "successful" culmination of his post-Zarathustran quest to take the measure of his age. Having set out to embody as many voices, drives, affects, and perspectives as possible, he eventually announces that he is "every name in history."[41] While it is perhaps unlikely that he ever envisioned the successful completion of his critical project in terms of the madness that engulfed him, he was not unaware of the personal risks involved in attempting to stand "between two millennia." Perhaps in the end he was simply unable to affirm the possibility that his revaluation might be in vain, that his shrill voice might never descend upon receptive ears. Perhaps his breakdown was necessary to the production of an audience that would carry on his life's work, a community that would trample even him in its purge of the priestly class.

A Decadent Antichrist?

Readers of *The Antichrist(ian)* commonly report that its author is virtually indistinguishable from the priests against whom he inveighs. His venomous attack on the Pauline priesthood actually exemplifies the priestly *ressentiment* he aims to expose, thereby implicating him in his own critique of Christian morality.[42] This problem of self-reference is widely held to be fatal to his project of revaluation: How can he possibly hope to mobilize his readers against the priests when everything he says about them holds true for him as well?[43]

Nietzsche's delusions of grandeur are perhaps best exemplified by the world-historical role he reserves for himself in the self-overcoming of Christian morality.[44] It is his destiny, he believes, to be born "posthumously" as the Antichrist and to preside over the founding of a post-Christian, tragic age. Just as he portrays Paul as the apotheosis of the Jewish priesthood who embodies the self-overcoming of the Law, so he fancies himself the apotheosis of the Christian priesthood in whom the self-overcoming of Christian morality becomes incarnate. As a representative exemplar of late modernity, he presents himself as a decadent scion of Cesare Borgia, whose overflowing, exotic vitality was emblematic of the age of the Renaissance.

Where Cesare Borgia failed, however, Nietzsche will succeed. Although he does not foresee his imminent election to the papacy, he does see himself as inhabiting the node of historical transformation within which the "other" of Christianity will be birthed: "Am I understood? – The self-overcoming of morality, out of truthfulness; the self-overcoming of the moralist into his opposite – into me" (EH:destiny 3). But the Antichrist is not to be confused with an anti-Christian. Nietzsche's avowed, visceral enmity for the priests may be genuine, but it remains, in the end, an undeniably priestly enmity. His performance of revaluation reproduces in every respect the resentment and hatred for which he takes the priests to task. Despite his genuine contempt for Christian morality, he is not, strictly speaking, its other.

As we have seen, Nietzsche's faith in the "inevitable" self-overcoming of Christian morality trades on a dubious appeal to a trans-historical verity he calls "the law of Life":

> All great things bring about their destruction through an act of self-overcoming [*Selbstaufhebung*]: thus the law of Life will have it, the law of the *necessity* of "self-overcoming" [*Selbstüberwindung*] in the nature of life – the lawgiver himself eventually receives the call: "*patere legem, quam ipse tulisti.*" (GM III:27)

Eschewing, as usual, the antiquarian custom of providing empirical verification, he supplies no instances of this "law" at work, nor any account of its alleged "*necessity.*" In fact, his appeal here to the logic of self-overcoming is strongly reminiscent of *The Birth of Tragedy*, whose clumsy recourse to dialectic, he later concedes, "smells offensively Hegelian" (EH:bt 1).

A similar stench pervades Nietzsche's dialectical critique of Christian morality. Exuding an optimism that borders on Socratic cheerfulness – which he identifies, incidentally, as a signal symptom of decadence (EH:wise 1) – he presents the self-overcoming of Christian morality as an inevitable consequence of the interrogation he initiates. He thus places great confidence in the irresistible march of "Christian truthfulness" toward its self-referential showdown with the will to truth (GM III:27), despite his own observation that *Christian truthfulness* constitutes an oxymoron of world-historical proportions. Although he understands that the self-overcoming of Christian morality clearly implicates him in the duplicity and anti-naturalism he seeks to unseat, he also believes that the inevitable sublation of Christian morality will somehow absolve him of his participation in its signature practices.

Whatever the ultimate merit of Nietzsche's appeal to dialectics, we are witness only to his complicity with Christian morality, and not to the logical transformation he supposedly instigates. He may be the most perfect Christian ever produced, but there is no evidence to suggest that he is the last. In judging his own historical moment to be pregnant with calamity, in fact, he yields to the grim seriousness and epochal self-presentation for which he chastises Socrates and other decadents. Falsely generalizing from the crisis within his own soul, he blindly diagnoses a crisis within modernity itself, a crisis that demands, or so he believes, an immediate and decisive response. By grandiosely presuming himself to stand at the crossroads of modernity and its successor epoch, he not only exaggerates the world-historical significance of his own halting agency, but also participates in the moralization of decadence.[45] Rather than produce the other of Christianity, his "explosion" merely creates a more resilient strain of Christian morality. The anti-Christian is simply a particular, mutant type of Christian from whom the diametric other of Christian morality may or may not evolve.

Nietzsche's failure to complete the logic of self-overcoming marks him not only as a type of Christian, but also as a type of Christian priest. His "children" may someday command the dialectical node of transformation that he claims to occupy, but his own anti-Christian sallies still bear the unmistakable imprint of priestly resentment. To appropriate his own pet analogy, just as Paul's betrayal of the Law continues the hieratic tradition of the Jews, so Nietzsche's betrayal of the priests conforms to the inner logic of their twisted mission. Rather than complete the internal logic of Christian morality and hasten its inevitable self-overcoming, his revaluation engenders a more perfectly evolved species of priest: the anti-priest, who furthers the teaching of decadence by pretending to oppose all priests. On this point, Zarathustra is considerably more savvy than his "father": "Here are priests; and though they are my enemies, pass by them silently and with sleeping swords . . . My blood is related to theirs, and I want to know that my blood is honored even in theirs" (Z II:4). In his attempt to execute the "law of Life," Nietzsche unwittingly instantiates his own image of morality as a "scorpion [that] drives its sting into its own body" (D P3).

Nietzsche knows that he is decadent, but he does not know precisely how his decadence affects his revaluation of all values. He seems to believe that he can insulate his "perfect" readers from the harmful effects of his decadence, but he is simply mistaken in this belief. While he expressly refuses both to "improve" humankind and to erect "new idols" (EH P2), his own account of decadence suggests that all such promises conceal lies. He would sooner be a "buffoon" than a "holy man" (EH:destiny 1), a "satyr" rather than a "saint" (EH P2), but his decadence overrides these preferences, prompting him to seek precisely what is most disadvantageous for him.

Although he fully expects his revaluation of all values to exhaust his residual vitality, he apparently does not expect his performance to subvert its own claims to authority. He is consequently ignorant, as usual, of the precise nature of the excess vitality he expends. He does not realize, for example, that the explosive squandering that gives birth to *The Antichrist(ian)* draws from a capacious reservoir of priestly resentment.[46] As the following passage self-servingly suggests, he believes that his explosive capacity prevents him from accumulating a toxic reservoir of resentment: "*Ressentiment* itself, if it should appear in the noble man, consummates and exhausts itself in an immediate reaction, and therefore does not *poison*" (GM I:10).

Nietzsche presents his reversal of St. Paul as a strict cancellation of priestly power, as a purely liberatory exercise, but his own decadence greatly complicates the reversal he actually effects. While he fully intends to reproduce the priestly stratagems of St. Paul and thereby reverse the original revaluation of values, he also reproduces, unintentionally, the priestly affect of his nemesis. *The Antichrist(ian)* not only documents the hatred and resentment that motivate the Christian priesthood, but also exemplifies them for all (but Nietzsche) to see. Indeed, if his readers are to endorse his case against the Pauline priests, then they must do so in spite of him, for his otherwise impressive exposé reeks of priestly resentment.

Nietzsche's attack on the Christian priesthood thus turns out to be self-referential in scope, for everything he says about the priests is true of him as well. As a decadent priest in his own right, he is not free merely to expose St. Paul as the high priest of the ascetic ideal. He also aspires to supplant the saint, to exploit him, as Paul exploited Christ, for his own priestly ends. Although he insists otherwise, no salient differences distinguish him from the historical and psychological type to which he assigns Paul. Both are self-proclaimed decadents who revaluate existing values rather than create new ones. In his assault on the Christian priesthood, Nietzsche matches his rival's every move and calumny. Even his transfigurative experience of eternal recurrence is derivative, bearing a suspicious resemblance to Saul's/Paul's epiphany on the road to Damascus.[47]

Nietzsche does enjoy the advantage of historical succession, for he may determine what his readers know about both himself and Paul, and he exploits this advantage to cast his rival in an unflattering light. Even this trick, however, he has learned from his nemesis: Just as Paul exploited the privilege of the successor to falsify the history of Judaism and the life of Christ, so Nietzsche provides his own revisionist account of the history of Christianity and the life of Paul. For example, while Nietzsche claims to cleanse the "text" of Christ's life of its Pauline accretions, thereby exposing the "real" Christ as an idiot, as a cipher incapable of resisting even conflicting interpretations (AC 32–34),[48] this claim devolves from a priestly stratagem he has borrowed from Paul.

Under the pretense of "interpreting" the Law, Paul insinuated himself between Christ and Christianity, thereby clearing a space in which he might perform his signature mischief. Under the related pretense of interpreting the Gospels, Nietzsche similarly insinuates himself between Paul and Christianity, thereby creating the conditions for his own peculiar philological violence. Because Nietzsche enjoys the advantage of succession, he may confidently advertise his heterodox interpretation of Christ's life as true, while merely adding his own distinctive scrawl to the palimpsest he claims to have wiped clean. Of course, this advantage is rendered virtually meaningless by the sheer weight of Pauline tradition. Nietzsche's chances of deposing Paul are no better than were Paul's prospects for toppling an empire.

Nietzsche, or his apologists, might account for this haunting symmetry by appealing to the successful execution of his guiding strategy. In order to orchestrate the self-overcoming of Christian morality, he must present himself as the *Doppelgänger* of St. Paul, shadowing his predecessor and precisely reproducing his priestly strategies. The *Doppelgänger,* his champions might say, is simply a role that he strategically assumes and declines at will. Any such account, however, trades on the dubious assumption that Nietzsche retains full control of his excesses, that he can neutralize the effects of his decadence.

Although consistent with the mode of self-presentation he favors in *Ecce Homo,* this assumption requires us to exempt him from his own account of the decadence that besets late modernity. Nietzsche is a teacher of decadence, and no array of rhetorical stratagems can purify his ensuing expenditures. As we have seen in the case of St. Paul, betrayal of one's kind constitutes the essence rather than the antithesis of priestly resentment.

Powerless to throw off his destiny as a resentment-driven double agent versed in the priestly arts of subterfuge, dissembling, and betrayal, he instinctually employs his priestly legacy to serve his own anti-priestly ends.

Nietzsche's decadence also complicates the terms of his summary dismissal of Socrates as a political rival. Like Socrates, he is a type of priest, and he too has contributed to the decadence of his age. Just as Socrates realized that he could not prevent the decay of Athenian culture, so Nietzsche interprets his earlier attempts to redeem modernity as symptoms of his own degeneration. In squandering his residual vitality, or so he believes, he thus avoids the fate of Socrates and enacts a more effective political response to the decadence of his age. As we have seen, however, he is largely ignorant of the nature of his explosion, and he is simply mistaken in his apparent belief that he can separate his excesses from his decadence. Unbeknownst to him, then, *The Antichrist(ian)* subverts the authority of the priestly class as a whole, but only by means of a self-consuming attack on the teachers of decline.

Nietzsche's inadvertent exemplification of priestly revenge punctuates his exposé of the Christian priesthood, but only at the expense of his own authority as an objective critic of Christian morality. As a consequence of this unwitting forfeiture of his remaining priestly authority, he is far closer to Socrates than he ever dreamed.[49] Like Socrates, whose *Apology* casts aspersions upon all self-proclaimed benefactors of Athens, Nietzsche exposes the twisted motives of all priests, including himself. Like Socrates, in fact, he consumes his own residual vitality in a desperate, vengeful act of philosophical "suicide." Nietzsche may fancy himself a heroic squanderer and Socrates a cowardly martyr, but in the end very little separates the desperate farewells of these two decadent philosophers.

Tableaux Vivants: An Embodied Critique of Modernity

As an enactment of Nietzsche's revaluation of all values, *The Antichrist(ian)* falls far short of his grandiose expectations for it. We need not endorse, however, his own idiosyncratic standards for success and failure. Indeed, his self-consuming assault on the priests may actually further the political ends he pursued, though by means unknown to him. Like all priests, Nietzsche advances a moralization of decadence, claiming that late modernity can only produce its own, timely end. As we have seen, however, moralizations of decadence often yield unanticipated productive consequences, insofar as the priests in question involuntarily body forth configurations of agency that are uniquely possible only for them. As intended, then, Nietzsche's revaluation must be judged a resounding failure. But this failure may spawn unintended successes that he cannot ascertain. Here too his fate mirrors that of St. Paul, who inadvertently and indirectly contributed to the creation of one Friedrich Nietzsche.

If granted the opportunity and critical distance to reflect on his performance of revaluation, Nietzsche would certainly deem it a failure, and rightfully so. Priestly resentment clouds his exposé of Christian morality, stealing the Apollinian light and clarity of which he boasts so immodestly. Promising to dispel the "lies of millennia" by recounting the *genuine* history of Christianity, he simply adds his own distinctive scrawl to an already crowded palimpsest. Rather than induce Christian morality to confront itself truthfully, he contributes yet another lie to its impressive repertoire of falsehoods. Nor is the failure of his grand exposé an accident, which he might have avoided by attending more scrupulously to the facts at hand. It was Nietzsche himself who taught us that all such discursive accounts of modernity are of interest primarily as symptoms. By the terms of his own symptomatology, then, his exposé of Christian morality holds philosophical value only as a symptom of his own decay. The question of its truth, of its objective validity, simply cannot be approached (TI 5:5). His diagnosis of modernity may strike us as scintillating, provocative, even persuasive at times, but we have no epistemic warrant for following him in pronouncing it true.

Nietzsche's grand exposé of Christian morality may be flawed, but it is not the only critique he delivers of modernity. In addition to the discursive critique he intentionally articulates, he also and unwittingly dispenses an *embodied* critique of modernity – just as he has led us to expect from the representative exemplars of any age. In order to advance an immanent critique of modernity, he must actually enact a representative type of life that faithfully expresses the fractured ethos of the age. In his explosive performance of revaluation, he actually bodies forth the signature tensions and contradictions that define late modernity as a decadent epoch. His strategic modes of self-presentation combine with his involuntary expenditures to produce a grotesque (albeit accurate) self-portrait, which, owing to his unique historical situation, also serves as a portrait of the age he involuntarily represents.[50]

Nietzsche's discursive critique of modernity thus directs his readers back to him, to his dying soul, as the physiological ground of the symptoms they have observed. He in turn delivers a comprehensive account of his age, which he involuntarily enacts in the fragmented performances of his life. His full critique of modernity is thus expressed not in his idle speculations about his age, but in the *absurdum practicum* he involuntarily enacts as he attempts to divine the logos of his age. In the course of pursuing his scheme to deliver an immanent critique of modernity, he has incorporated into his soul an unprecedented dimension of internal multiplicity and disarray. His painful experiences of the constitutive tensions of the age have fashioned his distended soul into a mirror and model of modernity.

By virtue of his misguided quest to take the measure of modernity, he has actually transformed himself into a sign of his times, riddled for all to see by the tensions that define the epoch as a whole. In this respect, his *Ecce Homo* stands as an unwitting testament to the fragmentation and chaos that rend his soul. We may certainly take issue with the idealized self-portrait essayed in this strange "autobiography," but it documents nevertheless the multivalency – indeed, the contradictions – of its author's life and career.[51]

In pronouncing his own decadence and fixing himself in the ensuing envelope of self-referential critique, Nietzsche comes to stand for his age as a whole.[52] Owing to his unique destiny as a representative exemplar of late modernity, he accommodates within his tortured soul the riddles and tensions that define his age. Any self-disclosure on his part, whether intentional or unwitting, thus contributes to our understanding of modernity as a whole. If only for a brief, time-dispersing instant, he embodies fully the contradictions of the age, postponing its implosion while personally illuminating the unique powers and perfections that reside within decadence itself. He expends his residual vitality not in the implementation of some half-baked political scheme, but in willfully preserving the structural integrity of his disintegrating soul, even as it fragments itself after the fashion of modernity. The peculiar accomplishments and failures of modernity, its potentialities and limitations, its insights and blunders, are all inscribed onto his dying soul and enacted in the spasmodic practices of his nomadic existence. If only for the "perfect day" dishonestly commemorated in the interleaf epigraph to *Ecce Homo,* Nietzsche bodies forth an involuntary critique of modernity, manifesting its hidden contradictions in his quixotic campaign to take the measure of his life and age.

Indeed, notwithstanding the explanatory power and visionary scope of his "official" diagnosis of modernity, this discursive critique is overshadowed by his involuntary enactment of the decadence he chronicles. He does finally become a sign, though not the Hyperborean beacon that illuminates the exit from the labyrinth of Western Christianity. He inadvertently becomes a sign of the disintegrating ethos of his dying epoch, reprising in his own life the signature foibles and *absurdum practicum* of modernity as a whole. Failing in his quest to divine the logos of modernity, he unwittingly contributes to the defining pathos of his age. His teachings compromised by an irrepressible anxiety of influence, his critique of Christian morality subverted by his own priestly mischief, his vitality sapped by instinctual disarray, Nietzsche embodies but does not resolve the plight of modernity as a whole. In death as in life, ontogeny recapitulates phylogeny.

In every epoch, whether healthy or decadent, the will to power announces its accession to a new configuration by leaving its stamp on a few, select individuals. The will to power thus inscribes onto these representative examplars a living record of its various historical instantiations, which collectively document the full complement of human powers and faculties. "Through Wagner," Nietzsche avers (though he could very well have selected any other exemplary specimen), "modernity speaks most intimately, concealing neither its good nor its evil – having forgotten all sense of shame" (CW P). Cesare Borgia, Kant, Goethe, Napoleon, Hegel, Schopenhauer, Wagner, and now Nietzsche: Each has served in turn as the canvas on which modernity has successively painted its self-portrait. These *tableaux vivants* collectively form a sublime, encrypted mural that faithfully records the curriculum vitae of modernity itself.[53] Hence the importance of treating Nietzsche as a sign of his times: He is the missing and perhaps final piece in the puzzle of modernity. In order to complete his critique of modernity, we must be willing not only to regard him as an exemplary specimen of his epoch, but also to interpret him as ruthlessly and objectively as he interprets the representative exemplars of predecessor ages.

Nietzsche's situation is complicated further by his inability to view and interpret the sign he has become. For the most part, he deploys his symptomatology to good effect, rendering astute interpretations of the instinctual traces he detects in others. His own symptoms, however, remain opaque to him, resisting stubbornly the self-serving interpretations he confects for them. If we take seriously his own account of genius, then we must conclude that he is not privy to the nature and effects of his explosive squanderings. His various (and self-serving) efforts at self-presentation are idle at best, for he is the least reliable witness to the critique of modernity that he enacts.

Indeed, if he were the sole practitioner of this symptomatological method of criticism, then his critique of modernity would remain forever incomplete, fatally compromised by its failure to incorporate an account of his own decadence. But he has in fact schooled his children in this new brand of philology so that they might bravely navigate the "open seas" before them. While he never intended this philology to be applied directly to him, as a means of wresting from him the "unconscious memoir" that he involuntarily essays, his children have also been sufficiently schooled in betrayal to transgress any residual authority he might have intended to retain for himself. Reflecting in their own lives this divided heritage, they resolve to pass his Promethean torch to the philosophers of the future, while indulging themselves in priestly pyromania along the way. Along with this ambiguous torch, Nietzsche's symptomatology will be handed down through the generations of his progeny in order that the founders of the new epoch might both understand and beware his vexed relationship to the Christian priesthood he claims to oppose.

In one respect, then, this attack on the priests is more successful than he ever could have imagined, for it manages to neutralize an unknown opponent to the rebellion he foments: Nietzsche himself. Having inadvertently raised the stakes of confrontation, he may force his nemeses to respond in kind, with self-consuming performances of their own. These performances furthermore identify him as the apotheosis of the internal disarray, self-hatred, pity, and resentment that he associates with Christianity. In exposing the signature calumnies of Christian morality, he actually becomes a sign of the destructive, anti-affective animus it shelters. As the most perfectly evolved specimen of Christian morality, Nietzsche himself stands as the greatest argument against its continued authority and existence – not primarily in his teachings, but in his performances, in the tortured life he involuntarily enacts. In the person of Nietzsche, fragmentation and self-division achieve monstrous proportions, forcibly transgressing the bounds of the recognizably human.

As he nears the end of his inconstant dalliance with sanity, Nietzsche apparently senses the stirrings of his resident *monstrum in animo*. Monstrous and inhuman images haunt his various self-presentations in late 1888 and early 1889. In addition to the ubiquitous twin personae of Dionysus and the Antichrist, he likens himself to a satyr (EH P2), a Hyperborean (AC P), a beast (*Unthier*),[54] the Phoenix,[55] the Immoralist,[56] the Crucified,[57] Astu,[58] and so on. Appropriating for himself the diagnosis advanced of Socrates by the peripatetic physiognomist (TI 2:3), he identifies himself as "a kind of cave" that hides from view his monstrous appetites.[59] That a single soul could accommodate this grotesque menagerie is simultaneously a testament to the spiritual achievements of Christianity and a sign of its irrecuperable corruption.[60] In the shadow cast over posterity by the monstrosity that is Nietzsche, humankind must either perish from its Christian disciplines of breeding or renounce them forever.

We know that both Dionysus and the Antichrist often appear in monstrous aspects, especially while consumed in the frenzy of their respective transfigurative labors. In *The Birth of Tragedy*, for example, Nietzsche evinces his enduring fascination with the satyr, who serves not only as as the bestial familiar of the god Dionysus, but also as the original prototype for the tragic chorus (BT 7). The Antichrist is popularly portrayed both as a draconic monster and, as in Revelations 13, as a hideous composite beast to which the dragon cedes its political and secular authority. If Nietzsche is to accede to the station of the millennial Antichrist or to complete his rite of initiation into the mysteries of Dionysus, then he too must lend voice and aspect to the monsters lurking within himself. This terrible transfiguration he unwittingly accomplishes within the self-obliterating squanderings that characterize his performance of revaluation.[61] By unleashing a torrent of excess hatred and resentment, he actually becomes the horrifying changeling produced by Christianity, the unspeakable monstrosity that will strike fear into the hearts of the founders of the successor epoch. To ensure that such a monstrosity as Nietzsche will never again wail and writhe:[62] This is sufficient reason for the philosophers of the future to expunge all traces of Christian morality from the foundation of the postmodern, tragic age.

Nietzsche ultimately failes to constitute himself as the "other" of Christianity, as the Antichrist, but he succeeds in constituting himself as a monstrosity of Christian provenance, which in turn bespeaks the possibility of the Antichrist.[63] His grand exposé of Christian morality fails to execute the "law of Life," but his explosion illuminates the benighted landscape of late modernity, revealing an array of potentially promising ends to which Christian "techniques of the self" might be constructively employed. His vaunted revaluation of all values fails to "break history in two," but his sumptuary performances forcibly disclose the decadence of late modernity as an unexplored field of experimentation within which alternative con-figurations of agency might be bodied forth and tested. Nietzsche himself turns out to be the best argument he could possibly summon against the continued authority of Christian morality.

This is not to say, however, that Nietzsche either intended to stand for modernity, at least in the way I have described him, or understood himself to have attained this standing. Although he has always intended to transform himself into a sign, into a beacon of excess that might illuminate the twilight of modernity, he has characteristically idealized – and thus misunderstood – the extent of his significatory power. While it is true that his revaluation signifies the (relatively) robust vitality resident within him, this explosion also confirms the provenance of his excesses in the hatred and resentment on which he involuntarily draws. In the end, he may take the measure of his age, although not by dint of the discursive critique he purveys in his post-Zarathustran writings.

Although he undertakes an immanent critique of modernity, deliberately situating himself in the besetting failures of the age, he also – and necessarily – misinterprets the nature of his participation in the project of immanent critique. He tends to issue himself a partial exemption from the decadence of late modernity, as if his painful immersion in the contradic-tions of his age had somehow conferred upon him a "postmodern," or "extramodern," status. When pressed to produce a representative exemplar of modernity, he typically summons Socrates, on whom he presents himself as an improvement. These strategies of self-exclusion are fully explained, however, by Nietzsche's general account of the typical pathologies of deca-dent philosophers. To proclaim oneself "other," thereby betraying one's age or people, is the very essence of the philosopher's art. More so than any other sign or symptom of decline, Nietzsche's alleged "escape" from moder-nity enacts the final, convulsive throes of his dying epoch.

Nietzsche does in fact deliver an immanent critique of modernity, but only insofar as he embodies and thus stands for the fragmented ethos of the age. As a sign of his times, he succeeds not in escaping the formative influence of modernity, but in banishing the *constraint* these historical forces had formerly imposed upon him. In standing for modernity as its representative exemplar, he momentarily bears responsibility for the failures and imperfections of his age as a whole. In this fleeting instant of embodiment and madness, Nietzsche manages to free himself from the constraint of history, from the oppression of the "It was," but only because his swollen, febrile soul momentarily accommodates the unfathomable richness and plenitude of modernity as a whole. "At bottom," he triumphantly announces to Burckhardt in January 1889, "I am every name in history."[64]

But alas, Nietzsche does not partake of the happy solution Zarathustra proposed to the problem of history (Z II:20). Ignorant of the reach of his embodied critique, Nietzsche is not free to announce the completion of his philosophical project with the triumphant refrain, "Thus I willed it!" This is not to say, of course, that he refrains from this refrain, but only that his occasional renditions of it ring painfully false to us. He could not have willed to stand for modernity as a whole, and any proclamation to the contrary is valuable only as another sign of his decay. Indeed, if he is to take the full measure of modernity, then the success of his immanent – and involuntary – critique must necessarily elude him. Lacking the requisite access to his own enactments and embodiments, he must rely on his imperfect readers to proclaim honestly the completion of his life's task; only then will he be "born posthumously."

In order to decipher this embodied critique, his readers must apply to him the symptomatological methods and analyses that he reluctantly bequeathed to them. The resulting violence to him, perpetrated by ungrateful, resentful heirs, is nevertheless performed in his name. Nietzsche could not have known the extent to which his readers would turn his instruments of torture against him, but he willingly supplied them nonetheless. It would be fitting, then, if some of the university chairs that are to be reserved for scholars of his *Zarathustra* might be awarded to those intrepid hermeneuts who attempt to refine and expand the terms of his own symptomatology.

Notes

1 *Friedrich Nietzsche: Sämtliche Briefe, Kritische Studienausgabe in 8 Bänden,* ed. G. Colli and M. Montinari (Berlin: deGruyter/Deutscher Taschenbuch Verlag, 1986), Vol. 8, No. 989, p. 248.

2 Robert Ackermann notes that "Nietzsche has been transformed from an incomprehensible foreigner into a safe and predictable contemporary. But when Nietzsche is presented in such terms, he is trivialized into a King-Kong-in-chains, appearing under heavy sedation to English-speaking academic au-

diences" ["Current American Thought on Nietzsche," in *Nietzsche heute: Die Rezeption seines Werkes nach 1968*, ed. Sigrid Bauschinger, Susan L. Cocalis, and Sara Lennox (Bern: A. Francke Verlag, 1988), p. 129].

3   In the preface to his translation of *The Antichrist(ian)*, Walter Kaufmann, in *The Portable Nietzsche* (New York: Viking Penguin, 1982), scrambles to preserve his thesis that Nietzsche was in fact an opponent of anti-Semitism, but his case succeeds only in showing that Nietzsche perhaps expressed more hatred for Christians than for Jews. Apprised perhaps of the failure of his case, Kaufmann proceeds to diminish the importance of the book: "Like Nietzsche's first essay, *The Birth of Tragedy*, *The Antichrist* is unscholarly and so full of faults that only a pedant could have any wish to catalogue them" (p. 568). Kaufmann also declines to translate certain paratextual components of *The Antichrist(ian)* – such as the revised subtitle, *Fluch auf das Christenthum* (A Curse on Christianity), and the particularly inflammatory "Gesetz wider das Christenthum" (Decree against Christianity) – perhaps because they would further militate against his proposed domestication of Nietzsche's thought.

4   Kaufmann, *The Portable Nietzsche*, p. 463. Werner Dannhauser similarly maintains of *The Antichrist(ian)* that "everything [Nietzsche] says is colored by his unbridled polemical passion and shaped by his desire to attack Christianity by any and all means" [*Nietzsche's View of Socrates* (Ithaca, NY: Cornell University Press, 1974), pp. 233–234].

5   In a draft of a letter to Brandes at the beginning of December 1888, Nietzsche likens *The Antichrist(ian)* to a "volcano," which "spews out the deepest mysteries of human nature" (*Sämtliche Briefe*, Vol. 8, No. 1170, p. 501).

6   See, e.g., Salaquarda, "Dionysos gegen den Gekreutzigten," pp. 288–295.

7   Zarathustra similarly distinguishes between martyrdom, or sacrifice (*Opfer*), and squandering (*Verschwendung*) (Z IV:1). John Sallis offers an ingenious reading of Dionysus as a principle of "résounding excess" in *Crossings: Nietzsche and the Space of Tragedy* (Chicago: University of Chicago Press, 1991), especially chapter 2.

8   My attention to the performative dimension of Nietzsche's thought is indebted to a number of sources, including Ernst Behler, *Irony and the Discourse of Modernity* (Seattle: University of Washington Press, 1990); Eric Blondel, *Nietzsche: The Body and Culture* (Stanford, CA: Stanford University Press, 1991); Charles Scott, *The Question of Ethics: Nietzsche, Foucault, Heidegger* (Bloomington: Indiana University Press, 1991); Gary Shapiro, *Nietzschean Narratives* (Bloomington: Indiana University Press, 1989); and Henry Staten, *Nietzsche's Voice* (Ithaca, NY: Cornell University Press, 1990).

9   On the "instability" of the libidinal economy of Nietzsche's texts, see Staten, *Nietzsche's Voice*, pp. 86–107.

10 The performative dimension of Nietzsche's revaluation illuminates the similarity he perceives between himself and Christ. He describes Jesus as "an incarnate [*leibhafte*] Gospel of love" (GM 1:8), and he credits "the Redeemer" with disclosing "a new way of life, *not* a new faith" (AC 33).

11 For an excellent account of Nietzsche's debts to Emerson as a performative (i.e., "provocative") thinker, see Tracy B. Strong, "Nietzsche's Political Aesthetics," collected in *Nietzsche's New Seas*, ed. Michael Allen Gillespie and Tracy B. Strong (Chicago: University of Chicago Press, 1988), pp. 153–174. Strong

persuasively shows how Nietzsche's performances "provoke" in (some) others a desire to found the authority of their judgments in the collective intuitions of a community (pp. 158–59).

12 In his draft of a letter to Brandes at the beginning of December 1888, Nietzsche describes the "Decree Against Christianity" as "marking the conclusion [*das den Schluß macht*]" of *The Antichrist(ian)* (*Sämtliche Briefe*, Vol. 8, No. 1170, p. 502). See also Mazzino Montinari's commentary on the "Decree" in *Friedrich Nietzsche: Sämtliche Werke, Kritische Studienausgabe in 15 Bänden*, ed. G. Colli and M. Montinari (Berlin: deGruyter/Deutscher Taschenbuch Verlag, 1980), Vol. 14, pp. 450–453.

13 My treatment of the Decree is significantly indebted to Shapiro's lucid discussion in *Nietzschean Narratives*, pp. 146–47. Shapiro also renders a felicitous English translation of the "Decree" (p. 146).

14 *Studienausgabe*, Vol. 6, p. 254.

15 Ibid., emphasis added.

16 Shapiro proposes that "*Ecce Homo* is substituted for a book that is not written. The text which was to serve as a kind of personal appendix to the event and text of transvaluation becomes a means of not completing either" (*Nietzschean Narratives*, pp. 145–146). While Nietzsche does not complete his original, ambitious plan for a quadrapartite *Hauptwerk*, he eventually understands this plan to be unrealistic. Nietzsche does complete his planned statement and performance of revaluation, if only because he can do no more.

17 Shapiro, for example, recommends a remarkably Apollinian recuperation of Nietzsche's excesses in *The Antichrist(ian):* "I suggest that we read the admittedly feverish imagery of dirt and cleanliness, body, blood and poison, which becomes more and more pronounced as one reaches the end of the book, as intrinsic to the strategies and economy of the text rather than as symptoms of a loss of control" (ibid., p. 139).

18 In the introduction to his massive study, Richard Schacht explains his decision to discount the "excesses" that obscure and occlude Nietzsche's genuinely philosophical insights: "I also have chosen simply to pass over Nietzsche's frequent rhetorical excesses, and the ill-considered shots he so often takes at various targets which catch his eye along his way. . . . I feel that dwelling upon them gets in the way of coming to terms with the substance of his philosophical thought. They blemish and mar its surface; but one must school oneself to look past them, filtering them out as so much unfortunate static, if one is to be able to get down to matters of philosophical moment" [*Nietzsche* (New York: Routledge, 1983), p. xv].

19 With respect to this question of Nietzsche's confrontation with Christianity, I am inclined to resist the apolitical, "aestheticist" orientation of Alexander Nehamas's excellent book *Nietzsche: Life as Literature* (Cambridge, MA: Harvard University Press, 1985). According to Nehamas, Nietzsche's experiment with "life as literature" has effectively removed him from the sphere of moral evaluation: "In praising people and deeds who are beyond good and evil [Nietzsche] has managed to situate himself beyond moral evaluation as well, in that the question of his importance has become more pressing than the question of his goodness. His own cruelty, his attacks on many of our ideas and values, on our

habits and sensibilities, are not reasons why we should turn away from him. On the contrary, they are reasons why we should continue to read him and why we should admire him even as we disagree with him" (p. 234). While I am aware that Nehamas's own "perspectivism" significantly restricts the compass of the "we" for whom he speaks, I nevertheless fear that his guiding aestheticism prematurely tables the question of Nietzsche's "goodness," which strikes me as more important (in certain contexts, at least) than the question of Nietzsche's "importance." A fully aestheticized Nietzsche may be more pleasing to contemplate, but "he" fails to embody the signature tensions of the age, from which we might gain a heightened appreciation for the guiding pathos of modernity as a whole.

20   Robert Eden thus observes that "so much intelligence has been invested in saving Nietzsche from the Nazi vulgarization that it is demoralizing to realize that Nietzsche intended a veritable jungle growth of such partial or misunderstandings to spring from the fertile soil of his writings" [*Political Leadership and Nihilism* (Tampa: University Presses of Florida, 1983), p. 226].

21   Nehamas's claim that Nietzsche is "always his own best reader" (*Nietzsche*, p. 234), aptly conveys his appreciation of Nietzsche's unparalleled powers of self-inquisition, but it also understates the delusions and self-misunderstandings that are induced by Nietzsche's decadence.

22   Draft of a letter to Georg Brandes at the beginning of December 1888 (*Sämtliche Briefe*, Vol. 8, No. 1170, p. 501).

23   In this respect, then, Alasdair MacIntyre is entirely justified in portraying Nietzsche as the logical culmination and prodigal son of the Enlightenment [*After Virtue* (Notre Dame, IN: Notre Dame University Press, 1984), pp. 113–118]. Yet Nietzsche's case against Christian morality is not reducible to the claim that it trades on metaphysical fictions and superstitions – hence the inadequacy of the analogy MacIntyre suggests between Nietzsche and Captain Cook (p. 113). Nietzsche's critique of Christian morality also targets the need cultivated in otherwise healthy individuals for the specific superstitions purveyed by the priests; Nietzsche's critical task thus comprises more than simple enlightenment.

24   This strongly cognitive interpretation of Nietzsche's revaluation, as a grand exposé of Christian morality, builds upon Walter Kaufmann's seminal reading in *Nietzsche: Philosopher, Psychologist, Antichrist*, 4th Edition (Princeton, NJ: Princeton University Press, 1974), pp. 110–115.

25   The author of *The Antichrist(ian)* and *Ecce Homo* is obviously not the Nietzsche who, according to Richard Rorty, "first explicitly suggested that we drop the whole idea of 'knowing the truth'" [*Contingency, Irony and Solidarity* (Cambridge: Cambridge University Press, 1989), p. 27]. Rorty's Nietzsche apparently authored only such undistinguished works as the unpublished essay "On Truth and Lie in an Extramoral Sense."

26   For a persuasive interpretation of *The Antichrist(ian)* as a "polemic against liberal Christianity," see Weaver Santaniello, *Nietzsche, God, and the Jews: His Critique of Judeo-Christianity in Relation to the Nazi Myth* (Albany: State University of New York Press, 1994), chapter 6.

27   In his 1886 preface to *Daybreak*, Nietzsche elaborates on his scheme to subvert

Christian morality: "We too are still men of conscience. . . . It is only as men of *this* conscience that we still feel ourselves related to the German piety and integrity of millennia, even if as its most questionable and final descendants, we immoralists, we godless men of today, indeed in a certain sense as its heirs, as the executors of its innermost will. . . . In us there is accomplished – supposing you want a formula – the *self-overcoming* [*Selbstaufhebung*] *of morality*" (D P4).

28   Nietzsche's insistence in *Ecce Homo* that he is not just another priest or prophet should be understood in terms of his unprecedented access to the truth. The "halcyon tone" of *Zarathustra*, for example, is evidence not merely of poetic inspiration, but of the author's descent into the well of truth (EH P4).

29   For a comprehensive reckoning of Nietzsche's complex orientation to truth, see Babette Babich, *Nietzsche's Philosophy of Science: Reflecting Science on the Ground of Art for Life* (Albany: State University of New York Press, 1994), especially pp. 227–235. By attributing to Nietzsche a "perspectival hyperrealism," Babich is able to isolate the precise contexts in which Nietzsche is both a "realist" and an "antirealist" (pp. 227–229).

30   On the complexity of Nietzsche's attempt to contribute to the overcoming of the will to truth, see Staten, *Nietzsche's Voice*, p. 30.

31   My attention to "Nietzsche's graffito" is indebted to Shapiro's eponymous essay, which appears in revised form as chapter 5 of his *Nietzschean Narratives*.

32   I borrow this particular use of the term *anxiety of influence* from Harold Bloom, *The Anxiety of Influence: A Theory of Poetry* (New York: Oxford University Press, 1973). I am also indebted on this point to Rorty's extension of Bloom's theory in *Contingency, Irony, and Solidarity*, chapter 2.

33   Henry Staten too detects Nietzsche's voice of despair, situating it within the complex libidinal economy of Nietzsche's texts (*Nietzsche's Voice*, p. 34).

34   Nietzsche includes himself among "the firstborn of the twentieth century" (BGE 214), and he predicts that he will be "misunderstood, misjudged, misidentified, slandered, misheard, and not heard" at least "until 1901" (GS 371). In a letter to Malwida von Meysenbug on 12 May 1887, he explains that his 1886 prefaces are designed to discourage the "crowd" from reading his books: "Owing to the indescribable strangeness and danger of my thoughts, receptive ears will open up to them only much later – and certainly not before 1901" (*Sämtliche Briefe*, Vol. 8, No. 845, p. 70).

35   The "voice" of *Zarathustra* "bridges centuries" (EH P4).

36   The "birthday" in question may be 30 September 1888, which Nietzsche identifies as "the day when the first book of the *Revaluation of All Values* was completed" (TI P).

37   Nietzsche also speaks from this posthumous standpoint in *Ecce Homo*: "I know my fate. One day my name will be associated with the memory of something tremendous – a crisis without equal on earth, the most profound collision of conscience, a decision that was conjured up *against* everything that had been believed, demanded, hallowed so far" (EH:destiny 1).

38   Additional, albeit indirect, evidence of Nietzsche's intention to address audiences of a distant posterity is found in his reference in *Ecce Homo* to Part IV of *Thus Spoke Zarathustra*, of which his readers in 1888 would have been utterly ignorant (EH:wise 4). Unless he is simply confused at this point – and he does

refer elsewhere to Part III as "the third and last part" of *Zarathustra* (EH:z 4) –
he can only have in mind an audience to whom the whole of *Zarathustra* has
been made available. In a letter to Köselitz on 9 December 1888, he declares
that "the proper time" for the publication of Part IV of *Zarathustra* will be "after
a few decades of world-historical crises – wars!" (*Sämtliche Briefe*, Vol. 8, No.
1181, pp. 514–515).

39   W. Bousset suggests that the mythology of the Antichrist "seems to have arisen
in the Persian eschatology (the battle of Ahura Mazda with Angra Mainyu) . . .
and to have penetrated from this source to the Jewish Apocalyptic literature"
[*Encyclopaedia of Religion and Ethics*, ed. James Hastings, Volume 1 (New York:
Scribner's, 1957), p. 578]. If Bousset is correct, then Nietzsche's figures of the
Antichrist and Zarathustra (Zoroaster) both arise from a common source in
Persian eschatology.

40   Nietzsche's hastily scribbled cards, letters, and drafts of letters from January
1889 alternately identify their author as Caesar, the Crucified, Dionysus, the
condemner of all anti-Semites, the would-be assassin of the young emperor,
Buddha, Alexander, Lord Bacon, Voltaire, Napoleon, Wagner, Prado, Astu, and
"every name in history" (*Sämtliche Briefe*, Vol. 8, Nos. 1229–1256, pp. 567–579).
On Nietzsche's madness-inspired turn to revolutionary politics, see Strong,
"Nietzsche's Political Aesthetics," pp. 153–174. Strong downplays the seriousness of Nietzsche's threats, attributing them to the onset of madness. For the
alternative view that Nietzsche "seduced" Ariadne by simulating madness, see
Claudia Crawford, *To Nietzsche: Dionysus, I Love You! Ariadne* (Albany: State University of New York Press, 1995), especially pp. 143–258.

41   *Sämtliche Briefe*, Vol. 8, No. 1256, p. 578.

42   John Bernstein presents a compelling case to this effect in *Nietzsche's Moral
Philosophy* (Cranbury, NJ: Fairleigh Dickinson University Press, 1988).

43   See Eugen Fink, *Nietzsches Philosophie* (Stuttgart: W. Kohlhammer Verlag), pp.
134–135.

44   Rene Girard draws attention to the complex situation of Nietzsche's delusions
of grandeur within the economy of his thought in "Strategies of Madness –
Nietzsche, Wagner, and Dostoevski," collected in *To Double Business Bound* (Baltimore: Johns Hopkins University Press, 1978), especially pp. 70–72.

45   For a perspicacious analysis of Nietzsche's misjudgment of the timing of his
revaluation, see Hans Sluga, *Heidegger's Crisis: Philosophy and Politics in Nazi
Germany* (Cambridge, MA: Harvard University Press, 1993), pp. 70–74. Sluga
suggests that the historical "crisis" to which Nietzsche alludes may be more
accurately understood as a personal, psychological crisis: "The crisis of which
Nietzsche spoke in *Ecce Homo* was in reality both more and less than a historical
happening. What he announced right before his final collapse was above all a
crisis in his own consciousness. . . . The subjective experience of a cataclysmic
present became the symbol of a world-historical process as well" (p. 71).

46   I am indebted here to Staten's discussion of the "transcendental *ressentiment*"
that motivates and informs Nietzsche's own diagnosis of priestly *ressentiment*
(*Nietzsche's Voice*, p. 38).

47   This parallel is noted and documented by Salaquarda ("Dionysos gegen den
Gekreutzigten," pp. 311–312), who in turn attributes it to C. A. Bernoulli.

48 For an excellent account of Nietzsche's physiological interpretation of Christ, see Daniel Ahern, *Nietzsche as Cultural Physician* (University Park: Pennsylvania State University Press, 1995), pp. 98–113.

49 For a compelling sketch of the "kinship" between Nietzsche and Socrates, see Dannhauser, *Nietzsche's View of Socrates*, pp. 269–274.

50 The double agency involved in Nietzsche's revaluation – his involuntary participation in the spectacle he organizes – provides a representative basis for Michel Foucault's account of the *episteme* that corresponds to the "age of man" [*The Order of Things: An Archaeology of the Human Sciences* (New York: Random House, 1970), especially chapter 9, "Man and His Doubles"]. I maintain here that Nietzsche's response to the epistemic crisis of modernity (like Foucault's) is to live within the terms of its constitutive contradictions, to embody the fragmentation of its signature ethos.

51 Acknowledging this problem of self-reference, Maudemarie Clark promptly issues Nietzsche an exemption from his general account of philosophers: "Nietzsche knows perfectly well that [his doctrine of the will to power] is not the truth" [*Nietzsche on Truth and Philosophy* (Cambridge: Cambridge University Press, 1990), p. 240]. Clark's Nietzsche is not only honest about himself to an unprecedented degree, but also solicitous of his readers' welfare and progress as philosophers in their own right: "He gives us the clues we need to figure out that [the doctrine of will to power] is actually a projection of his life-affirming (and self-affirming) ideal" (p. 240). Clark does not explain, however, why a creature endowed with such abundant self-knowledge, self-restraint, and care for his readers must (or does) resort to the byzantine strategies of self-disclosure deployed by Nietzsche. If he really is more honest and beneficent than all other philosophers hitherto, then why must he be so secretive and indirect in his teachings? Whence his esotericism at all?

52 My account of Nietzsche's standing as a representative exemplar of late modernity is indebted to Stanley Cavell's similar account of Emerson in *Conditions Handsome and Unhandsome: The Constitution of Emersonian Perfectionism* (Chicago: University of Chicago Press, 1990), especially pp. 56–63.

53 Characterizing the enduring significance of the post-discursive Nietzsche, Alphonso Lingis maintains that "Nietzsche's discourse . . . does not formulate simply his closed and immanent organic vitality but the surgings of the forces of Dionysian nature, of the waves breaking on the cliffs at Ez and the sun blazing over the glaciers at Sils Maria, for which his own organism is the conduit. In addition it is, like every impulsive stream of life that formulates itself in discourse, addressed to someone. But this someone is not us, representatives of the discourse we today have established as sane" ("The Irrecuperable," *International Studies in Philosophy*, Vol. 23, No. 2, 1991, p. 74).

54 Letter to Emily Fynn on 6 December 1888 *(Sämtliche Briefe,* Vol. 8, No. 1175, p. 507).

55 Letter to Köselitz on 9 December 1888 *(Sämtliche Briefe,* Vol. 8, No. 1181, p. 515).

56 Letter to Malwida von Meysenbug on 5 November 1888 *(Sämtliche Briefe,* Vol. 8, No. 1138, p. 463).

57 Various letters written in January 1889 (*Sämtliche Briefe*, Vol. 8, Nos. 1238, 1239, 1243, 1247, 1248, 1253–1255, pp. 572–577).

58 Letter to Burckhardt on 6 January 1989 (*Sämtliche Briefe*, Vol. 8, No. 1256, pp. 577–578).

59 Letter to Reinhard von Seydlitz on 12 February 1888 (*Sämtliche Briefe*, Vol. 8, No. 989, p. 248).

60 On the significatory importance of Nietzsche's polycentric soul, see Gilles Deleuze, "Nomad Thought," trans. David B. Allison, collected in *The New Nietzsche*, ed. David B. Allison (New York: Delta, 1977), pp. 142–149. Deleuze writes, "These proper names that come and go in Nietzsche's texts are . . . designations of intensity inscribed upon a body that could be the earth of a book, but could also be the suffering body of Nietzsche himself: *I am all the names of history.* . . . There is a kind of nomadism, a perpetual displacement in the intensities designated by proper names, intensities that interpenetrate one another at the same time that they are lived, experienced, by a single body" (p. 146).

61 Sensing, perhaps, the horrifying nature of the excesses unleashed in *The Antichrist(ian)*, Nietzsche explains in his letter to Köselitz on 30 October 1888 that *Ecce Homo* is supposed to muffle, if only temporarily, the monstrous reverberations of his explosion: "I do not want to present myself to people as a prophet, savage beast *[Unthier]*, or moral monster *[Moral-Scheusal]*" (*Sämtliche Briefe*, Vol. 8, No. 1137, p. 462).

62 In his letter to Erwin Rohde on 31 December 1895, Overbeck describes his final meeting with Nietzsche: "I saw him only in his room, half-crouching like a wild animal mortally wounded and wanting only to be left in peace. He made literally not one sound while I was there. He did not appear to be suffering or in pain, except perhaps for the expression of profound distaste visible in his lifeless eyes. . . . He had been living for weeks in a state of alternation between days of dreadful excitability, rising to a pitch of roaring and shouting, and days of complete prostration" [letter cited in Ronald Hayman, *Nietzsche: A Critical Life* (New York: Penguin, 1982), p. 348].

63 Lingis detects in the depths of Nietzsche's madness an extrahuman "language" that points, perhaps, to the future of humankind: "And after the neurochemical collapse, in those last ten years when Nietzsche no longer wrote texts, even postcards, but howled and screeched and hissed at night, it is only *our* inevitable interpretation that we take those utterances of his neurochemically collapsed body as a rhetoric desperately addressed to the doctor, representative of our institutions and our established discourse. . . . Nietzsche's utterance of his last ten years, lost to us, reverberates only for his lions and his eagles and his serpents" ("The Irrecuperable," p. 74).

64 *Sämtliche Briefe*, Vol. 8, No. 1256, p. 578. This letter states more succinctly the theme of a letter written three days earlier to his "beloved Princess Ariadne" (Cosima Wagner), in which he claims to have been Buddha, Dionysus, Alexander, Caesar, Lord Bacon, Voltaire, Napoleon, Wagner, and the Crucified (*Sämtliche Briefe*, Vol. 8, No. 1241, p. 573).

CONCLUSION: ODYSSEUS BOUND?

But I with my sharp sword cut into small bits a great round cake of wax, and kneaded it with my strong hands, and soon the wax grew warm, forced by the strong pressure and the rays of the lord Helios Hyperion. Then I anointed with this [wax] the ears of all my comrades in turn; and they bound me in the ship hand and foot, upright in the step of the mast, and made the ropes fast at the ends to the mast itself; and themselves sitting down smote the grey sea with their oars.

The Odyssey, XII. 172–179

I am still waiting for a philosophical *physician* in the exceptional sense of that word – one who has to pursue the problem of the total health of a people, time, race or of humanity – *to muster the courage to push my suspicion to its limits* and to risk the proposition: what was at stake in all philosophizing hitherto was not at all "truth" but something else – let us say, health, future, growth, power, life.

The Gay Science, Preface, Section 2 (emphasis added)

How clever was Herr Nietzsche? Clever enough to equate morality with diet (EH:clever 1), apparently, and to prefer the lusty naturalism of Rossini to the constipated gravity of "German music" (EH:clever 7). Clever enough to husband the depleted vitality and dwindling creativity at his disposal, never striving "for *honors*, for *women*, [or] for *money*" (EH:clever 9). Clever enough to attend carefully to the "small things which are generally considered matters of complete indifference" (EH:clever 10), to the quotidian nuances

246

of nutrition, place, climate, and recreation (EH:clever 8). Clever enough, in the end, to have become what he was by following his "formula for greatness in a human being": *amor fati* (EH:clever 10).

This testimony to Nietzsche's cleverness is drawn, however, from an exceedingly dubious source: his own ersatz autobiography, *Ecce Homo*. While this bristling little book yields a wealth of insights into Nietzsche's life and career, its aspirations to hagiography should pique the suspicions of even his most adoring readers. This is an author, after all, who has already suggested that "modern men" could not "stand a *true* autobiography," for they could not "endure a single *truth* 'about man'" (GM III:19). Remarking on the reluctance of modern readers to see their heroes and villains as they really are, he asks, "What prudent man would write a single honest word about himself today? He would have to be a member of the Order of Holy Foolhardiness to do so" (GM III:19). In light of such remarks, we are obliged to approach Nietzsche's own autobiography with heightened suspicions of his honesty. Indeed, unless we are prepared to take his feckless (or prudent) word for it, we must look elsewhere to gauge the true range and depth of his abiding cleverness.

A successor psychologist, Sigmund Freud, reportedly opined that "[Nietzsche] had a more penetrating knowledge of himself than any other man who ever lived or was ever likely to live."[1] This platitude certainly concurs with Nietzsche's familiar account of himself, but it also dodges the pragmatic question of determining the precise depths to which his "penetrating" self-knowledge actually reached. Did he achieve a level of self-knowledge commensurate with his general knowledge of human psychology? Was he sufficiently apprised of his own failings – his decadence, resentment, romanticism, anxiety of influence, and so on – that he was able to arrange for their pre-emptive neutralization?

Let us grant that Nietzsche's understanding of decadence is, as he insists, both unprecedented and unrivaled. "In questions of *décadence*," he may very well be "the highest authority on earth."[2] But how familiar was he with the particular manifestations and eruptions of his own decadence? How exacting was he in applying his general diagnosis of modernity to his own psychic disarray? He knew, for example, that decadence typically expresses itself in symptoms unknown and unimaginable to the agents in question, who generally stand in the worst possible position to detect and interpret the signs of their own decay. He also knew that decadence characteristically manifests itself in various delusions of grandeur, such as the perception of oneself standing "between two millennia" or the conviction that one can manage the effects of one's own decay. This impressive fund of general knowledge corroborates his claim to authority in all matters of decadence, but it does not yet suggest an intimate familiarity with the specific facts of his own condition. Our guiding question thus stands: To what extent was Nietzsche able to subsume his own erratic life under the general theory of decadence that he advances?

Nietzsche was not as clever as his most loyal readers tend to suggest. He did not possess sufficient self-knowledge to close the circle of his thought and complete his critical project.³ Nor did he finally attain the panoptic standpoint he disallows to other thinkers. Most important, he succeeded neither in resisting the philosopher's temptation to exempt himself from his own blanket diagnoses nor in defending the exemption he surreptitiously issued to himself. Having exposed the recidivistic error to which all philosophers naturally fall prey, he was powerless to resist this error in his own right. Like all previous systems of thought, Nietzsche's philosophy "creates the world in its own image; it cannot do otherwise" (BGE 9).

The fatal flaw of all philosophers and psychologists hitherto, he announces, lies in their common failure to forge the final, self-referential link in the concatenation of their own pet insights. Philosophers are all "advocates who resent that name, and for the most part even wily spokesmen for their prejudices" (BGE 5). Nietzsche himself presents no exception to this general truth, despite his occasional protestations to the contrary. He may have been more successful than his predecessors in applying his signature insights to his own situation, but in the end, he too fails to subject himself to the withering critical gaze he trains on others. Having told us that all philosophers "tyrannically" excuse themselves from their own critical inquisitions, that the presumption of philosophers constitutes "the most spiritual will to power" (BGE 9), he promptly corroborates this claim by issuing himself an exemption from his otherwise inclusive diagnosis of modernity. Precisely *because* he is decadent, he perversely insists, he has taken the measure of his age (EH:wise 1).

At this juncture, however, it would be premature to reject Freud's assessment of Nietzsche's "penetrating" self-knowledge. He neither pursued nor claimed for himself the transparency of soul that would invite a definitive self-examination. While accounting for the genius that distinguishes himself and his fellow genealogists, he candidly remarks: "We are unknown to ourselves, we men of knowledge – and with good reason. We have never sought ourselves – how could it happen that we should ever *find* ourselves?" (GM P1). Reprising this curious maxim in his "autobiography," he offers to share the secret of his prodigious cleverness: "To become what one is, one must not have the faintest notion *what* one is" (EH:clever 9).

By treading this *via negativa*, Nietzsche actually joins his former nemesis, Socrates, in obeying the imperative of the Delphic oracle: "Know thyself." Like Socrates, moreover, Nietzsche embraces the oracle's pronouncement in the full force of its defining irony. He pursues self-knowledge, that is, despite his guiding insight into the futility of any such quest. The irony of the Delphic injunction, as of the twinship of the philosophers it joins, thus arises from the unattainable nature of the goal it assigns to the votaries of the oracle: "Consequently, given the best will in the world to understand ourselves as individually as possible, 'to know ourselves,' each of us will always succeed in becoming conscious only of what is not individual but 'average'" (GS 354). In order to obey the Delphic imperative and resolutely pursue the goal of self-knowledge, one must already understand that a definitive self-knowledge is impossible to attain: "We are necessarily strangers to ourselves, we do not comprehend ourselves, we *have* to misunderstand ourselves, for us the law 'Each is furthest from himself' applies to all eternity – we are not 'men of knowledge' with respect to ourselves" (GM P1).

Nietzsche's interpretation of the Apollinian oracle thus reveals the Dionysian wisdom encrypted within the Delphic injunction. Issued to a healthy people, for whom self-knowledge is coextensive with spontaneous self-expression, the imperative "Know thyself" is otiose, if not unintelligible. Nothing comes more naturally to the representatives of a healthy people or epoch than an unquestioned, pre-reflective, embodied self-knowledge. It is a hallmark of healthy peoples and ages that self-knowledge never becomes an issue to be addressed, much less a lack to be overcome. Issued to a decadent people or epoch, however, the Delphic imperative amounts to a sibylline joke played by malicious gods on enfeebled mortals (GS 335). The stipulated need for self-knowledge points not to the possibility of actually gaining self-knowledge, but to the irreversible decay that this need signifies. Anyone who lacks self-knowledge will most assuredly never attain it.

Socrates indirectly confirms Nietzsche's interpretation of the oracle's pronouncement when he locates his alleged "wisdom" in the knowledge that he does not know.[4] This nihilistic insight, celebrated by Socrates and Nietzsche alike, is attainable only by decadent philosophers, who pathologically call into question the unjustified, pre-reflective practices that define a people or epoch. As they expertly unravel the instinctual fabric that binds their respective peoples and epochs, decadent philosophers are left clutching a single, nihilistic thread. They may know nothing else, but they at least know that they know nothing. Here, one step removed from the self-consuming wisdom of Silenus, decadent philosophers presume to pass judgment on the (meaningless) whole.

One's obedience to the imperative "Know thyself" thus leads not to self-knowledge, but to the enactment of one's inevitable self-destruction. While a healthy soul "knows" itself immediately and without oracular prompting, a corrupt soul will sooner expend its residual vitality than surrender its innermost secrets. *Nosce te ipsum,* Nietzsche candidly concedes, thus constitutes a "recipe for ruin" (EH:clever 9). Is it merely a coincidence that Socrates alone pursues the oracle's gnomic pronouncement to its absurd, self-consuming conclusion, whereby he obliquely accuses his fellow Athenians of collective impiety? Or that Nietzsche, two millennia removed from the suicide of Socrates, would dare to court madness and self-destruction in order to become what he was?

For nihilists like Socrates and Nietzsche, then, the point of obeying the oracle's imperative cannot be to gain self-knowledge. Indeed, if the primary justification of the pursuit of self-knowledge were to lie in the promise of its successful attainment, then one would be foolish to engage in its pursuit. While it is true that one might receive in the process a negative, tragic insight, this humble morsel of wisdom could never be considered an adequate justification for the pain and hardship endured. For both Nietzsche and Socrates, the real justification of the pursuit of self-knowledge lies elsewhere, in a vague anticipation of the type of person one might become in the process. Socrates thus explains that if we continue to seek that which we do not know, we will become "better men, braver and less idle" – even if we never gain knowledge of anything.[5] Nietzsche similarly insists that his own genealogical investigations contribute to the constitution of a fructifying regimen of self-overcoming, a therapeutic "technique of the self" that may enable him to explore further the undiscovered country of decadence. He remains forever unknown to himself, but his pursuit of self-knowledge nevertheless yields indirect, unanticipated benefits for his ongoing struggle with the decadence of late modernity.

The hunt for self-knowledge will always fail to turn up its elusive quarry, but it may nevertheless succeed in transforming the hunters into *signs* of the excess vitality required to participate in the sport. The quest for self-knowledge thus furnishes an effective ascetic pretext for the expenditure of residual vitality. One is still a fool for seeking self-knowledge, but one becomes a significatory – and therefore significant – fool in the process. Strictly speaking, however, even this justification remains indirect and external, for seekers of self-knowledge are unable to determine in advance the dialogic meaning of the signs they will become. To quest for self-knowledge in order to embody a *particular* sign is to confuse cause and effect.

The most that decadent philosophers can hope for from their quest for self-knowledge is to reveal themselves fully to others in the embodiment of their inexorable decay. As I have suggested, this dialogical self-revelation is the source of Nietzsche's mitigated triumph in the "dangerous game" he plays. While he fails to provide a definitive account of his age, he successfully transforms himself into a sign of his times. He thereby contributes to our appreciation for the governing pathos of his age by bodying forth (albeit unwittingly) an incarnate critique of modernity. Although ultimately unknown to himself, he trained his successors to probe the self-referential blind spot that vitiates his critical enterprise. Regardless of its success or failure, any attempt to take the measure of Nietzsche will lead to the parastrategic dissemination of his teachings.

The hard truth of Freud's insight thus lies in the tragic formulation of his appraisal of Nietzsche's "penetrating" self-knowledge. Nietzsche may have failed to attain the Promethean measure of self-understanding that would make him whole again, but his knowledge of himself nevertheless outstrips that of most mortals. While no philosopher ever gains a definitive self-knowledge, some active nihilists are free to continue their quest even in the face of its acknowledged futility. Nietzsche's foolish pursuit of self-knowledge is doomed to failure, but it might contribute nonetheless to his readers' understanding of the age he involuntarily represents. If this is true, then how best might we describe and convey the unparalleled self-knowledge he attained?

I have portrayed Nietzsche as pursuing the sort of transfigurative limit experience that would occasion an enhancement of humankind as a whole. He aspired to be born posthumously as the Antichrist, an achievement he equates with the calamitous self-overcoming of Christian morality. In many respects his pursuit of a limit experience resembles that of Odysseus, who similarly sought to advance the recognized frontiers of the human condition. Odysseus longed for an experience previously unknown to mortals: to survive the thanatonic song of the sirens. While bewitched by the sirens, he knew, any mortal would dash himself on the nearest rocks. Such a state, in which one unthinkingly craves what is most disadvantageous for oneself, is not unlike the condition Nietzsche calls "decadence." His agency bounded by a horizon of distinctly human experiences, Odysseus could not have known in advance what it would be like to hear – and survive – the song of the sirens. He could know only that he would be transfigured by the experience and that the extant complement of human perfections would be permanently expanded.

On his own, Odysseus knew, he was not equal to the limit experience he sought. He too would dash himself on the rocks if tempted by the sirens. Guided by the goddess Circe, he consequently implemented measures designed to insulate his pursuit of a transfigurative experience from his own, all-too-human limitations. He famously instructed his crew to bind him to the mast and to sail within auditory range of the sirens' lair. Having pre-emptively compensated for his all-too-human weaknesses, he would be free to experience the reveries of sirenic intoxication without fear of accepting their invitation to die. If his initial orders to his crew were to prevail as securely as the lashes that would soon bind him to the ship's mast, then he would need first to prepare his shipmates for the adventure that lay ahead. They must be disciplined to ignore the subsequent, countermanding orders that he knows the sirens will elicit from him. By sealing his shipmates' ears with wax, Odysseus effectively founded a community that would compensate for his own acknowledged weaknesses, a community that would not permit him to recoil from his moment of transfiguration. Once bound to the mast by his newly deafened comrades, he could neither refuse nor resist the epiphany he craved. No twinge of ambivalence would be permitted to deflect the limit experience he sought.[6] The wisdom of Odysseus, justly celebrated in the circulatory myths of Greek antiquity, thus emanates from an unflinching appraisal of his own, all-too-human limitations. As Nietzsche might say, the wisdom of Odysseus lies in his uncanny ability to turn his destiny to his advantage.

In his desire to "stand between two millennia," Nietzsche resembles Odysseus before the mast. Cognizant of his own decadence, if not of its precise manifestations, Nietzsche must insulate his pursuit of a limit experience from his own, all-too-human weaknesses. Unable to confront his own decadence in its immanence and specificity, he frames a plan for enlisting others to do so for him. He thus anticipates and potentially compensates for the unknown effects of his own decay. He knew, for example, that he would need to recruit readers who would continue his incipient rebellion against Christian morality. Such readers, he also knew, must heroically resist the blandishments of discipleship, lest they succumb to the spell of a clever priest. Hoping to induce the self-overcoming of Christian morality, he strove to extend his formative influence into the coming millennium, at which time he would be recognized and revered as the Antichrist. In order to prepare himself to stand between two millennia, he experimented with parastrategesis, which he thought might neutralize the effects of his own decay while attracting a fellowship of anti-Christian successors.

Like Odysseus, Nietzsche is not equal to the limit experience he seeks. Having briefly tasted epiphany before in the form of the adventitious thought of eternal recurrence (EH:z 1), Nietzsche understands that his conscious pursuit of transfiguration is severely jeopardized by his all-too-human weaknesses. He must consequently enlist the help of others, and he must discipline these others to execute their original charge, despite the subsequent demands he knows he will make of them. If he is to succeed in orchestrating for himself the transfiguration he craves, then he must first seal his readers' ears to the decadent longings that emanate irrepressibly from his writings.[7] Duly trained, such readers would turn a deaf ear to the entreaties of Nietzsche's decadence, just as Odysseus's crew ignored his crazed demands to be unbound and released to his death. Guided by the divine patronage of Dionysus, Nietzsche reprises the self-neutralizing strategy of the clever Odysseus. His experiments with parastrategesis are designed to found a community of readers who will safely transport his teachings across the "open sea" of late modernity (GS 343).

Like the loyal members of Odysseus's crew, Nietzsche's perfect readers would belay, if necessary, any subsequent orders that might divert them from their appointed course. They would heed only his original call to arms, ignoring his subsequent and inevitable wish for spineless sycophants and fawning disciples. It is no coincidence that his favorite image for his perfect readers is borrowed from Zarathustra's heartfelt address to his intrepid shipmates:

> To you, the bold searchers [*Suchern*], researchers [*Versuchern*], and whoever embarks with cunning sails on terrible seas – to you, drunk with riddles, glad of the twilight, whose soul flutes lure astray to every whirlpool, because you do not want to grope along a thread with cowardly hand; and where you can *guess*, you hate to *deduce* – to you alone I tell the riddle that I *saw*, the vision of the loneliest. (Z III:2.1; partially cited in EH:gb 3)

Here, however, the Odyssean parallel ends. Nietzsche did not enjoy the luxury of an exclusively mythic existence,[8] and his experiments with para-strategesis have failed to reproduce the resounding success of the clever Odysseus. Whereas Odysseus could rely confidently on his loyal, battle-tested crew, Nietzsche must count on unknown readers whom he neither trusts nor admires. While his desperate situation imbues his pursuit of a limit experience with a degree of danger unknown to Odysseus, it also seals his inevitable failure. To be sure, Nietzsche did eventually attain a sort of limit experience, which he described to his friend Heinrich Köselitz, under the macabre signature of "The Crucified," as gloriously ecstatic: "Sing me a new song: the world is transfigured [*verklärt*] and all the heavens rejoice."[9] This transfiguration is more regularly called "madness," however, and it bears no resemblance to the calamitous limit experience he led us to expect on his behalf. Rather than deafen his perfect readers to the siren song of decadence, he now lends his own voice to its ubiquitous chorus, even as he clamors for silence. In fact, if we appeal to the evaluative standards that he consistently invoked in his post-Zarathustran writings, then we must pro-nounce him a loser in the "dangerous game" he desperately plays.

From Nietzsche's own decadent perspective, his campaign to unseat Christian morality would appear to be a failure. He has attracted all the wrong readers, and the madness that enveloped him is certainly not the limit experience he sought. Instead of the philosopher-commanders who would oversee the era of "great politics," legislating the transition to the successor age to modernity, he has sired lawgivers manqué, political bullies and thugs, and papier mâché *Übermenschen*. For every Stefan George or Thomas Mann (decadent artists in their own right), Nietzsche has inspired a legion of graffiti artists, hack playwrights, and adolescent songwriters. It would appear, then, that he cannot afford the readership he desires. His decadence enforces instinctual needs that subvert the cultivation of the perfect readers he envisions. His ingenious experiments with parastrategesis ultimately fail to insulate his readers from his decadence. Not unlike an-other mad Teutonic genius of the nineteenth century, Nietzsche creates monstrous children whom he ultimately cannot control.

In arriving at an "objective" assessment of his influence, however, we must beware of accepting uncritically his own criteria of evaluation. Although he claimed to pursue an experience that is altogether new and would permanently augment the complement of extant human perfections, he characteristically assessed his progress in terms of what was known and familiar to him. His diagnosis of modernity was similarly unoriginal in its Protestant anticipation of demise and apocalypse, whereas his hazy vision of the postmodern, tragic age to come betrays his bourgeois, romantic yearnings.[10] Nietzsche vowed to "break history in two," but the rupture he eventually celebrates only reinforces the hegemony of the traditions from which he claims to stray. He promised to deliver "dynamite," but he has apparently attached to this dubious ordnance an interminably long fuse.

While his need for slavish readers is certainly symptomatic of decadence, his desire for masterly readers is equally so – especially insofar as it manifests a romantic anachronism. As we have seen, Nietzsche subscribes to a romance in which he would personally train an intrepid vanguard of swashbuckling warrior-genealogists. These perfect readers must complete their apprenticeship by disowning their master, only to return later as his equals and compatriots (Z I:22.3). Steeled by this manly rite of initiation, they swear their unerring fealty to Nietzsche and pledge their lives to the destruction of Christianity. Regardless of how we might ultimately judge his unique rendition of this masculinist romance, his idle speculations on the likely consequences of his explosion are no more authoritative than Odysseus's imaginations of the sirens prior to his transfigurative experience before the mast. As his own theory of decadence expressly indicates, his discursive critique of modernity holds philosophical value only as a symptom of his own decay.

Nietzsche's apparent failure to endue his philosophy with the novelty and originality he promises should come as no surprise to his readers. Did he not teach us to beware of priests and philosophers who claim to bear "glad tidings?" Did he not warn that anyone who discovers a new route to the enhancement of humankind will invariably present this path as impassably strewn with obstacles and barriers, such that all would-be pilgrims are dependent upon the "assistance" of the resident expert guide? In order to explore the undiscovered countries of the human soul, he sensibly insists, we must forcibly negate the colonizing influence of the philosophers who initially point the way. But what of a philosopher who stands under the name Nietzsche? On this point of self-reference he remains uncharacteristically silent, unable in his besetting decay to entertain for long the possibility that he too postpones the enhancement of humankind.

Nietzsche has failed to assemble the readership he sought for his war on Christianity, but his books have in fact attracted readers who are uniquely suited to toil in the twilight of the idols. He envisioned a vanguard of warrior-genealogists whom he would personally train in the arts of manly contest, but his actual readers are nook-dwelling creatures of *ressentiment*, versed in the "effeminate" arts of subterfuge, duplicity, and deception. He yearned for disciples who might tear him to shreds in a pique of maenadic possession, but he instead attracts treacherous followers who will betray him and distort his teachings to suit their own designs.[11] His readership is not what he hoped for, but it accurately reflects what his own critique of modernity would lead us to expect of any decadent philosopher. Although he would certainly disown such readers as unworthy of his legacy, he would do so only because they bear an unbearable resemblance to him. Like their reluctant father, these readers are agents of decadence who anachronistically expend their residual vitality in the service of heroic ideals. Following him, they advance the campaign against Christianity through the use of priestly weapons and stratagems, all the while mouthing a litany of noble pieties.

Nietzsche's irrepressible decadence might appear to compromise his experiments with parastrategesis, but only if we also accept without question his preferred standards for success and failure. The warrior-genealogists whom he hoped to muster would certainly be an impressive sight, especially against the blighted backdrop of late modernity. But they would also be stunningly ill equipped, much like Sophocles' Ajax, to negotiate the shades and shadows of a decadent epoch. The contestatory arena within which such heroes thrive presupposes an age or people that can afford to defend the *agon* against those scoundrels and malcontents who would change the rules of the contest in order to reward their own underhanded "virtues."[12] Since late modernity can afford neither to stage nor to defend a heroic *agon*, Nietzsche's nascent rebellion is much better served by the shifty rogues and dissemblers who bear the unmistakable imprint of his decadence. They alone can summon the requisite deception and trickery to vanquish the last surviving priests of Christendom, and they alone can be counted upon to consume themselves in the priestly Armageddon that will (supposedly) bring modernity to a close. Most important, they alone will betray even Nietzsche in their hateful campaign to exterminate the priestly class.

Although he could not conceive of his readers needing to trample him in the service of the anti-Christian rebellion he foments, he trained them to beware of all priests, especially those who, like him, strike the pose of the anti-priest. Unbeknownst to Nietzsche, then, he cultivated a readership that would grant him no quarter were he to reveal himself as an obstacle to be overcome. He furthermore and equally unwittingly armed his successors with the priestly weapons they would need to vanquish him and all other anti-priests. So although he was unable to assess honestly the nature and effects of his own decadence, he actually compensated for this failing when training his successors. His actual readers are free to pursue his anti-

Christian ends through any means necessary, including a renunciation of him and his signature teachings. Through his participation in the dangerous game, that is, he inadvertently created the audience he wants rather than the audience he needs. His experiments with parastrategesis inaugurated an intergenerational torch race whose participants may successively illuminate the gloaming until the arrival of those who will greet the dawn of the postmodern epoch.

It may be possible, of course, and perhaps even desirable to chart the parallel descent of other alternative lineages of Nietzschean readership. Diligent genealogists may even succeed in identifying the heroic lineage he desired or in locating those perfect readers who quietly toil in the twilight of the idols to disseminate the transformative teachings that will redeem modernity. I am concerned here to trace one particular lineage of Nietzschean readership, which I take to have descended from the mitigated, unanticipated success of his confrontation with modernity. From the perspective of this particular line of descent, his books appear to have attracted readers who continue his political project while questioning the formative influence he exerts over them. Although it would be precipitous to claim that these readers have broken free entirely of discipleship, it is undeniable that they have forged for themselves a significant critical distance from him.

Versed in the critical strategies that they have learned from observing Nietzsche in action, these readers inoculate themselves against his own peculiar strain of priestly pathogenesis. These readers know that he is not to be trusted, that his enmity for the weak and misbegotten is also directed at them. These readers are better prepared, when the time comes, to betray even him to further the ends of the rebellion he incites. By the same token, however, the apostasy of his children is never complete. They may turn on him, denounce him, even profane his teachings, but they do so only by implementing the insights and strategies he has bequeathed to them. Indeed, the recent campaign to auscultate the idol of Nietzsche and to depose him from his exalted station as a "master of suspicion" may be the greatest testament to the power of his parastrategic experiments.[13] In the end, he may be born posthumously after all, in spite of himself.

Although Nietzsche's "revaluation of all values" fails to achieve the grandiose goals he set for it, it may nonetheless serve the greater ends of his erratic rebellion, albeit by means unimaginable and unpalatable to him. It is entirely possible, in fact, that his actual readers, whom he would despise precisely for the decadence they have inherited from him, have already contributed to the self-overcoming of Christian morality. The pernicious moral concept of sin, for example, is gradually yielding its privileged place to diagnoses of sickness, addiction, and other organic dysfunctions. As a consequence, contemporary physicians of culture command ever more confidently their appointed standpoint beyond good and evil. That this transition from evil to sickness would disgust Nietzsche, that he would expose the therapist-kings of late modernity as cleverly disguised priests, tricked out in tweed, is, in the end, irrelevant. His fantasies of a heroic redemption of modernity must be treated as symptoms of, rather than solutions to, the besetting decadence of the epoch. The eventual demise of Christian moral-ity may follow any one of a number of descensional trajectories, and his contribution to its disintegration need bear no resemblance whatsoever to the leading role he reserves for himself.

Nietzsche has in fact exerted a powerful influence on the course of twentieth-century thought, and he commands an ever- growing influence as we approach the turning of the millennium. That this influence deviates from his fantasies about it, that he has been lionized by sundry permutations of the reviled "man of *ressentiment*," is, finally, beside the point. He has created a readership in his own decadent image, and for better or worse, this audience will determine the fate of his anti-Christian rebellion. He may have failed to create the intrepid warrior-genealogists who would bravely escort him across the threshold of the new millennium, but this failure need not crush his incipient anti-Christian rebellion. In fact, his weakness for this hackneyed romance of male bonding may actually serve to align his political agenda with his unique historical situation.

The recent academic campaign to discredit appeals to authorial inten-tion might discourage us from attributing to Nietzsche the conscious designs that the disposition of his current readership obliquely suggests. Some critics might argue that the parastrategic devices that I have discerned in his writings are more properly attributed to my own unexamined readerly response. Still others might explain his enduring influence in terms of the fascination his iconoclasm holds for a decadent culture arrested in a state of protracted adolescence. Reservations about authorial intentions, especially when motivated by legitimate epistemic concerns, are salutary possessions for any careful reader. I fear, however, that the attack on authorial intention all too often manifests a latent resentment of genius itself, a contempt for aesthetic productions whose design outstrips those of ordinary mortals in originality and audacity. While it is clear that most of Nietzsche's readers could never have anticipated and compensated for the deleterious effects of their own decadence, it does not necessarily follow that Nietzsche himself was similarly limited.

If, as Freud claims, Nietzsche amassed an unprecedented wealth of self-knowledge, then perhaps we should be prepared to attribute to him au-thorial designs so elaborate and complex as to suggest the inspiration of genius. As I have suggested, Nietzsche may very well have known that he would quail before the transfigurative task he set for himself and that he must enlist others who would inflict on him the violence that he would, in the end, spare himself. In light of this "penetrating" self-knowledge, is it not possible that he schooled his readers in suspicion and symptomatology so that they might assist him in an attack on Christianity to which he knew he was not equal? Is it not possible that his experiments with parastrategesis have succeeded in compensating even for those weaknesses of which he was ignorant? Is it not possible that he has cleverly sealed our ears so that we would not heed his cries of surrender to the siren song of decadence? Finally, is it simply a coincidence that his books have in fact contributed to the production of readers who continue his life's work, despite the obstacles he has planted in their path?

In the end, Freud may be right about the pioneering reaches of Nietzsche's penetrating self-knowledge. Like the clever Odysseus, he objectively surveyed his all-too-human limitations and implemented corrective measures. He may have failed to attain the final, self-referential insight that would have completed his critique of modernity, but he presided over the training of those who might yet do so for him. He may have flinched from beholding himself in the full, terrifying embodiment of his decadence, but he furnished the symptomatological tools that others would need to plumb the murky depths of his lacerated soul.

Nietzsche's decadence is thus responsible for the crowning irony of his life and career: It is only as a decadent, as the consummate man of *ressentiment*, that he commands anything like the power and influence he regularly claims for himself. Had he somehow succeeded in creating the audience he needed, his anti-Christian rebellion surely would have foundered. It is only insofar as he has failed to control his readership, attracting readers whom he summarily disowns, that his political agenda remains viable at all. If his self-engineered "explosion" succeeds in clearing the way for a new, tragic *agon,* it does so only because he has unwittingly tapped an abundant store of priestly resentment.[14] His rearguard attack on the Christian priesthood succeeds not because he induces Christian morality to take a fatal, self-referential turn, but because he trumps St. Paul with his – and modernity's – sole remaining card: He betrays even himself in a self-consuming assault on the Christian priesthood. Only as a martyr, and not as a squanderer, does he hasten the self-overcoming of Christian morality.

To all appearances, Nietzsche remained blind to the secret of his limited success. Soothed by the tonic melodies of his marathon piano improvisations, confident in his mad resolve to assassinate the political and religious leaders of Europe, he never fully confronted the reflection of his own visage in the yawning abyss of decadence. Spared a final, devastating self-examination by the onset of insanity, he blissfully acceded to the station of the millennial Antichrist. Had he suspected that his exit from the labyrinth would pursue the low road, tracing clandestine paths through malodorous swamps and lowlands, tunneling through dimly lit subterranean nooks and chambers, he never could have embarked upon this Hyperborean expedition: "We sail right *over* morality, we crush, we destroy perhaps the remains of our own morality by daring to make our voyage there – but what matter are *we!*" (BGE 23).

Notes

1 Cited in Ernest Jones, *The Life and Work of Sigmund Freud,* Volume 2 (New York: Basic, 1953), p. 344.

2 Letter to Malwida von Meysenbug on 18 October 1888 [*Friedrich Nietzsche: Sämtliche Briefe, Kritische Studienausgabe in 8 Bänden,* ed. G. Colli and M. Montinari (Berlin: deGruyter/Deutscher Taschenbuch Verlag, 1986), Vol. 8, No. 1131, p. 452].

3 According to Maudemarie Clark, Nietzsche creates the world in his own image, but unlike all previous philosophers, he does not do so self-deceptively: "Nietzsche knows perfectly well that [his doctrine of the will to power] is not the truth" [*Nietzsche on Truth and Philosophy* (Cambridge: Cambridge University Press, 1990), p. 240].

4 *Apology,* 21 c–e; 23 a–b. Gregory Vlastos argues that Socrates' irony shelters an implicit epistemic distinction between two species of knowledge, in *Socrates: Ironist and Moral Philosopher* (Ithaca, NY: Cornell University Press, 1991), especially pp. 21–44. In contrast to Vlastos's influential interpretation, I follow Nietzsche in interpreting Socrates' claim as an unironic statement of the nihilism that defines his peculiar life. It is not so much, as Vlastos suggests, that Socrates knows (but lacks/refuses the analytic tools to articulate) that knowledge admits of multiple dimensions, as that he knows that knowledge, once acquired by decadent philosophers, is useless to effect political change. As kindred nihilists, Socrates and Nietzsche thus understand that the Delphic imperative shelters an esoteric teaching that is available only to those who have already gained insight into the natural cycle of growth and decay.

5 Plato, *Meno,* trans. G. M. A. Grube (Indianapolis, IN: Hackett, 1976), p. 20; 86 b–c.

6 My understanding of Odysseus's self-neutralizing strategies is indebted to Jon Elster's perspicacious discussion of "binding" and "precommitting" in *Ulysses and the Sirens: Studies in Rationality and Irrationality* (Cambridge: Cambridge University Press, 1979), chapter 2.

7 Nietzsche borrows this Odyssean motif to advertise his own "strange and insane" task. Likening the allure of metaphysics to the bewitching song of the sirens, he vows to scour the "eternal basic text of *homo natura*" of all supernatural accretions: "To translate man back into Nature; . . . to see to it that man henceforth stands before man as even today, hardened in the discipline of science, he stands before the *rest* of Nature, with intrepid Oedipus eyes and sealed Odysseus ears, deaf to the siren songs of old metaphysical bird catchers who have been piping at him all too long, 'you are more, you are higher, you are of a different origin!'" (BGE 230).

8 Alexander Nehamas maintains that Nietzsche largely succeeded in living his "life as literature": "In engaging with [Nietzsche's] works, we are not engaging with the miserable little man who wrote them but with the philosopher who

emerges through them, the magnificent character these texts constitute and manifest" [*Nietzsche: Life as Literature* (Cambridge, MA: Harvard University Press, 1985). p. 234]. Nehamas does not explain, however, how "the miserable little man" escapes our engagement with Nietzsche, or why we should allow him to do so; nor does Nehamas identify the readership that comprises the "we" to which he refers. In any event, Nietzsche himself does not restrict his focus to the "magnificent character[s]" who are constituted in and through literature. He insists, for example, that "a Homer would not have created an Achilles nor a Goethe a Faust if Homer had been an Achilles or Goethe a Faust" (GM III:4).

9   Letter to Köselitz on 4 January 1889 (*Sämtliche Briefe*, Vol. 8, No. 1247, p. 575).

10   Jürgen Habermas points out, for example, that "[Nietzsche's] idea of a new mythology is of Romantic provenance, and so also is the recourse to Dionysus as the god who is coming. Nietzsche likewise distances himself from the Romantic use of these ideas and proclaims a manifestly more radical version pointing far beyond Wagner. But wherein does the Dionysian differ from the Romantic?" [*The Philosophical Discourse of Modernity: Twelve Lectures*, trans. Frederick G. Lawrence (Cambridge, MA: MIT Press, 1987), p. 88].

11   Michel Foucault thus maintains that "the only valid tribute to thought such as Nietzsche's is precisely to use it, to make it groan and protest. And, if the commentators say I am being unfaithful to Nietzsche, that is of absolutely no interest" ("Prison-Talk: An Interview with Michel Foucault," *Radical Philosophy*, No. 16, 1977, p. 15).

12   Like Nietzsche, Bonnie Honig candidly acknowledges the difficulties involved in sustaining the *agon* in late modernity: "But the agon is less easily protected in late modern times in part because it is less easily located and in part because it is threatened not by a single individual possessed of great force but by numerous, overlapping forces, some of which are hegemonic in their aspirations, others of which are simply the expressions of the human, all-too-human yearning for a freedom from politics or contest, a freedom Nietzsche identifies with death" [*Political Theory and the Displacement of Politics* (Ithaca, NY: Cornell University Press, 1993), p. 209]. Unlike Nietzsche, however, Honig nevertheless retains her faith in the contest as a viable model for participatory political activity in the liberal democratic societies of late modernity. Why she does so is less clear, since she offers no historical or empirical arguments to support the continued viability of her preferred model of contest. While she confidently insists that "the lesson of the contest of virtue and *virtù* is that politics never gets things right, over and done with" (p. 210), this "lesson" does not establish that the "contest of virtue and *virtù*" either could or should continue in late modernity. Honig boldy invites her readers "to accept and embrace the perpetuity of contest" (p. 210), but she never seriously considers the grim possibility – raised by Nietzsche in his post-Zarathustran critique of modernity – that meaningful contestation is no longer a viable option for most late modern agents. As Nietzsche's diagnosis of modernity indicates, "freedom from politics or contest" need not require death, for advanced decay also brings an end to the fructifying contests of Western European cultures. In light of Nietzsche's critique of modernity, in fact, would an enduring faith in "the perpetuity of contest" not appear as yet another instance of what Honig calls "the displacement of poli-

tics?" Is it not possible, following the principles of Nietzschean symptomatology, to interpret Honig's faith in the perpetuity of contest as a sign that the contest of virtue and *virtù* has in fact ended?

13   Hence the recent appearance of *Pourquoi nous ne sommes pas nietzschéens,* ed. Alain Boyer et al. (Paris: Éditions Grasset et Fasquelle, 1991). For a sensible treatment of the recent turning away from Nietzsche by French intellectuals, see Alan Schrift, *Nietzsche's French Legacy* (New York: Routledge, 1995), chapter 5.

14   Robert C. Solomon calls attention to the potentially productive expressions of resentment in his essay "One Hundred Years of Resentment: Nietzsche's *Genealogy of Morals,*" collected in *Nietzsche, Genealogy, Morality: Essays on Nietzsche's "On the Genealogy of Morals,"* ed. Richard Schacht (Berkeley: University of California Press, 1994), pp. 95–126. Solomon maintains that "an ethics of resentment is not just a matter of good character/bad character or good emotions and bad emotions. It is also – contra Nietzsche (and MacIntyre) – a question of justification, of the political and social context and the legitimacy of motives and emotions" (p. 124).

INDEX